PENGUIN BOOKS

WITH JUSTICE FOR NONE

Gerry Spence is the author of three other books: *Gunning for Justice*, *Trial by Fire*, and *Of Murder and Madness*. He maintains a national practice from his offices and home in Jackson, Wyoming, and lectures widely across the country.

WITH
JUSTICE

Destroying

FOR NONE

an American Myth

GERRY SPENCE

PENGUIN BOOKS

PENGUIN BOOKS
Published by the Penguin Group
Viking Penguin, a division of Penguin Books USA Inc.,
375 Hudson Street, New York, New York 10014, U.S.A.
Penguin Books Ltd, 27 Wrights Lane,
London W8 5TZ, England
Penguin Books Australia Ltd, Ringwood,
Victoria, Australia
Penguin Books Canada Ltd, 2801 John Street,
Markham, Ontario, Canada L3R 1B4
Penguin Books (N.Z.) Ltd, 182–190 Wairau Road,
Auckland 10, New Zealand

Penguin Books Ltd, Registered Offices:
Harmondsworth, Middlesex, England

First published in the United States of America by
Times Books, a division of Random House, Inc., 1989
Published in Penguin Books 1990

10 9 8 7 6 5 4 3 2 1

Grateful acknowledgment is made to James Nielsen for permission to reprint
an excerpt from "The Flaw in Our Law Schools," *Newsweek*, June 11, 1984.
Copyright © 1984 by J. Nielsen.

LIBRARY OF CONGRESS CATALOGING IN PUBLICATION DATA
Spence, Gerry.
    With justice for none: destroying an American myth/Gerry
Spence.
        p. cm.
    Reprint. Originally published: New York, NY: Times Books, 1989.
    Includes bibliographical references.
    ISBN 0 14 01.3325 9
    1. Justice, Administration of — United States.   I. Title.
KF384.S66   1990
347.73 — dc20   90–7017

Printed in the United States of America

To our children,
who first learned of injustice
from us

Contents

Starting

I feel like a farmer who has spent all of his life on forty rocky acres and one day thinks he's qualified to tell you something about the state of agriculture in America. Yet a man can't talk much about anybody else's farm without first knowing his own—where the soil is thin and the cockleburs take over every spring after that first long drizzle leaves both man and mule slicked down like newborn calves. A man learns other things, too—how the politician steals his vote and the owner of the only elevator in town steals his oats while they slap him on the back and ask about the wife and the kids.

This is a book about the law, but it's presented from the standpoint of one who has plodded and staggered in the furrow. If you put this book to the test as a scientific treatise on the justice system, you will be disappointed—as will I. What do scientists know about growing a crop when the old mule is stove up and the weather is bent on doing in both man and beast? Although I respect the valuable insights of some academicians, and shamelessly cite them as authorities whenever it serves my purpose, I believe their conclusions are often flawed, for they have failed to expose themselves in the workplace of the law, in the pits where the killing is done and the most pungent truths revealed. Naturally my kind likes the boast of Thomas Hobbes: "Had I read as much as other men, I should have known as little as other men."

I have spent most of my life representing ordinary people against the corporate giants. Sometimes I feel like the farmer on his forty acres who has to take on God and all of the elements. Yet in this tangled, frantic, commercial society, can we expect justice except by the immutable rules of Darwin? In our system, money is power. As long as we play the money game, we all make a bargain: In place of our equal share, we accept hope—the hope to acquire *more* than our share. As a consequence of that bargain, not everybody can have yachts and castles in Spain, or the best lawyers money can buy. Today, like a pernicious blight that ruins a good crop of oats, the power of money invades every cell of the justice system and destroys its promise. I won't accept that kind of justice. That was not in the bargain I made—not for me, or the people I represent.

I have no use for the Milquetoasts and the mealymouthed. A good advocate is never evenhanded. I'll leave balanced reporting to the anchormen whose empty eyes stare into the TelePrompTer as they "report" the evening news. To me, it's immoral to make a balanced report when one knows things are lopsided. It's true that corporate America complains about justice, too, about the vicious mobs and greedy lawyers who feed off the corporate body like ticks on a dog's back. But corporate America can buy all the silver-tongued spellbinders and anchormen and magicians from Madison Avenue it needs to present its case. Therefore, I leave the corporate case to others.

Every day, I meet people who have been bullied or cheated or injured. They say they're going to hire a lawyer. They say they're going to sue and get justice. But they'll likely be disappointed, and that hurts me, especially when I see how people innocently cling to the belief that justice is theirs for the asking. Sometimes when I talk about justice, I get angry, and people tend to turn off when you're angry. They think you're mad at *them*. Or you seem unreasonable or—because you think differently than they—radical. Nobody wants to hear some firebrand raging about what's wrong in America when there are so many things right. You see these wild-eyed screamers all the time in the cities, standing on boxes while the people walk on by without even turning their heads. But the fellow on the box is there for himself. He'd say what he has to say even if he were only hollering into the wind. I love the guy. It takes a certain courage to be a fool, and there is still a need in this country for the pariahs and the common scolds. That they irritate us often tells us more about *us* than about them. And that they tell only part of the story is better than their not having told us anything at all.

I would prefer to assure you that there's nothing wrong with justice in America. After laboring in the system for over thirty-five years, I love it the way the farmer loves his pile of rocks and his old mule. But he doesn't have any illusions about them. He knows that the mule is likely to kick hell out of him whenever he feels like it, and that the forty acres only grows a reasonable crop of oats every fifth year or so. Sometimes the truth is hard to listen to. It can be cold and plain and sad, and we do the best we can to hide from it. We buy face-lifts and youthful clothes, and when the truth finally catches up with us, they haul us out under a sheet and pay someone to make us look alive and then bury us fast. We stay the hell out of the ghettos so we don't have to see the filth and poverty and pain, and we never visit the asylums where the people are screaming, and we buy a lot of worthless things in pursuit of our pervasive goal—happiness. So the farmer, too, had just as well go on hoping for a miracle—that one day he'll get one hell of a bumper crop off his forty acres behind his old mule. That's the way it is with justice in America. The system doesn't often deliver justice to the people, and it never has, but we cling to our hopes and to old myths that are much more comforting than the truth.

Before I am finished here, we will look at the justice system as if we were children taking a watch apart, and I make no representations we can get it back together again. We'll examine the pieces: how the crimes of nonliving corporations cost the rest of us ten times more than all the crimes of all the street thugs and mobsters and crooks and scam artists combined; how the great nationwide insurance fraud presently threatens to cheat us of our sacred rights; how lawyers, too, are merchandised, and how they are trained to fight for "the nonbreathers" against the people; how law schools have become factories producing replacement parts for the large corporate-law machines, and judges have become the high priests of the marketplace, beholden too often to the new king, corporate America. We'll learn the predicament of American workers, who are substantially without rights in the workplace, and who have become property and are often consumed like grease rags. That is the key—*the commoditization of America*—the conversion of our people, our institutions, our lawyers and our judges, even our victims, into *things* for sale in the marketplace.

This book is an argument. It is often a sermon, one I have taken a lifetime to prepare, and one that sometimes lays down a trail resembling tracks I once saw left in the snow by a one-winged bird. Yet a one-winged bird has learned certain truths the rest of the flock has never learned. I can assure you of one thing, however: There's nothing very ponderous coming up here. The problems as I see them can be simply stated, because most truths *are* very simple. In talking to juries, I've learned it doesn't make any difference how complicated the law or the facts, they only *appear* complicated. It's the lawyer's job to understand his client's case so he can explain it to anyone. It's when the lawyer doesn't understand that he resorts to the big words and the fancy phrases and the jargon. And you can almost always tell the truth when you hear it. It's so easy to recognize, you think it's something you knew all along.

Arguments that bring no new understanding, that foster no change, waste everyone's time. I propose to offer some solutions. But the first step toward reform is to acknowledge how things *are*— to strip away the myths, to fling open the door and listen for the sounds in the night that have snatched us from our sleep, and to shine our light where they lie hiding until they finally slink away. Sometimes I feel heady when I think of the kind of justice we could deliver to the people if we set ourselves to it and sought honest solutions. The invitation for change I extend in the second part of this book displays awesome possibilities. The question is not whether these schemes have merit, but whether they demonstrate that we *can*, if we will it, amend our system to deliver justice to most of the people most of the time; so, indeed, the voice from the soapbox will cease wailing that there is *justice for none* and will, instead, step down to join a people offering *justice for all*.

Gerry Spence
Jackson Hole, Wyoming

PART ONE

JUSTICE FOR NONE
What's Wrong?

1 | JUSTICE
The Divine Mist— the Interminable Search

The truth is there is no justice in America for the people. And there never has been—not from the beginning. There is no justice for the wealthy surgeon at Mercy Hospital, or the scrubwoman who cleans up after him. There is no justice for the dregs of our society who plague us with their crimes, or for the workers, or for women. There is no justice even for Jerry Falwell, who loves God and votes Republican, or for the poor in the ghettos. They've never heard of it. There is no justice for the farmer who works his guts out for the banks. And don't forget the children—there has never been justice for them.

We search for justice in fearful places—in cities encrusted with crime, in the workplace where people are mere units on the production line, in a world where justice, if it exists, has become only another commodity for sale. We huddle behind barred doors, wired to expensive burglar alarms, and when the wind blows and rattles the door in the night, we awaken, our hearts in our throats, because nothing can make us feel safe anymore. Yet fiercely we cling to old myths that give comfort—justice is out there. Somewhere.

What has happened to justice in America? There stands the court-house, solid, stately. Inside, we still find great judges, men and women dedicated to the law, presiding over our cases. In the court-rooms, we hear our hometown lawyers pleading to a jury of our neighbors. But there will be no justice, for a new king dominates justice in America, a sovereign whose soul is pledged to business and whose heart is geared to profit. The new king, an amorphous agglomeration of corporations, of banks and insurance companies and mammoth multinational financial institutions, maintains a prurient passion for money and demands a justice of its own, one that is stable and predictable, one that fits into columns and accounts and mortality tables, one that is interpretable in dollars, so that a little justice is a few dollars and a lot of justice many. The new king cannot deal with the soul, the fire, and the unpredictability of human justice. Profit is the lifeblood of business, and if there is no profit in justice, people are not likely to receive it.

Like the citizens of any kingdom, we tend to take on the style of the sovereign. In this corporate world, people have become corporatelike themselves. Our hearts have become synchronized with the corporate heart that beats in dollars, and with the corporate spirit that worships dollars. In the Age of the Yuppie, we have become so insanely obsessed with things that we have willingly pawned the heritage of generations, battered the earth, and poisoned the oceans in order to possess whatever dollars will buy. We seek to become salable commodities ourselves; students pursue an advanced degree, not because they yearn to learn, but because they wish to make themselves more marketable. Businessmen buy respect with the dollars they accumulate and with which they score the game of profit. Ideas seem valueless unless they are salable. Workers have become expendable parts for sale in the ordinary course of commerce. The detection, punishment, and prevention of crime are fungible goods. Rapists and robbers and thieves and their victims have become wares that stock the system's shelves. Lawyers are too often expediters, and judges are dedicated to keeping the cases flowing in deference to the commerce of law. Our leaders are often elected because of their purchasable images on television. Even eternal salvation has become something sold in the marketplace. And justice—whatever it is, and it is different for each of us—has finally become a mercantile matter, where profit is the paramount concern of all.

Yet a steady gnawing in the night awakens us. It is an awareness that the love of *only* money, and devotion to *only* things, leaves us as empty and dead as dollars, that the worship of *only* property transforms the living into the dead—dead forests, dead rivers, dead towns and deserted communities. When we petition for a *human* justice, one that does not sell us like so many pork bellies, we often make demands on the system to which it cannot respond. But every system must finally be judged by the character of justice it delivers, and a justice attuned to the needs of only the nonliving, to the demands of the new king, provides justice for none.

What is justice? Clarence Darrow insisted, "There is no such thing as justice. In fact, the word cannot be defined." Darrow was right. Justice, like life, cannot be adequately defined. Justice is the divine mist, and is something inexorably connected to the state of being. But Darrow understood clearly the meaning of *injustice*, and all his life fought against it. The black child in the ghetto begging for his supper knows the meaning of that word, and so does the innocent man rotting in prison. Even the coyote chained to a stake near the gas pumps to entertain the tourists understands the meaning of injustice.

Yet justice usually fails without law, for it is the office of the law to restrain the powerful. The black child, given power, may, in turn, starve the children of his oppressors, and the innocent, once freed, may, given power, kill those who have wrongfully imprisoned him. Justice is not a willow in the wind; justice is the great tree that stands immutable against unjust forces, and the law, the massive trunk of the great tree, must resist the tempests that storm upon it.

Most of us maintain vague notions of justice, but its precise meaning escapes us until we are deprived of it. As long as the coyote was free to roam the prairies, and as long as the child was fed and loved, neither understood very much about justice. The human organism can withstand unspeakable physical pain. It can be starved. It can endure grief and bear all nature of misery. Yet the human soul cannot tolerate injustice. We must have it. We beseech God for it. Why, we demand, do You claim to be just and yet deal our fate so willy-nilly? Job, that devout and righteous man, confronted God, and in his sublime suffering exhorted God to reason with him and to be just: "Here is my signature, let the Almighty answer me," he cried. "Thou knowest I am not wicked . . . yet thou dost destroy me . . . !" Nowhere is there a clearer cry for justice. But God often stands silent.

I knew a man who lived on the Wind River and helplessly watched his wife and children turn to char and cinders while their small cabin burned. They say he cursed God. They say he would have killed God with his bare hands if he could have found Him. Being helpless to obtain justice, he did the only thing he could do—he disavowed Him. If God exists, he argued, He would be a just God, for man cannot worship an unjust God. After the fire, he lived alone and grew very old. At night he played his guitar to himself until he fell asleep, and in the morning he tended his garden like a living scarecrow. He said he grew certain high-altitude corn and squash he himself had perfected, not God.

Whether at the hands of man or God, the deprivation of justice drives human beings to insane places. In each of us, there is a smoldering terror that injustice will descend upon us as it did on Job and the old hermit of the Wind River. "God is always watching," my mother said. God has made paranoids of us all.

Justice requires atonement, and justice demands reform. It teaches its lessons and insists that we change. I remember when our small Wyoming town was stunned by the death of one of its most exceptional progeny—a beautiful young woman I'll call Donna. She was a gifted and popular student, and a loving daughter. She died in the wreck of a new car her father had given her for her birthday. The manufacturer's own tests had shown that the car went out of control under certain braking conditions, and we were prepared to prove these conditions existed in her case, that the company knew of the defect but had refused to correct the design before the car was marketed to millions of unsuspecting drivers. The evidence I saw supported our allegations (and those made by hundreds of others in similar court cases) that the manufacturer's haste to market the car, despite its knowledge of the dangerous design, was motivated by its desire to beat the Japanese to the marketplace. It was the same old story—profit over people. We filed suit on behalf of the girl's stricken family. All they wanted, they said, was justice.

A few days before the trial, we settled. These are, indeed, hard cases to win. The car manufacturer has teams of experts selected not so much for what they know but for their ability to convince jurors of whatever defenses the company may raise. It has skilled trial lawyers and huge support staffs. For my part, I dreaded dragging the parents through the agony of their daughter's death again, this time amid the glare and clamor of the media. Even if they won, there would be the expensive and lengthy appeals, and, in the end, the only justice they would receive would be, of course, money. At the last minute, faced with the strain of the upcoming trial and offered a sum of money by the company that permitted them to argue that they had at least won something, the parents opted to end the war. People usually do.

But the manufacturer's offer required that the amount of the settlement remain confidential. Hundreds of similar cases waited in the wings. Millions were at stake, and the company wanted protection. We could argue to the parents, and did, that we had beaten the company. The company claimed this was the largest settlement it had ever paid in this kind of case. Yet we did not win. There would be no punishment of the corporation, or of its officers, who had known from the beginning that the car was dangerous. There would be no admission of guilt. To the contrary, the settlement papers specifically recited that the corporation admitted no wrongdoing of any kind. Only the gross payment of money to the living for the dead marked the transaction. When the company paid up, it did not even flinch. To thus punish the manufacturer for exposing thousands to injury and death was as satisfying as getting even with the United States government at income-tax time by slamming the door at the post office.

I think of those nights I dumped myself heavily into bed and lay listening to my heart while I fought through the case. I think of the months my staff hunted down the facts and the law. I think of the family's grief, and that all of this human pain and striving should come down to a mere accounting entry made on the company's computer in some obscure room by a bored operator waiting for "Miller time."

Now that the case was settled and the money in my clients' hands, they didn't know what to do with it. How could they take money in place of their child? They did not get justice. They were delivered, instead, a bagful of guilt. A few days after the settlement, one of the dead girl's sisters wrote me:

"It's all over. It's gone, and [Donna] is too. What's left? An empty feeling with nothing to do about it . . . the money is nothing—pocket change to a corporation that makes billions of dollars. What bothers me is that we settled and that one of the conditions of the settlement was confidentiality. It is an admission of guilt on their part, but a *secret* admission. It's as if they are saying, 'Let's settle this now— we were wrong—here's some money—now let us get back to *business as usual.*'

" 'Business as usual'—the business of making automobiles profitably, not safely, and hoping no one finds out that one of the decisions made in a big corporation is to make cars they know will kill. It's just not enough. Part of our lives is gone; revenge is impossible; the perpetrator is too strong . . . our silence was bought, and we all lose—all of us."

The other sister addressed another side of the issue. "I think the settlement was definitely in my parents' best interests. I dread to think what a long ugly trial would have done to them and to me.

"All of us had ideas and dreams of how we would get justice— or revenge on the company. As you know, in different ways, we were somewhat disappointed that we couldn't really make the company pay by adverse publicity, and such. However, it dawned on me . . . that although we were unable to get justice as we know it or want it, there is, after all, *divine justice.* God sees all, and these people *will* pay, whether it be in this world, or the next. There *is* justice. This I know to be true, and it gives me a sense of hope, and resolution, and comfort." A pity, I thought, that in America we must wait until the "next world" to receive justice.

Even though, as Darrow insisted, justice cannot be defined, it is something that can be felt. But the feeling of justice requires that the wrong be righted. The Old Testament ideal of an eye for an eye speaks to that need. We no longer hold vengeance among the most worthy of human emotions, yet vengeance, too, is found at the heart of justice. It is not enough to free the innocent who has been wrongfully imprisoned for many years; he requires something more. The money the family receives from the manufacturer for the wrongful death of a child will never satisfy them. Something is missing. Daily we deal out our own justice in small ways that are more satisfying. When a careless driver cuts us off by a left turn from the right lane, we slam on the brakes, but we give him the horn and perhaps the familiar sign. In the office, we avenge slight slights with small snubs. No insult goes without its tit for tat. At home, a wife extracts her own justice against an errant husband—she may withhold sex or civility or overspend the family budget. A child, believing he is mistreated by a parent, may reciprocate outside the home and become a delinquent. Some psychologists contend that even some forms of psychosis are retaliatory in nature. Humans are specialized in vindictive behavior. Ah, revenge! "Sweeter far than flowing honey!" exclaimed Homer. But vengeance is like salt. Sprinkled in the oatmeal, it lends body and flavor, but salt alone is not food— nor is vengeance justice.

In most societies, including our own, revenge is the state's sole prerogative. Were it otherwise, we would live in lawlessness. Victims may look to the law for justice, but in criminal cases many report that getting satisfaction in the nation's justice system is equivalent to leaving the Church in charge of sex. We are taught, correctly, that forgiveness is sublime, but often forgiveness leaves us unjustly suspended in emotional conflict. When the state mumbles its bland rationalizations about reforming and rehabilitating those who have harmed us, and when vicious criminals are coddled and turned loose on the streets to again pursue their commitments to evil and to injury, we, the victims, feel abandoned, and, worse, we feel injured again. While we could not live in a society where the citizen is free to torture and kill at will to gratify a vengeful heart, try to explain that to a husband whose wife has been brutally raped and murdered. The state's bargain for clemency is yet another crime against him. The husband craves revenge. He must have it or his sorrow will spoil like milk left in the sun.

I can no more precisely define that phenomenon we call *justice* than could Darrow, or Justinian, who himself was able to come up with no better definition than "delivering to every man his just dues." Yet I have learned certain things: I know that the human need for revenge and the mysterious powers of forgiveness that oppose it have waged their battles, one against the other, throughout the history of man, and in my career they have proven to be inseparably entwined. Nowhere was that terrible war fought so hard and with so little as in the case of a young woman I'll call Maria. Let me tell you her story, for, although I don't fully understand its lesson, it speaks eloquently of the elusive, the mysterious, the magical qualities of what we call *justice*.

I have piled hundreds of cases over her memory, and yet even now her open, cheerful face peers through, not the face of a child, but of one who struggled for innocence and nearly won. Maria said she loved this man I'll call Leyland. She loved him in ways that were never quite clear, but one does not demand explanations in matters of love. Leyland was even younger than she, or perhaps he only seemed to be. He was the son of a decent and enterprising self-made millionaire, and because his father underwrote his son's business, Leyland had the means to follow his hollow passion—"the art of fun-seeking," as he actually was to call it.

Leyland drank excessively, I suppose not only in his quest for fun, but to fill a certain restive emptiness that haunted him. Frequently, Maria held him and listened and counseled as any good mother would a son. I thought I understood that. We have all been hurt at some time, or felt lost, and there are times when we all need to weep. I tried not to be judgmental. Every plant in the forest is not the mighty Douglas fir. For reasons peculiar to Maria, she was attracted to the irresponsible child in Leyland that characterized his behavior and that also exposed, especially when drunk, the dangerous side of him. Before she opened the door to his house that terrible night, she knew he was drunk and that he had a gun, and she must have known that drunk, he was no more trustworthy than a three-year-old.

He shot her. He claimed it was an accident, although later the officers found the gun in the garbage can. Why would he intentionally kill her? He said he loved her, and he wept.

The bullet slashed the spinal cord in Maria's neck. Leyland tried to stop the blood. He tried to phone for help. Crying with real cause, he begged her not to die. He prayed. There is an old saying: Be careful what you pray for, lest your prayers be answered.

Later, she said that when the gun, a .357 Magnum, exploded, she felt as if the bullet had taken off the whole side of her face: "I thought if I could hold myself up, I wouldn't die. Everything got kind of dark. I went down on my knees. It was pretty peaceful, because I knew that I would be with my favorite aunt, who had just passed away."

Maria's life hung in the balance for a long time. The prosecutor announced that if she died, he would charge Leyland with first-degree murder. There was no doubt he shot Maria. But were the essential elements of first-degree murder present—malice and pre-meditation? Too many prosecutors overcharge an accused—with murder, say, when he is guilty only of manslaughter. It is the frightful technique of intimidation. Often, in panic, the accused will admit to the lesser charge without a trial. He thinks he will save himself from being found guilty of the greater crime he did not commit (even though the prosecutor may well know that's true). Some argue the abuse is an acceptable part of the justice game. If so, no one should condemn an attorney for pleading his guilty client "Innocent," and thereafter holding the state to its burden of proof.

I didn't like the case from the beginning. Although the charge of first-degree murder was properly defensible, I felt uneasy about representing Leyland. Perhaps I should have left the case to another lawyer. But I felt a certain pity for his parents, who had done everything they knew to insure the success of their son. I have sons of my own.

I tried to argue away my misgivings. Wouldn't any doctor worth his salt labor fervently over the bleeding body of a heinous killer to save his life? No one would condemn the doctor. He acts out of the most humane ethics of his profession. Why, then, should lawyers be called to task for protecting the rights of the accused under the Constitution? Is not the highest calling of a lawyer to defend the damned? Still, the facts repelled me. I made further arguments to myself. I always do. Perhaps Leyland's heavy drinking had hurled him into psychosis. Perhaps I could enter a "Diminished Capacity" defense on his behalf. But cases, like people, change when you get to know them better.

In Leyland's case, the more we investigated, the worse it got. We interviewed scores of witnesses, one being Mabel, a woman who owned a watering hole favored by Leyland and his fellow "fun-seekers." "When he was sober, he was one of the nicest people in the world, and when he was drunk, he was the meanest son of a bitch I ever met," said Mabel. "He was a very violent person. You could see it in his eyes. I see a lot of drunks. Some go to sleep and some get silly, and then there's the kind who get mean. There's a look they all get—just black in their eyes. One second he'll be fine, and the next he'll get that black look."

Mabel said Leyland and his friends, including one called Jamey, didn't have anything to do in this world but to sit around and play cops and robbers. "To them, it was a game, and those two had very large feelings of inadequacy. They carried guns because it made them feel important." That's the nicest thing about bartenders nowadays: They'll not only listen to your problems but psychoanalyze you, too—all for the price of a drink.

One night, they say, Leyland came to Mabel's bar with five guns, and Mabel's bouncer had to take the guns off the guy. "Leyland sat there and screamed that he was going to kill my bartender," Mabel said, "and he carried on and climbed over the bar, and they had to physically hold him down to the floor." Then, she said, he went out to his car, and came back with a submachine gun and waited a while in the lobby for the bartender to come out. The next day, Maria came to the bar and retrieved the guns, and Leyland and Jamey brought Mabel a big bouquet of flowers and said their sorrys, but she barred Leyland from the premises anyway. Leyland sent notes begging her to let him come back, and the other fun-seekers threatened to boycott the place if she didn't. Finally Mabel relented, upon Leyland's solemn promise that he wouldn't drink on her premises—not a drop.

One time Maria told Mabel how Leyland had come to her home, put a gun to her cheek, and pulled the hammer back. He'd done it more than once. "Why do you let him in if he's going to do that?" Mabel asked.

"Well, he'll come to the door and say, 'I just want to talk to you. Everything's cool.' Then, later, we'll have a hassle and he'll pull the gun, and when I freak out, he just looks at me and says, 'I won't hurt you, you know I won't hurt you.'"

"You really don't believe Leyland will ever pull the trigger?"

"I believe he's capable of it," Maria answered. "I told him that until he got his life straightened out, I wasn't going to see him again. But he's been so upset over his wife, he just can't get it together." Then she quietly said, "I have really high hopes that Leyland will get his life together and we'll be able to do something." Something.

The wife tried to keep a check on him. One witness claimed that in a single month she had sixty-two charges on her phone bill, all attributable to the woman's attempt to keep tabs on her husband—long-distance. Another witness close to Leyland said, "Their marriage has been very strange. In a little over three years, they haven't spent a fourth of their married life together. When she gets mad, she'll pack up and sneak out and run home to Mother. This is his second marriage. I know Leyland hates losing it."

The day before the shooting, Leyland had been at a popular restaurant, where he and Jamey were drunk. They had a couple of toy cannons with them; Leyland fired one off the bar, and the police threw him in jail overnight. He was bonded out the next morning, but he went right back to the same restaurant and started getting drunk again. Maria tried to persuade him to go with her to Jamey's house—"Fort Blotto," they called it—for Mexican food, but Leyland stayed put at the bar and got drunker. Finally Maria left him there and went with Jamey for dinner, and afterward she drove to Leyland's parents' home to talk to them. In the meantime, Jamey went back to the bar to find Leyland.

"Where's Maria?" Leyland asked.

"I think she went home," Jamey said.

Then some loser piped up. "Come on, Jamey, tell him where she *really* is. What did you and Maria *really* do?"

"No, she's home. I don't know. She isn't coming down here," Jamey said, trying to keep things going straight.

"Why?" Leyland asked. He was probably getting that black look, but he was too drunk to understand, and anyway, as Jamey said later, "Maria didn't want to see him while he was this ripped." In the meantime, Leyland phoned everybody he could think of trying to find her, and later, blind drunk, he staggered home. From what Mabel said, Leyland had always been the jealous type. Once before, when he caught a woman he was dating just sitting at the bar with another guy, Leyland had threatened to kill him.

On the night of the shooting, Leyland's wife called him about some bills a housepainter had incorrectly charged, and Leyland had exploded. The painter, a friend of the family's, was at Leyland's parents' place when Leyland came storming in trying to get the man to fight him. Leyland's father had jumped in between them, and Leyland took a swing at his father, and then the two of them backed Leyland up against the wall and held him there until he calmed down. When he wouldn't leave, his father finally called the sheriff, but before the sheriff arrived, Leyland stomped on back to the bar, and only when he was nearly comatose did he go home. He must have slept for a while and then awakened to find himself alone, perhaps frightened by certain demons, and at about one-thirty in the morning he called Maria. He demanded that she come over. Then he shot her.

At the time of the preliminary hearing in February, Maria was still clinging to life. At the rehabilitation center, she had learned to operate a mechanical wheelchair by blowing into a tube, and the therapists had attached a device to her that permitted her to form audible words. Her mother had cut her long hair as short as a boy's. She couldn't move her head. It was in this condition that I remember seeing her as her father wheeled her into the courtroom. Only the judge would decide if the evidence presented was sufficient to bind Leyland over for a later jury trial on a charge of assault with a dangerous weapon. That charge carried a maximum of twenty years, and some thought that wouldn't be enough.

I saw that the bullet had not dimmed Maria's eyes, but what I remember most were her arms—sticks affixed to a wheelchair—and her fingernails. They grew, while everything else seemed dead. They were longer than the claws of a grizzly, perfectly groomed and polished bright red. A polyester pantsuit hung on her bones, and on her feet someone had stuck a pair of too-large cowboy boots. Her mother stood guard at her side as she had every day and every night since the shooting.

On the witness stand, I have taken to task the heads of great corporations and wrestled with world authorities on every subject from nuclear fission to the engineering and design of automobiles. I have cross-examined the cagiest psychiatrists, the most articulate professional witnesses—those habitually hired by the insurance companies—and, of course, the smoothest-talking of them all, the agents of the FBI. Yet this helpless child propped in her wheelchair like a rag doll, unable to move a single finger or a single toe, unable to speak without mechanical assistance, presented the most formidable witness I had ever faced. I looked at this small, huddled remainder of a woman, and all I wanted to do was to get the hell out of there. She was, of course, the state's star witness. How does a lawyer take on one so horribly wounded? She demonstrated the prodigious power of helplessness. I didn't belong there. I wanted to run. I looked over at Leyland, and he was weeping.

Maria answered the prosecutor's questions with raspy words usually coming in clusters of no more than two or three. One had to listen carefully. The packed courtroom was as silent as snow. "We were good . . . friends," she said, but he was getting serious about her and was "making accusations . . . that I liked . . . other people . . . that I was probably sneaking . . . around . . . on"—she paused to gather the strength to get the word out—"him." There was the motive for the killing! There, as bright and clear as if it were spelled out across the courtroom in neon: He tried to kill her out of jealousy. Then the prosecutor nailed it down. He called a woman who testified that Leyland had phoned her the night of the shooting when he was looking for Maria, and when the witness told Leyland she didn't know where Maria was, Leyland had muttered, "She's history."

Maria tried to explain why she had come to Leyland's house that night. He had called, and he was mad. If she didn't come over to his house right away, he was coming to hers, and she didn't want that. When she arrived, he was in the kitchen, pacing and storming.

"He wouldn't . . . sit . . . down," Maria said, struggling with each word. I wanted her to stop, to be saved the misery, and to save me. "He had a mean . . . look . . . in his eye. I . . . couldn't tell . . . why." She said he continued to demand where she had been all afternoon. "I tried to . . . settle him down. He grabbed the . . . whiskey bottle, which . . . I was pretty fed up . . . with," but when she got up to leave, he stomped out of the room and came back with the gun. "I put my purse . . . back down. I said, 'Okay, I'll stay.' Then he pointed it . . . at my face . . . and it went . . . off."

Her memory carried her back to that hellish place, and she shuddered. I saw her sob and begin to choke. Her mother was right there, of course, and we were afraid Maria would die. After her mother inserted a suction tube down her throat, and she seemed finally to recover, the prosecutor took her back to that hideous scene once more.

"What did his face look like?" he asked in a hushed voice that was supposed to reflect a special level of sensitivity.

"It was mean. Very mean. I couldn't . . . believe it. It was a look of . . . revenge. That's the one thing . . . that stuck in my mind . . . for seven months . . . that face . . . and how scared I was . . . when I saw it. I knew it. I knew he . . . was going to." My objections would only have been overruled. I remained silent.

The case, of course, would turn on Leyland's intent, and now she underlined it for us: "It was *intentional*," she whispered.

Automatically I got up to object, but again I caught myself and sat down without a word. Now, Maria began sobbing and choking, and her father and her mother were crying. It was horrible. Leyland was sitting beside me, and he was sobbing, too. Then the prosecutor, satisfied, said, "I have no more questions."

It was my turn to cross-examine. What could I say? I stood there feeling ugly and out of place, a large man towering over this crumpled child. I asked the judge if I couldn't sit down to examine her; I think he felt my discomfort and wished to hold me to it. "You know the rules of this court, Mr. Spence," he said.

As I looked down at Maria, I remembered the small deer I had wounded as a boy. My bullet had broken its back, and the deer lay helplessly in the snow, paralyzed, bleeding, staring up at me with round, soft eyes in which I could see the reflection of my own face. I looked insane. "Get up!" I screamed, and it did! The poor creature lifted itself up on its wobbly front legs and then dragged its hind-quarters behind it. After it staggered a step or two, it fell back down in an awful heap with a groan and lay at my feet panting. I shot the poor beast in the head to save it from its misery, and me from mine. That much was the least expected of a hunter who had made a bad shot. I felt the same pressure now. There were certain expectations of me.

"Maria, I wish neither one of us were here," I began in a very subdued voice.

"I do . . . too," she gasped through her talking machine.

"I know my job isn't nearly as hard as yours. It's easier for me to ask the questions than for you to answer them, and I wish I didn't have to ask them. Do you hear me?"

"Yes, sir."

"You don't need to call me 'sir.' We are just two human beings struggling through this thing together."

"All right," she said through her raspy machine. Then she told me she hadn't been looking for any permanent connection with Leyland, just friendship, because in a few months she was going to work for Western Airlines as a stewardess. "But he needed somebody."

"I suppose he shared his feelings and his life with you?"

"Yes," she said. But he loved his wife and wanted her back. Maria even called his wife, who said if Leyland would stop drinking, she would come back. Maria testified that she said to the wife, "Oh, please . . . I will do . . . anything. I will help . . . you. Just come back . . . because he really . . . loves you." She claimed she had worked very hard with Leyland toward that end. "We got to . . . do this," she told him. "Number one . . . we got to quit . . . drinking. You got . . . to get away . . . from these girls . . . that your wife . . . is hearing about." But after she convinced Leyland's wife to come back to him, Leyland had gone to meet her at the airport—drunk! That's when Maria gave up.

I asked, "Did Leyland ever suggest to you that one of the reasons he got drunk was because he really didn't want to go back to his wife?"

Suddenly she began to choke again, and her mother rushed forward once more to stick the suction tube down her throat. I felt a cold sweat. I was disgusted by the sound of my own voice. After minutes, her answer came.

"No."

She admitted that once she had gone antelope hunting with Leyland, and that she had shot an antelope and broken its back and that Leyland had had to finish it off. When she told of that, the visions of my own wounded childhood deer returned, and I wondered why those same avenging fates hadn't struck me down as they had Maria.

Maria also admitted that Leyland had pulled a gun on her maybe fifteen or twenty times before, sometimes in the presence of others. He used the gun when he wanted to make her stay with him, and he used it when he wanted to make her go with him. I wasn't quite sure what their game was. He hated being alone, she said. The guns seemed to give him the power he needed. He was obsessed with them, and as his drinking mounted, she saw his personality begin to change—for the worse.

"What would you say was the most obvious change you saw?" I asked.

"Insecurity," she said.

"He got more and more afraid?"

"Yes."

"In your whole life, Maria, had you ever heard or known of anybody who was so wrapped up in this strange use of guns as Leyland was?"

"No, sir."

"And it *was* strange, wasn't it?"

"Yes, sir."

Later, she testified that when she saw Leyland in the bar the night of the shooting, he was glassy-eyed drunk. "He really wouldn't . . . look at you. It was like . . . he was staring . . . into another world." That was the launch I needed into the defense of "Diminished Capacity"—insanity.

"And would he say *strange* things on such nights?"

"Yes."

"Could you give me examples, Maria?"

" 'I am going to . . . get them,' he'd say."

"And who was he talking to?"

"Nobody."

"Did you ever ask him who he was talking about?"

"It was the people . . . after him. But there wasn't . . . anybody after him." And she said that on such occasions he also had "that mean look on his face," but not nearly so mean as he'd looked on the night of the shooting.

Maria said Leyland would shout, "I have to get them for talking about me."

"And you would comfort him?"

"Just by a very . . . nice talk . . . soothing talk . . . reassuring him . . . that nobody was trying . . . to hurt him," she said, struggling to breathe and to speak.

Near the end, I asked if at any time after the shooting she had been given any message from Leyland about his continuing love for her.

"No."

"No?" I asked, surprised. "Did you know he tried to get that message to you?"

"How?"

"He wanted to come to see you and wasn't permitted to do so. Did you know that?" She looked confused, stunned.

"Did you know he was asked not to come to the hospital by your parents?" The prosecutor objected. "Irrelevant!" he hollered.

"Your Honor, this has something to do with her understanding of what this man *intended*. She has probably come to some wrong conclusions about his intent. I think that if I were Maria, lying there this way, and there was this man who had previously professed his love but who had never come to see me and who had never spoken to me afterward, it might be easy to conclude he didn't care. In fact, Leyland tried very hard to see her in the hospital, but was always prevented from doing so."

The judge sustained the prosecutor's objection, but I had said to Maria what I had wanted to say, and what I said was true. I looked over at Leyland. There were large tears welling up in his eyes again.

"I have no further questions," I said.

The judge's antagonism toward me had grown as the case proceeded. No matter how I tried to be gentle and caring, I was still that large man with the deep voice leaning over that defenseless child. Nothing could make the contest fair, and the judge had reacted to it. Now, it was time to argue to this judge that Leyland ought not be bound over to the district court for trial. That such a task was impossible was no reason for an attorney not to give his best.

I began quietly. "There has been an unspeakable tragedy here. But this tragedy is contagious. There is only one victim so far— Maria, a young woman without fault—innocent, decent, loving. She was healthy and happy. She was useful. Her parents and the people who knew her were justly proud of her. Then, one morning, this young woman lay in the hospital a hair from the grave, totally helpless.

"The outrage of seeing a child transformed from what she was to this—by a single crass and purposeless act—causes outrage beyond description." I looked at the judge. His eyes were squinted, hot. "At this point, we might feel justified to drag this man away to some dark place and leave him there forever.

"Now, Your Honor, how can I look you in the face and argue that a crime wasn't committed here? If my child were run down by a driver in a Mack truck who sped through the school zone, I would surely think a crime had been committed. But it wouldn't be a crime under the charge in this case unless there was a *malicious* intent, and what I want to talk about now is whether a preponderance of evidence establishes such a *malicious* intent."

I reviewed the evidence, and argued, of course, that there was none. As to Maria's testimony, how could she know Leyland's mind? And her statement that he intended to kill her had no probative value under the law, and couldn't be considered by the court.

"And so, Your Honor, if you bind my client over for trial to the district court, I will understand. If I sat in your chair, I might do the same. But what I ask you to do is to take a courageous step, one that won't be popular. The people up and down the streets of this community want Leyland's blood. The citizens who sit in front of their television sets want his blood. The people who read the newspapers—all want his blood. Everybody I have talked to wants him crucified. Give him to the mob! It is the easy, the popular, thing to do. Every person on the street will pat you on the back. Every person who knows of this case will crown you the hero if you bind him over." Then I told the judge I was sorry we had to present this painful case to him, and I sat down.

Now the judge looked over at the defendant and opened his eyes very wide, as if to release all that had been dammed behind them. "Would the defendant please stand up?" he commanded. Leyland rose, stiff, self-conscious, afraid. His face reddened.

The judge's voice was hard. "It will be the finding of this court that there is probable cause that you did commit the offense as charged, and I bind you over to the district court for trial." He said nothing more. He didn't need to. Leyland would now plead his case before a jury of his peers, and, as I saw it, the judge's ruling was Leyland's sure ticket to the penitentiary. Thereafter, Leyland entered a plea in the district court of "Not Guilty" and "Not Guilty by Reason of Mental Deficiency or Illness," which includes both the medical and legal notions of insanity. The pleas would put the state to its proof, and that is as it should be.

This was just the beginning of Leyland's problems. The total cost of Maria's hospitalization, the months she had spent in rehabilitation, the special nurses, the attendants and equipment she required, had already totaled nearly $100,000. Her father ran a small, successful business, but he was by no means able to satisfy the endless demands of her medical expenses. Such cases cry out for multi-million-dollar verdicts, and, naturally, her father hired one of the leading trial lawyers around, who now filed a civil suit against Leyland for damages.

Considering the severity of Maria's injuries, and the likelihood that the jury would add a large award to punish him, I thought Leyland's exposure to liability could total as much as $10 million. How could he pay her? Although he ostensibly ran his own business, all of his assets were fully encumbered. He did have a homeowner's insurance policy that provided him with liability coverage for his *negligent* acts in causing injury to his guests. Maria was his guest, all right, but the policy contained a standard provision that denied any protection to Leyland if his acts were *intentional*, and no one, least of all the insurance-company lawyers, could forget the well-publicized testimony of Maria at the preliminary hearing that "I know he . . . had meant . . . to do it. . . . It was *intentional*." By telling it as she remembered it, Maria had seemingly hurt herself badly. Although she could doubtless obtain a very large award from the jury, under the terms of Leyland's insurance, which were the only substantial monies she could get from him, the company would not be required to pay *any* sum as damages resulting from Leyland's *intentional* acts. Moreover, the total amount of Leyland's insurance policy was $100,000. I demanded that the company pay it to Maria immediately.

To an insurance company, every penny is its dearest offspring, and no company will surrender any of its children without a terrible fight. In the home office of one of the nation's largest insurers, there were, however, broad and confident smiles, for Leyland's company had a clear way out—Leyland had shot Maria intentionally, and therefore the company had no liability under its policy. To make sure, however, that the company was fully protected, its lawyers sued Leyland in what is known as a declaratory judgment action, the object of which was to obtain the court's finding that Leyland had, indeed, intended to shoot Maria, thus excusing the company's nonpayment of any sum to anybody for anything.

I had already concluded that Maria's testimony—that she knew Leyland intended to shoot her—would never be permitted at trial. The law does not empower one to read another's mind. On the other hand, every person charged with a crime is entitled to testify to his own intentions. I thought these simple rules of law would leave the insurance company facing Leyland's uncontradicted testimony that the shooting was purely an accident. He had no intent to shoot

Maria. The jury could conclude otherwise, of course, but gradually the insurance-company lawyers began to realize their position wasn't as solid as they had originally thought.

What the company hadn't anticipated was the counterclaim I filed. That launched a new and dangerous war against them. I alleged that the company knew that the "injuries to Maria are so horrible to behold and create such pity for her and such hatred against the defendant that any jury will be outraged and will punish him by convicting him." Then I called the insurance company's game on the public record. "It is the tactic of the company to refuse to pay [Maria] the just sums due her, hoping, instead, that [Leyland] will be found guilty of the criminal charge." I alleged this placed the company in *conflict* with its own insured. An insurance company is supposed to protect its insured, not injure him. Here, the company had hired one set of lawyers to do him in with a declaratory judgment action, and another to defend him in the suit brought by Maria against Leyland for her damages. Proof by the insurance company in the declaratory judgment action that Leyland had acted intentionally could aid the state in convicting him, not to mention that it would relieve the company of any obligation to pay Maria the $100,000—which, of course, so far as the company was concerned, was the object of their game. My counterclaim against the company alleged both the company's bad faith and its intentional violation of Leyland's civil rights. I asked for $1 million to compensate him for his pain and suffering, and $10 million to punish the corporation—punitive damages.

Now, those calling the shots for the company began to realize that the whole damn case was getting too risky. What if the jury found Leyland was insane or that his capacity was otherwise so diminished by drinking he could harbor no intent? What if the jury believed it was an accident? Accidents are not intended.

At the last minute, the company caved in. Don't forget, a jury might hit the company big for having run wild and loose with Leyland's rights, in which case some claims supervisor could end up in Nome, Alaska. But now the company men made another bad move, precipitated, I think, by the panic that often sets in once the enemy is routed and in full retreat. So desperately did the company want to save its pennies that, after paying its $100,000 to Maria, it completely withdrew all its attorneys from all of the cases, leaving Leyland without any representation in Maria's damage suit against him. Some company big shot didn't think that one through, because the company had a duty under its policy to provide Leyland a defense, including an attorney, at the company's expense. The way I read the situation, company strategists probably thought I would enter the case for Leyland, and when I didn't, the company was wide open for the moves I would now make to force the company to pay Maria beyond the limits of its policy.

I asked Maria's attorney to make Leyland an offer of settlement. As soon as the judge had set Maria's damage suit for trial, her lawyer did just that. He offered to settle her case for $5 million. I wrote the insurance company a nasty letter. The company had turned its back on Leyland, I wrote. His defense required skillful attorneys, and now he had no one to defend him. The company had no right to first throw its attorneys into the battle, and then, after it paid Maria, "to run and hide, leaving Leyland defenseless. The law will not permit that. It is outrageous conduct." Didn't the insurance company want to take a fresh look at what it had done? But as is often the case with large corporations, the company now seemed unable to make a decision at all.

Because Leyland had pled "Diminished Capacity," the law required that he be sent to the Wyoming State Hospital for observation, and after that institution had discharged him as sane and tryable, we hired our own psychiatrist to examine him in a private sanitarium. Now that Leyland was sober, the horrible dimensions of his act began to close in on him, and, more than anything else, he longed to make whatever small amends he could. He gathered up all the property he owned—his guns, his home, everything—and sold it, paying the proceeds, some $13,921.37, to Maria. Further, he agreed to pay her $1,500 a month so long as she should live, and to assign to her the net proceeds, if ever any, from his suits against his insurance company. In turn, on the advice of her parents and her lawyer, Maria agreed that any judgment she might obtain against Leyland in her lawsuit against him would be satisfied if he fully performed his agreement.

The day of the trial, I stayed home. No one appeared on behalf of Leyland, and a default was, of course, entered against him. Now I wrote the insurance company attorneys another letter. "Your company has one last chance to set aside the default and to try to keep the damages down. You don't have much time. Won't you please get on the telephone and tell the company to help Leyland? It will be a lot easier for the company to do what should be done now rather than make technical, legal, mealymouthed, lawyer-type arguments to the jury later on when Leyland sues your company for his damages resulting from the company's failure to act now, as they should." The company buried its head.

A short time thereafter, the judge set Maria's damages against

Leyland at $6,598,172 and I filed suit in the state court against the company for this same amount, and I demanded punitive damages as well. Now the company was in the soup, and its attorneys promptly removed the case to the federal court. On January 13, 1980, facing an impending trial, the insurance company entered into a settlement with both Leyland and Maria for an undisclosed amount. All of the money was paid to Maria. The settlement agreement provided that its terms would not be divulged, and, bound thereby, I am to this day unable to reveal what additional sums of money Maria received, but I can tell you that the amount was, under the circumstances, agreeable to Maria's parents and to her lawyers and, most certainly, to Leyland.

In the meantime, Leyland, still awaiting trial on the criminal case, was finally permitted to visit Maria. He pled with her to believe him when he swore it was all a horrible accident. How could he have intended to kill her? He loved her. I could hear Maria gasping, one word at a time, one sob at a time. I could understand her conflict. In her heart, she knew that if Leyland had not been drunk, he would never have harmed her. She knew of the great lengths to which we had gone to force Leyland's insurance company to pay not only its policy limits but much, much more. And bound by her own Christian ideals in that ungodly conflict between forgiveness and revenge, she had no choice. Whatever her reasons, Maria now interceded on Leyland's behalf with the prosecutor.

My associate in the case, Dallas Laird, a bright young lawyer whose talents were then just beginning to be revealed, had convinced the trial judge in the criminal case that much of the state's evidence, including the gun, was inadmissible as having been unlawfully seized without a warrant, and the court's ruling would cause all the scientific tests performed on the evidence to be excluded as well— such as proof that the gun in the state's possession was the gun that was used to shoot Maria. How much this actually weakened the state's case I don't know. But a little over a year after the shooting, the state dismissed its criminal charge against Leyland. The prosecutor spoke to the press, claiming he was "surprised and dismayed" that Maria had changed her mind about prosecuting Leyland. He said, "It is apparent the testimony she would give at the trial would not support a criminal conviction." As I saw it, the criminal charge would have been very hard, if not impossible, to defend, with or without Maria's testimony. There had been over thirty articles appearing in the local paper reporting the most morbid details of the case, not to mention a constant barrage on television. Every citizen had seen that picture of Maria being rolled into court in her wheelchair. I had moved for a change of venue, but the judge had denied my motion despite the widespread furor in the community against Leyland. A jury wouldn't care if the act was intentional or not. The jurors would convict Leyland and demand his punishment. But finally, even the prosecutor himself must have been reluctant to force Maria into court to testify against the man she had now forgiven.

The state's dismissal of its case deprived me of the chance to deliver my final argument to the jury, but Maria probably knew that any argument I might have made would fail to save him—that only she in her powerlessness had such power. Perhaps she chose to save herself from what she foresaw as the ravages of vengeance. Some may think her change of heart was connected to her desperate need for the money she would receive, but I think she simply had to forgive him. What else could she have done? I have no doubt she loved Leyland, maybe more as a mother, but that is worse, since mothers must forgive, and mothers do. Always. Even as her son swings on the gallows, a mother loves him and has already forgiven him. And yet Maria must have despised the day she met this man. She must have hated him for what he had done to her. And pitied him. She could never have revenge, for the more she sought justice, the more she would be hurt by it.

One month after Maria withdrew her charges against Leyland, she died.

It must have been maddening to Maria's parents that Leyland should go free, and that some soulless insurance company treating this human tragedy as just another entry in its profit-and-loss statement should be permitted to stand in for Leyland—to stand in for justice. Soon thereafter, Maria's parents, long married, were divorced. Perhaps, had they been able to witness justice together, it might have been different. They had wanted Leyland punished, that much I know, and to them, the system had failed. Perhaps, finally, they had no other place to lay their anger than upon each other.

As for me—well, once in the case, I had a duty to defend Leyland. And strangely, I still felt the need to defend myself for having done so. I had argued to the prosecutor that locking Leyland in the foulest prison would never provide the funds necessary to purchase the small comforts required to help Maria face her suffering. I admit that in aiding her to recover the monies from the insurance company, I had also helped Leyland escape punishment. But I did as the system demands: I zealously defended my client. Still, the most powerful of all defenses, the one that in the end resolved this tragic case, was forgiveness. I admit I worked to gain it for Leyland, and when I did, I hurled its might at the state and smashed its case. "To forgive is blessed," and forgiveness is as much a part of justice as revenge. Gandhi once said, "If everyone took an eye for an eye, the whole world would be blind."

Yet the pure rage that stems from an unredressed injury can be more fearsome than that produced by the original wrong. For any system of justice to survive, it must be respected. Too often, our Christian ideals against revenge leave the system appearing palsied. Forgiveness alone solves no human need. If I slap you on the right cheek and you turn the other, what may appear to be forgiveness is only masked anger. We shall never be friends until both your anger is dispelled and my guilt atoned. When we fail to justly punish the criminal, the community sees justice aborted. With its own ignoble voice, blood does, indeed, cry out for blood. Revenge, too, is always at the heart of justice.

But that single bullet had destroyed Leyland as well as Maria. I was powerless to salve his guilt, but I felt my own. By helping Leyland escape punishment at the hands of the law, I had also deprived him of the right to know the healing power of just punishment. Despite the foppish shell he had presented as the leader of the "fun-seekers," I had thought there was something worth saving in Leyland, although then it was never clear to me precisely what it was. When the great spruce tree burns, its cones explode, and the seeds of a new forest are planted. I held to the faith of that metaphor—that infamous fires father new life.

After Maria's death, Leyland moved away and tried to start over. He wandered in and out of alcohol-rehabilitation centers, and I lost track of him. But I wanted to know how to write the last chapter of Maria's story, and I found Leyland through his parents. He was glad to hear from me. His voice seemed strong.

"I've been going to write to you," he said. "I've wanted to tell you about my life and to thank you. It's been nearly eight years since all that happened. I've always remembered that one thing you told me—you said, 'Leyland, it is *your* choice as to what happens to the rest of your life.'" Then he told me that he had joined Alcoholics Anonymous, and that it had been five years now since he'd had a drink.

"I am very fortunate, and I'm sharing what I've learned with others. I give guest lectures at the college to the Health and Education classes. I don't just cut it short and tell them I had a drinking problem, I tell them the *whole* story."

"The *whole* story?"

"Yes, everything. It doesn't have any impact if I just say I had 'legal problems.'"

"Perhaps that's a part of the atonement that goes into making you whole again," I said. A modern-day version of the stocks and pillories of the pilgrims.

"Yes," he said.

"Do those ghosts ever sneak in and shake at you?"

"Yes," he said. "But I don't want to totally brush them away. I want them in my life."

"You don't want the ghosts to go away?"

"No. They will always have a part to play."

"You sound different," I said. "You sound mature. You've grown up."

"I've made mistakes. I can't change that. All I can do is to live today to the best of my ability."

Then Leyland spoke to me about how both his misery and his joy had been contagious. "Besides Maria and her family, the thing that hurt me the worst was the pain I brought to my parents. But one month after I stopped drinking, my father also stopped. And then my mother quit, too. We came together as a family. We are very close," he said. Leyland's resurrection and all that went with it gave me a new sense of fulfillment and became the magical legacy of Maria in her search for human justice.

But what of Donna—that young Wyoming woman I mentioned who died in an automobile with brakes the manufacturer had known all along were defective? She was needlessly sacrificed in the company's competitive war with Japan. Despite the settlement the company paid to the family, there was no justice. There was not even an apology. Never once did her young face flash across the mind of the president or its chief engineer as they monitored the track of the company's stock. They never heard of Donna or her family. They never knew of the parents' lawsuit in a remote Wyoming court. The case was just another digit in the company's litigation portfolio that was tended to by the company lawyers. The death, the grief, the waste, were commingled in the corporation's profit-and-loss statement like a small bug mixed into the concrete of Hoover Dam. The company made no offer to change. There has been no admission of guilt. There never will be. There will be only the family's memories, and, of course, the expedient payment of money.

At first, the grief consumed them. But the grief turned to horror with the family's realization that her life had been wasted and that nothing could be made of it, except money. I suggested they endow a scholarship fund in the name of their daughter with some of the money and some of my fee. And they did. Now, every year for fifty years, there will be a bright young woman, perhaps someone like Donna, who will go to college and who will thereafter make her contributions—and the corporation's dead money will, indeed, be transformed into something living.

Clarence Darrow was right. Justice cannot be defined. And to the same extent that justice cannot be defined, neither can it be realized. Yet is not our great challenge to form a system that harmonizes such noble ideals as forgiveness with such a human impulse as revenge? At the heart of justice is a divine spirit. It sprouts from the same seeds as life itself. And although we can define neither life nor justice, we are able to recognize injustice, the supreme form of which is to surrender to the status quo and to sanctify the myths and fantasies that breed it, among which is the national legend that in America there is liberty and justice for all.

I feel like a man groping through a dark and dangerous room. Even though my eyes are adjusted to the dark, I can still see very little. I stumble, although I've passed through this room long ago, often in the same places as before. I rely mostly on my feelings. I am afraid. Sometimes I recognize a danger and call out a warning. Occasionally a brief beam shines through the window denying the dark. "Justice for none" is as much a slogan as "justice for all." Still, in a society in which we are free to explore for better ways, to embrace the fiction of "justice for all" terminates the search. Though the fool seeks solutions to the unsolvable and struggles to know the unknowable, such has also consumed the souls of messiahs and saints. The providence of man is never to know, but to search— always to search. So let us get on with our business.

2 | LAWYERS
Hawkers and Merchants

One can no more search for justice through the entangled labyrinths of the law without a lawyer than one can trod through fearsome, uncharted jungles without a guide. There is, however, no scarcity of these sons of canon and code, and daughters of order and ordinance, to lead us through such perilous places. Lawyers are everywhere. They abound in our hamlets and swarm in our cities. They overcrowd our legislatures, flourish as the heads of state and, like dead fish too long in the water, rise to the top of our great corporations. What is happening in America that we should provide our citizens with 2.67 lawyers per thousand people while Japan needs only 0.10? Two-thirds of the lawyers on earth live in the United States, while we account for only 6 percent of the world's population. In our nation's capital, there is one lawyer for every sixty people. There were 355,000 lawyers in the United States in 1970. Between 1970 and 1975, admissions to the bar increased a staggering 91 percent, and today, 40,000 additional lawyers are produced annually in our universities. Already there are over 675,000 lawyers in the country, and at the current rate there will be over a million by the middle of the next decade.

Why the proliferation of these legalistic creatures in a society that has rarely embraced them? The abhorrence of the profession is documented throughout Anglo-Saxon history. Shakespeare's Dick the Butcher in *King Henry VI* exclaimed, "The first thing we do, let's kill all the lawyers!" And Dickens wrote, "If there were no bad people, there would be no good lawyers." Poor Richard in his *Almanac* said, "God works wonders now and then; Behold! a lawyer, an honest man." So scorned were lawyers by the colonists that they were depicted as "lawyer-birds, with their long bills" and "lawyer-fish, always slippery." Both Massachusetts and Rhode Island prohibited lawyers from serving in their colonial assemblies. Brigham Young, upon establishing his utopia in the Utah desert, characterized lawyers as "a stink in the nostrils of every Latter-day Saint," and described the courtroom as "a cage of unclean birds, a den and kitchen of the devil." Early in the nineteenth century, the Baptist preacher John Leland attacked "a host of lawyers who infest our land . . . like the swarms of locusts in Egypt that eat up every green thing." Even in Riverton, Wyoming, the uncelebrated genesis of my legal career, the townsfolk spoke disparagingly of the profession. I remember once hearing Emmett Osborne of Osborne's Shoes talk about lawyers at the morning coffee klatch. "A lawyer is like a fly in a dog's ear," he said. "Makes a man go plumb crazy."

The California Bar Association brings us worse news. Its recent survey shows that 75 percent of the people form their bad opinion of the profession not on idle gossip and jokes but from direct dealing with lawyers themselves. That study concluded, "Overall, the general public's view of lawyers is not encouraging. . . . Indeed, lawyers are perceived as arrogant people who create problems, not solve them, and who are unconcerned about their clients or the public at large." Only 19 percent of the respondents gave lawyers high marks for maintaining honest and ethical standards. The negative words and phrases most frequently chosen to describe lawyers were "greedy," "arrogant," "they charge too much," and they are "not nice people." Forty-five percent of lawyers themselves thought their peers self-serving, and 59 percent thought their members overbearing. Ironically, a society committed to the rights of mankind, we have always seemed to hate the one profession that is charged with the preservation of such rights.

In the minds of the public, lawyers who represent people are often associated, even implicated, with those they represent, and since there are usually two sides to a case, lawyers stand damned by half of the public most of the time. I daresay that if doctors were charged with the morals of those they treat, the medical profession would be in as much trouble as their brothers and sisters of the bar. But it was Watergate that finally dropped the profession into its seemingly bottomless stinkhole. We all remember—the White House occupied by a lawyer who, in turn, had surrounded himself with lawyers, almost all of whom were found guilty of burglary or perjury or obstruction of justice or worse. Anthony Lewis of *The New York Times* wrote, "The record of the lawyers around Richard Nixon is one of the most appalling aspects of his Presidency. . . . Lawyers made their names symbols of contempt for the law." John Dean exclaimed, "How in God's name could so many lawyers get involved in something like this?" The Nixon lawyers confirmed the underlying suspicions of the country—that *lawyer* was synonymous with *shyster* and *crook*. After Watergate, it just got worse.

During Watergate, I comforted myself with the memories that Jefferson and Madison and Hamilton and Adams had all been lawyers, too, and that Jefferson and his colleague Madison had framed perhaps the most revered instrument in human history, the Constitution of the United States, with its venerable Bill of Rights. Theirs was the holy work of lawyers. Hadn't these gentlemen guaranteed liberties to the citizen that had never before been bestowed upon the human race? The first Congress of the United States was dominated by the legal profession. Abe Lincoln was a lawyer and so was Roosevelt, and I tried to remember that Hitler himself said, "I shall not rest until every German sees that it is a shameful thing to be a lawyer." And even in our times, hadn't lawyers and judges pried the nation free from the ugly grip of racism in *Brown* v. *Board of Education*, and hadn't the profession fought for women and struggled for our constitutional rights under *Miranda* and *Mapp*? During the painful days of Watergate, I held to the belief that the legal system and the lawyers in it would save the nation, and indeed it was lawyers, both as prosecutors and judges, who brought their errant brothers to justice. Wasn't old Sam Ervin a lawyer, and Judge Sirica, too? Yet a pervasive sense of shame hung over our profession. Lawyers began to understand how clients felt who were charged with crimes they hadn't committed. Guilty or not, one felt guilty. I also felt angry.

During Watergate, I impatiently waited for the American Bar Association to rise up in defense of its membership, but I heard only feeble, quavering sounds from headquarters. I told a gathering of the ABA that its vigorous and forthright defense of the profession had all the potency and sway of those mysterious noises I used to hear as a child when I listened to my grandmother in the morning in the bathroom. What black magic, what sorcery, was being performed behind that locked door? Later, I discovered it was only a sweet old woman cleaning her dentures and putting them back in her mouth, after which she said the same grandmotherly things to me as always—and that, I told the ABA, was how the bar sounded to me in its defense of the profession.

After Watergate, Chief Justice Burger decried the trial bar as a house bursting at the seams with incompetents, and he further fomented the public's hatred against us like Pope Innocent VIII, who, in the Dark Ages, launched his infamous hunt for witches that would last for centuries. We lawyers, like witches, were being blamed for nearly every nature of evil in our society. We were the slickers finding loopholes in the law to turn criminals back on the streets. We were the shysters who were into every business deal jamming the honest flow of commerce with fakery and fraud. We were the greedy ambulance chasers representing rancorous clients who clogged the court dockets. Given the chance, the public would have torched us with our own law books. I took the attacks personally. Although I agreed with Judge Burger that many of the profession were unfit for their work, had he forgotten that many of his "brethren" in the judiciary were once among those he now charged as incompetent?

I railed at the bar in my speeches. I wanted them to get up on their hind legs and do battle. If they lacked the courage to fight for themselves and for their good names, how could they fight for anyone else? They were too passive, too frightened, too intellectual, too dehumanized, and too surrendered to the system to represent the people. They had become the system. They didn't care as much about who they had become as how they *appeared*. Yet I loved lawyers, and I thought I knew what was wrong. I wanted lawyers to *care*—about themselves and about their clients—and to fight for their clients. I spoke to public defenders, to groups of young struggling trial lawyers. I complimented them. I scolded them.

I told them stories—of Sir Francis Drake, the most feared seaman of his time, a pirate for the queen, a glorified robber knighted for his criminal excellence in stripping the Spanish of their gold. Yet Drake had been aided by a secret weapon. After months on a diet of salt pork and hardtack, his opponents grew weak from scurvy, a common and dreaded disease among sailors. Often men went blind, their teeth rotted and fell out, and some died. They blamed the Devil. But Drake learned that a little lime juice kept his men healthy (and that, of course, is why the English are, to this day, called Limeys). Such a small thing, so powerful, so magical, this fruit that, unknown to them, contained vitamin C. I told lawyers they would never be knighted by any queen, and certainly they would be charged as pirates for their raids against the great corporations on behalf of their injured clients. But the secret I was about to give them would vest them with a terrible power—one their adversaries knew nothing of, one as magical as Drake's lime juice. It is the magic of *caring* for one's clients, because caring is the secret of winning. Juries feel its irresistible power and respond to it, and even judges are not immune to its magic. I asked the lawyers, "How can you expect a jury to care for your client if you do not? Caring is contagious," I said.

Sometimes a young lawyer would ask, "But how could anybody love some of the types we have to represent?" I knew that public defenders don't have the luxury of choosing their cases. Habitual petty thieves and drug addicts dumped on top of their already bulging caseload become their newest clients. Look at it this way, I suggested: "Imagine newborns in a bright nursery. Which was you and which your criminal client? What happened to that child after he was bundled up and hauled off to some dark ghetto to begin those long years of festering? What scars deformed him, so that even you, who stand for him in the courtroom, are repulsed by him? What have they done to him? And to you?"

I preached on.

"Perhaps you can care only for that tiny child inside. If you cannot love your client, could you at least love the child? Perhaps you can hate what has been done to him. Behind those hard faces and vacant eyes are injured people who have been too afraid and too desperate too long. And if you can't love your client, maybe you can love yourselves. What we do is blessed. It is only we—alone and in lonely places—who stand between tyranny and liberty. When we zealously defend the lowest, the forgotten, and the damned, we preserve the system that protects all of us." I sounded like the Methodist minister of my childhood.

Yet it is one thing to preach and another to survive in that jungle called "the law business." "It's hard to defend the Constitution when the people don't want you to defend it, when the people want to hang your clients, and the judges have grown calloused and bitter," says Richard Sherman, noted Los Angeles criminal defense attorney. "What the people want is more police, more prisons, not more rights—and not more of those damnable lawyers." I told my lawyer audiences, "I know how tired you are of being stoned by the mob as you try to drag the limp and drowning body of liberty to safety. I know how tired you are of being told you are incompetent by judges whose sense of justice has shriveled up and hardened into something that looks like an old prune seed."

I hated being hated. Once I overheard somebody talking about me in the next booth at a restaurant in Jackson. "He's worse than the criminals he represents. *He* knows better." Later, my youngest son told me a kid at school said he wished our house would burn down, with me in it, and even friends often asked very confidentially, "How can you represent those guilty people?" as if my clients had already been tried and convicted as soon as they were charged. In the aftermath of Watergate, the people began to seriously hate lawyers. The people abandoned their rights like men at sea dumping their precious cargo overboard from a sinking ship. They passed legislation against themselves. Caps were installed in many states on the amount people could recover for their own injuries. The death penalty was reinstated across the land, and the courts trimmed the protection of its citizens against unreasonable searches and seizures. The press unabashedly jeered at the profession. We were hated, all right. One day somebody stopped me on the street. "Hey, Spence," he said. "Do you know why they're using lawyers now instead of white rats in the laboratory?" I went along with him. "Well," he said, "there're a lot more lawyers. Sometimes they get attached to the rats, but"— he paused to let me know the punch line was about to come—"there are certain things a rat just won't do." Then he laughed like hell and swaggered on down the street.

Yet if a lawyer represented the local bank or the railroad or the insurance companies, and lived in the right part of town and belonged to the right clubs, well, that was different. He was seen as one of "the gentlemen of the profession." I thought it strange people didn't realize that whenever the bank gave the nod, the *gentlemen* of the bar would foreclose on the people's homes and farms, and whenever the people were hurt or their loved ones killed, the *gentlemen* of the bar, for their standard hourly fee, would defeat their just claims, while the *rabble* of the profession still fought for the little guy.

I tried to preach our profession out of the doldrums. It was like a captain blowing against his own limp sails. I told my audiences that it was all right to tell the jury the truth. I quoted Lincoln: "Resolve to be honest at all events: and if in your judgment you cannot be an honest lawyer, resolve to be honest without being a lawyer. Choose some other occupation, rather than one in the choosing of which you do, in advance, consent to be a knave."

"Tell the truth, Mr. Spence?" one young turk asked. "You want us to tell the truth? We can never win if we tell the truth. We are judged by our skill in skewing the truth."

"Yes," I repeated. "Tell the jury the truth." Then I tried to explain the great power of truth, and of a lawyer who cares for his client and who tells the jury simple, honest things. "Isn't what we're afraid of that we'll fail our clients? Well, tell the jury. If you care, they will also care. Caring is contagious," I preached again. Some listened. One year I gave over fifty speeches to as many different groups. I was a cheap program—I went without fee anywhere they asked. My sermons were a labor of love. I told lawyers, "We occupy a high place in this land. Ours is a fearsome duty—to fight for justice, for people. We can win for them by being truthful. We can win their respect once more by being real, by caring. And the people long for the return of their warriors—for us."

Yet, sadly, we, too, had become commodities that were offered for sale, and often what the people bought they didn't like. The people were angry. They wanted lawyers who would fight for them. They wanted their champions back. I told lawyers we could no longer sell our lives, one hour at a time, like some poor street vendor selling his tricks and his toys. We were more than mere commodities. We were warriors. We had to lay it all down for that one small, frightened person who clung to us because we were all he had.

When I was in law school, the people thought differently of lawyers, and we students held the local Laramie attorneys in consummate awe. For me, they were magnificent. Whereas my father attended church in a shirt with a collar that curled up at the ends like dried pasta and wore the same suit every Sunday until the knees bulged like a weary maternity dress, these gentlemen of the bar who came to speak to us at the law school were spiffed-up in their well-pressed, three-piece pin-striped suits with white shirts and stiff starched collars, and they wore shiny black shoes that shone like jewels. They spoke with authority, if not elegance, and they charmed us, and I wished above all else to be like them. One day right after the war, I saw Al Pence, Laramie's leading lawyer, driving a brand-new black Chevy sedan right down Main Street, the first I had seen of the postwar models. By then, my father had a '37 Ford. It was the family's only car, but he drove it to godawful places hunting in the high backcountry, and in town, you could hear the damned old rattletrap coming down the street from a mile away. The fenders flapped in the breeze, and the engine coughed and wheezed like an old man on his last legs. It was embarrassing to be seen in it. Oh, to be a lawyer. Oh, to have a new black Chevy! Those were mighty ambitions for a young man from Wyoming.

The day I was notified I had passed the bar, I went to town just to feel the pride of walking down Main Street as a lawyer. As I passed the townsfolk, they never gave me a second glance, but I spoke to them under my breath. "I am an attorney-at-law, sir. Yes, sir! An attorney-at-law." I remember coming to a line of people standing in front of a mobile X-ray unit operated by authority of the state public-health service. The general welfare, according to prevailing wisdom, required the citizenry to submit to chest X rays to facilitate an early diagnosis of tuberculosis. I got in line along with the rest of the sincere citizens, none of whom had TB or even thought that they might, but all of whom agreed to be X-rayed because that was what good citizens were doing that morning. When it came my turn, the volunteer who was filling out the cards asked me my occupation.

"I am an attorney-at-law, ma'am," I said, almost choking from pride.

The woman looked at me very closely over her spectacles. At twenty-three, I still suffered from adolescent pimples. Irritated, she asked my occupation again, and now I raised my right eyebrow—one of the prerequistes of any good trial man—and once more I protested, "I am an attorney-at-law, ma'am." Then she wrote something down and let me have my chest X-rayed anyway.

By this time, I already had a wife and two children to support. But what I really wanted to do was to fight and to hunt. That's what lawyers were for—to fight for the people, and somehow I had got hunting mixed in there, too. It had something to do with being a man. I had no ambitions to achieve great wealth or power or fame. All that was beyond the understanding of a small-town Wyoming boy. I had hardly heard of Wall Street. I had never been to Washington, D.C.

Then, the bar took for granted that its members had a clear duty to represent the poor. I was impressed that the poorest lawyers were usually the most willing to give of their lives. Now, in practice, I soon learned that the so-called "fathers of the bar" were generally too busy representing the banks and the utility companies and certain wealthy oil men in important litigation. Everybody seemed to understand this—that theirs was important work—and when their names came up on the list to defend some impecunious wretch, they were usually successful in begging off. They were close to the judges, while the younger, poorer lawyers were not, and, besides, they made their contributions to society by giving occasional speeches at the monthly lawyers' meetings on ethics. I thought it strange that the young lawyers, the poor lawyers, the lawyers representing the indigent, were never respected for their ethics. Ethics was, instead, mysteriously connected with position, prestige, and power—with money. I remember clearly the lecture I received from the president of the bar when, upon my opening a practice, the Riverton paper published a small news item announcing my arrival in town. That was advertising, charged the revered elder of the bar—among the worst crimes a lawyer could commit, right along with ambulance chasing and jury tampering. If a new lawyer came to town, the rules were that nobody should know it, lest, I suppose, a few dissatisfied clients of the established bar might seek him out.

In those days, clients tried to sneak into your office without anybody seeing them. It was shameful to need a lawyer. And people talked. That's why most lawyers in Riverton had their offices in the upstairs rooms in the Masonic Temple Building along with the accountants and the dentists. A client could hold on to his jaw, and people would assume he was headed for a tooth extraction. The leading citizens were rarely in court. They met every morning for coffee at the Teton Hotel, where a consensus was achieved on all local, national, and international issues. The town fathers were a close-knit brotherhood. They did business with each other, entertained each other in their homes, and belonged to the Elks so they could drink together on Sundays. For one to sue another would have been a divisive act not easily tolerated. Somehow things got worked out—but usually not in court.

To keep the family fed and the rent paid, I ran for prosecuting attorney, knocked on every door in the county, including all the doors on the adjoining Indian reservation, and, to my surprise, I was elected. I began to prosecute a lot of criminal cases—murders, rapes, and all the rest—and in the years that followed, I got fairly proficient as a trial lawyer at the state's expense. As I look back to those days and the nearly two decades that followed before Watergate, it seems to me that the legal profession held up pretty well. I liked being a lawyer. I was proud of my profession, and I thought, perhaps out of naïveté, perhaps only wishfully, that the people thought well of us. After Watergate, however, hope that the profession might regain any semblance of its former position of acceptance and respect seemed to vanish. Today, the latest joke going around about lawyers is: What do you call ten lawyers on the bottom of the ocean? The answer: a good start.

But lawyers reflect the standards and values of the people who hire them. J. P. Morgan, confronted by a lawyer who did not tell him what he wanted to hear, said, "Your job is to help me do what I want to do." On the other hand, we are not a nation that summarily disposes of our criminal population with a firing squad. If the guilty as well as the innocent must have a fair trial, then lawyers must be permitted to vigorously defend the rights of those who are accused of wrongdoing—including those they know are criminally culpable. If we are not to be a nation that tortures the accused for confessions, condones police brutality, and permits the law to burst open our doors in search of evidence against us, then lawyers must throw up a shield of technicalities to protect us—and, consequently, to protect criminals as well. If we value our right to tell our lawyers everything in order that they may know the truth to defend us, then lawyers must also keep the secrets of dopers and murderers. If we expect our lawyers not to judge us, but to fight for us, even when our cases are legally weak or morally thin or indefensible, we must expect lawyers to take cases that do not pass the scrutiny of reason or satisfy our ideas of justice. The people create the cases, not their lawyers.

The heart and soul and face of America is changing, and so are her lawyers. Our attitudes respecting the family have undergone a drastic mutation. Divorce suits clog the courts. Anguished couples spend years fighting over their children. Our moral structure has been altered. We sue for palimony. Gays are no longer closeted. Abortion is legal. Crime is on the rampage. We sue for sex, race, and age discrimination. We sue for the rights of those who wish to die, for those who wish to live, for those who want their children bused and for those who do not. We sue for victims of corporate crime, and, endlessly, we sue over money and things. We are not a passive and peaceful population. Our mothers are no longer in the home. And our lawyers, some of whom are mothers, are only reflections of who we are. We want success—whatever that is—and we want money—whatever it stands for. And our lawyers are no different. Judge John F. Grady of the United States District Court in Chicago, speaking to the American Bar Association, recently said, "What I see happening is that a growing percentage of the bar is not only primarily concerned with pecuniary gain but is preoccupied with pecuniary gain to the exclusion of everything else. . . . [E]thics," he said, "have been harnessed in the service of pecuniary gain." We also want our rights, and by damn, we will sue for them. Nobody would have us go back to "the good old days" when people were born in poor backwoods towns and lived and died in obscure drudgery, when minorities were second-class citizens and women household slaves. In "the good old days" when I launched my legal career in Wyoming, the "Equality State," the first state in which women were given the right to vote, there were only two women engaged in the practice of law. Today, the profession is surging with them.

America is changing. Over fifty years ago, when I was a boy, my family knew no lawyers, good or bad. Except during hunting and fishing seasons, we trudged off to church every Sunday and held our potluck suppers in the church basement and everybody knew everybody—and we trusted each other. I never knew a lawyer, never heard my parents even speak of one. My father never had a will. He worked for wages, and whatever business agreements he entered into were few, made on a handshake, and kept. A man did right by his neighbors. When my father brought home an elk or an antelope, he hung it up in the garage to age, and when it was prime, he delivered a quarter to the widow across town, who didn't have a man to hunt for her, and gave another to the barber across the street, who was pretty well strapped because everybody, including us, cut their hair at home.

In the summertime, I slept in the backyard in a tent, and we rented our bedrooms to tourists for a dollar a night. They always paid. We never locked the doors. Nor did they. I sold the sweet peas I grew in our backyard garden to the ladies at the village brothels (my mother never knew), and I sold my mother's fresh cinnamon rolls door to door, to the people across town, but I never knocked on the door of a lawyer, so far as I know.

My mother never stopped working—never wanted to. She roasted wheat in the oven and ground it by hand in an old coffee grinder for our breakfast cereal. She fed the chickens and gathered the eggs, and when my father was off hunting, she milked the goat, and she watered and hoed the garden and canned the garden vegetables, and in the early fall, while my father fished for trout, we gathered wild chokecherries and plums for her jellies and jams, and she also canned the fish my father caught. She made all our clothes, including our leather winter coats, which she sewed out of the hides of deer and elk my father brought home and had tanned, and, of course, she cut our hair. It was she who papered our rooms and did the painting. We had a sense that *we* were in control of our lives. We didn't need a lawyer to sue a corporation for false advertising. We made our own or did without. We didn't need a lawyer to sue for the botulin in the corn that had been canned in some distant factory. My mother canned it herself. We didn't need to sue Delta Airlines for the loss of our luggage or our lives. We never flew in an airplane. There was no need to sue Ford for a car manufactured with defective brakes. We putted along in our Model A at thirty miles an hour on empty country roads. There was no call to sue for the rights of women. Few were thinking of women's rights—least of all, women themselves. Martin Luther King, Jr., had yet to march to Selma. Civil-rights suits were unheard of. Most of the nation's blacks congregated in the large northern cities or lay subdued in the South. In Sheridan, Wyoming, a small town at the foot of the Big Horn Mountains where I grew up, there was one black child in our school, and he was there for only part of the year. Most folks still lived in small, self-supporting towns where local businessmen were both responsive and responsible to their customers, and were honest. Folks walked to work, and young people strolled with their dates on a night out. The daily frantic rush through the combat zones of our nation's freeways was an experience unknown to most of us. We could not envision the mammoth body of litigation engendered by the modern automobile—suits against manufacturers for defective cars, claims against drivers for injuries in wrecks, criminal charges for drunk driving.

America has changed. We are a manifoldly more complex culture, and our "national personality" is making new demands on both the legal system and the legal profession. Lawrence Friedman, in his thoughtful book *Total Justice*, says, "To understand what is happening inside the legal system, it is best to start from the outside, by looking at great general movements of social force. America has made the legal system what it is; the legal system has not made America." Our morals, our ideals, our values—and hence, our laws—keep changing. Today, certain major segments of our citizenry—blacks, gays, women—have gained rights that were never dreamed of a generation ago and reflect the nation's new intense yearning for equality. Although many of our citizens remain powerless to enforce their newly won rights, and many of their gains seem more a nodding rhetoric than a practiced reality, we are, nonetheless, a nation that litigates—not because of lawyers, or because there is something insidious and decadent going on in the moral understructure of the country, but because the national personality has changed, and along with it our expectations of justice—a justice we demand on the job, in our schools, in our homes, on the streets, within our families—a justice Friedman calls "total justice." That is not all bad. In fact, it is not bad at all. Individual rights are not bounteous in Russia or China. No profusion of lawsuits clogs the courts of Cuba. There is no "litigation explosion" in the poor countries of the Third World. That Americans continue to use their courts and employ lawyers tells us something of our growing appetite for human rights and suggests the possibilities of realizing the American dream of justice—justice for all.

Still, everywhere we hear the same old cry: "Too many lawyers!" Former Chief Justice Burger thought so. So does the established bar. We are told there are too many lawyers out there scrambling over each other to make a dollar. The specter we are shown is horrible—hungry lawyers drumming up business, inventing new rights, and encouraging groundless litigation. Yet today there are not too many lawyers, but *too few*—too few of the right kind; too few who are trained as fighters; too few who will represent the people. There are too few warriors and too few committed to a just cause. Like us, our young lawyers search, not for justice but for what someone called the "twin Holy Grails of American life—money and success." Skillfully, designedly, our young have made themselves salable to corporate America as replacement parts for the legal machine that grinds away in corporate law firms at lush hourly rates. Many students are recruited by the large firms before they have graduated, and at salaries larger than those we pay our veteran judges. The new lawyers flock to our large cities and descend in hordes on Wall Street and Washington, D.C. There many will spend their lives dotting i's and crossing t's in high-floor cubbyholes—human sacrifices to the profit gods of their corporate employers. Already, only a fortnight past puberty, they scorn such sentimental idealisms as justice. "Justice?" They laugh. "What is justice? But *this* is a dollar." Our young, I fear, only bear our own familiar stripes.

That we disparage the profession charged with protecting our personal rights and privileges reveals something of ourselves, for our lawyers, these "crooks" and these "shysters," were chosen from among our "best and brightest." They are *our* sons and *our* daughters. It is not my mission at this late date to launch a new defense of the profession, for, indeed, a justice that is more accessible to the people relies upon an uplifting of the entire justice system, the very success of which depends, in large part, upon the kind and character of our lawyers. I don't argue that there is nothing wrong with lawyers both as to their competence and their conscience. Nor do I argue that people have no right to expect their lawyers to display a more durable moral fiber than their own, for there is a greater trust imposed on lawyers. But that the lawyers of America disappoint us tells us something of our dreams and our own goals for justice. It also demands that we investigate anew how our lawyers are selected, and how they are trained to fight for us.

There *are* many who struggle in anonymity for the rights of people and for justice. We do not find them on the golf courses or lounging in the private clubs. They labor in dingy offices and struggle for the next month's rent. Their goal is not money, but freedom for a client charged with a crime he did not commit. They fight for justice for a woman who was harassed by her boss at the workplace. They fight for those who have been cheated by their landlords and manipulated by their banks. They are likely shunned by the elitists of the profession. They likely hold no offices in the bar or attend its functions in Hawaii. They are among the masses of lawyers scorned by the public. But they count among them the few who still guard the liberty of the people. When I go to law schools to speak, I recognize them immediately. They sit up front, and I want them to know before they start to doubt themselves that one person really can make a difference. So I launch into my story of Ralph Nader.

Can a single man still make a difference in America? What about Ralph Nader, a quiet, dedicated man who dresses no better than my father did when he got ready for church. He still lives in a small studio apartment, and after all these years of service to the public, he draws a salary smaller than I pay some of my beginning clerks. The *New Republic* says there is no one living today who is responsible for "more concrete improvement" in the lives of Americans. Two decades ago, Nader's book *Unsafe at Any Speed*, a surprise best-seller, led to federal legislation that has saved untold lives and given rise to a new era of consumerism. We wouldn't have such standard safety features in our automobiles as seat belts, padded dashboards, collapsible steering wheels, and shatter-resistant glass if it weren't for Nader. Today, if your airline is overbooked despite your reservation, you won't lose your seat and receive only the airline's apologies. The airline will get you a seat even if it has to buy it at a dear price from another passenger. Ralph Nader forced into American law the idea that airlines that take the risk of overbooking must pay the price of making it right with their passengers if they lose, and it was also Nader who was responsible for the no-smoking sections in today's planes.

Nader learned early on what it's like to fight the big corporation. When, in *Unsafe at Any Speed*, he attacked General Motors' Corvair, an engineering catastrophe that put chrome and company profits ahead of safety and human life, GM decided to defend itself, not by correcting the fatal defects in its car, but by smearing Nader. A Senate committee documented how GM hired detectives to dig up dirt about Nader's private life, but to GM's embarrassment, its sleazy attempt was discovered and exposed, and later the company was required to publicly apologize.

Here is a lawyer who, almost single-handedly, made us aware of our rights in a society that had accepted a jaded business morality, one that held it was permissible to exploit the nearly helpless consumer with dangerous products and unjust practices. Today, he and his young, idealistic "Raiders," most of them lawyers, fight the insurance industry's counterfeit "lawsuit crisis" engineered to cause the people to give up more of their rights for promised lower premiums that are never delivered. He supports organizations that expose and struggle against corporate crime, and he has launched a new campaign to preserve the American jury. He is one lawyer—*one*. Across the land, there are thousands of other lawyers who are often poorly trained and poorly paid for such great battles as they carry on at terrible odds, wars they wage on behalf of people whose cases we will never hear of. We owe our freedom to these anonymous champions.

But despite some advances, justice, whatever it is, has, like our lawyers, too often come to reflect our modern mores, to become a *commodity*—something bought and sold in the marketplace. Too often it is a luxury item—that is a central theme in this book—and lawyers are changed in the process, for in such a milieu they become mere hawkers and merchants seeking customers who will pay the price of their wares. Like the great tree that has been felled and its finest heart timber fashioned into expensive violins, as soon as justice becomes a *thing for sale*, its features and its availability are also changed. Once the tree stood strong and sturdy to shade and shelter everyone, but the violins made of it were procurable only by those who possessed the price. As peddlers peddle their expensive fiddles to the monied, so lawyers most often sell justice. But most of the people never hear the music.

And one thing more: The scoundrel in Shakespeare's *King Henry VI* who made the remark about killing all the lawyers had revolution in his mind. He knew that no government could be overthrown without first ridding the kingdom of lawyers, for at that time the profession was a bulwark for law and order and the protector of the rights and privileges of the people. Such was then and has always been the highest calling of the profession.

3 | LAW STUDENTS

Spare Parts for the Legal Machine

If we chose our fighters—those in the ring—the way we choose our lawyers—those who fight for us in court—they would barely break into a sweat before they retired to the clubhouse for cocktails. That, I surmise, is why golf, not boxing, is the principal pastime of the profession. I remember when some of my friends, consumed with delirium, peeled off large chunks of their savings to buy an enterprising young Adonis who had captured their collective imagination at about the time of *Rocky II*. They would support him, provide for his training, give him a stipend to live on, and he would fight for them; and since he was young, white, and beautiful, and a dedicated as well as natural athlete, and since he was intelligent, too, he would learn the game easily where others had failed. He would become the Heavyweight Champion of the World. He had played football in college and claimed he had an instinct for battle. All he needed was the training and the opportunity; to my friends, he symbolized "the Great White Hope." My friends offered me a piece of him. I said he couldn't win his first fight, even if it were fixed.

Who had ever heard of a world-champion boxer whose parents were upper-middle class, who grew up with a room of his own, was a member of the high-school debating team, and was an officer in the DeMolays? With rare exceptions, world champions are bullied and beaten into fighting shape on the streets. They are nurtured by hate and honed by fear. That America has produced so many world-champion boxers is only a tribute to the violence of her steaming ghettos.

I thought it amazing that this Adonis found the courage to crawl into the ring against a younger, smaller, Lower East Side black, who was also making his debut. You could see it in the black's eyes, and you could see it as he warmed up in his corner—on his toes, moving, striking out viciously at the air. He was committed to kill anything he contacted. He struck at his own breath, again and again, ripped at it, hated it. I thought he should have been chained to the corner post. At the opposite side of the ring stood this beautiful hulk who looked as well formed and as succulent and white as a Christmas turkey. His warm-up consisted of several deep knee bends and a few foot shuffles like a girl skipping rope, and he smiled at someone in the crowd as if he were acknowledging a neighbor at a church picnic, and when they touched gloves in the center of the ring, he smiled in the same lazy way at his opponent. Then the bell ruined it for everybody. The Adonis was finished in the first seconds of the first round, and the winner actually wept, not out of joy for his victory but because he felt unfulfilled.

He had been cheated of his first fight. Maybe someone would think the match was fixed. "I come to fight," he said. "That guy don't belong in no ring. That kind can ruin the fight game."

So it is with the young prospects we throw into the pits of the courtroom. A trial is also a fight. The maiming is done with words. My more refined brothers and sisters of the bar will not accept that metaphor. To them, a trial is a debate among the learned and the clever, but after they crawl into the pits with a kid raised in the Bronx or a tough miner's son from Butte, Montana, they soon learn differently.

I train for a trial, run in order to be physically fit, eat right, and sleep right. To prepare mentally for it, I concentrate on the justice of my client's case, on my anger. I cherish it, contain it. Feel it. Anger is the fuel of the fight, the life force of the trial. If lawyers cannot feel their own anger rising out of the injustice imposed upon their client, how can they expect the jury to feel it and to render justice? In the courtroom, my opponents feel my anger, know my physical presence, and sense my commitment to my case; as the trial stretches into weeks, perhaps months, they learn that that anger continually replenishes the energy for battle and the will for victory.

A trial lawyer is a fighter, one struggling to accomplish justice under the great disability of a legal education. Whether he has graduated from Harvard or the University of Wyoming, it is mostly the *person* who accounts for the successful trial lawyer. Young lawyers ask me, "How can I get better in the courtroom?" They know something vital is missing. For although they were chosen when most were not, and although they have endured the torment of cruel professors and the agony of boring classes, and survived the punishment of the bar examination, they still suspect they are mysteriously wanting—but how? Why?

They have been taught by their professors that feelings are exhibited only by the intellectually puny; they are not to be trusted. I tell them they must learn to feel again. The ability to feel is the principal distinction between man and machine. Justice itself is a feeling. If one cannot feel, one cannot understand his client's case. If one cannot feel, one cannot understand the jury—or even the judge, for contrary to the suspicions of many, judges do feel. The lawyer who *thinks* the words but does not *feel* the words will seem disingenuous to jurors who themselves feel, but who, despite his words, are able to sense that the lawyer does not.

We have injured our young, and now we wish them to run fast and long. We have frightened them and made nodding sycophants of them, and now we wish them to fight with style and courage. We teach the young like we program computers, and then complain they do not perform like human beings.

In a study of students who decided to abandon the law as a career and whose decision was not related to their academic potential but rather to the student's personality type, based on a Jungian introversion-extroversion measure, the "thinking types" had a dropout rate of 11 percent, while the "feeling types" quit at the rate of 20 percent. An even higher dropout rate, 28.1 percent, correlated with those who were especially idealistic and people-oriented. Moreover, it was discovered that this extroverted type was underrepresented in the law schools to begin with, compared to the undergraduate population. These researchers concluded that those law students who remained in school "are not primarily concerned with implementing individual judgments about the restructuring of society to improve social justice."

The fact is, we are selecting too many of the wrong kind for our fighters. Those who are fit for fighting are sent away. Many of those who can hear the people and speak their language cannot speak the language of the computer that stands guard at the door of our law schools. Where are the blacks and the Chicanos? One sees a smattering of them here and there on the otherwise white linen that is set before us. We can, of course, point to the token few, but in Chicago for example, where 32 percent of the population is black, only 3.5 percent of the legal profession is, and about one-third of 1 percent of black lawyers practice in firms. Only 5 percent of our law students are black, and the figure is declining. Hispanics account for 2.7 percent and less than 1 percent of the bar is Hispanic. Many who do survive the entrance cut are soon disgusted and leave, for law school is no place for human beings who care about other human beings. Too many of the pampered are left, too many intellectual mechanics who, like their professors, love the more mathematical processes of the law and little of its human side survive law school. Most are scarred by the law-school experience. Some, of course, go to law school out of benevolent hearts, and some courageously; a few effectively serve the people. They are the ones who are held up as proof that the legal educational system is working. Where is the Chicano whose father slaved in the lettuce fields? Where are the sons of longshoremen and black factory workers from the South? I am not arguing that only the poor and the desperate can be whole persons and good lawyers. I do not wish to disenfranchise the fortunate, but one thing I know: We cannot serve justice to the people from a silver spoon.

Peter J. Liacouras, president of Temple University and formerly the dean of its law school, writes, "What has not been fully realized . . . is that white ethnic minorities are also being turned back by the same professional school gatekeepers." Professor Jerold S. Auerbach, in his classic book *Unequal Justice*, speaks of this legal aristocracy and how the prestigious schools continue to recruit from "elite family backgrounds," their students still "represent[ing] a privileged economic, racial, and religious sample." He describes the historical objective of the white elitist bar—it was to keep it "clear and clean," to fence out Eastern Europeans and Roman Catholics and other ethnics who would "dilute" or "undoubtedly deteriorate" the "high standards," "order," "congeniality," and "ethics" in the legal world. James Beck, former Solicitor General of the United States, in 1930 wrote these frantic words: "If the old American stock can be organized, we can still avert the threatened decay of constitutionalism in this country."

It takes a sturdy, tough kind of beast to carry the load up the rocky trails in the backcountry of the American justice system. Fighting for the rights of the people is more a matter of caring, of passion, than of breeding. Some say the "gentlemen of the bar" lend the dignity and stability the profession needs at a time when lawyering seems to be disintegrating into anarchy and ambulance chasing. Yet a large portion of the lawyers of Watergate and, more lately, of Irangate and those involved in insider-trading scams came from the carriage trade. Society places heavy demands on these who have been so fragilely grown and so poorly tested by life itself.

Every country must finally be judged by the quality of justice it delivers to its people. But given the screening processes now in place, most young men and women accepted into law school are those least qualified to fight for our rights. We specify criteria for the selection of our future lawyers that are not specific to the fighting profession. Scholastics? To be sure, lawyers should be comfortable with scholarly endeavors, but there is little correlation between grade-point averages and the success of the graduate as a practicing lawyer. It is a well-known old saw among professors that the top students will also become professors or, worse, drones in a large firm, the middle students will produce most of the judges, and the bottom will provide the most successful trial lawyers. The professors laugh at the irony but ignore the message—that academic skills and fighting skills may not often coexist. They may even be antagonistic.

But there are other reasons why the fighters for the people have been largely excluded from our law schools in favor of those whose hearts seem to beat more in cadence with corporate America. The computer mostly makes the choice. The Law School Admission Test (LSAT), a three-hour, multiple-choice test with the alleged purpose of identifying those who may most readily be trained to "think like a lawyer," has long ago proven itself an unreliable indicator of the likely success either of the student in law school or the lawyer in practice. Originally the test was devised, given, and graded by Education Testing Service (ETS) of Princeton, New Jersey. According to studies presented by ETS itself as long ago as 1977, the LSAT is only 13 percent accurate in predicting first-year grades. This means that in 87 percent of the cases, candidates for law school could be ranked equally well by a random process, such as rolling the dice. When supplementing undergraduate grades as a selecting tool, the LSAT delivered 20 percent accuracy in law-school grade prediction, and it predicted graduation from law school only 5 percent of the time better than mere chance. A study published in the legal journal *Law and the Social Order* concluded, "There is no empirical evidence of a significant correlation between LSAT scores and probable 'success' in the practice of law." Chesterfield Smith, former ABA president, admitted that "there is no authority suggesting that the LSAT can predict success," and even ETS's president conceded that he "would not say that a low score on the LSAT would be an adequate basis for saying to a student, 'you'll never make it as a lawyer.' " But that is exactly what the law schools of this country tell applicants turned away because of low LSAT scores.

Dean Liacouras said, "What the LSAT does not even purport to measure—and what is not seriously and systematically measured in most general admissions processes—turns out to be so much of what *does* count in lawyering and good community leadership: *common sense, self-discipline, motivation, judgment, practicality, idealism, tenacity, fidelity, character and maturity, integrity, patience, preparation, the ability to listen, perseverance, client-handling, creativity, courage, personality, oral skills, organizational ability and leadership,"* and I would add the propensity *to give a damn.* If a high-scoring Charles Manson and a low-scoring Mother Teresa both took the LSAT, the former would be ranked favorably by the computer and the latter rejected. Little wonder the profession finds itself in such straits.

What kind of students are being selected for us by the machine? As the available seats in our law schools become scarcer and scarcer, the schools' admissions policies border on fantastic. The average LSAT score of students accepted by Stanford in 1985 was an unheard of 745 out of 800. But the chosen students are not those who have already proven their merit as citizens or who have demonstrated a desire to struggle for justice. Instead, those who are chosen are simply the elite of the test-takers. One investigator reported, "At least in terms of the average LSAT scores of their entering classes, every law school today is more selective than 80% . . . were in 1961."

How will these individuals boasting such specialized intelligence turn out as lawyers? As I have experienced them, they seem frighteningly similar. Perhaps the specter of *Brave New World*, or worse, has come to pass. Perhaps there is some evil, secret crossbreeding going on between man and machine. A computer-driven test creates a fellowship of siblings all born of the same mother. I have spoken at many law schools throughout the country and talked with their students for endless hours, and listened, and what I always hear are strange noises that certainly sound as if they were emitted from the same machine, a pedantic droning of legalisms and logic. What I have seen are students who emotionally and intellectually seem alike and act alike.

I ask my student audiences simple questions, like, "Why are you here?" Some look at each other and grin. A few admit they are there because their fathers were lawyers. Over a fifth of the students are in law school because they are indecisive about any career and have simply decided to try law. Harvard's President Derek Bok charges that our law schools have become "the refuge of able, ambitious college seniors who cannot think of anything else they want to do." They are also there because we usually measure the success of our children by the money they make, and they think they can make money in the law. John Hart Ely, former dean of Stanford Law School, says, "The students automatically assume from the moment they're here that a job with a large corporate law firm is the brass ring. . . ." Ely admits that one of his goals is to convince his law students that an avowed attraction to public-interest law careers is not "evidence of mental illness."

Everyone does not need the same kind of lawyer, yet our lawyers are becoming standardized. They often seem more like replacement parts than people. Perhaps most will work well in offices. Perhaps they will excel at struggling through the maze of government regulations and prosper in the concrete and paper jungles of commerce. But when I ask my student audiences if any of them are in law school from a desire to better the human condition, they smile again. Ralph Nader and Allen Nairn, who researched the LSAT in depth, found it utterly unrelated to the issues of social justice. Dean Liacouras claims the LSAT "inhibits well-roundedness in all of our youngsters. It tends to pollute our educational processes with too much instant result-orientation, glorifies quick cleverness and, unchecked, may produce a superabundant monotony of sameness in our professions and nation. Such overreliance," he warns, "may soon provide the nation not with a corps of renaissance persons and pragmatic professionals, but with a brigade of skilled test-takers, hip-shooters and crossword-puzzle whizzes."

Professor Roger Crampton of Cornell Law School predicts, "On average [today's students] will have better analytical ability and greater verbal skills," and although he believes these changes will produce a more qualified profession, he fails to tell us what they will be more qualified to do. He acknowledges that these new lawyers "may be less interested in people, less inclined toward empathy and sensitivity in interpersonal relations, more inclined to talk than listen, and unprepared to devote their considerable intellectual talents to the mundane realities of routine service to the middle class and the poor. As intellectual capability has expanded, experience of people and of life may be decreased."

Nader and Nairn further assert "that the LSAT systematically filters out certain kinds of people and tends to rank applicants *according to how much money their parents earn*. As reliance by the law schools on the LSAT has increased, the number of black students in predominantly white schools has decreased, to virtually nil. Overreliance on the test has excluded white ethnic minorities as well. The median scores for students from two colleges with substantial numbers of Slavic or Polish-American students (Alliance and Illinois Benedictine College) was 473 and 468 (about 28th percentile). The median scores at two predominantly black universities, Howard and Fisk, were 418 and 400 (about 15th percentile). These scores compare with the MIT median of 674 (93rd percentile). But Dean Liacouras asks, "[I]s the median MIT student necessarily more likely to be a better lawyer or community leader . . . in a pluralistic society than the median Alliance or Fisk student?"

Despite the lack of evidence that the LSAT correlates with the student's success either in law school or as a lawyer, the ABA requires all its approved schools to screen their applicants with an "acceptable test," and the only test mentioned in the ABA rules is the LSAT. By 1979, the LSAT was required by all 168 of the nation's accredited law schools, and in many the LSAT has become the principle measure by which those seeking admission are selected. *Computers*, not humans, too often select our future lawyers. But unfortunately the computer cannot judge human beings; it can only select as superior those candidates who possess traits the computer itself understands, whose minds are compatible with it.

After having heard the horror stories of many students who had taken the LSAT, once, on a whim, I decided to take it myself. I was furnished with the sample tests students are given to practice on. I sat down with pen in hand and began. I was confident. Why shouldn't I be? Surely I could match wits with mere college students.

"Wait a minute," said the young man who was administering the test to me—a kid getting ready to take the test himself. "Wait just a minute! I gotta time you. Start when I say go."

I took the test, and my score was considerably lower than his. Then, mostly because of the humiliation, I took several more tests on successive evenings. The more intimidated I got, the lower my scores got, until I heaved the damned thing across the room. That machine would have never chosen me.

"In 1961," says ETS research fellow Dr. Barbara Lerner, "the median LSAT score of students at 81 percent of the nation's law schools was below 485." Lerner, formerly staff director of the National Academy of Sciences Committee on Ability Testing, observed in a paper delivered before she joined the ETS staff, "What this means in comparative terms is that most American lawyers and judges practicing today would never have gotten into law school at all if they had had to compete against the inflated standards which now govern admission."

Our law schools are jammed. The number of students enrolled in ABA-approved law schools doubled in the twelve-year period from 1968 to 1979. By 1987, we had 117,813 students in ABA-approved law schools. Although there are supposedly too many lawyers, although the marketplace is said to be full, nevertheless the students continue to pour in. It is a very strange scene—our schools crowded to overflowing with law students, the world teeming with avaricious lawyers, but when the people need a lawyer, someone to hear and care about them, and to fight for them, there is no one to be found. Where did all the students go after law school?

Most went off to the cities, of course. Ten percent of America's graduating lawyers took up work for the government, including ten thousand judges in our federal and state courts. Another 10 percent grabbed up jobs in private business as salaried lawyers, or drifted into management. Thirty-two percent are professors in law schools, politicians, insurance executives, bankers, or are in real estate. But 68 percent are in private practice, and "the best and the brightest" have, as always, been snatched up by the large firms that represent corporate America, firms often with over two hundred members— one with over seven hundred. At Stanford, during the height of America's stampede to law schools in 1982, only one graduate from that university joined a public-interest law firm.

The reason? The eternal and pervasive lure of the dollar. "I have to make a lot of money to pay off my debts," one student told me. "I plan to work for a large firm for a few years and then leave." I have heard that many times before. It is also a matter of what is considered prestigious and what is not. Studies based on personal interviews with lawyers established the viewpoint of the profession itself—that specialities serving big business carried more prestige, and that general practice, divorce, personal injury, consumer, and criminal law were at the bottom of the hierarchy.

In 1983, Harvard's President Bok charged that the law schools of America were geared to supply new and exclusive talent for corporate firms that, in turn, deliver quality representation to the wealthy and the powerful. Bok further asserted that the poor and the middle class find their access to the courts blocked by prohibitive costs and a bewildering array of complex rules and procedures. Dean Roscoe Pound of Harvard was making the same complaint more than fifty years ago, calling for study, for reform. But today at Harvard, things go on as usual. There are the sporadic complaints from those with prickly consciences, and occasional, much-publicized pronouncements from those on high intended to lull the waters temporarily, but nothing really changes.

Today, at our great law schools, an overwhelming majority of the graduates are seduced into the large firms, while the poor still search for lawyers to fight for their rights. And "the best and the brightest," as Ralph Nader says, "labor for the polluters, not anti-polluters, for sellers, not consumers, for corporations, not citizens, for labor leaders, not the rank and file, for, not against, rate increases, for highway builders, not displaced residents, for, not against, judicial and administrative delay, for preferential business access to government and against equal citizen access to the same government, for agricultural subsidies to the rich but not food stamps for the poor, for tax and quota privileges, not for equity and free trade."

Still, there are those who originally chose the law as an opportunity to expedite social change. What of them? They soon become what Harvard's Bok calls a "massive diversion of exceptional talent into pursuits that often add little to the growth of the economy, the pursuit of culture or the enhancement of the human spirit." It doesn't take long in law school for lofty notions to evaporate. The teachers, the method, and the curriculum blaze away at tender minds like the midday sun on dew. "The law school classroom at the beginning of the first year is culturally reactionary," says Duncan Kennedy, a Harvard professor who has wrestled with the dilemma. "I take it as a given that the second- and third-year program is a failure, for both students and faculty. Over the last five years I've sat in on many meetings in which old and young, experienced and novice . . . bad students and good students, casual and conscientious—all agree that it just doesn't work." He describes law-school professors as "overwhelmingly white, male, and deadeningly straight and middle-class in manner."

The case method of study, by which past cases are read and analyzed and from which certain principles of law are to be extrapolated and reasoning skills are supposedly honed, has long been condemned as a waste of time. Professor Jerome Frank of Yale Law School compared this method of teaching the law to a dog-breeder who sees only stuffed dogs. He thought what usually resulted from the exercise was an "overproduction of stuffed shirts." Students complain. The case method, they claim, is frustrating, humiliating, and "absolutely stultifyingly boring." Professor Lawrence M. Friedman of Stanford asks rhetorically, "Is there a more backward, slow, inefficient way for providing knowledge?" Haverford College's president, Robert B. Stevens, concludes that so long as we continue to teach our young by this antiquated method, the question will remain whether elite American law schools are "more than high grade schools of rhetoric" that seem to produce "analytic giants but moral pygmies."

Yet law schools understand the dollar as well. By the case method, both cheap and easy, one can teach two hundred students as easily as twenty. Many universities see their law schools as businesses generating pure profit. The average cost of educating a law student by using the casebook methodology is about 10 percent of the cost of educating a medical student, albeit medical students learn the skills of their profession while law students only learn to think about theirs.

In the final analysis, it is the established and practicing profession itself that is responsible for keeping our law schools fettered to old stakes. The leading schools have become, as Professor William Cohen of Stanford Law School says, "an adjunct to the hiring hall." David Margolick, writing for *The New York Times Magazine*, said that when he visited Stanford's campus, "I found that one-third to one-half of the second-year class were away on 'fly-backs'—lavish hegiras, primarily to New York and Washington, financed by corporate law firms wooing recruits." He claims that 85 percent of the first-year class were working during the summer for law firms. He quotes Stanford Professor Robert Weisberg: "Students become socialized into the law-firm world incredibly quickly these days, and whether they like that world or respect that world doesn't matter. There are students who can hardly spell 'tort' and who really aren't sure what consideration for a contract is who know the names of all the law firms and purport to know really subtle distinctions between them." Margolick reports that in the year of his visit to the Stanford campus, 425 law firms had come looking for recruits.

Once, a pleasant young woman from the American Bar Association came to Jackson Hole to interview me for an article she intended to write.

"Mr. Spence, why are you so different from most of the lawyers in the country?" I didn't answer. I didn't know what to say. She tried again. "Is there something wrong with the American Bar Association? Is there something wrong with our law schools?" Now, I didn't know which question to answer first. I looked out to the west at the Tetons and thought a long time.

"Well," I began, "I'm different from other lawyers because I wasn't as well educated as most." She looked surprised, as if I had admitted to bad ancestry. "I was never taught to 'think like a lawyer,' or if I was, it never stuck. This business of teaching young men and women to 'think like lawyers' is a euphemism for brainwashing them."

"Do you accuse the law schools of brainwashing?" she asked. She looked troubled.

"Yes," I said. And when I said nothing more, she abruptly changed the subject.

Most Americans know little more of our law schools than what they've seen of television's razor-tongued Professor Kingsfield of *Paper Chase*, whose great delight is to sadistically reduce the hapless law student to a shambles of blubbering sentences and non sequiturs.

We laugh. The professor will not be satisfied until the student is "thinking like a lawyer"—that is, thinking like him. Until the student conforms, he will be humiliated and punished. He will learn to be polite and passive, not to speak out, not to inquire, although he has an inquiring mind, not to invent, although his greatest joy is to create. Those whom we send to school to become our warriors will not learn the fine art of fighting, but how to patronize and to play along. It is a pity we so deform plastic minds and so cripple young psyches.

It is a mistake to leave our students to be trained as fighters with those types, most of whom have never entered the courtrooms, who disdain the forensic art, who have chosen academia instead. This truth was observed long ago. Once, at the urging of the well-meaning citizens of Virginia, the Indians of the Six Nations sent their finest young men off to one of those eastern schools for the white man's education, one supposedly superior to their own. But when their young men returned, the Indians complained to their benefactors that "they were bad Runners, ignorant of every means of living in the woods . . . neither fit for Hunters, Warriors, nor Counsellors, they were totally good for nothing. . . ." However, the Indians had a sense of justice and made the following offer in return: "To show our grateful sense of it, if the Gentlemen of Virginia will send us a dozen of their sons, we will take Care of their Education, instruct them in all we know, and make Men of them."

We can no longer trust the law schools of this country to select the people's champions under the shriveled fist of the ABA. Clothed in self-interest, the American bar has had nearly two centuries within which to devise a fair and effective means of choosing and educating our courtroom warriors. Instead, beholden to Power and devoted to money, the ABA, along with the law schools it dominates, have condoned a process of selecting our nation's lawyers that views our young as numbers and scores to be sorted and chosen by formula, and in so doing, they have failed *our* test of *them*. Our test did not originate on the campus of ETS in New Jersey, nor has it been rendered by a computer. Our test has been administered by a nation's citizens in search of justice, and they have rejected the product. They distrust their lawyers, their own champions. In the final analysis, we, the lawyers of America, have failed the most important test of all, the *people's* test, and that is the shame of it.

4 | LAW SCHOOLS
Factories

Maybe the tumor won't be malignant. After all, there can be all kinds of benign lesions in the brain. As the nurses wheel you to the operating room, your family walks beside you tearfully, and you say something silly, like, "When I get out of this, you'll like me a lot more. They're only gonna cut out the parts that made me cranky," and you think, Oh, God! That's maybe the last thing I'll ever say to them, and then you're in a room that seems very bright and cold and smells antiseptic. You don't recognize any of the people. They all wear masks and are gowned in surgical green, a dreadful color unmatched in any growing thing on this earth. Then a man dressed like the others comes into the room carrying an armload of books.

"Who is that?" you ask.

"That is your surgeon." You feel a small wave of fear. Someone is sticking a needle into your arm, and you are being hooked up to a machine.

"What do you have those books for?"

"Just a handy reference," you hear the friendly voice of your doctor reply.

"Well, you have done one of these operations before, haven't you?" you ask. You can't remember what he answers—something that seemed unspecific. Things are getting hazy now, and as you start to drift, you see your doctor looking at a full-page drawing of a human brain in color. Now, you feel true panic. You jerk upright.

"What the hell are you reading, Doctor?" One of the nurses rushes over and tries to force you down, but you fight back. "What the hell are you reading?"

"Oh, I'm just checking out a detail or two. Don't worry."

The doctor nods to the anesthesiologist, and suddenly things become very distant. You begin to drown in your own waves, wave after dark wave, until the bright room is dark, and the sound of your doctor's voice has drifted away.

The doctor had gathered up six books, all the latest on the anatomy of the brain and on the surgical technique demanded. He began his procedure by reading aloud to the others in the operating room, and as he read, they handed him the necessary instruments and helped him identify the special places he must cut, and he was very conscientious. Nobody accused him of not trying his best. The operation took several hours, including the Code Blue at the end, when other doctors came running into the operating room and administered their desperate lifesaving procedures that, of course, failed.

They say the doctor performed eight of these operations before one of his patients survived. Some critics who did not understand the problem of medical training claimed the doctor stacked up the dead and maimed like cordwood, but perhaps that is the small price we pay for good medicine. The doctor was quick to learn from his mistakes, and had a certain cavalier courage that served him well. He was able to take his early defeats in stride and to dismiss them as part of his education.

While the foregoing is merely a frightful fantasy, its parallel is a reality so far as the education and training of trial lawyers is concerned. Every year, the law schools disgorge their latest graduates, thousands of eager, wide-eyed young men and women who finally pass the bars of their states and are thereby authorized to practice law with no more training before they are loosed upon the unsuspecting American public than a surgeon whose only experience has been the dissection of a frog in biology class.

Although every law school offers a course in trial practice, and while some permit their students to take part in certain clinical programs in which the students experiment with the rights and lives of the poor so that at graduation the student can honestly claim he actually saw a real client and actually saw the inside of a real court, the truth is that no law student in America receives competent training in the art of advocacy, and left to their own devices, many never acquire it, let alone perfect it, in an entire career at the bar.

Of course, all young men and women do not depart our law schools with the intent of trying cases. Some recognize that they are not suited for this sort of combat and have resolved to engage in an office practice, similar to the doctor who never intends to grasp a scalpel. Still, even the radiologist or rheumatologist first takes an internship and then a residency in a teaching hospital under the supervision of clinical experts, and sees literally thousands of patients before he ventures out on his own. But most of the training of young lawyers in this country has been entrusted to professors who have never engaged in the actual practice of law or, if they have, have abandoned it after a short and usually disillusioning exposure for the more sedate life within the university.

If the students intend to become experts in, say, contract law, they will likely be taught contracts by a professor who has never sat across from a living client, who has never considered the grave, long-lasting personal and social consequences of the agreement he is to write. Generally the students will never draft a contract themselves, nor likely ever see one in law school. Should they open individual offices on their own, which today is rare, some legal publishing company will send its representative around to sell them— on easy monthly terms—a set of form books containing contracts that other lawyers have drafted, contracts neophytes can copy and afterward present to their clients as though they had written every word, along with a fee commensurate with authorship.

I have taught young trial lawyers from across the land for many years in various trial seminars, and to my dismay, I find that most do not know how to conduct the simplest cross-examination, or how to get an exhibit into evidence or to impeach a witness with a prior inconsistent statement—skills equivalent to a doctor being able to take a patient's blood pressure or examine his tonsils. Yet these lawyers, without the most rudimentary tools, are thrown into every kind of trial from wrongful death suits for widows and children to the defense of capital murder cases for the accused. James Nielsen, a professor at Hastings Law School, said, "It is a fact that a student can graduate from this, the fourth largest law school in the United States, without ever having written a pleading, a contract, a will, a promissory note, or a deed. It's worse than that. It is a fact that most students graduate from this law school without ever having seen a real, honest-to-God pleading, or contract, will, promissory note, or deed. A student can graduate without ever having set foot in a courtroom and without ever having spoken to, or on behalf of, a person in need of advice of counsel. A student can graduate without once being exposed to the operation of the rules of court. . . . Whatever else may be said about this license issued by the state bar, let it be said that for these students and their clients it is a cruel hoax."

Professor Alan Dershowitz, the youngest professor ever to obtain tenure at Harvard, writes, "I had never actually tried a case at that time, having gone straight from law school to a pair of judicial clerkships and then on to teach at Harvard Law School. . . . Having made my decision [he was about to represent his first client], I did not have the foggiest notion of where to begin. They didn't teach that sort of thing in law school."

Several years ago I had the opportunity to speak about this predicament to a national convention of law-school deans. I had them trapped in a single room in Jackson Hole, and I wasn't going to let them go without first torturing them with the pesky truth I thought they already knew and were mostly helpless to overcome. I was cruel. I said, "I've seen these bright kids come, gawking, into a courtroom, their brains full to overflowing like foam off the head of a badly drawn beer. They know the law and can cite the cases and they have learned to look intelligent because they have emulated you, and some have even read the dialogues of Plato. But standing there in the courtroom, they are as impotent as a herd of fat steers." The deans stared back.

"It's pitiful," I said. "Makes you want to cry. It isn't that these young men and women are stupid. It isn't that they don't desperately want to be competent in their life's work, or long to be worthy and successful trial lawyers. But the truth is that they are released after all those years of toil and agony at your hands and they are still worthless. I have scores of bright, well-educated young men and women from your universities apply for employment to my office every year. The letters of application would break your heart. They want to be trial lawyers. They have labored endlessly to digest what you have fed them, in order, of course, that they may later regurgitate it in their examinations—like one of my old cows calls up her cud. They have been probed and tested; they have been run through the cutting chutes of the educational system and they are the survivors, but they are still worthless. They are the victims of the system you perpetuate." One of the deans got up to leave the room.

"Where are you going?" I asked. "I'm not finished with you."

"I'm finished with you," he said.

"Your law students never had that choice."

"I do," he answered, and slammed the door behind him. I saw a look of slight concern come over several of the remaining faces. But most looked as passive as a band of freshly shorn ewes.

"Shall I continue?" I asked. "Or is this too damned painful for you to bear?"

A man in the front row with an easy smile and sleepy eyes said, "Continue, Mr. Spence. Maybe we need to hear this."

"It's free," I said.

"So is a kick in the teeth," somebody else said, and got up and left.

"Go ahead, Mr. Spence," the man in the front row said again, and so I continued.

"Most of these young men and women have had no other role models to follow, and so they tend to think like you, to make their faces look like yours, and even to walk like you. But most of you are not qualified to walk into a courtroom. I talked to a renowned trial lawyer in Denver the other day who told me he never hires young lawyers to help him anymore. 'I hire nurses,' he said. 'Nurses?' I asked. 'Yeah,' he said. 'They've been taught to ask intelligent questions of the patient and to listen to someone who is hurt or frightened. They have been taught to care about the patient and write reports that others can rely on. They can get to the bottom of a case for me. Young lawyers just get in the way. They want to legalize everything, dehumanize every client, categorize every case, box up people into causes of action and understand them in accordance with stare decisis. And after a year they demand a partnership for their good work.' He was right. The next day, I hired a local nurse myself, and she has been a great help to us ever since." The man in front smiled again, slightly. He shouldn't have. It only encouraged me.

"I was asked by my son the other day what law school I would recommend to him. I said, 'Well, we'll try to find the school which is likely to teach you the *least*, because in that way you will have the least to unlearn before you can become useful as a lawyer.' Now what's the matter here? People across the land are crying for lawyers who are qualified to represent them, who will fight for them. Why have we become the most hated of all professions? Don't you really know? You have been members of those numerous committees mandated to discover what is wrong with the legal profession, and you have heard the speeches, including the cruel indictments by Chief Justice Burger, and you have read the countless articles in your plentiful pedagogical publications, and it is all very entertaining. But nothing changes."

I was flogging the innocent. What could the deans do? They, too, were caught in a system that had long ago been dominated by another group of elitists, the legal professors, the fussy savants of the law.

The professors were not training young attorneys to represent people. They were teaching their students only what they themselves knew—the art of studying law. It had not always been so.

Throughout most of the nineteenth century, law-school professors obtained their teaching credentials by distinguishing themselves in the practice of law. But in 1870, Harvard made its infamous gift to the education of the American lawyer in the person of one Christopher Columbus Langdell, dean of Harvard Law School, who held that "what qualifies a person to teach law is not experience in the work of a lawyer's office, and not experience in dealing with men, nor experience in the trial or argument of cases, not experience, in short, in using law, but experience in learning law."

The supercilious was followed by the sanctimonious. Charles W. Elliott, then Harvard's president, proudly proclaimed, "In due course . . . there will be produced in this country a body of men learned in the law, who have never been on the bench or at the bar, but who nevertheless hold positions of great weight and influence as teachers of the law, as expounders, systematizers, and historians. This, I venture to predict, is one of the most far-reaching changes in the organization of the profession that has ever been made in our country." He was, of course, quite correct. Generations of students followed who at graduation were utterly unqualified to do anything except what their professors did—study the law. Harvard's Thomas Reed Powell described the brain being fashioned as "one that could think of something that was inextricably connected to something else without thinking about what it was connected to." The professors created students in their own image.

"It will scarcely be disputed," said Christopher Columbus Langdell, "that the law is one of the greatest and most difficult of sciences, and that it needs all of the light that the most enlightened seat of learning can throw upon it." That lofty notion spread like a virulent germ into every law school in the nation. Young would-be lawyers were no longer sent to "read the law" in the office of a practicing attorney. They were taught to "think like lawyers," a mysterious cerebral exercise that disqualified most to think thereafter like human beings. During the fifty years between 1870 to 1920, virtually every law school in the nation adopted Langdell's casebook method of instruction and revamped its faculties so that these teachers enriched with years in the practice were replaced with professional scholars.

Judge Lois G. Forer, at present serving on the bench in Philadelphia, tells us, "The aim of the law schools and their professors was, as it has been for decades, to train the 'brightest and the best' to staff the ever-expanding elite law firms that steadily raised their fees and symbiotically served their wealthy clients." Journalist Herbert Croly, describing the "betrayed promise of America," argues that the lawyer is no longer trusted to interpret and lead American constitutional democracy because he has abdicated his role in order to defend special interests instead.

But our law schools, like General Motors, try to discover what the consumer wants and to produce it, and the message the law schools have heard is that the system wants more of the same. It is the wrong message. Our law schools have set their casts and dies and machinery to produce the same old product—replacement parts for the great corporate legal machinery of America. General Motors suffered from a similar defect, and the Japanese took over half of the market. The problem is, of course, that there is no competition waiting in the wings to compete with American law schools. That the new graduate is essentially unqualified to help ordinary people is of little concern to the large corporate law firms who are the law schools' most visible customers and their greatest supporters, and people are not the principal business of the large firms. Instead, these firms represent corporations in mergers and takeovers where senior partners in a major New York law firm may typically charge $350 an hour for their services.

Today, corporate law firms still recruit "the best and the brightest" of each year's crop of graduates, each year vying for the top students like bidders for horseflesh at the annual Keenesland sale of thoroughbred colts. These law firms make the young recruits whatever promises are necessary to fulfill their dreams—start them at salaries often exceeding the stipends paid their professors; give them memberships in exclusive clubs; and after a few years as associates, offer them partnerships. Some students, still bearing the frayed remnants of a social conscience, are promised the freedom to do a certain amount of public-service work each year, but such crisp ideals are soon sopped up in the high demands of the money-making legal machinery.

But I wasn't through with my speech to the deans. The rage had been building for too many years. My performance was not sweet. "What you produce are monkeys skilled only in making monkey talk." I waited for a reaction. There was only a room full of eyelids blinking slowly, rhythmically, like dripping faucets. "You do your work dutifully, seriously, religiously. You write your own articles in monkey talk. But the monkeys you produce are smarter than the corporations that cage them, because the monkeys have convinced the corporations that to survive they must have their monkeys. But

I am repelled not as much by what you do as that you do it so piously." I looked around for the slightest sign of life. I felt as if I were addressing the College of Cardinals and was automatically being forgiven for every word I said.

I got quiet for a moment. "You must get tired of working in your factories—one class of freshmen must finally come to look like the next." I could feel the sadness. "One class must fade into another. Parts are parts. And they come out of your law schools tested and sorted and graded ready for their monkey cages." I finally got a reaction. One of the deans up front murmured, "You mustn't mix your metaphors."

"I know, I'm bad about that. But listen," I continued. "The people want their lawyers! The people of this country are *entitled* to law-yers, men and women who can hear them, who care for them, who will fight for them.

"Folks, there is a great market out there for people's lawyers. You are in business, and you are missing a great business opportunity. Your school could leap ahead of the pack. The demand for people's lawyers is so great you could never fill it. And you would no longer be producing merely parts. Do you hear me?"

They didn't hear me. They had never listened. In 1905, Theodore Roosevelt addressed Harvard on the same subject and they thought him too rustic a populist to be taken seriously. He said, as if he were speaking today, "Many of the most influential and most highly re-munerated members of the bar in every center of wealth make it their special tasks to work out bold and ingenious schemes by which their very wealthy clients, individual or corporate, can evade laws which are made to regulate in the interest of the public the use of great wealth." These new professional elite, he said, were fostering growth of a "spirit of dumb anger against all laws and of disbelief in their efficacy."

In 1910, Woodrow Wilson also tried to tell them. He said the constitutional advocate, once the pride of the profession, had vir-tually disappeared, to be replaced by "lawyers who have been sucked into the maelstrom of the new business system of the country. They do not practice law. They do not handle the general, miscellaneous interests of society. They are not general counselors of right and obligation." Wilson charged that corporate attorneys were "intimate counsel" to all that had been going on. "The country holds them largely responsible for it. It distrusts every 'corporate lawyer.' " Jer-old S. Auerbach, distinguished author and legal historian, observed that corporation lawyers were mistrusted not because they were inherently evil, but because "corporate interest were ipso facto antithetical to social interests." Harvard was delivered the same message by Louis D. Brandeis, who told his audience that "able lawyers have, to a great extent, allowed themselves to become adjuncts of great corporations and have neglected their obligation to use their powers for the protection of the people. We hear much of the 'corporation lawyer' and far too little of the 'people's lawyer.' " Nothing changes.

I hadn't known how deep my anger went during that speech until later. Well, I knew about some of it. When I was a few years past forty, I had begun to feel a certain panic that if I were to die at that instant, my life would have stood for nothing at all except a variety of empty self-indulgences. Then I had gone to the dean of the Wyoming Law School and tried to get him to hire me on as a professor. I told him I'd done everything a lawyer could do. I had both prosecuted and defended the accused. I had represented the insurance industry in some of the celebrated civil suits in the Rocky Mountain area. I pled my case. I bragged about myself. Surely he would understand. I had something of value to offer his students. I had represented the injured against America's greatest corporations. I owned the record for the largest jury awards in the state's history. I hadn't lost a case to a jury for over a decade. I'd had rich experience in the appellate courts of the land, but more important, I had examined abstracts and drawn deeds and written farm leases and represented husbands and wives against each other and probated dinky estates and collected bills for the credit bureau, and in short, I'd done everything a country lawyer, or any lawyer, could do, and after all, wasn't that what the state needed—lawyers who would trickle out into the small isolated towns and villages of Wyoming to represent the people?

"You don't fit the profile of the law-school professor," the dean said, while he sorted through a stack of papers on his desk.

"Why?" I asked. "I was your top student in 1952. I'm as long-headed as the rest of the crew you have up here. I can engage in pettifoggery with the best of 'em." I laughed. He wasn't amused, and he didn't look up.

"We're not looking for the experienced practitioner. What we want is a young honor graduate from Harvard or Yale or maybe Michigan or Stanford who has been in a large New York firm for a year or two. That's the kind. With all due respect, you wouldn't help our standing with the ABA accreditation very much. Besides, we don't usually hire our former students as professors—something incestuous about that."

"You still hold it against me that I was your first honor graduate to flunk the bar, don't you? That must have embarrassed you a lot."

"Didn't bother me in the slightest," he said. "You were always unpredictable. You'd be unpredictable as a professor as well."

"Is that bad?" I asked.

"Predictability is not only a virtue in the law but in lawyers and law professors. Law is a science," he said. "It is a very difficult science." Then he excused himself for a meeting.

A special task force of the American Bar Association itself concluded that the lawyer's training is wholly inadequate and that candidates for the bar are not properly tested: "Neither the multiple-choice nor the essay examinations can ensure that students have adequate lawyering skills to enable them to engage in the practice of law. Bar examiners should continue to experiment with the possibility of expanding the bar examination to include measurement of at least some of the lawyering skills not tested in the traditional formats." Among the recommendations of the task force was that "Law schools should make more use of experienced lawyers and judges in law school instruction." That report was made in 1983. The law-school curriculum remains substantially unchanged.

Several years ago, I gave a speech at Stanford Law School, and afterward I was driven to the airport by a top senior. He told me that except for a single B in the fifth grade, he had a straight-A average throughout his entire scholastic career. Both his parents were physicians. He had gone directly from high school to Stanford for undergraduate studies and then law school, and now he was being courted by one of the large New York firms of several hundred lawyers. "What should I do?" he asked.

"How would I know? I've practiced most of my life alone or with a couple of partners in little towns in Wyoming."

"You know something you're not telling me," he said. Indeed, he was bright.

"Well," I said, "why don't you tell me what's troubling you?" He didn't hesitate. He immediately began to recount how the summer before he had been whisked off his feet by a Wall Street firm that provided him with a convertible automobile and paid him $900 a week. After graduation, they promised he would start at a salary in excess of $70,000 a year.

"I feel dirty," he said. "I feel bought."

"You shouldn't feel too guilty," I said. "The firm will bill your time out at a hundred and fifty an hour or more, and you'll make them a lot of money, like the sale of any commodity at a profit."

"I'm not a damned commodity," he said. I didn't reply. "Well, damn it," he said, "I'm not something to be bought and sold like a—" He couldn't think of the right word.

"Don't feel bad," I said. "They're paying top dollar. It's sort of like the women they used to run up in the whorehouse in Laramie when I was a kid. They charged five dollars a trick. They got to keep half and the madam got half. The more women the madam had working for her, the more she made. The prettier they were, the better the madam's business, and you're as pretty as they come— 'the best and brightest,' as they say. And if you work long enough and hard enough, someday you may even become a madam yourself."

I shouldn't have said that. The kid drove along through the green hills of California without saying a word. The silence grew painful. Finally I said, "I'm sorry I came out with all of that. At your age, I'd have given anything for a chance like yours. I'm sure you'll be happy there."

"No, I won't!" he almost shouted. "But it'll make my parents happy. That's all they've ever talked about—me being in one of the big firms and making the big money and being successful. That's their religion."

"You better try to make *yourself* happy," I said. "I agree with you. You're more than something that's bought and sold. A lot of people out there need you. Those corporations you'll be working for can do without you, but the people can't."

I knew the kid was trapped. Finally I said, "What's going on with you?"

"Not a damn thing," he said. "Not a goddamned thing." Then he was silent again for a long time.

Most of the students I talked to at Stanford wanted to be recruited by one of the large law firms at a big salary. Some had entered into employment agreements after their first year in law school. The same was true at Harvard, where for several years I'd taught a week-long seminar in trial practice. Like college athletes, the students wanted to be a first-round draft choice. A Cravath partner once made the point: "The business connected with corporations and general office practice is much more profitable and satisfactory, and you will find that the 'better class' of men at our bar prefer work in this line." Such has been the elitist attitude of the American bar from the beginning.

Vast numbers of the so-called "leftovers," comprising the majority of the nation's 675,000 lawyers, do not fare so well. In the cities, many young lawyers must fend for themselves in the best way they can. Disabled by their poor training and a paucity of useful experience, they hang around the courts hoping for a court appointment to defend an indigent for a total fee of perhaps $300. They hire out to do collections against the poor for a percentage of the blood squeezed out of the turnip, and take other cases that never seem to find their way to any "respectable lawyer."

The kid from Stanford finally broke the silence again. "How do you set up a practice?" he asked. "It costs a lot of money, and I don't know anything about practicing. I'd starve to death."

"It's hard," I said. "It would be the hardest thing you ever did."

"How did you do it?" he said.

"It was easier in those days," I said. "I just went to the part of the state where the mountains were, where there was good hunting and fishing, and I was lucky. I found an older lawyer who thought he needed some help, and he put me to work for two hundred dollars a month, but I had to do my own typing, because he didn't want his wife, who was also his secretary, doing my work. In six months, he was appointed judge, and then I didn't know what the hell to do. I didn't know how to file even the simplest collection case in the justice-of-the-peace court." The kid was a good listener, and we drove on. "How did you learn the practice?" he asked.

"Well, I learned it a little at a time. Shorty Anderson taught me a lot. He was a craggy old hide-and-wool buyer who sat as the justice of the peace, and he held court in his warehouse. I remember the stink. The heat of his wood-fire stove made the grease from the wool melt, and it smelled like hell! 'The stink of the wool ain't as bad as the stink of the law,' old Shorty used to say. He taught me how to file a case, and I practiced arguing in his court in front of all the old sheep pelts. But I had a lot of trouble."

"I didn't think you ever had any trouble litigating," he said.

"I never have been a litigator," I said. "I'm a lawyer. You people from Stanford are the litigators." I said the word so it sounded bad. "I remember standing in the district court before old Smokey Lewis. I was as stiff as a petrified stork—scared speechless. I was representing a young boy who had been injured playing in the railroad yards on a large cable spool. My theory, of course, was 'attractive nuisance.' "

"That's first-year torts."

"Yeah, it was when I went to school in Wyoming, too," I said. "The boy's mother was a widow who supported herself and her son entirely from baby-sitting, and she didn't have any money for doctors. They lived in a hovel in Shoshone, a town of maybe a couple hundred—a few bars, a hardware store, a drugstore, and a whorehouse that also served as the bus stop. Oh, how I wanted to win! The railroad was represented by Wyoming's greatest living trial lawyer at the time, the patriarch of the bar, William Werhli, and I remember the horror of the trial. His simplest objection left me speechless.

" 'I object,' he'd say. 'The question is leading,' which, of course, it was.

" 'Sustained,' the judge would rule. 'Rephrase your question, Mr. Spence.'

"It was so pitiful. I couldn't think of how to rephrase the question. I remember standing there getting red in the face and my mind going blank. The judge was a kind man. He wanted to help me, but he couldn't. 'Well, Mr. Spence, rephrase the question and let's get on with it,' he'd say. I remember looking at the jury. They were embarrassed for me. Most of them were looking at their hands, and then the judge said, 'Well, Mr. Spence, do you have any more questions?' And I said, 'Yes, Your Honor, I do, but I can't think of how to ask them,' and I struggled on for a while. I lost the case. And I lost the next four."

"Jesus," the kid said. "I thought you never lost a case."

"Everybody loses cases," I said. "But that was a hard one to lose. I was all the lawyer that she could get. They trusted me as much as they could, and I tried, and old Bill Werhli was a gentleman and was patient with me, and the jury was sorry. I could see it in their faces when they returned their verdict. It was hard for them to look at me. After that case was over, a motherly sort on the jury came up to me.

" 'I'm sorry,' she said. 'It wasn't your fault. I took an oath to decide the case on the law and the facts, and the law and the facts were just against you, that's all.' And she had tears in her eyes. But I knew why I lost the case, and so did she and so did my client."

"How did you get good?" he asked.

"I just kept trying cases. I kept piling up the dead bodies until I finally learned how. I owe the people a lot," I said.

I thought of all the cases I had needlessly lost, and I felt sad again. And I felt sad for all the young lawyers who wanted to win and didn't know how. I felt sad for the people. I thought of the few great lawyers I knew. Most of them were tucked away anonymously in small towns, in wayward places where people had come to take them for granted. And I thought of the law schools, and my sadness turned to anger again. A pity we can't train lawyers for the people.

Then I said good-bye to the student and walked into the terminal. When I looked back, he was still staring in my direction.

5 | JURIES
The Great
American Myth

Somewhere in this country a man tosses in sleepless torment, the threats of the banker still pounding in his ears, his eyes staring up into the blackness where he sees his wife and kids standing frozen, the pans and kettles, their clothes, everything, piled up in cardboard boxes stacked up in the street in front of the house. Where will they go when the bank forecloses and the sheriff comes? The man's wife reaches across the bed covers and pats him gently on the shoulder and says, "Don't worry, honey. No jury in the country will do that to us, not when they hear our side of it," and finally the man's eyes close. But a jury will never hear their side of it. Foreclosure, a matter of money and property, is for judges, not juries.

At the same time, across town another man lies paralyzed in a bed of pain, his spine ripped in two by one of those trucks that bears down on you on the highway like a runaway freight train, a truck owned by a large transport service and driven by a dopehead who slipped through when the company began hiring damned near anybody who could hold on to a wheel and would work cheap. The truck smashed the man's small car flat, with him in it. He has been bedridden now for over two years. He has sores on his body and on his soul, and slowly he disintegrates—while the insurance company stalls. The one thought that keeps seeping through his misery is that someday his case will go before a jury, and then he will be awarded enough damages to hire a nurse to relieve his exhausted wife and to pay for therapy that will help the torturous cramping in his muscles, and to stop the phone's incessant ringing and the bill collector's shrill voice, and maybe there will also be enough left to buy a small house in a nice neighborhood with a ramp up the front entry for his wheelchair.

The injured man's case will be heard by a jury all right, but the controlling issues in his case will first be decided by a judge—a judge the insurance-company lawyer probably knows pretty well, a man he can predict, a judge who may not let the injured party's case even go to a jury at all if he thinks the evidence does not fit into certain precise legal boxes. And if the judge allows the case to go to the jury, and even if the jury finds in the man's favor, before the insurance company has to pay out a penny, a panel of appellate judges—not a jury—will actually decide his case. Thankfully, nobody told the man that.

In the same town, a young lawyer just starting out in her storefront office has herself a case. Her client is a nursing student, but she could have been a store clerk, a mechanic, or anyone who lives from payday to payday. The student was parked at the grocery store and was broadsided by a careless driver who was insured by a well-known insurance company. We have seen the honest faces of the hometown insurance representative on television ads, face after face, year after year. Upon the default of our Maker, the insurance company, through these saints, their hands extended to us, will save us. Yet not one of these companies will pay a just claim until it is more profitable to pay than not. The nursing student's insurance company would not pay her doctor bills or her lost wages or her other debts, and finally she had to drop out of school. Maybe she will never go back. Small things cause great changes in fragile lives.

Her young lawyer has, of course, threatened the company. "Pay up or I'll take my case to the jury," she warns. But you cannot threaten that which cannot feel fear. The company will not pay, because the company knows that while it stalls, it draws interest on the student's money, and it knows it can settle cheaper when things get tougher for her.

Over 90 percent of all civil jury cases are settled before trial, and the great stall is a standard part of the game. Finally, when reality takes over—that is, when the nurse has to move back home with her folks and goes back to work at the drugstore, and when her lawyer faces her own overdrafts and the landlord is hounding her for the rent again—they will both come to their senses. No jury will award justice. The young woman will settle out of court for peanuts, and, after her lawyer gets her share, there won't be enough left for the young woman to get started in school again.

In the same town and on the same day, a government vehicle driven by a federal employee runs a red light, crippling an old woman. But neither the old woman nor thousands like her who are injured and killed each year as the result of the negligence of federal employees will ever be given a jury trial. They must, under the law, present their claims to another federal employee, the federal judge, who alone will decide their cases.

In the same town and on the same day, an attendant at a filling station falls through a manhole cover his employer had left open, and he suffers severe brain damage. He and hundreds of thousands of employees like him, as part of a bargain they never made, have given up the right to sue their employer and their right to have their case heard by a jury. They get only workers' compensation. I can usually get more for a lost thumb from a reasonable jury than many widows will get for the lives of their husbands under the workers' compensation law. Across the country, injured workmen with their families live in the most degrading conditions of poverty while their employers are permitted to continue their dangerous practices, for the payment of workers' compensation has become a mere cost of doing business, and the workers themselves have often become disposable commodities.

The idea of workers' compensation was easy to sell. Before, when workers were injured, they were unable to win any sum from their employers. Even if the workers were able to find lawyers to represent them, and most could not, their employers fought them with their stables of attorneys who asserted judge-made laws against them. Under such laws, if the employer was 99 percent negligent, the worker could recover nothing if the jury found him even 1 percent at fault. He could recover nothing if he was aware of the risk even when ordered into the danger by the boss. Nor could he recover if his injury was inflicted upon him by a fellow worker. These and other legal entanglements were erected by the judges of this country to keep the new industrial nation safe from the claims of injured workers. From the bench, the judges rarely saw the workers living in abject misery or dying or their families starving, for the view from the bench has most often been blurred to human suffering.

But the injured continued to plague the system with their suits, and finally a bargain was struck. Workers would all get the same for the same injury, although we know that no injuries and no workers are the same. It was an interesting spectacle—observing our leaders, rock-hard in their commitment to the free-enterprise system, socializing, of all things, justice itself. Businessmen are not regulated to receive the same profits, nor is the sale of their products regulated to bring the same price; nothing else is regulated except justice for the worker. The employer could still sue anybody, for anything, for any amount. Only the workers were required to give up their right to sue their employer, no matter how gross the employer's negligence, and they would also have to agree to a uniform pittance for their injuries. True, the employees would now be compensated even if the boss was not negligent or even if the employees were negligent themselves, but that was to concede little, for, in reality, what worker lays himself open to injury or death on the job except as the job requires? Under Wyoming's run-of-the-mill law, the worker might get $45,000 for the loss of a leg. In the same case, without the prohibition of workers' compensation, I have often recovered ten times that amount. The worker has no right to a jury trial. He doesn't even have a case. He has only a claim for his injuries.

We cling to the myth that when we need justice we can turn to a jury of our peers and justice will be ours. But as with all myths, reality keeps intruding. I have written about the case of Karen Silkwood at length elsewhere, but I would like to examine it again as a classic example of a well-kept secret—that Americans have lost their right to a trial by jury.

The saga of Karen Silkwood was of a modern woman who some claimed knew too much and talked too frequently about how her employer, Kerr-McGee, was dealing with the deadly man-made element plutonium. She was particularly concerned for young workers who were being contaminated and didn't know the dreadful consequences of that exposure. Further, she had discovered certain photomicrographs she believed had been touched up to hide defects in the welds of the plutonium fuel rods. These fuel rods were used to feed the experimental "breeder reactor," a treacherous contrivance that could breed more plutonium than it consumed in a never-ending process of self-renewal.

Ms. Silkwood had agreed to meet with David Burnham of *The New York Times*, fully intending to expose Kerr-McGee. But she never made it to the meeting. Her small Honda was found smashed against a concrete culvert within eyesight of the plant. She was dead. Based upon the report of a reconstruction engineer, it was claimed she had been hit from behind and run off the road. Kerr-McGee charged she was doped up with Quaaludes. But according to a fellow worker, just before she had left to meet Burnham, Ms. Silkwood had shown her a file she said contained the incriminating evidence. After the accident, the file was never found, and the cause of the accident has remained in violent dispute to this day.

Ms. Silkwood's father, Bill Silkwood, a housepainter who lived in Nederland, Texas, brought suit against Kerr-McGee on behalf of Ms. Silkwood's children, seeking the damages he claimed his daughter suffered during her lifetime at the hands of Kerr-McGee. She, too, had been contaminated by plutonium, the element named after Pluto, the god of the dead. Bill Silkwood's attorneys undertook a search for a trial lawyer. His job would be to convince an Oklahoma City federal jury that Kerr-McGee's operation was a menace to its workers. He would seek from the jury large enough damages to assure society that these dangers would, in the future, be eradicated. For reasons best known to them, they offered the case to me.

I wish you had been in Oklahoma City with me. I wish you had heard the voice of Karen Silkwood speaking to Steve Wodka of the Atomic Workers' Union. Before she died, Wodka had recorded their phone conversation, and we played the tape to the jury. Hers was the tiny, plaintive voice of a Texas woman full of worry and love. "Steve, in the laboratory, we've got eighteen- and nineteen-year-old boys and they don't have any schooling, so they don't understand what radiation is. They don't understand. They don't understand, Steve. They don't understand." They had received little training on the job, and had not been plainly told that plutonium caused cancer. Spills were routine, contaminations were treated indifferently, and nobody in charge seemed to give a damn.

I wish you could have seen the faces of that Oklahoma City jury: an engineer, a retired schoolteacher, a businessman, a housewife—honest people who were worried about what was happening in America. I wish you could have heard the physician and nuclear chemist Dr. John Gofman explain to them how infinitesimal amounts of plutonium in the lungs will guarantee lung cancer. "So, when people say a small amount of this won't hurt you [which Kerr-McGee had alleged], that is so absurd one wonders how anyone can think it. Expecting that an alpha particle will go through a cell and not do horrible damage is like ramming an ice pick through a fine Swiss watch, or shooting a machine gun through a television set and saying it will function just fine."

I wish you could have seen the faces of the jury as the awful specter of the future unfolded before them. Workers and innocent citizens were being contaminated with small quantities of radiation that sealed their deaths by cancer while the government stood by impotently and the company told its workers they were safe. What that Oklahoma jury saw was a scene of terror, of an insidiously slow, agonizing death for uncounted Americans, and, for the first time in the history of the world, a jury was to hear the sworn testimony of the experts on radiation and hear them cross-examined by skilled trial lawyers.

Dr. Gofman continued, "So when somebody says, 'We only lost one thousandth of a pound of plutonium,' and 'That isn't very much,' well, let me tell you something." Dr. Gofman looked very long and intently at each of the jurors. "A thousandth of a thousandth of a thousandth of a pound of plutonium is a very great deal with respect to the life and health of a human being concerned about the development of cancer."

Understatement is as much a misrepresentation as exaggeration. Gofman pulled no punches. "No plant should operate that can give rise to any quantities like that. No plant has any right to talk of safe amounts and permissible amounts. Those words have no meaning." He told the jury we were being fooled by the government when its agencies set up "safe standards." To tell workers they had not as yet reached the "permissible" dose and that they could thereafter go back for more was an unmitigated lie. "There is no such thing as a safe amount. The 'permissible' is simply a license to give you a poison that can kill you." Not once did the jurors take their eyes from him.

"Doctor," I asked, "have you seen the documents on the autopsy of Karen Silkwood?"

"I have."

"What amount of radiation did she have in her lungs?"

"Five nanocuries . . . which means she had 1.3 times as much plutonium as was required to give her lung cancer. And there is no way to stop that process, because once plutonium is there . . . you inevitably launch the process of cancer." The amount of plutonium in her lungs at the time of her exposure was considerably greater, because its traces had dissipated by the time of her autopsy by probably half.

"Doctor, are you saying that at her death she had lung cancer?" I asked.

"I'm saying unequivocally that Karen Silkwood was married to cancer. They are inseparable."

"Do you have an opinion as to whether failure to adequately train is negligence?"

"I do."

Kerr-McGee objected.

"I think he's about to hit pay dirt on this one," Judge Theis said, overruling the objection, and Dr. Gofman answered.

"My opinion is that that is clearly and unequivocally negligence."

The jury heard Kerr-McGee's expert, Allen Valentine, a health-physicist responsible for establishing the plant's original safety program. He said he had taken special care to create a manual that adequately warned the workers of the dangers of plutonium. "I thought it was fair game to tell workers about malignancy as a major hazard of plutonium," he testified. Interestingly, the word *cancer*, the word that strikes terror into the hearts of everyone, seemed to have been carefully avoided. He admitted obtaining much of the material for his manual from a 1959 publication. Even then, Valentine had omitted critical portions of that publication, about "bone cancer, chronic anemia, osteoporosis and bone necrosis . . ." and other symptoms of radiation poisoning that had been clearly identified in the article, and the information that the "high incidence of cancer" in radium workers had been known for over four hundred years. Instead, Valentine had chosen to "inform" the nineteen-year-old farm boys and the ordinary unsuspecting workers at the plant of precious little, and even that in the high-flown language of the scientist, words that seemed more obscuring than enlightening.

On cross-examination, I asked Valentine, "Now, if you told the workers what you actually knew and what was actually in this article from which you quoted [about the bone cancer and radiation poisoning and all], you couldn't have gotten a single soul to work in that plant, could you?" I turned my back on him and looked long and hard at the jury.

"The answer to that question would be subjective on my part." It was not a good enough answer for me. I asked the court to allow an amendment of our claim for punitive damages against Kerr-McGee from $10 million, a mere one-half of 1 percent of Kerr-McGee's $2 billion annual income, to one for $70 million. "This may be *the* significant case of the century," I said to His Honor in chambers. "And I don't think I'm overstating it. In the Scopes trial, we were concerned about man's freedom to think, but in this trial we are talking about whether our children will inherit the face of this earth." Judge Theis sat back in his chair and peered over his glasses at me. His face was still and stern and serious. I said, "I watch these young people get on the stand, open-eyed, open-faced, ignorant of what was happening to them, carrying this destruction in their bodies that will kill them . . . in twenty or thirty years . . . the man could have just as well said to you, 'My name is John Worker at the Kerr-McGee plant. I'm dead.' "

What right did Kerr-McGee have to put minimal information in that manual, and to obfuscate even that minimal information with technical jargon? Dr. Gofman had said if he'd written the manual he would have included the word CANCER in capital letters on every page. "We see Kerr-McGee's own people sitting here with clear facts of the cancer-causing effects of plutonium in their possession and concealing those facts from these young people. To me, that has to stop, and it can't be stopped when we are dealing with one-half of one percent of their corporate assets," I said. Later, Judge Theis ruled we could ask the jury for any sum we wanted—$70 million, or even more than that, if we chose.

I had the jury read the now-infamous letter of the chairman of the board, Dean McGee. It had been sent to the workers, telling them that the company's problems could be laid at the feet of their own union. McGee called the plant a safe, clean operation, and said that because all the dangers of plutonium were known, the nuclear industry is the "safest . . . ever developed." In front of the plant, the company had erected a large sign blithely informing the workers just how safe they really were: 594 DAYS SINCE A LOST TIME ACCIDENT. SAFETY PAYS, ON AND OFF THE JOB, the sign read.

The jury heard the testimony of other well-regarded scientists. I called Dr. Karl Morgan, the most "conservative" of our experts, the father of health-physics, who had worked in the heart of the nuclear beast for thirty years at the AEC's Oak Ridge lab. "I felt this was one of the worst operations I have ever studied," he said, and Kerr-McGee's requirement that workers labor in contaminated areas in respirators meant for emergency use only was "inexcusable and irresponsible." He judged Kerr-McGee guilty of willful and wanton disregard for the safety of its workers, then added his own judgment—it was "callous," he said.

Dr. Edward Martell, then our country's foremost environmental physicist, gave his opinion about Kerr-McGee's burying radioactive material on its own property. "The kind of radioactive waste they are handling out there is the most dangerous kind. You are not just going to affect the people living out there now; you are going to affect the larger population that may live there for future generations. It is illegal to bury this anywhere. . . . We are dealing with the health and welfare of future generations." The half-life of plutonium is twenty-five thousand years. But who cared? Certainly the government didn't. Kerr-McGee actually recorded 574 incidents of worker contamination and had been cited by the federal regulatory agency no less than 70 times for violations of that agency's safety rules. Despite these facts, the government never leveled so much as a twenty-five-dollar fine against that corporation. Perhaps you and I could talk an ordinary traffic cop out of ticketing us for driving over the speed limit in a school zone once, but seventy times? What was going on here? Juries may not understand the niceties of nuclear energy, but they can distinguish right and wrong. It is disgustingly common to discover that those who today work for an industry at large salaries once policed the same industry for the government at small ones. Moreover, as Dr. Martell put it, "You don't let a 'vested interest agency' decide what the health effects of their activities are." You don't let the Atomic Energy Commission, while promoting America's use of nuclear energy, guard the health and safety of American workers any more than you depend on the bullsnake to watch over the robin's nest. Thomas Jefferson was correct when he described the jury as "the only anchor ever yet imagined by man by which a government can be held to the principles of its constitution." And we were presenting our case to an American jury.

Jim Smith was a working man who came up through the ranks of Kerr-McGee, and he knew how to handle radioactive substances and stay alive. He testified about Kerr-McGee's uranium plant. "I never saw anything so filthy in my life."

"What was Kerr-McGee's attitude as to the safety of its workers over there?" I asked.

"If you ever walked into it, you could hardly breathe when you went beyond the door. The ammonia fumes and the uranium around there was just one big pigpen." Smith also disputed Kerr-McGee's claim that the forty pounds of missing plutonium wasn't actually missing but was simply hidden somewhere in the plant's piping system. That amount of plutonium was enough to build a couple of bombs like the ones we dropped on Hiroshima and Nagasaki. Smith said when the plant was shut down for cleanup in December 1975 the pipes were thoroughly flushed with boiling acid. "We spent many, many thousands of hours. It was a super cleanout." The plutonium wasn't there.

He told of how contaminated workers had driven a contaminated truck into town and had gone into a restaurant, and how later the workers and the truck were decontaminated, but the restaurant, with Lord knows how many unsuspecting people and employees exposed, was never surveyed. People could walk in or out of the plant without anybody checking them, and workers testified to forgeries of their records—it was a nightmare.

I wish you could have seen the jurors' faces when they heard the testimony of how Karen Silkwood herself had been contaminated with the dreadful stuff. She would leave work clean, but when she came back the next morning she would set off the alarms. Once, she had ten times the AEC limit on her right forearm, face, and neck, and she was panicked because her readings kept getting higher.

She thought someone was intentionally poisoning her, or maybe, she thought it was coming back out of her *lungs*. She took the company men to her tiny apartment in search of the source of the contamination, and they found plutonium everywhere—in the bathroom, the bedroom, her sheets, the refrigerator—even on the bologna for her sandwiches. Kerr-McGee wanted the jury to believe she had contaminated herself. She had been working with the Oil, Chemical and Atomic Workers Union to get the plant unionized. There was conflict. Some of her co-workers in the lab were dead set against the union and had access to her urine-sample kits and to raw plutonium as well. Some believed anti-union co-workers had contaminated her urine-sample kit to make it look as if she were contaminating herself and to thus discredit her. Those contentions went to the jury.

During the last weeks of her life, she had called her sister Rosemary, who testified, "She was scared. She asked me to come and visit her, to come see her—she needed to speak with someone. . . . She told me something was happening to her. She was hysterically upset, and she wouldn't tell me anything over the phone. . . . She was crying. She couldn't get the words out."

These jurors, honest men and women, saw the faces of the witnesses, and heard their voices, saw a hand clutch the arm of the witness chair and heard the tightening of throats. There was a truth being revealed that transcended the written word of the record.

I wish you could have heard the defense, heard the lead counsel for Kerr-McGee argue with the judge in chambers that he should be permitted to smear Karen Silkwood. I wish you could have heard him say, "In view of the flavor of Mr. Spence's opening statement I think we ought to be relieved of your ruling not to make mention of drugs and suicide in my opening statement."

"Why don't you comment on the forty pounds of missing plutonium?" I asked Kerr-McGee's lawyer.

"I will, Mr. Spence."

"You know, my friend," I said, "she could have been the dirtiest hog in the world, which you know she wasn't, and that has nothing whatever to do with the fact that your people let forty pounds of plutonium go."

The law is that if one handles an inherently dangerous substance and it escapes the possession of the owner, the owner is responsible. I went to the blackboard and in front of the jury wrote in large letters, IF THE LION GETS AWAY, KERR-MCGEE HAS TO PAY. The lion, of course, was plutonium. If a lion keeper brings his beast into the village in a cage, I argued, it made no difference that the man was careful, and locked the cage, or even double-locked it. It made no difference even if someone else let the lion out, because if it escaped and injured an innocent person, the lion keeper was responsible. It was a case not against nuclear power but against irresponsibility. I told the jury, "I don't want to see the workers of America cheated out of their lives anymore. I don't want to see people deprived of the truth, by the cover-ups, the word games, the mumblings. It's ugly. With your help, I want to stop it!"

I argued that the callous manner in which Kerr-McGee permitted its workers to be infected, the townspeople to be contaminated, and the environment to be destroyed had to be stopped. It takes less than a pound of plutonium to irradiate every human being in the world! What about the forty pounds Karen Silkwood claimed were missing? Ask the gentlemen in gray, as I called Kerr-McGee's lawyers. Ask the gentlemen of the bar. Ask its lead counsel, the former president of the Oklahoma Bar Association. They were dignified men with stiff white shirts and shoes as shiny as black marble. And they all said Kerr-McGee had done nothing wrong. Their voices were full of conviction and reason and they had that sweet, right look, like Methodist ministers. There was no plutonium missing. It was Karen Silkwood who had spiked her own urine samples. They found plutonium in her house! It was she who contaminated herself, the gentlemen in gray said.

How does one make an earless monster understand except to bleed it slightly—bleed it of its own green blood, its money? I argued to the jury, "If one of your children lied about something that had to do with the life and health of his brother or sister and he said that they were safe when he knew that he had exposed them to death— I suppose you might not find it unreasonable to take two piddling weeks of his allowance away to punish him." Should a corporation receive less proportionate punishment for having contaminated its workers with deadly plutonium? Should the lifeless corporation be entitled to a special privilege under the law that is not afforded to our children by responsible parents?

The case lasted nearly three months, the longest in Oklahoma's history, and we had invested hundreds of thousands of our own dollars and time. But as I saw it, the safety of thousands of American workers rested on the jury's decision, and the jurors worried, too, and sorted through the evidence and, after deliberating the better part of three days, came to a judgment they thought would do justice—that would maybe change things. They awarded a verdict of $500,000 actual damages and $10 million in punitive damages— damages to punish Kerr-McGee for its willful and wanton handling of the world's most dangerous substance—for letting the lion get away—and to assure society that the nuclear industry would do better for its workers in the future.

Of course, Kerr-McGee appealed to the United States Court of Appeals for the Tenth Circuit. The appeal took years, and, to no one's surprise, the judges reversed the case. The majority of the panel spoke in long, dreary intellectualizations about the jurisdiction of the state of Oklahoma to punish an industry engaged in the nuclear business, proclaiming that the right to regulate the nuclear industry was preempted by the federal government. By rendering $10 million in punitive damages, the court said the jury had encroached on that exclusive territory of the Nuclear Regulatory Commission (formerly the Atomic Energy Commission)—a bureaucracy that had already proved it absolutely would not enforce its own rules and regulations for the benefit of the people. Therefore, the court reasoned, Kerr-McGee would go unpunished except as the NRC might wish to levy its own fines from time to time, which, of course, it never did. The court made no mention of more than five hundred contaminations and the scores of violations that had already been found against Kerr-McGee for which no citations were ever issued. The court did not address itself to the rights of American workers to be protected in the workplace from the terrible dangers of plutonium. Besides, if Karen Silkwood had been injured by plutonium, the injury must have been associated with her job, the court said, and, therefore, she was barred by workers' compensation from suing her employer, despite the undisputed evidence that her contamination occurred off the premises. In short, it was not the health and safety of human beings that concerned the court, but the obligation of the corporation to pay punitive damages—not the right of workers to be fairly informed about the dangers of radiation, but the jurisdiction of the court to hear the case in the first place.

Judges, not juries, decide our cases in America.

And it is difficult for judges to see the living—and the dead—through the heavy paneled walls of their chambers. It is not that all judges lack human compassion, but the frightened faces, the pained faces of the human beings that the jury has seen are not before them. The judges cannot hear the deep sounds of agony or sorrow the jurors have heard. The misery of the people seeking justice is no more vivid to the judges than reading about any other tragedy in the morning's news. Judges see paper, not people. They see the lifeless briefs heaped upon their benches like great mountains in stark black and white.

And none of us will see that worker with the red face from the Kerr-McGee plant when he comes home one night maybe twenty years from now. But his wife will see him. Perhaps she will be standing at the stove turning the potatoes, and the room will be warm and filled with good kitchen smells. The husband will take off his hat and throw it on the chair. The coffeepot will perk away while his wife dishes up the potatoes on a big white platter and says, "Get washed up."

"The doctor says there's something wrong with me," the man will say in a quiet voice. "The doctor says I got cancer."

And then there will be a long silence, and pretty soon the wife will set down her spatula very softly.

When the man goes to the company and asks to be put on workers' compensation so he can get medical attention, the company will very kindly point out that he cannot prove his cancer is work-related. After all, it's been twenty years since he was at the plant. He never reported anything wrong with his lungs then, and they will argue that he worked within the safe limits of radiation approved by the Nuclear Regulatory Commission of the United States government. I can't see the rest of the misery and the dying. I can't stand the pain of it. Not for that man or the countless others like him.

After the Tenth Circuit Court of Appeals reversed the jury's verdict in the Silkwood case, we appealed to the United States Supreme Court, and after a long time that court sent the case back to the Tenth Circuit, where it lay dormant while the lawyers filed more motions and briefs and while Kerr-McGee appealed again to the Supreme Court. In the ensuing years, the children of Karen Silkwood grew to college age and were in serious need of money, and finally, seven years after the case had first been tried, Kerr-McGee and the Silkwood children settled out of court for little more than a single year's interest on the jury's original award, which was plain and simply nothing to Kerr-McGee; after the costs of the suit and the administration costs in the estate were paid, there was pitifully little for the children, and the lawyers got a pittance as well. But if the case hadn't been settled, it could easily have gone on for another seven years, and perhaps the kids would have got nothing. The estate was exhausted and the lawyers were drained—emotionally and financially. But the gentlemen in gray went on to bigger and better things. Kerr-McGee's lead counsel became the general counsel for Phillips Petroleum, and Kerr-McGee hired another great firm of Washington, D.C., lawyers to represent it.

But what about the work of those Oklahoma jurors? They had faithfully contributed nearly three months of their lives to the case, because they were told it was their duty as Americans to do so. They had listened intently and weighed the evidence for three days before they made their decision. They tried to do right, and they hoped they could do justice. But no one had told the jurors that judges in Denver would actually decide their case. The jurors had hoped that because of their verdict America would be safer. But no one told them that judges and lawyers would take nearly seven years to argue and bicker over the language of statutes and over the meaning of obscure cases in briefs and opinions that would fill hundreds of thousands of sheets of paper. And before the jurors' efforts were thrown out as irrelevant, no one had even stopped to mumble two small words to them—"Thank you." And, of course, the jury would not be there when the red-faced farm boys of Oklahoma come home to their wives on one of those black nights, already sick with cancer. No one would hear them except, perhaps the ghost of Karen Silkwood.

Many judges believe that all good to the people dribbles down to them from the plenitude of business, and that it is the solemn duty of the judiciary to remain ever vigilant, to protect the people from their own excesses, as if the people are not to be trusted any more than children turned loose in a candy factory—as if the appellate judges who saw and heard nothing of the trial know everything, but the twelve jurors who saw and heard everything know nothing. The consuming danger to the people is seldom the people themselves.

Yet our system could not work without judges to correct the miscarriages of justice that occasionally occur in a jury trial. We must have compassionate appellate judges to protect us when a tyrant on the trial bench prejudices the jury or interferes with an attorney's fair presentation of his case. We must have thoughtful appellate judges to review the evidence to make certain that the jury's verdict was based on the facts presented, not on prejudice. It is the duty of judges to protect the jury's verdict, to respect it, to guard it against judicial intrusion except where it is most clear that the process has failed, as occasionally it may. Appellate judges must protect us, not dictate to us, not arrogantly flick away the verdicts of juries as if they are of no greater import than lint on the cuff of their coat sleeves.

But in the Silkwood case, there was a pernicious principle at work that damned the jury's verdict from the moment the foreman put his signature to it. There is one cardinal postulate carved into the foundation stone of American justice that must never be violated. It is a rule that is never recited aloud by the judges, and never appears in writing. This axiom, like all great axioms, is simply stated:

LITTLE PEOPLE ARE ENTITLED TO
LITTLE JUSTICE.

That rule asks tight-fisted questions. Ten million dollars? Wouldn't such a huge award unjustly enrich these children? Imagine the immediate wealth that would accrue to the children's lawyers, who would share in the award. But such questions only give rise to others. Is it all right for Henry Ford III to be endowed with enormous wealth by the accident of birth, while the Silkwood children should be deprived of the well-conceived justice granted them by a jury? Is it all right that huge windfall profits enjoyed by mammoth American corporations gleaned from the suffering of a nation at war be assiduously protected by judges, while the occasional large award rendered to an ordinary citizen is set aside because it "shocks the conscience of the court"? I do not argue for a socialist's solution. To the contrary. I argue against the socialization of justice, against the prevailing notion that somehow justice for people must be more nearly equalized and spread out among the masses either by the operation of statutes such as the Workers' Compensation Act or its judicially imposed equivalent.

Judges in their secret chambers ask other questions. Can judges trust juries to regulate such a sophisticated and perilous endeavor as the nuclear business? That is a task requiring the finest minds of science and reason, not the emotional twaddle of the housewives and laborers who supposedly make up American juries. And if the judges won't trust the jury, would they rather trust Kerr-McGee? Or how about the Nuclear Regulatory Commission, which has habitually betrayed its trust to the American people? Shall we trust that bureaucracy one more time but distrust our own honest citizens? It is not that juries occasionally go wrong. It is that judges too frequently reveal that haughty conceit that has surely done us in—the idea that judges are wise but that ordinary people are not, that judges know, but that the people do not.

I remember when a Wyoming jury tried to take on *Penthouse* magazine to stop pornographers from exploiting the good names of innocent people for profit. I have written at length on that case as well and will not attempt to do so again, but it classically demonstrates the actual, as distinguished from mythological, power of the American jury. I can see my client, Kim Pring, sitting on the witness stand struggling to explain to the jury what had happened to her. She was born with a clubfoot, but early on her mother enrolled her in baton twirling. She took to it like a good pup to a point, and after the many operations on her foot and the lessons and the years of single-minded dedication that go into the making of every champion, she finally achieved her goal: She was crowned the Woman's Grand National Baton Twirling Champion of 1978. Wyoming was very proud of her. After all, we had never had a Woman's Grand National Baton Twirling Champion, nor many other champions, for that matter. And so the people chose Kim Pring to represent us as Miss Wyoming, and proudly sent her off to Atlantic City to the big affair.

At the same time, a writer for *Penthouse* magazine was covering the Miss America Pageant, where he saw Kim perform. She was far and away the crowd's favorite—a marvelous athlete who could perform magic with her baton. She could throw three batons in the air at once and do something called a "mouth-roll" and a lot of other difficult exercises that easily won her the talent award in the pageant that year. But that wasn't what the *Penthouse* story was about. As Kim later tried to explain to the jury, in less than three thousand words *Penthouse* transformed her from the greatest baton twirler in the nation to the greatest blowjob artist in the history of the world. The story claimed Miss Wyoming was so good at oral sex she could actually levitate a man. People read the story and laughed. Whenever they saw Kim, they pointed and laughed. She couldn't understand why *Penthouse* had done this to her. She had done nothing to *Penthouse*, and she certainly hadn't given them permission to write a story about her. She had never even met the author.

After the story, wherever she went, people hollered at her. "Hey, Penthouse, are you really as good as they say?" "Hey, Penthouse, how 'bout givin' me some of that?" They called her at night and breathed obscenities to her over the phone, and they wrote "Give me head" in the fresh snow on the windshield of her Volkswagen. The psychiatrists at the trial told the jury that Kim had been devastated. It was as if she had been raped, because rape is when someone takes from you what you don't want to give, and what *Penthouse* had done to Kim was to take her privacy and her good name, and they wrapped it all up in one obscene article they hadn't even bothered to label as fiction, and sold it to the 25 million men who, according to *Penthouse*, constituted the readership of that month's edition.

The jury wanted to stop pornographers from despoiling the good names of innocent women, and I told them I knew how they could do it. I argued that every time someone read that article, Kim was raped, and that the jury should punish *Penthouse* by charging them a mere dollar a rape. That amounted to $25 million—that should be fair, and it ought to stop that sort of thing once and for all. The jury agreed. They returned a verdict of $26.5 million against *Penthouse*,

$1.5 million as damages for Kim and $25 million to punish *Penthouse*. Later, Robert Guccione, the owner of the magazine, told the press that the jury's verdict wasn't worth the paper it was written on. And, of course, he was right. He fully understood the operation of the "little people—little justice" rule. Besides, Guccione knew what every publisher knows—that during the last two decades jury verdicts in the federal courts have been reversed more than 70 percent of the time.

Again, the same Tenth Circuit Court of Appeals reversed the case. There would be nothing for Kim. Nothing! Why? Because what *Penthouse* had published wasn't a libel at all, they said. Every reader of *Penthouse* knew that no matter how good you are at the art of fellatio, you can't actually cause a man to levitate. The court found that the article was obviously mere fantasy, and since it wasn't intended to be believed and couldn't be believed by a reasonable reader, the case should be dismissed. The court never mentioned the "little people—little justice" rule. Courts never do.

Nowhere in its decision did the court acknowledge there was a human being who had been injured and who had petitioned a jury for justice. Perhaps it would have been different if the judges had been in the courtroom and had seen Kim through the eyes of the jury—had seen her locked in her room staring at the walls, afraid to venture out for fear someone would jeer, "Hey, Penthouse, how's about levitatin' me?" Perhaps it would have been different if the judges had seen her when she finally mustered up the courage to go looking for a job—seen how it was when now no one would hire her even though she had been a good student and had earned a degree in business administration. At one time, she had her application in at fourteen different places, and the prospective employers either laughed at her or leered at her. Finally, in desperation, Kim joined the United States Army as a private, and she says that even after all these years men still holler, "Hey, Penthouse—are you really as good at—well, you know what I'm talking about." And then they laugh at the joke of it.

Nor did the court ever acknowledge that once more a jury of good citizens had labored to do justice and to effect change. The jury wanted to stop this First Amendment abuse. But, as usual, it would be judges, not juries, who made the decision in money cases. We applied to the United States Supreme Court for certiorari, which simply means we asked the high court to hear our case on appeal, but it refused. Maybe they thought she got what she deserved for parading around on television in a bathing suit. Maybe they didn't think about it at all. They didn't say. They don't have to. Their proceedings on pleas for certiorari are secret. And there was no other court for a further appeal.

Much later, I finally got around to talking to one of the jurors who had heard the case. He said the jury had made a bad mistake.

"I've been thinkin' a lot about that case lately," he said. "If we had given a million instead of twenty-five million, the judges might have let you keep it. Pornography is one thing to those judges, but letting a citizen have twenty-five million dollars is something else. I guess the judges figured what we did to the pornographer was a worse crime than what the pornographer done to Kim. We shouldn't have given you so much," he said. "We done wrong, I guess."

Sometimes I wonder why we pay our judges such a pittance. For as much harm as some sometimes do, they should be better compensated. But perhaps it is wise that we sparingly reward those in charge of our money. Insurance companies and banks learned that long ago, and are equally parsimonious with their adjusters and loan officers. An insurance adjuster making under $30,000 a year seems to have a natural aversion to paying some poor laborer a million dollars for his injuries, and the million dollars of loose change that falls through the crack of many corporate floorboards is an incomprehensible sum to most judges.

Judges affect society by their decisions much more than the presidents of McDonald's or Coca-Cola or Revlon, who are frequently paid ten times as much. Perhaps if our judges were paid more, they would resent large jury awards less. Yet the "gentlemen of the bar," who represent the monied interests of the nation, never fight very hard for larger salaries for our judges, although they rarely miss an opportunity to tell judges the opposite. The "gentlemen of the bar" understand the truth—that even if we paid our judges on the same scale as the president of General Motors and gave them a big expense account and a private jet to fly around in, we could never successfully change who the judges really are. Large salaries do not change the composition of a man's soul or sensitize a leathered heart.

That the law is not law at all but only what a majority of judges happen to say the law is on a particular day is no more clearly illustrated than in a recent session of the United States Supreme Court in which twenty-nine of sixty-six decisions were decided by only a single vote. If the judges themselves cannot agree as to what the law is, how are we to know it? In both the Silkwood and *Penthouse* cases, the decision was by a majority of one, and in both instances there were vigorous dissenting opinions. How strange that we require juries to return unanimous verdicts but permit the more learned judges to get by with a mere majority. We are told that judges are left to settle the law because we must have predictability in a commercial society. But my experience has been that juries are far more predictable than judges, and certainly they are not prey to years of petty in-house feuds and small slights that, as all lawyers know, may intervene in the judges' decisions. My experience is that jurors are more likely to see justice as something alive and relevant to the human beings before them, while appellate judges, who do not know the litigants and have never seen or heard them, tend to apply their private philosophical or political views to their decisions.

If we wish to return to the promised land where juries truly administer justice for the people, we must first rip away the old myths. Juries do not decide our cases—judges do. Today, no jury is permitted to hear a case in the first place unless the trial judge permits the case to go to trial. At the close of all the evidence, the judge alone determines if the party has presented a sufficient case for the jury to hear, and if the judge decides not, the case is thrown on the judicial garbage heap. Many times I have seen the judge direct the jury to return a verdict against an injured party—to sign the verdict form as he, the judge, provides, and always jurors do as he orders. They must. The judge is the law.

In every trial, civil or criminal, the judge shapes the case. Before and during the trial, the judge makes rulings that determine what procedures will be followed, what evidence will be permitted to go to the jury, what law will govern the trial, what arguments will be allowed, and how long such arguments will last. The case is no longer the parties' case but the judge's, and he will fashion the case to suit his fancy like any sculptor hacking away at his own private piece of rock.

If, after the jurors have tediously labored through the evidence, and have bludgeoned each other into a unanimous verdict, and have unanimously answered each of the pestiferous questions the judge has given them, all correctly—if, even then, the judge does not like the jury's decision, he has the power to set it aside and to order a new trial for any one of scores of reasons that may tickle his whimsy. He may claim the winning party's attorney prejudiced the jury by something he did, or that the judge himself permitted the jury to hear inadmissible evidence. Or he may pare the jury's award down to whatever size suits his fancy by ordering what is called a remittitur, claiming the size of the award has "shocked the court's conscience" (thereby presuming a fact not in universal agreement among lawyers). But should the party refuse to accept the lesser sum, the judge will order a new trial and will continue thereafter to order one new trial after another until a verdict is returned that suits him or until the party has finally become exhausted or impoverished or loses his case or submits to the judge's order.

Sadly, too many judges worry more about being reversed by the appeals court than they do about rendering justice in the case before them. Too often a trial becomes a contest between the trial judge and the appellate court, and justice is forgotten. One judge I know thinks of the appeal in terms of the upper court "grading his papers." Another I know refers to the appellate judges as the "Five Old Know-It-Alls." To be reversed means that the trial judge is publicly found to be deficient in his knowledge of the law, and he suffers a sense of frustration and even shame. How is it to hear whispers behind one's back that you are the most reversed judge in the state? The trial judge must not commit an error, and every decision he makes in the case—and he makes hundreds of them every day of the trial—presents an opportunity for a reversible misstep. Instructions to the jury must be technically correct. As a consequence, the trial judge does not draft his instructions to the jurors in easily understandable language. Instead, they are written in the dead, heavy language of the law, often quoting passages he has lifted verbatim from some prior decision of the appellate court, all of which may satisfy the appellate court on the appeal but most often leaves the jury utterly in the dark as to what the law is. Sometimes even the lawyers cannot make heads or tails of the instructions.

The illusion that juries are deciding our civil cases is encouraged by the judges themselves. When appellate judges agree with a jury's decision, we will read in the opinion that "the jury's finding of fact binds the court." But the truth is that nothing binds the court except what the court says binds it. On the other hand, when the judges disagree with the jury, the opinion may say that "the jurors were led to an improper conclusion as a result of prejudicial error," a phrase that covers a host of supposed evils, from the introduction of improper evidence to some forbidden argument made by one of the attorneys. The same supposed error may be prejudicial in one case, thus requiring a reversal of the jury's verdict, or utterly harmless in another, depending on how a majority of the judges wish to decide the case. Yet no matter how the judges decide, they will always give lip service to the inviolate power of the jury's verdict, thereby preserving the myth that justice in this country is still a product of a jury of our peers.

Today, our cases are decided by a jury of judges whose attitudes and prejudices and personal philosophies are often at violent variance with those of the injured citizen. More often than not, our cases on appeal are decided by a jury of judges composed of persons most lawyers would have challenged summarily from any jury panel. An attorney for a party injured in an automobile collison might be guilty of malpractice were he to accept a juror who had spent his life working for a liability-insurance company. But on appeal, his case will often be decided by judges who, before they rose to the bench, spent their lives and amassed modest fortunes defending insurance companies in similar cases.

Yet juries have not always been disenfranchised in America. Not until the nineteenth century did judges begin to regularly set aside the jury's verdicts. Originally, jurors were given the power to nullify the law if their consciences demanded, because jurors were expected to perform that vital function in a democracy—to stand firm for the individual against the tyrannical yoke of unjust rule. Our Founding Fathers argued passionately for the unrestrained power of the jury. John Adams said in 1771 that it is not only the right of the juror but "his duty . . . to find the verdict according to his own best understanding, judgment, and conscience, though in opposition to the direction of the court." Even Alexander Hamilton, a lawyer representing the commercial interests of the time, stated in 1804 that the jury in a criminal case is duty-bound to acquit, despite the instructions of the judge, "if exercising their judgment with discretion and honesty they have a clear conviction that the charge of the court is wrong." John Jay, the first Chief Justice of the United States, in a jury trial before the full Supreme Court (that court, at its inception, actually heard jury trials), told the jurors, "Gentlemen, you have a right to determine the law as well as the facts in controversy." Jefferson himself described the function of the jury: "If the question relate to any point of public liberty, or if it be one of those in which the judges may be suspected of bias, the jury undertakes to decide both law and fact."

The right of the jury to nullify the law was the restatement of the spirit of the American Revolution by men who had despised the king's absolutism and were leery of the power of the new state they had created. Alexis de Tocqueville observed in 1840 that the American jury was a political as well as a judicial institution, which "places the real direction of society in the hands of the governed, or a portion of the governed, and not in that of the government," so that "the primary purpose of the jury [was] to prevent the possibility of oppression."

But before we applaud the generous and democratic spirit of our Founding Fathers, we must understand one simple fact: They never intended that any but the "gentlemen" of the new nation, their own class, should sit as jurors. It was to be a jury of their peers, all right—

that is, a jury of landed gentlemen. Our constitutional fathers, the elitists of their times, trusted the ordinary people the way a hawk trusts a flock of pestering magpies. They never intended that juries should be selected from "the rabble and the riffraff." They never intended to give either the right to vote or the power of the jury to the poor, to blacks, or to women. Because juries were made up only of trusted members of the ruling class, they were also freely given the right to nullify the law.

The Founding Fathers never dreamed that the system they invented would be expanded to include the class, ethnic, and social variety of the nineteenth century. Once common men were given the right to sit on juries, it was no longer deemed safe to leave it to them to decide disputes involving the interests of money and property. With the onslaught of the Industrial Revolution, the power of the jury had already been wrested from them by the judges. But the history of the decline of the American jury has also been the history of the decline of democracy in this country, for the jury has always been at the heart of the system.

In 1895, in the case of *Sparf and Hansen* v. *United States*, the Supreme Court terminated the power of juries to nullify the law, and shackled juries for all time to the judiciary. Today, in every courtroom in the land one may hear some judge sternly admonish the jury, "Ladies and gentlemen of the jury: It becomes my duty as the judge to instruct you concerning the law applicable to this case, and it is your duty as jurors to follow the law as I shall state it to you." Failure of the jury to follow the law as dictated by the court is, of course, grounds for a judge to reverse the jury's verdict.

Ironically, in the criminal case, where only the life and liberty of the citizen are at stake, where the poor are usually the accused, and—more important—where money and property are not at risk, juries are trusted somewhat more with the decision. An accused, once acquitted by a jury, cannot be ordered to stand trial again, because of the constitutional prohibition against double jeopardy, a rule that remains essentially intact today. But usually its enforcement does not jeopardize the business community. As one scholar observed, "Although the American jury is still praised as a bastion of democracy standing between oppressive governments and the people, most of today's American judges in fact do everything they can to emasculate the jury until the only role left for jurors is to review the facts and then rubber-stamp the application of the law for the government." Every lawyer who has ever defended a criminal case knows he speaks the truth. In modern times, juries have often become that "docile, regimented group" who, as good citizens per-

forming their duty, follow the judge's instructions like children following the admonitions of the father, for in the courtroom the judge
is father, teacher, God, the source of all knowledge and wisdom,
whom all good citizens are taught to obey. And all jurors are sworn,
upon their solemn oaths, to do the same. Nevertheless, in the occasional criminal case, the old ideals of jury nullification may still
temper the rock-hard justice of the law with the common sense and
compassion of human beings judging other human beings.

I think back over thirty years to the case of Maude Hackleman.
She was a grizzled old woman with a beer belly and voice to match,
and she knew something about justice. At the time, I was the prosecuting attorney of Fremont County, with my office in Riverton. I
was questioning Maude on the complaint of her neighbor, Benny
Etalope, a Basque sheepman, who claimed she had shot at him, run
his pickup in the ditch, dragged him out, and beat him up—actually
pistol-whipped him. The sheriff had pictures of Benny. His eyes were
swollen shut, his lips looked like hamburger, and he had a couple
of broken ribs where Maude had kicked him when he was down.
Maude admitted it all to me. That was before Miranda.

"Why did you do it, Maude?" I asked. "I mean, he's got you
charged with assault with a deadly weapon."

"Well, Mr. Spence," she said, and Maude could look very respectful and reverent, and make her wrinkled old face innocent and sad,
"it was justice. It was plumb justice and it felt good." Suddenly she
erupted and jumped up, and began pounding the table with her fist.
"I would run the dirty little bastard down and do it again, if I had
to chase him to hell!" Then she looked at me with a small apology
for having gotten so carried away, and she whispered, "He roped one
of my mares and sewed her lips shut with bailing wire." And then
Maude began to cry.

"He did what?" I asked.

"You heard me," she said through her sobs. "He musta throwed
her and tied her, and then he took bailing wire and punched it
through her lips and wired her mouth shut. She couldn't eat. She
had a colt. I never found the mare for a long time afterward—come
on to her up at the reservoir one day. She was tryin' to suck water
through them lips . . . a horrible mess. The colt died. I had to shoot
the mare. Then I went out lookin' for that little son of a bitch."

"How did you know Benny did it?" I asked.

"Don't gimme that lawyer talk. Everybody knows that little bastard done it," she said, having now recovered. "He done it once
before to Jim Halson's stud. Caught that stud in his hayfield and
sewed his lips shut just like he done to my mare. Jim was too old

to do anything about it 'cept shoot the little bastard, and Jim said shootin' was too good for him. I told Benny if he ever done that to any of my stock I'd kick him till his pants were full, and I did."

"Was your mare also on his property, Maude?" I asked. Property rights in Wyoming are important.

"Don't make no difference. It ain't a matter of property. He ain't got a right to do that to any livin' creature anywhere."

"I asked you a question, Maude."

"Well, that mare was a little breachy," she said. "But all he had to do was run her and her colt back through the gate again."

Later, Maude admitted it all to the jury, trusted them, told them the whole story; but the judge charged the jurors, each of whom had been duly sworn to follow his instructions, that, in effect, people can't go around kicking the hell out of other people for having wired a mare's mouth shut. There might be a charge against Benny Etalope for cruelty to animals or malicious destruction of property or some such thing, but that was for another case at another time. He told the jury that the law forbade them from taking into account that Maude may have thought she was justified. "It is not lawful for a citizen to take justice into the citizen's own hands. Retaliation and retribution, if ever exercised, are solely the function of the state. Were it otherwise we would live in chaos and anarchy."

The judge in Maude's case had the eyes of a predator. Once he had been a prosecutor himself. He was the kind who would let a lawyer plead for mercy for a client until the lawyer was exhausted and then the judge would stare down at the lawyer like an apathetic coyote inspecting a gopher he'd just cornered under a rock. "You plead for justice, Counsel?" You could hear the sneer in his voice. "If you can define justice for me, I'll deliver it to you." The judge was a part of the divine joke, for it was he, this judge, who would deliver justice, and we all knew that however he defined justice, it didn't include mercy. In Maude's case, he thought he had the jurors where he wanted them and that they would have to follow the law as he dictated and find Maude guilty. Within a few minutes, the jury, mostly ranchers, returned a verdict of "Not Guilty." Dumbfounded, I asked the foreman, a crafty old devil and a rancher himself, how they could make such a decision under the court's instructions.

"The judge trusted us to do justice," the foreman said. "Now you wouldn't have wanted us to violate his trust, would you? That judge knew we wouldn't go along with all that legal horseshit as he was readin' us." In his rustic way, the juror had, of course, announced the old principle of jury nullification, and it had worked in this case just as the Founding Fathers had intended.

Yet even in the criminal case, modern juries are placed under the severest restraints by judges. Often juries return verdicts they know are unjust, verdicts they would not have returned but for the imposition of the judge's will upon them. In the celebrated case of Dr. Benjamin Spock, who was convicted by a jury of conspiring to violate the draft laws, one juror confessed he didn't want to vote for conviction. "I agreed wholeheartedly with [Dr. Spock] but . . . I felt that technically he did break the law." And more recently it was reported that the jurors wept upon returning a verdict of "Guilty" against a doctor who, out of love and mercy, had gently ended the life of his wife to spare her the last unspeakable agony of a terminal cancer.

Today, justice is no longer tied to the ideals of ordinary people, or grounded in what ordinary people think. Instead, justice is a commodity designed by a hierarchy of judges still dedicated to the interests of Power. Our forefathers, that lawless minority who revolted against the king and were led by such alleged enemies of law and order as George Washington and Thomas Jefferson, argued that no law was valid if it deprived man of his natural rights. "The jury, which is the most energetic means of making the people rule, is also the most effective means of teaching it to rule," Alexis de Tocqueville said of the nineteenth-century jury. But judges, not the Constitution, not the dreams of our Founding Fathers, decree justice in America today. Like a man growing old, the law has stiffened and calcified.

Yet the myth of the jury persists, and why not? We can still walk into any courtroom anywhere in the country and see the jury at work, its members carefully listening, weighing the evidence. There sits the jury—that grand old institution of democracy, still intact, still meting out justice to the ordinary citizen, to the injured, to the forgotten, and to the damned. And things seem safe, and things seem all right again.

6 | JUDGES

Priests in the Marketplace

Who are these judges who wield such power over us, a power reserved for God? Who are these mere humans with the power to wrest children from their mothers and to condemn men to death or cage them like beasts in penitentiaries? Who possesses the power to strip us of our professions, our possessions, our very lives? The judges of America have more influence over the course of the nation than Congress and the president. They interpret the laws, apply them, change them to match their private vision of the world, and extend their collective nose into every manner of private or government business.

Judges decide whether the janitor was fired for just cause and whether GM is engaged in price-fixing. They review the hospital board's suspension of your doctor's surgical privileges and decide the constitutionality of the university's enrollment policies that gave a coveted slot to a minority student with lower grades and test scores than your child. They make law. They have the power to force children to be bused into strange places, make abortion legal, and determine whether a quadriplegic who wants to die may be permitted to do so. They may take away your wife or your good name or your freedom or your fortune or your life. They are omnipotent. And the question is: To whom have we so carelessly granted that power? Are they the kind who would understand you, who from their experiences would know something of the fears and struggles you have faced? Will they care about you or about justice?

The profile of the typical American judge is a white, Protestant male of about fifty years of age from an upper middle-class family, who has labored without stellar success as an attorney. He has been in politics, but there he was not a rising star, either. He is more likely to be from a large firm than a small one, and has had, during his practice, a variety of corporate clients but little experience in representing those charged with crimes, those who have been injured, and the poor.

The ascension of the judge to the bench does not, of course, alter his personal history, erase the memories of his experiences, modify his genes, change his parentage, or blot out his prejudices. Every president knows that, and achieves a sort of immortality by extending his influence over the nation through the judges he appoints. Moreover, the mating of a human being to the federal bench seems to produce an offspring that lives approximately forever.

Not long after his second term had begun, President Reagan had already appointed over half of the nation's 744 federal judges, including a new Chief Justice of the United States Supreme Court. The profile of these judges is starkly homogeneous: 91.6 percent are men, 92.6 percent white, and 89.5 percent Republican. Nearly twice as many were from moderate to large firms as from small ones, nearly half have been prosecutors, 60 percent went to Ivy League or private law schools, and 64.2 percent are Protestant. Seventy percent of the appeals-court judges and nearly 60 percent of the district-court judges have a net worth of between $200,000 and $1 million, and over 20 percent of the district-court judges and nearly 18 percent of the appeals-court judges appointed by Reagan have a net worth in excess of $1 million. These judges, who as private lawyers represented numerous corporate clients, will now hear the cases of people seeking justice against corporate America; as former prosecutors, they will now sit on the cases of citizens charged by the government with crimes. William Jones once said, "There is very little difference between one man and another; but what little there is, is very important."

No one took the federal bench during Reagan's administration who could not demonstrate a political philosophy compatible with the president's. Before they were approved for appointment, the Reagan judges were "shook down and wrung out" like crowbaits being bought by a horse trader. The candidates were required to answer a ten-page questionnaire, followed by a daylong personal interview. A special administration committee made further inquiries into the candidate's attitudes toward abortion, school prayer, criminal procedure, and affirmative action; then, finally, the prospective judge had to pass muster with the attorney general himself. With few exceptions, those who received the administration's nod were not especially renowned for their fondness of the people or the people's rights. Only three of the appointees were black, and four Hispanic. Elaine Jones of the NAACP says, "[Reagan's judges] will just be hitting their stride in fifteen years. In any question that pits the rights of the individual against the power of the state, we are going to see individual rights suffering."

During Reagan's second term, Chief Justice Burger, in a sacrifice fly to the right, stepped down from the court, thereby allowing the president to appoint a younger man, Justice William Rehnquist, his successor. This move also gave the president the right to appoint Rehnquist's successor, another avowed conservative, Judge Scalia. Archibald Cox, who was the special Watergate prosecutor fired by Nixon, fears that this kind of politicizing will endanger the fundamental purpose of the court. He cautions, "The idea of judicial independence may be at risk."

Alan Dershowitz, noted author and Harvard Law School professor, writing in *Penthouse*, says, "[A] president who seeks to change the jurisprudence by appointing judges committed to carrying out his political agenda endangers our delicate system of checks and balances. Judges are supposed to serve as a counterweight to political excess, not as the president's yes-men. . . ."

The New York Times left little doubt that the restructuring of the court is already being felt: "The conservatives on the Supreme Court dominated the term that just ended to a degree unmatched in the Court's recent history." The *Times* reported that judges were now permitted to impose the death penalty even though a jury had refused to do so. That ruling upheld a Florida law and will affect more than eighty inmates on Florida's death row whose sentences were changed by judges from life in prison to death. Now, illegally obtained evidence may be used against the accused if it can be shown that the evidence would have "inevitably been discovered" by legal means, thus delivering up our constitutional rights to mere speculation. Searches of private property for illegal aliens can be made without a search warrant. The court ruled that the requirements of "public safety," whatever that is, "could justify the police in questioning a suspect without first giving the familiar warnings against self-incrimination." The court thus created the first exception in eighteen years to the Miranda rule. In the workplace, the right of blacks to maintain their job quota is no longer guaranteed against whites with greater seniority, and juveniles who have not yet been tried for their supposed crimes can be detained to prevent them from committing other crimes—the first time in our history that the court has allowed preventive detention, despite the fact that under the Constitution these children are presumed innocent. At the conclusion of the term, Burt Neuborne, legal director of the American Civil Liberties Union, said, "Americans are far less free today than they were a year ago. When the Supreme Court functions not as a vigorous guardian of the individual but as a cheerleader for the government, individual constitutional rights cease to have independent meaning. Instead, they mean whatever the government wants them to mean."

While the court was awaiting the appointment of its ninth member after the Senate's rejection of Judge Robert Bork, Robert Streetman was put to death in Texas. He had petitioned the court to stay his execution pending review. The court was deadlocked four to four (it would take a majority court to stay his execution). Of the conservatives on the court, White, O'Connor, Scalia, and Rehnquist, *The New York Times* lamented, "not one was willing even to wait for the vote of a ninth judge." Justice William Brennan observed in a stinging dissent that if Streetman had been a convicted bank robber, the court's decision on whether to hear his case would have been put on hold until the ninth justice was appointed. In calling for special safeguards in capital cases, the court has previously admitted that "death is different" from other kinds of cases. Justice Brennan wrote, "Death is certainly different, but I had never believed it to be different in this way." The erosion of a nation's concern for life, and for individual rights, has always preceded the intrusion of tyranny.

The American Bar Association, its dominant membership in tune with the new conservative court, has provided little inspirational leadership for the nation's lawyers to fight for the rights of the individual. That is nothing new. Fifteen years earlier, Chief Justice Earl Warren castigated the ABA for its nonfeasance in the area of human rights: "In all candor, I cannot say that in my view the organized bar of the nation has, on the whole, discharged that obligation in praiseworthy fashion. Throughout the McCarthy era, and for years following that shameful period, while the federal courts were struggling to make the Bill of Rights and the Civil War Amendments meaningful in our society, the organized bar of the nation did precious little to assist. On the contrary, it occupied itself with trying to establish to the world that the Supreme Court of the United States was the handmaiden of Communism and the greatest friend the Soviets had in America." None of this must have surprised the good judge, assuming he had even a scant knowledge of the ABA's history.

Nearly from its inception, the American Bar Association has held affectionately to its pallid bosom its favorite child, the wealthy white male Protestant from selected parentage. Blacks were not admitted to the organization until 1953. The ABA's Standing Committee on the Federal Judiciary, which passes judgment on all nominees to the federal bench, was, from its birth in 1946, restricted in membership, cloaked in class bias, and composed of lawyers from the "fast track"—the said "best and brightest" of the Anglo-Saxon elitist bar. More than half its membership came from the very corporate law firms that have perennially held the reins of the bar. None of the committee members in these crucial years specialized in criminal law or family law. For the two decades ending in 1967, not a single black person held membership on that committee. It was all-male and as pure white as a Wyoming snowstorm.

The ABA's approval of the first woman appointed to the Supreme Court was given with as much enthusiasm as that of a groom at a shotgun wedding. Yet except for gender, Justice Sandra O'Connor seemed identical to the American Bar Association's profile of a duly qualified judge. She was a graduate of Stanford Law School, a member of a prestigious law firm that represented the corporate sector, and she was conservative. She did not disappoint her mentors. By her third session, she was already standing as close to the archconservative of the court, Justice William Rehnquist, as would be proper for a robed woman. In twenty-nine of the cases decided by one-vote margins she had joined Justice Rehnquist in all but three.

The Judicature Society, devoted to the uplifting of the American judiciary, took pains to scrutinize the ABA's evaluation of judges. It concluded: ". . . the strongest possible relationship which emerged in our analysis was that between the American Bar Association rating [of nominated judges] and the candidates' white male status. Higher marks were bestowed on the judicial candidates who practiced predominantly before federal and appellate tribunals, those who practiced predominantly in civil litigation and in the traditional subject areas of the law; those who were born in the jurisdiction of their appointments; those who attended the elite law schools; those who at one time had achieved a prestigious legal clerkship, and those who earned relatively higher incomes than other candidates."

The study further revealed that the ABA had not taken into account the not-so-subtle political influences of the candidate toward his own appointment—such as his hefty financial contributions or those of his sponsors, or the ever-present cronyism, or the relationship of the candidate's firm to the members of the ABA committee or to the approving congressional committees, or to the president himself. Partners of senators and powerful congressmen are, with unusual predictability, endorsed by the ABA and appointed to the federal bench.

The Judicature Society reported that half of the male federal judges were active in party politics before their election to the bench. Some held high political office. Others had been advisers to prominent politicians. Almost every appointee had either directly or indirectly through his partners made substantial contributions to his political party, so that the clear margin between politics and judging became blurred. By the beginning of President Reagan's second term, the ABA, working overtime, had rated over half of Reagan's first-term nominees to the district court "exceptionally well qualified" or "well qualified." Given the foregoing, I should have thought those judicial nominees receiving the ABA's punctilious kiss of approval would have found the same as disquieting as being over-greeted by a whore in church.

These judges, many of whom have spent a majority of their years as corporation lawyers, are, upon ascending to the bench, just as much the corporate progeny as a skunk raised in a litter of kittens is still a skunk. These judges will continue to make their decisions with the same mental apparatus that only a fortnight before they had called upon during an entire career to forward the interests of their corporate clients. Are we to suppose that such a judge, like a blacksmith who, for all of his life, has beaten swords from plowshares, will, merely because he has moved to a better address, beat plowshares from swords? Oliver Wendell Holmes and others debunked the orthodox doctrine that judges, despite the method of their selection, upon assuming the ermine would faithfully apply existing rules of common justice in deciding cases. These so-called "legal realists" argued the obvious, that judges actually decide cases according to their own political, ethnic, and moral preferences, and in payment of their political obligations.

State judicial selection procedures are even more severely criticized. Robert E. Woodside, a former judge, testifying before the Pennsylvania State Legislature concerning the selection of state judges, asserted, "Today . . . [they] are sold over television like soap, and the selling costs lots and lots of money. . . . That money comes from lawyers and those special interest groups who are involved in frequent litigation. This system puts the judges into direct obligation to lawyers and litigants who consistently appear before them."

On the other hand, consider what might happen to the game of football if we permitted any damn fool who ever played the sport in college to run for referee, and whoever got the most votes would officiate the next contest between the Bears and the Skins. Suppose, further, that the Bears' organization contributed heavily to the campaign of one of the candidates, and that the candidate bought a lot of posters with the money and stuck his smiling face on little stakes in the front yards of his neighbors. Do we know anything about his competence, his experience, or his honesty? The fans, of course, vote for him, and he wins. But what kind of a job will he do officiating at the next Bears game?

In some states, judges are elected like any other official. In others, a committee made up of judges, lawyers, and laymen—another of those anonymous committees that always seem to run things from behind the scenes—submits three names to the governor to fill a judicial vacancy, and the governor picks one of the names from the list. Thereafter, the appointed judge is periodically required to run against himself—that is, no one is permitted to run against him, so that the sole decision left to the voters is: "Should Judge Smith be retained?" If half or more of the voters agree that he should, he will be free to wreak his havoc on us for another term. This travesty is called the "Missouri Plan," after the state in which it was invented, and Wyoming has adopted it. I know of no state, including Missouri, in which those who have experienced the plan's operation believe it has materially raised the quality of the state's judiciary. Contrary to its promise, the plan does not remove the selection of judges from politics. The governor, a political being, still appoints judges and creates political obligations thereby. Moreover, the committee that presents the governor with the lists of names from which his appointment of the judge can be made is often dominated by special-interest groups, who attempt to make the appointment themselves. In Wyoming, where the governor is presented with three names, I have known the committee to include the names of two candidates wholly unacceptable to the governor, leaving as his only practical choice the candidate the committee itself had chosen. Once the judge takes the bench, unless he gets involved in his own Chappaquiddick, he will probably remain in office for the rest of his life. Only two judges have been turned out of office since Wyoming adopted this method of judicial selection nearly twenty years ago. The fact is, the Missouri Plan is a sort of backdoor method of installing the federal plan of life tenure in the state judiciary without the voters ever having realized it.

If the Missouri Plan, as it has sometimes operated in Wyoming, were instituted in the National Football League, we would see the commissioner picking a referee from three names submitted to him by a Referee Selection Committee. That committee might be composed of a referee who had once been a Bear himself, a former member of the Bears' front office, and several Bears fans in good standing. Of the three names submitted to the commissioner, one is blind and one wheelchair-bound. The third is, of course, an ex-Bear, and, being the only candidate the commissioner could appoint, he is appointed and will now probably officiate in every Bears game for the rest of his life. It is argued that because the referee has de facto life tenure and cannot be kicked off the field no matter how bad his calls, no matter how old and frail he gets, his overall officiating will somehow be superior and, therefore, out of the purity of his heart and a short memory as to whom he is indebted for his job, he will be most likely to call them as he sees them.

We hear of judges being bribed, and occasionally overt bribery does occur. The infamous Graylord cases of Chicago come to mind. I remember an incident several years ago that raised troublesome questions in the mind of a semi-innocent country lawyer from the mountains of Wyoming. What is bribery? And under what circumstances might we actually consider bribing a judge? I had just finished speaking to a group of criminal-defense attorneys in Chicago, and after my speech I took an empty seat next to a seedy-looking character who, I soon discovered, was half-drunk and, by his abrasive remarks, wanting to get my attention. I was trying to be polite and get through dinner without any trouble and then get the hell out of there.

"What do you do?" I finally asked.

"I bribe judges," he said. I looked around to see if anybody heard him. The entire table was listening.

"What do you mean, you bribe judges?" I started to get up, but the drunk threw his arm out in front of me.

"Wait a minute, Spence!" I sat back and folded my arms in resignation. "Let me just tell you a little something! Judge-bribing is an honorable profession. If you wanted a judge bribed in Chicago, you used to come to my father. Now, if you want a judge bribed, you come to me. You lily-pure bastards make me sick. You bribe judges all the time, but you're not honest about it."

"Oh, yeah, tell me about it," the guy across from me piped up.

"You play golf with the bastards and let 'em win, and you laugh at their jokes that aren't funny and kiss their asses and make 'em feel like they are King Shit, and you give 'em awards at your fucking bar meetings and you put a lot of money in their campaign funds. You bribe 'em, but you don't want anybody to think you're bribing 'em. I just put the money in the judges' hands, like that. It's clean. It's honest bribery."

"How many judges have you bribed?" the guy across from me asked.

"Why? Do you want a judge bribed?"

"Heavens, no," the guy said, as if he were about to be kissed on the lips by a leper. Then the drunk came up with a hypothetical case to make his point. "Suppose your kid is a little drunk and drives into a tree, kills his girlfriend, and he's charged with manslaughter by the D.A. It's your boy now, not your client's boy. He's a good kid. I got a kid of my own in law school. Now let me ask you: Do you want to take ten grand and go out and hire a good lawyer and let the kid take his chances, or do you want me to take the same ten grand and bribe the judge? It's your choice."

The guy across from me said, "I'll take my chances."

"Don't bullshit me," the drunk said. "You know damned well the kid's gonna be convicted. He had a blood alcohol of point two-oh. Ain't no lawyer in the world gonna get 'im off." The drunk laughed.

The guy across from me didn't say anything. He looked pale. "Excuse me, I have to take a little trip," he said. "Be right back." The drunk turned to me.

"What's right depends on whose kid it is, don't it?" he asked. Then the evening's master of ceremonies proceeded to introduce a respected veteran trial lawyer who would present the association's Judge-of-the-Year Award to a certain eminent jurist, and after a very long and laudatory presentation by the lawyer and a short acceptance speech by the judge, he made one last remark before he sat down.

"And if any of you think that because of this award I'm likely to be any easier on your clients who are convicted in my court, you got another think coming," the judge said, and everybody laughed.

I have known many a judge who was bribed—by the tears of an anguished father or the wailing of a motherless child or the quiet plea of an old friend. But in an entire career, I never knew a judge who I believed was bribed by raw money. Yet most judges I know are beholden to Power—by that I mean unalterably pledged to the dominant force of the system. Sometimes the dominant force is public opinion and sometimes the ward boss, but in America it has more often been the power of those colossal corporate creatures— those paper omnivores that feed on our culture and our lives and that often have taken possession, one way or another, of the lawyers who become our judges. When justice is defeated, whether by an overt bribe or when the judge, because of who he is, honestly views justice through the eyes of the corporation so that the just claims of people are more easily defeated, the result is the same. When judges are saturated with notions respectful of the rights of man, and join in the singing of hymns that glorify humans over things and people over profits, there will be little demand for the likes of the lawyer in Chicago whose business it was to bribe judges.

Throughout history, judges have faithfully served Power, for the law, whether in a democracy or a totalitarian state, has but one function—to perpetuate Power. Judges administer the laws of both saints and tyrants. That we live in a democracy only obfuscates the issue, for a democracy merely defines the means by which Power obtains power—presumably by the will of the people. It does not identify those who *wield* the power—a junta, an inner circle of elitists, a corporate oligarchy that advances a spirit and a force at odds with the interests of people.

To the people, justice is an ideal, not an instrument of Power. To the people, justice is as Justinian defined it—"the firm and continuous desire to render to everyone that which is his due." But the legal system is not predominantly attentive to notions of equality and the rights of the individual. The legal system is concerned, instead, with law, and law is pledged to Power. As a consequence, law will most often stand against such human rights as threaten Power. The virulence of Power is not the question. By reason of Power's preoccupation with its own goals, all Power tends to function as if the system were designed to destroy the individual, for Power, by definition, can never permit itself to be subordinated to the individual. As a consequence, justice will be delivered to the people only when it is in the best interests of Power to deliver it.

Power! Man himself has a passion for power that brings on a strange and noxious malady. I have seen judges reeling in the throes of it. Once, I watched a judge waving jauntily down from the bench to his cronies who had come to court to engage in the sadistic sport of witnessing a young convicted murderer beg for his life. I saw the judge winking and smirking, more interested in being recognized by his friends than in hearing the condemned's piteous plea. Later, the man was executed. The judge never heard him and never intended to. I saw a judge throw out the just case of a widow whose husband had been murdered, because the jury's verdict would have been an embarrassment to the governor who had appointed him. I saw a judge permit the prosecution of an innocent man because the man was unpopular in the judge's club. I have seen hundreds of millions of just jury awards against corporations taken from the injured, from bereaved parents and orphaned children, by judges who claimed their consciences were shocked that a human being should receive so much money—so much of the corporate blood. I do not forget the true missionaries of justice—the good, the decent, the devoted judges—they also have power. But they are uncomfortable with it and shy from it. They are the few giant trees in the forest—but the weeds, not the majestic cedars, choke us.

How, then, can we choose the right judges? I have seen good citizens ascend to the bench, and seen them, as if by the touch of hell, change into despots. Power does strange and evil things. I have seen whole forests of competent lawyers quaking like aspens in a windstorm before a cruel judge who relished not justice, not fairness, not truth, but his own precious power. I have quaked myself before these tyrants, and still do, and did the first time I came before one many years ago.

I was a beginning lawyer representing a farmer in a civil dispute. A local slicker had purchased my client's crop of hay and, after feeding most of it to his sheep, refused to pay for it, claiming that the hay was moldy and he'd been defrauded. I'd been out to my client's farm and seen the hay myself, and it was as sweet and clean as the day it was put up. Nothing in this world smells better than good fresh hay. The price of the hay was all the farmer and his family had to live on for the winter, and after the man refused to pay, the farmer went to the bank for enough to squeeze by until spring. Now, the bank wanted its money, and under its pressure the farmer made another mistake—they usually come in bunches—he hired me, and I sued.

The courtroom was upstairs in the old courthouse, and in August it was sweltering. I knew for a fact that the judge didn't wear his suit coat under his robe, and I was suffering in the lightest jacket I owned with the collar unbuttoned behind a wide knotted tie. When it came time for my client to testify, he took the witness stand in his bib overalls. They were all he owned, but they were freshly laundered and pressed, and to show his respect he wore his blue denim shirt buttoned tight. The judge had been reading the court file. When the judge looked up to see him in the witness chair, he slammed the file closed, turned red as a garden radish, and screamed, "Get that man down from there!"

"What's the matter, Your Honor? I mean—"

"Get that man off that witness stand."

"Why, sir?"

"Don't ask me why!" the judge erupted. "Don't you know you never ask a judge why? Get him off of there!"

"But, Your Honor. This is my client. He has a right to testify."

"I know he's your client. You know my rule, Mr. Spence. That witness is not properly attired to take the stand in my courtroom!" The judge had once posted a rule that all witnesses who testified were required to wear a coat.

"Well, yes, Your Honor. But my client doesn't own a coat."

"Well, he's not testifying in my court without one," the judge said, and he slammed his gavel down and exited the courtroom in a fury, leaving the poor man sitting there and both of us speechless and humiliated. The court reporter was so embarrassed for us he wouldn't look up. I didn't know what to do. But farmers are a resourceful lot.

"I got a coat down in my pickup truck," the farmer said. "It ain't pretty, but it's a coat if that's whatcha need." In a little while, he came up dragging a tattered sheepskin coat covered with grease and dog hair and various other debris. "I leave it in the back of my truck for my dog to lie on," the farmer said, "but she sure is a coat, ain't she?" He held up the dirty rag for me to behold.

"You can't wear that in here," I said.

"Don't know why not," my client said. "A pig's a pig and a coat's a coat." He put it on and sat down on the witness chair again. "Go get the judge."

I nodded to the clerk, and momentarily the judge came back, took the bench, and glanced down at the witness and exploded again.

"What's the meaning of this?" he screamed. I thought he was going to have a stroke. "Are you trying to make a mockery of this court?" Judges never speak in the first person. They are not a person, they are "the court."

"No, Your Honor. I apologize for how this coat looks, but a coat's a coat, I mean . . ." Finally I blurted out, "Your rule doesn't specify what *kind* of coat."

"Well, I specify what goes on in this courtroom when an officer of my court attempts to make a mockery of my rules. Your case is dismissed, Mr. Spence." Now he added the salt of sarcasm to the fresh wound. "If, of course, you disagree with my ruling, you have your right to appeal."

"But, Your Honor, my client can't afford an appeal. You know that." Red-faced, the judge stormed off the bench and slammed the door to his chambers in reply. Later, I threatened the slicker with an appeal. My client really didn't have the money, but neither did the slicker. He offered to pay 25 percent of the bill, and we finally settled for a third. It was a very long, hard winter for the farmer, but for the judge—well, from the warmth and safety of his bench, he sent twenty-seven Arapahoe Indians to prison that one winter alone—mostly for bad checks they wrote to pay for their addiction to the white man's whiskey.

Power! We see it, but sometimes it confuses us. It is mysterious. It may even seem holy. From the earliest times, the work of judges was deemed nearly equivalent to the work of God, and when a judge passed by, the people tipped their hats, willingly extending to the judges all due reverence, while the judges often ordered the whip and the chains against them. And when the people finally rose up, Power suppressed them, usually through the judges. When the villagers of Cumberland fought against eviction from their homes, Henry VIII ordered his judges "without pitie or respect" to execute "a good number of the inhabitantes of every town, village and hamlet . . . by the hanging of them uppe in trees . . . or by quartering of them, and the setting of their heddes and quarters in every towne, great and small as a ferefull spectacle" in order to assure their obedience.

Even the common law could not protect the people against Power. I think of Dr. Fian (John Cunningham), who stood trial in 1602 in the infamous Star Chamber for the crime of having aroused the wind that made stormy the royal passage from Denmark. The English common law prohibited the use of torture to obtain a confession. But torture was applied and Fian confessed, only to retract his confession later. Enraged, the king, James I of England, turned to his private judge, the Lord Chancellor, who thereupon proclaimed that, insofar as such an exorbitant offense was charged against Dr. Fian, the court, by the exercise of its "extraordinary powers," could always supersede the common law. In deference to the king, the judge ordered that the culprit's leg bones be broken into small pieces in "the boot," an iron device employed for the purpose. Still lacking a confession and adhering to the king's wishes, the judge ordered the use of turkas, pincers employed to pull the nails from all of the prisoner's fingers, after which the judge ordered that into each socket two needles should be thrust up to their heads. But when Dr. Fian remained steadfast in his plea of innocence, the judge only commented that his stubbornness proved how deeply the Devil had entered his heart. Slaughter and torture declared by judges as the law lurk in the shadows of our history.

In the Dark Ages, Power was the Church. Galileo at seventy, sick and nearly blind, was brought before the Church's judges to be condemned for his proofs that the earth revolves around the sun, contrary to the geocentric doctrine of the Church. The judges ordered him to go to Rome, and there, kneeling in the presence of a great assembly, to place his hand upon the Gospel and to renounce the great truths he had discovered; but under his breath he is said to have whispered, "Nevertheless, the earth does move." Thereafter, the great scientist was sentenced by judges to house arrest in his villa near Florence, where he died five years later.

It was in the witch trials that the exquisite symbiosis between Power and the judiciary is perhaps best illustrated. Much of the cloth of fifteenth-century peasant society was woven around a pagan belief in forest spirits, a love and worship of nature that was to make its reappearance in America over two centuries later with the coming of Emerson and Thoreau. The people relied on shamans and witches to attend to their sick and to act as their midwives. Most witches were women, often aged derelicts who wielded great influence over the people. That such power should be vested in women obviously threatened the patriarchy of the Church and the king, and, moreover, competed with their faithful servants, the physicians. Power became committed to misogyny. It had its tactics. To maintain an undiluted influence, the judges destroyed the glue that cemented the poor— their Celtic beliefs in forest gods and gnomes and witches, and the judges ordered the helpless women who represented those beliefs burned before the eyes of the people.

To carry out the prerogatives of Power, in 1486 Pope Innocent VIII gave the judiciary its most venerated legal authority, the *Malleus Maleficarum* (*The Witches' Hammer*). Its avowed purpose was to aid the judges in the identification of witches and to set the procedures by which judges should rid the kingdom of their pestilence. According to its English translator, the Reverend Montague Summers: The *Malleus* "fastened on European jurisprudence for nearly three centuries the duty of combating the Society of Witches. The *Malleus* lay on the bench of every judge, on the desk of every magistrate. It was the ultimate, irrefutable, inarguable authority. It was implicitly accepted not only by Catholic but by Protestant legislatures." Applauding its omnipotence as few have dared, Summers wrote, "In fine, it is not too much to say that *The Malleus Maleficarum* is among the most important, wisest, and weightiest books of the world." At least fourteen editions between 1487 and 1520, and at least sixteen between 1574 and 1669, issued from the leading presses of the day in German, French, Italian, and Latin; its infamous influence spread to America and emerged like a carbuncle in the Salem witch trials of 1692.

Then as now, judges felt more at ease burning some poor wretch if they had a confession in hand. The problem was understood in the *Malleus*: The law, to retain its control over the people, must afford the appearance of justice. The great power of the state must not be brought down upon the obviously innocent, for if it were, the people would lose faith in the law, and its usefulness as a tool of Power would be diminished. Therefore, the *Malleus* proclaimed, ". . . common justice demands that a witch should not be condemned to death unless she is convicted by her own confession."

Ah, the appearance of justice! I once saw the great gentlemen of the American Bar Association hoist their glasses to the prayer of their honored speaker: "May the legal profession always appear just, even when it fails." We proclaim our motive is justice in rendering the death penalty, but before we accomplish our killing, the accused must endure endless appeals and further appeals, consuming an average of more than seven years and a cost of more than a million dollars a case—mostly to create the appearance of justice. The toll in dollars and in human energy, the excruciating wear and tear on victims and their families, the taunting cruelty suffered by the accused from such lengthy proceedings, argue exquisitely for the abolition of this barbarous penalty. If the economy of killing or sweet revenge is the best argument we can concoct for capital punishment, then let us face the truth: The fact is, we can house for life those convicted of capital offenses cheaper than we can kill them, and if we must have revenge, why not stretch it out over the full life of the accused?

Confessions then and now made executions easy. The *Malleus* provided a series of practical steps by which a confession might be extracted from a witch: The judge should order the woman stripped and subjected to his "own persuasions and those of other honest men zealous for the faith to induce her to confess the truth voluntarily: and if she will not, let him order the officers to bind her with cords, and apply her to some engine of torture; and then let them obey at once but not joyfully, rather appearing to be disturbed by their duty."

Today, courts still follow the spirit of these mean and moldy precedents. There is rarely a case involving a woman in which she is not in some way stripped—of her privacy, her dignity, her equality. In a rape case, her most furtive past will likely be exposed one way or another, and in the most vicious and devious ways she will probably be raped again by the proceeding itself. In the 1981 case I tried for Kimerli Jayne Pring, Miss Wyoming, against *Penthouse* magazine, one of the magazine's principal defenses—a falsity, to be sure—

was that she was a woman of low morals, and presumably it was therefore permissible for the magazine to portray her as the greatest fellatio artist in the history of the world. In the Karen Silkwood trial, the evidence Kerr-McGee most frequently offered in defense was that Karen Silkwood was somehow sexually and morally deviate, which must have made it acceptable for the company to contaminate her with deadly plutonium. Only rare jurists in both cases prevented such typical defenses from exposing these women in the public courtroom as cruelly as if they had been stretched naked on the medieval rack.

It is fascinating to watch how the judges in those dark times tricked women into their confessions. Listen to the *Malleus*: "If she has no friends, let some other trustworthy man, who is known to be congenial to the accused and to some extent a patron of hers, enter to the witch one evening and engage her in a protracted conversation. And then, if he is not an accomplice, let him pretend that it is too late for him to return and stay in prison with her, and continue talking during the night. And if he is an accomplice, let them eat and drink together and talk to each other about the things they have done. And then let it be arranged that spies should stand outside in a convenient place, and listen to them and take note of their words, and if necessary, let them have a scribe with them."

Today, it is accepted practice for the state to plant informants in the cell of an accused who, in his solitude, understandably longs for some compassionate human ear. The spy, usually a prisoner himself and under promise of beneficial treatment by the state, offers his friendship and concern to the accused, and should the latter confess any part of the crime, the spy will immediately report it, or whatever he concocts, to the officers in exchange for whatever judicial perks have been offered. The reliability of such testimony is almost zero. Yet thousands of citizens have been convicted on such misinformation, the precedent for such techniques having proceeded in a direct line from the treacherous times of the *Malleus* itself. Today, the state may employ undercover agents who falsely hold themselves out as persons they are not. In the name of justice, judges find it acceptable for the state's witnesses to be actors, liars, and cheats. The John DeLorean case is one case in point, in which, as we remember, federal agents were pretending to be engaged in an illegal narcotics transaction with the accused while they recorded the same on videotape.

Similarly, in the days of the *Malleus Maleficarum*, judges permitted such artifices: "When all the above have failed, let her [the witch], if possible, be led to some castle; and after she has been kept there under custody for some days, let the castellan pretend that he is going on a long journey. And then let some of his household, or even some honest women, visit her and promise that they will set her entirely at liberty if she will teach them how to conduct certain practices. And let the Judge take note that by this means they have very often confessed and been convicted." We may lament that so little change has occurred in such a long time, and wonder not so much at the system's merits but at its immutable foundations.

In both the days of the *Malleus* and in modern times, the struggle has continued unabated between Power and the great suppressed masses of the people, the poor. The middle class—the physicians, the scribes, and the artisans—have never offered a threat to Power. It has always been that smoldering horde that could come surging over the walls and through the gates that has so frightened the king and his conjugal partner, the Church. It has been the poor, the disenfranchised, the helpless, the utterly powerless, who have been most feared and, consequently, most despised by Power.

To the exclusion of all other classes, the poor constitute nearly the total population of our prisons, and those who are the most easily identifiable among the poor, the blacks, represent nearly half the country's inmates. As Power perceives it, the poor receive their just dues, for they have chosen sloth and crime over honest labor, and as the poor see it, the system has deprived them of an equal opportunity to succeed. To them, the justice system is a mockery, another cleaver in the hands of Power. Today, the spirit of the *Malleus* still wields its might against the helpless and the poor as though they were witches of old.

Yet in bright moments it is our judges who have led us out of the dark. One thinks of Justice William O. Douglas, who was up for impeachment for having stood for the rights of man against the forces of Power, and, more recently, of Justice Rose Bird, who chose to be expelled by the voters from office rather than compromise her position against the death penalty. And what of Brandeis and Holmes? What of Hand and Cardozo? What of the host of caring, compassionate trial judges who have struggled in near anonymity preserving our rights, judges like Frank Theis of Wichita, and Irving Norman of Chicago, Harl Haas of Portland, and Judge Miles Lord of Minneapolis? Multitudes of unremembered American judges have, indeed, distinguished the judiciary with an uprightness of purpose, a passion for duty, and a devotion to liberty that is unmatched in the history of civilization.

Great offices have often sired great men, notwithstanding the Power that spawns them. Chief Justice John Marshall fathered the

American system of government by both defining and confining the power of Congress in the famous cases of *Marbury* v. *Madison* and *McCulloch* v. *Maryland* despite the fact that Theodore Sedgwick, Speaker of the House and the leader of the opposition to his appointment, labeled him as indolent and wanting in integrity—a man "attached to pleasures, with convivial habits strongly fixed." In fact, Marshall was not even President John Adams's first choice. I think of my own former law partner, Justice Robert R. Rose of the Wyoming Supreme Court, who became one of the most renowned jurists in the nation. The wide acclaim he still enjoys is attributable chiefly to his insistence that the preservation of human dignity come before the preservation of sterile doctrine. I remember Earl Warren, the son of a car repairman for the Southern Pacific Railroad, a lawyer of little experience in private practice who was chosen by Eisenhower to be his conservative legacy to the nation, a selection that he later denounced as "the biggest damn fool mistake I ever made." A year after the appointment, Anthony Lewis was to write in *The New York Times*, "It is a delicious irony that the appointment of Chief Justice Warren may go down in history as the single most important act of Eisenhower's presidency."

What makes these men and women different from the masses of judges who mutter their liturgy at the alter of Power? To these judges, the foundation of all Power *is* Justice, so that finally Justice and Power become indistinguishable. But although great judges have intervened from time to time to redirect the course of a nation in landmark decisions such as *Brown* v. *Board of Education*, *Roe* v. *Wade*, *Miranda*, and many others, the great promise of justice has been otherwise consistently denied the people. There is no equal justice. There were brief times when we heard the freedom songs of Whitman and Sandburg and the crisp, clear advertisements of Thoreau and Emerson for the natural rights of man, but their voices were soon drowned in the noise of machinery, and the law, as always, reflected Power, soon to become the surging force of the Industrial Revolution.

Now, judges, in deference to a new industrial Power, proclaimed the common law too uncertain, too unpredictable, too costly to serve the interests of commerce. Judges, wielding the authority of legislators, cut new trails into the legal wilderness, often circumventing the rights of people for laws more amenable to the goals of business. The legal historian Morton J. Horwitz asserts, "During the first two decades of the nineteenth century judges began to conceive of themselves as the leading agents of legal change." In a trailbreaking decision in 1802, the New York High Court of Errors held that the state was not bound by the common law and was "at liberty to adopt such a construction as shall most subserve the solid interests of the growing country." Horwitz writes, "By 1820 the legal landscape in America bore only the faintest resemblance to what existed forty years earlier. . . . Law was no longer conceived of as an eternal set of principles expressed in custom and derived from natural law. Nor was it regarded primarily as a body of rules designed to achieve justice only in the individual case." Although the judges liberated themselves from precedent, they still served as the handmaidens of Power, and as the nation fell to its knees before industry, the judges offered the throne to the new king—to corporate America.

We are a trusting people. We believe in our leaders and our country and our judges. We assume that the judge, whoever he is and wherever he came from, is fair. We assume that the referee in today's game between the Broncos and the Redskins knows the rules and will apply them honestly. We accept officiating, whether in the courts or on the playing fields, as a fact, like the weather. Yet when those in the football business are not satisfied with the quality of the judging they get, their referees are easily replaced. In the business of justice, the quality of the judge is the most important factor in any trial—more important even than the composition of the jury.

The evil I perceive in our judges is not in the heart, not a native perniciousness abounding in bad men. No. These are the upstanding citizens, the clean and the antiseptic. These are the men and women who go to church and despise crime and lead exemplary, predictable lives. They coach at Little League and roar with their brethren at Lions meetings and stay out of the bars. When you skim the cream off the community's milk, the judges are there along with the bankers and doctors, and the owner of the local grain elevator. With them, you will also find the bank's lawyer and, of course, the preacher. If you opened up the judges' souls, there would no malicious demons lurking. Yet after one subtracts the small margin of great judges, there is something wrong with the remaining lot of them. Perhaps it is their parentage at the bench. Too often they are the offspring of Power. The medieval judges served the Church and the king and were the instruments by which the people were dominated. One would have hoped for more progress in five hundred years. But the principal office of the law has not been to discover justice but to preserve Power, to hold fast to the status quo.

I speak of the anomalies at both ends of the spectrum—those judges who do, in fact, serve the people, and those who serve only themselves, and how the rest of the judicial corps keep time to the beat of Power and harmonize with its music. That is an evil, not of intent, not of bad judges, but one inherent in the way they are chosen. Today, most of our federal judges have been handpicked by Power as men (and a few "right thinking" women) who embrace the philosophy that profit and morality are mysteriously connected. Even in states where judges are elected, the political process necessitates a covenant not with the people, not with justice, but with politics, and with whatever the political exigencies of the moment are as may affect the judge's longevity in office.

Freedom begins by exposing false notions. As Judge Frank Theis, chief judge of the federal court in Wichita, likes to say, "Before you can clear up the water, you've got to get the hogs out of the spring." One such "hog" is our belief that because we have delivered our rights and our lives into the hands of honest judges, justice will most often result. Such ideas, born of hope, confirmed by exception, and nurtured by the liturgy of both the innocent and the desperate, obscure the truth. Lawyers, without an alternative to faith, must believe in their judges, and daily froth up the waters with Fourth of July rhetoric that glorifies the system and canonizes the judges in it. The politicians, the schoolteachers, the media, all teach the same fables—that justice is safe in the hands of the judiciary. The innocent public, believing in its judges, also jump in, so that finally the waters are, indeed, muddy, and little is seen of the bottom where lies that elusive gem, the truth. We must acknowledge the religious fervor in the mainstream of current judicial thought, one that accepts as just the commoditization of human beings, one that righteously grinds away in sync with the machinery of business, that tends to see people as parts, as expendable, as subordinate to the rights of the new king, of corporate America. But if we hope to realize the American promise of justice for all, we must clear the waters, and when we do, we shall see we must find a better way to choose our judges.

7 | TRIALS

The Barbarous Sport

A trial is a barbarous sport conducted in accordance with certain civilized rules. We no longer run our adversary through with a pike or behead him with a broadax. Yet the contest is as deadly as before, and often crueler. Rarely will the fight be fair. As in most sports, those who can afford the best players generally win. Robert Frost said, "A jury consists of twelve persons chosen to decide who has the better lawyer." The notion that winning the trial and winning justice are somehow related is like arguing that if the Raiders are victorious on Sunday their owners are without sin—at least until the next Sunday.

As in most contests, there is a referee who oversees the combat. But in the trial, the judge, of course, has more power. He can postpone the game or cancel it—permanently. He can decree one side or the other the winner whenever he chooses—even before the game starts—or he can rule that the side declared the winner by the jury is not the winner at all. His power is almost absolute. If the loser believes his opponent's victory was the result of a foul, or an error on the part of the judge, he may appeal to a panel of overseeing judges, as in professional football, where the replay judge reviews the action on the television screen. But appeals in the law usually take thousands of yards—sometimes miles—of paper covered from top to bottom with hard print, and they require many months—sometimes years—of anxious waiting before the appellate judges deliver their wisdom.

There are also spectators at this sport, and of late, the television industry, always attuned to the entertainment value of people in mortal struggle, brings selected parts of the most sensational cases into our homes. Once a trial was almost holy work. Now, the most important cases are reduced to everyday soap operas, with all of the attendant Madison Avenue vulgarities—the ads for mini-pads and underarm deodorant.

Justice, like professional football, is a game controlled by the rules of economics. In a society where the search for profit is a national virtue, it is predictable that our justice system should also reflect this ideal. The modern trial is a contest in which justice is defined in easily understood, monetary terms—dollars. For football to be profitable, the spectators must be entertained. No one would pay to watch the Chicago Bears take on the Broncs of Jackson Hole High School. Yet, in the justice game, the mismatch between the opponents is usually that ridiculous. If we are maimed by a drunk in the most ordinary automobile accident, rarely will we be taking on the drunk himself; rather, one or more of the world's great insurance companies will secretly be standing in for the drunk, supplying him with the best lawyers, the best witnesses, the best defense money can buy. If your spouse and child are burned to death in a defective automobile manufactured by Ford, that company can call upon its fourteen thousand engineers who, by sophisticated experiments especially conducted for the case, can prove in court that their cars walk on water, and it can tap at will its resources of $15 billion or more to buy the great trial lawyers and hire the renowned experts necessary to defeat your claim. Usually, by the time any wrongfully injured person comes to court, he will be out of work and deeply in debt and desperate to feed his family. But to get justice he must take on one of the great corporations of the world and win—not only with the jury, but with the judges as well. It is a game few spectators would pay to witness.

Lopsided duels are part of our heritage. For centuries, our English predecessors witnessed the king's champions demolish their opponents. The prevailing wisdom was that God unfailingly threw His power to the side of justice. Later, trial by ordeal increased the accused's chances of proving his innocence, for now he could establish that God was on his side if he could hold on to a red-hot iron or walk through a bed of coals without crying out. Such ideas of divine intervention still prevail, for if not through the power of miracles, how else could justice emerge as the product of our unequal courtroom duels?

In the eighteenth century, Oliver Goldsmith complained, "Laws grind the poor, and rich men rule the law." Perhaps our system has deteriorated. Today, even rich men do not rule the law, for that is the nearly exclusive domain of megacorporations that in comparison reduce our richest to paupers. The justice game was never designed to be played between human beings and these corporate leviathans. No credible system of justice can tolerate such a farcical imbalance of power between contestants.

Early in my career, I was introduced to this business game of justice. When I began my practice in Riverton, Wyoming, I represented anyone who vaguely hinted at paying me a fee. I was willing to take on any honest contest—a $200 fender-bender for a third of what I collected, or a divorce. And I didn't care which side. I had a young son and a pregnant wife, and everybody, including me, wanted to eat regularly.

One day, a contractor was ushered into my office by my secretary as if he were one of the Rockefellers. He'd made it big in construction, and wanted to retain a lawyer who would become intimately acquainted with his business and represent him in his various dealings. He offered $100 a month, which to me fell only slightly short of reckless extravagance, and I was a candidate for the job. Within a few weeks, I was in federal court up to my lobes in lawsuits, most of which dealt with my new client's refusal to pay his subcontractors.

Since I have made it a rule not to lie to a client, I assume reciprocal honesty from him. It was, therefore, several years before I saw through the contractor's tactic—one I've learned is commonly employed by nearly every insurance company and commercial enterprise in their daily affairs. It works like this: If I owe you $50,000, there is no logical reason why I should pay you. I already have your $50,000 and can use your money for as long as I keep it. Moreover, if I contest payment on one ground or another, perhaps I can force you to take $30,000. After the payment of attorney's fees and costs, the difference saved is pure profit. It's not seen as immoral—it's merely business.

But back then I took my client at his word. I prepared my defenses down to the last detail, and tirelessly gathered up every scrap of available evidence that might support my client's contention that the subcontractor's work failed to meet some specification. I was dogged, creative. I labored over the law books until I had exhausted the legal authorities and myself. Of course, I wasn't skilled at my art. But I was thorough and driven by a will to win, and I attacked like a cornered Comanche. And, most of all, I naïvely believed in the justice of my client's case.

Over the several years I represented the contractor, I never lost a case for him, but the truth gradually began to seep through to me. I saw subcontractors accepting fifty cents on the dollar because they had to have the money to keep their sinking ships afloat. I saw beaten men give up their profit and their pride in order to meet their payrolls and pay their taxes. If they didn't accede to the contractor's demands, they were threatened with me, his new mad dog of the Rockies, and they soon folded—in court or out.

On the job, I saw government officials giving my client favor for favor, contractors joining together to rig the bidding and to split up the spoils, and I heard contractors bragging on the deals they had made through payoffs of one kind or another. I was told this was the way business was conducted. It was all a part of the game, and the holy creed, as my client phrased it, was, "Root, hog, or die." As I later found out, that ethic was to apply to me as well.

One summer afternoon after I had won another case for the contractor, we sat in his office basking in the glow of victory. A sort of reverie set in—probably more from the good sour-mash whiskey than anything else.

"You never lost a case for me, have ya, kid?"

"Guess that's right," I said. I took another big slug of Cabin Still and passed the bottle to him. He was gazing out into a yard filled with the various pieces of construction equipment he owned. There was a long silence. I expected him to acknowledge that I'd done a damn good job for him, and I was thinking about being humble and saying something about how it just went to prove that you couldn't trust those damned subs—the whole sorry lot of 'em. And I was going to give credit to the system for consistently delivering to him his just due—"Damn good system," I was going to say. After he wet his whistle again, he handed the bottle back to me.

"I made it big, Spence, and that ain't on account of my education." He looked at me with slight disdain. He'd quit school after the eighth grade to help his old man, a plumber, get through a pinch. Now, he pointed to a new piece of machinery I knew had cost several hundred thousand dollars. "Ya see that piece a' iron over there?" I nodded. "I bought it just like I buy engineers and accountants—and lawyers— to do me a job. Ya can buy those college kind for a dime a dozen," he said. "A man don't need an education. Ya just need to know what to buy and what to pay for it." I didn't think he was referring to me.

He pointed to his new machine. "Ya know what I do with that piece a' iron when the son-of-a-bitch don't do the job no more?"

"What?" I asked, taking another long draw on the bottle.

"I trade it off for one that does." Then he turned suddenly from the window and looked me squarely in the eyes for a long time, waiting for me to acknowledge that I got his clear meaning, and when I didn't answer, he said it again. "I get me another piece a' iron, Spence."

At first, it was hard for me to understand the "Root, hog, or die" principle. I had never seen myself as just a "piece of iron," a machine that performed for profit, failing which I would be replaced like any other inefficient piece of junk. I was a lawyer, a professional man who worked within a set of professional ethics. The system wasn't perfect, of course, but, as everyone said, it was the best damned one around.

When it came to paying just debts, I found out the contractor asked hard business questions: How much would it cost his creditor to force payment? Could he discount that cost from his bill? Would his refusal to pay hurt him in further business dealings? In other words: Did the creditor have any power? Could that power be used against him at a later time? He might pay a bill to Pacific Power and Light because that corporation could turn the electricity off, but he might contest the bill of an independent fuel jobber when there were plenty of others around who were hungry for his business. He always paid the banks, and he paid all other incontestable bills on time. He kept his credit spotless. He never went into court without "a story"—that is, a seemingly reasonable tale tinged with moralistic overtones: The jobber's gasoline was contaminated and caused serious damages to his equipment, resulting in costly downtime. Lost time was usually the best hook to hang his hat on, because lost time represented lost profit, and the courts were sympathetic whenever you could show lost profits. The contractor had ready records to back him up, and a shop foreman to testify that the bad fuel caused it all. No jobber wants that kind of publicity. Besides, the jobber had bills of his own to pay, and so he sometimes settled for half or less, depending on how good the story was. But if the independent jobber happened to be on the County Planning Commission, the bill was promptly paid in full. Lawyers were, indeed, mere profit-making machines.

Businessmen who played the game with skill and style were always respected by their peers and honored by the community. The contractor himself became a valued member of a Cheyenne bank and was on the bishopric of the church. He supported certain Republican candidates for public office, gathered up considerable influence in Congress, and went on to become one of the most highly regarded and influential entrepreneurs in the state, with mammoth interests in atomic energy and electronics. His pastimes became

trading commodities on the futures market and collecting butter-
flies. He made millions in the highly competitive school-book publishing business under the sure guidance of that one simple business
ethos: "Root, hog, or die."

As for me, after more than ten years of struggling to learn the
rudiments of trying lawsuits, my reputation as a successful trial
lawyer began to spread, and one day an insurance company offered
me a case to defend. Oh, I was proud. Imagine me, this small-town
Wyoming lawyer, representing the large insurance companies of
America. I had finally made it. And when I won that suit, the company brought me more cases, and then other companies began coming to my office. Now, I was defending against the suits brought by
workers for their injuries and the poor for the deaths of their loved
ones. Most folks hired their own hometown lawyers to bring their
suits. But it was business as usual. The companies never asked,
"What is justly owed?" but "What do we have to pay?" A workman
had to take $40,000 when both of his legs were amputated by a
defective crane, because his kids were actually hungry. The company
would have paid $200,000 easily, but his lawyer panicked at the last
minute. Johnny Longtree, an Indian I knew, was paralyzed from the
waist down in an automobile accident caused by a drunk who hit
him on the wrong side of the road. Johnny also desperately needed
money, and his lawyer couldn't take a chance on the trial and settled
a case worth several million at the courthouse steps for under
$100,000.

I got so good at defending cases for the insurance companies that
they began sending me to neighboring states to troubleshoot the
tough ones. The jury, then as now, was never permitted to know
there was an insurance company behind the party being sued. Many
times the folks I represented appeared more destitute and more pitiful than the poor injured party who brought the lawsuit in the first
place. The insurance companies hid behind my old coats and baggy
pants and my boots with the run-over heels. To the jury, I was just
that young country lawyer, that sincere kid representing a poor
client. I appeared naïve, dedicated, and honest. Indeed I was. I believed in the system. It was my job to put in all the evidence I could
muster for the insured, to undermine as much of my opponent's
case as possible and leave it to the system to sort out justice, and I
never stopped to give the moral questions any thought. I saw it this
way: I worked harder, and longer, and I cared more about my cases,
and that was moral and that was ethical. I performed my duty to
my client. If the system failed, it was no fault of mine. Anyway, it
was all supposed to magically balance out.

But finally the challenge of the contest grew stale and empty. I began to see the law as a cruel game played against my own kind. I felt like a traitor to the people, "a man who protected the greedy against the needy," if one were to devise an appropriate aphorism. Then, one day, after fifteen years at the practice, I suddenly decided to abandon the law. All that I had labored to achieve during those long years began to turn to nothing. Like a man who has had one too many and feels as though a heavy, nauseating blanket has dropped on him, I could stand no more—not for another moment.

Earlier, I'd taken up painting. That seemed more real, more honest, than what I was doing in the law. The paint was real, the brushes, the strokes on the canvas, the emotion. I'd built a small studio behind the house, and one day the contractor, needing some immediate advice on his latest deal, dropped by to see me. I was standing in the backyard nude, painting a full-length self-portrait—a nude madman in the sun painting, not working on a regular workday—and painting his own naked self! The contractor approached me with obvious caution. He stopped quite a ways back. "Hey, Spence," he hollered, "are you all right?"

"Yeah!" I hollered back. "Come on over and pull up a chair." He kept his distance and scratched his head of thick white hair. "I'll be back in a little while," he said, and that was the last I saw of him for several years.

I would become a painter. I would follow one simple ethic: that every stroke on the canvas would be as honest as I could make it, nothing facile, nothing for the sake of shock, nothing to gain attention, no mindless dumping of cans of paint on innocent cloth, no silly dribbles, nothing sentimental and pretty. I wanted to paint the honest painting, to seek truth in art. It embarrasses me to tell you. I wanted to learn more than I had been able to teach myself in that isolated little Wyoming town where the cultural event of the year was the Dubois Art Show, which gathered up the creations of a few-score local artists and hung them all in the Dubois High School gym on the second weekend in August.

I sent my portfolio of paintings to San Francisco State University and petitioned for admission to their master's program. I had no formal training in art—had never taken a course in my life; it was that arrogance of mine. And they accepted me. I left my beloved profession abruptly in confusion and sadness—I have written of it previously. But once in art school, I soon discovered that art, too, was a game. The idea was to peddle the wholly outrageous, to skillfully market (although not necessarily to skillfully execute) whatever eruption might escape. I thought the critics were trapped. They could either feign respect for these new "schools," or they could be left behind as—God forbid—plodding traditionalists. Obviously, I was not in the flow. I had never been in the flow—that was the trouble with me. I was a failure. Then, with no place else to go and nothing else to do, I went back to Wyoming.

I remember shortly after my return I ran into the contractor at a bar during the so-called "happy hour." He seemed glad to see me again and gave me that long, deep look of his to satisfy himself that I had finally regained my senses. Over the magic of straight Cabin Stills and Coors chasers we began to reminisce.

"You were crazy, weren't you, Spence?" he finally demanded.

I said, "Yes."

"I thought so," he said. "That's why you left, ain't it?"

I said, "Yes."

"You all right now?"

I said, "Yes."

"It's 'Root, hog, or die,' " he said. "You gotta learn how to play the game, Spence."

I said, "Yes."

"I play it and keep score by counting the dollars. I don't need the fuckin' money. You know that. You can only spend so much money, and after that it don't make no difference."

Then, I don't know what got into me—maybe the whiskey, maybe my yearning to speak to a jury once more, any jury. I had been away too long from the law. I was a lawyer, not a painter and not a piece of profit-making iron. I jumped up on a bar stool and began making a speech. The place grew suddenly quiet. I knew most of the people there, and most of them knew me or thought they did. They probably thought I was crazy all along. I didn't care.

"Ladies and gentlemen," I began. They watched to see what was going to happen, some amused, some alarmed. "I want to tell you a story about a man who plays a very strange game. Do any of you want to hear about it?" The room was silent. "His game is to make money. It's his vocation and his avocation, and he keeps score by counting his money. Do you think that's all right?"

No one answered.

"Of course it is," I said. "It's legal, so it must be all right. Isn't that true?" Silence. "Let's think about it. Suppose every dollar represents a loaf of bread. That's what a loaf of bread costs these days, isn't it—about a dollar? Suppose you have a hundred million dollars in the bank, as I know this man has, and suppose we were to convert it, instead, to a hundred million loaves of bread, and then suppose further that we put a fence around it so no one could steal the bread.

That is my hypothetical, as we lawyers call it. Is that all right? Of course it is. That would be legal, too."

I saw some people beginning to whisper as if they thought somebody should call the loony wagon. "How large an area do you think it would take to pile up a hundred million loaves of bread? An acre? Ten acres? Can you see the high fence this man has put around all of his bread so no one can steal even part of a loaf? Can you see the guards walking around the fence running off the people who ask for only part of a slice for their hungry children?"

The contractor unfolded his six-foot seven-inch frame, got up from the bar, and glared down at me. "You're still out of your fucking mind, Spence," he said as he stomped out. But that didn't stop me.

"Greed is only human, they say. But greed is a disease, and like many diseases, it is both contagious and dangerous. I have represented many poor, deranged madmen, murderers, those blank-eyed creatures who rage and jabber and sing to the empty air and who scream in terror at their hideous visions. We protect ourselves from them, from their disease. We lock them up in cruel places. But we do not protect our starving children in this world from being murdered by the greedy."

"Hey, turn on the television," somebody hollered.

"Leave him alone," somebody else hollered back.

"Every child in the world who starves is being slowly murdered," I said. "We even argue the virtues of starvation. Why, the other day I heard a man say that if it weren't for blessed starvation, the world would soon be overrun with humankind, and there would be no room left for the likes of us."

"Are you about through?" the bartender asked, with a bored look on his face. He motioned to the TV over the bar. "The game's comin' on."

"Yeah," I said, "I'm about through. But let me warn you. Greed is contagious. I know. I, too, have caught it. I have played for higher scores than I need. I seek more. Always more."

Then the smart aleck in the rear hollered, "Well, why don't ya set 'em up for the house then, and we'll all get well together?" I nodded to the bartender. "We even honor these great gluttons who have become our world leaders, our socialites, our jet-setters. They are praised and glorified as the epitome of success, and we emulate them while we watch babies beg in the streets of the world and die in those filthy gutters. And whenever a person diseased by greed endows a chair at the university in his own name and returns one-tenth of one percent of his hoard to the people, he is widely lauded as a philanthropist. In truth, he has merely purchased a license to grab still more."

"Here's to Spence!" somebody hollered.

The bartender turned on the television.

I shouted louder. "We have become so accepting of the disease of greed and the human suffering it causes that one needs to take care lest such criticisms as these cause a man to be labeled a pinko-commie or some far-left socialist bastard—and that I am not."

"Hey, watch your language," the bartender said. "There's ladies present."

"One must watch what he says or he may be audited by the IRS and investigated by the FBI. It's insane. It's as if we ourselves have gone mad, and worship madness. But the greedy are to be pitied. They suffer from a dangerous disease that has alienated them from the family of man.

"My friends, I thank you." Unsteadily, I got down. A few clapped, but I think it was in gratitude for their drinks. Most were watching the Broncos now. Nobody said anything to me, but the bartender set up another Cabin Still and Coors. "Here's yours," he said. "I already charged ya for it."

Then, as I was leaving, a little middle-aged man with a potbelly came up to me. "I was audited by the IRS once," he said.

"No kiddin'?" I said, and I gave him a look of one brother to another, and walked on out.

I began the practice of law anew in Casper, Wyoming's largest town. But we are victims of our history: The insurance companies began bringing me their cases again. I took them. I offer no excuses. I had discovered one thing—I was a lawyer, and I wanted to practice my profession. I fought for the companies. Mostly I fought for myself. Even if justice cried out for the injured party, I didn't hear. He didn't exist. I was concerned again only with winning. I told the insurance claimsmen not to settle the cases they brought me. If they wanted to settle, they should hire a negotiator. I was a gun. I had one purpose, and that was to take on the opposing lawyer and to beat him, and I did. But it didn't work. Again I began to suffer. Despite my focus on my opponent and my view that trial law was a sport, eventually I couldn't stand plying my skills against my own, against the ordinary citizens who were the victims, who were the injured and the grieving and the helpless. I have written about it several times before—of an old man who looked at me with kind eyes and forgave me for having beaten him out of justice, and how one day I realized I wasn't put on this earth to fight for the great insurance companies and the banks and the big money against little people. The power of that old man's forgiveness hurled me out of a dark hole into a new life.

The next morning I wrote to every insurance company I had ever represented. They'd have to find someone else to do their work. I was through. Suddenly I felt like a man standing in the wind with his hide ripped off. Raw. Frightened. Free. I would thereafter never again represent any of those corporations—any of them. New insights came rushing in. It seemed permissible in America, even honorable, to exploit the Mexican, to work him and his pregnant wife and his kids in the fields until they dropped, and to house them in a shack no better than a chicken coop. And when he was out of work and couldn't support his large family and the kids got hungry, that, too, provided opportunity. We could hate him for being poor. We could call him lazy and rage about the cost of welfare and pass immigration laws and hand out baskets at Christmas and feel warm and charitable. Out there it was still "Root, hog, or die." I saw it was no greater crime to permit a child to starve anonymously on the wrong side of the track in Rawlins, Wyoming, than to permit his father to die in the electric chair for lack of an adequate defense. On the west facade of the Supreme Court of the United States is inscribed the great American legend EQUAL JUSTICE UNDER LAW. In accordance with the high resolve of that great court to speak the truth, I thought the inscription should be amended to read "Equal Justice Under Law—to All Who Can Afford It."

There is a price tag on the best defense. In this country, even those who commit crimes against our president have a right to a fair trial, and John Hinckley's wealthy parents provided him with his. They could buy the services of one of our great law firms, and they could hire expert psychiatrists to show the jury that their son was insane. That was their blessed right. But a fair trial is also the right of an unemployed black on the streets of Harlem who robbed a liquor store out of the desperation of his life. If he didn't plead guilty, and most do, he would be represented by a public defender of little experience, and the likely result in his case would be prison for twenty years. We are a country that professes a belief in equal justice, but daily the most shameless injustices are committed against those who do not possess the price.

I would estimate the cost of Hinckley's defense attorneys, their support staff, and their expert witnesses at no less than a million dollars. One compares the best defense to one presented in twenty minutes by a public defender with a half-dozen other cases he must dispose of in the same day. One leading authority claims that in this country the average accused receives less than two hours of trial time. In some metropolitan courts, a single judge may hear as many as twelve cases a day—cases in which the lives and liberties of American citizens are at stake. Many juvenile-court judges dispose of up to thirty-five cases a day—cases in which children will be wrested from their parents or locked in a juvenile jail. The President's Commission on Law Enforcement and Administration of Justice has called such courts the "five-minute children's house."

We have learned to shrug our shoulders at such disparities. After all, wealth and opportunity are not distributed evenly in a capitalist society. And so it is in the law. Long ago, Anatole France observed, "The law, in its majestic equality, forbids the rich as well as the poor to sleep under bridges, to beg in the streets, and to steal bread." Yet our yearning for justice is as urgent as our need for nourishment. Both Hinckley, who was found innocent by reason of insanity and sent to a hospital for treatment, and Nathaniel Walker, who was found guilty of crimes he did not commit and spent the better part of the last decade in New Jersey prisons serving a sentence of life-plus-fifty years, had the same rights. But their equal rights were not to *justice*. They had only the equal right to *buy* justice.

Today, justice has become a luxury item reserved for the few. Still, the prevailing view in America is that there is too much justice and too many rights. Crime has become a rampant plague. We are so frightened by the crack addicts and the dope fiends who will kill us for the price of a hit that we have come to deplore our sacred rights. They no longer stand for what has made America unique among the civilizations of the world, but provide, instead, the loopholes through which our enemies can escape. Daily, I hear responsible citizens exclaim, "We should take them out and shoot them." We long for safety. We cherish security. The mood of the country is that any price is worth the eradication of this scourge—even if the price is liberty, for how can a society offer equal justice to criminals who jeer at its laws and whose survival depends upon their ability to successfully break them?

Yet I cannot accept a justice that loves only the rich. In the end, our choices are simple: We must deliver justice to all, including our enemies, including the thieves and the thugs on the street, or we must deliver our rights to the state. We must endure the crimes of a people free to commit them, or we must suffer the crimes of a totalitarian government, the ultimate crime of a people against itself. We must live with crime in our streets or turn our streets over to the brownshirts who will not only eradicate our enemies but take their place and beat down our doors at will and haul us off to their prisons and their gas chambers. The best antidote for crime is justice. The irony we often fail to appreciate is that the more justice people enjoy, the fewer crimes they commit. Crime is the natural offspring of an unjust society.

Anyone who has traveled in Third World countries is aware that the favors of public officials are customarily and blatantly for sale. It's a fact of life that by simply dropping appropriate monies at appropriate places, one may usually buy his way out of most predicaments, even murder. We are proud of our own system of justice, for, indeed, it is populated with honest judges and dedicated prosecutors, and the system struggles to provide our accused with public defenders, many of whom are the unsung heros of the law with their pathetic budgets, poor training, and heavy caseloads. We are assured that in this country every accused is entitled to a fair trial—the Hinkley case itself presenting cause for celebration—for although we were outraged by his act, only in America could one attempt to murder the president without being summarily shot or dragged away to rot forever in some dank hole. In America, we have juries that stand between the people and the unleashed power of monolithic government. We are, indeed, a nation of the law, and every citizen is guaranteed certain minimum rights. Yet the difference between buying an official in a Third World country and buying justice in America by loading up the odds in favor of the privileged few is a difference in method, not substance. The result is often the same: Those with money get off. Those without do not.

Today, even the government staggers when it takes on multinational monsters like IBM. On January 17, 1969, Attorney General Ramsey Clark, as his last official act, signed a well-founded complaint that charged IBM with monopolization in violation of Section 2 of the Sherman Act. Eight years later, the government threw in the towel after having spent in excess of $50 million to prosecute the case. Even with its seemingly limitless resources, the government could not match those that IBM had committed to the fight, including the services of one of the largest law firms in America, Cravath, Swaine & Moore of New York City—the sprawling historic home of "the best and the brightest."

IBM assigned hundreds of lawyers to the case. It leased office space that could have housed a small town, and rented fleets of cars. The corporation had more than 3 million documents recorded in full text on one of the world's largest main-frame computers, and an additional 17 million documents were entered in code for ready identification. Over eight hundred depositions were taken of witnesses concerning the activities of other companies engaged in the computer business, not to mention another two hundred depositions taken by IBM attorneys of the government's witnesses. One Cravath attorney scored a triumph for the firm that became legendary. He claimed he flew to California, worked in the plane, and, because of the change of the time zones, was able to charge for *twenty-seven* hours in a single day. Billings were made to IBM at the rate of $15 million a year. Once, one associate of the firm had been droning on for forty-five minutes concerning some technical aspect of a computer connection until a partner finally cut him off. "Why would they be stopped, when no matter how much time and energy they wasted, IBM would pay the bill? The longer they worked the more IBM paid," commented another partner later.

After the case was over, Ray Carlson, the principal government lawyer, acknowledged Thomas Barr, Cravath's lead counsel, as "one of the dozen most able lawyers I have ever come up against. David Boies and Paul Dodyk [also of Cravath] are two of the other twelve." He said, "They did things marvelously well. Of course, everything was done in a way that cost a fortune. If they wanted ten people working on one motion, they assigned ten lawyers. They always had the company jets or flew first-class; they had the best of everything."

And the best of everything was enough for IBM's lawyers to bring the government to its knees. At the end, there wasn't a single Justice Department attorney still working on the case who had been assigned to it in the beginning. Even so, one could argue that such a case merely tends to average things out. In most criminal cases, it's the government that unloads its Olympian power against us. As one old country lawyer used to rationalize when he was criticized for winning too often, "When I was young, I lost a lot of cases I should have won. Now that I'm older, I win a lot of cases I should lose. Justice gets averaged out." But what about Hurricane Carter, who was found guilty of a murder he didn't commit and spent eleven years in prison? Tell *him* about averaging out justice.

Most citizens manage to hire a lawyer and go to court for a divorce. But when the company you've worked for all your life discriminates against you because of your age and you're put out on the street without a pension at a time in your life when you can't compete in the job market; when your boss promotes the woman who has been giving him sexual favors, and you, with superior skills and seniority, can't seem to move up the corporate ladder; when you are wrongfully accused of child molesting and although utterly innocent are banished from the whole world; when you are a school administrator and are publicly accused of having embezzled funds and your reputation has been forever destroyed and you can never get another job in another school; when the IRS decides to harass you with its fearsome powers and you go to bed at night and fight the terrifying fantasies of bankruptcy or, worse, of Leavenworth; when you want General Motors to stand good on its warranty on your new Chevy that turned out to be a ripe lemon and you have to make your payments to the bank anyway; when you want to obtain justice against the contractor who skimped on the footings under your house and the whole north wall has caved in; when you and your family have been contaminated by corporate pollutants and you're sick but you can't prove it was the corporation you worked for that poisoned you; when any of these or countless similar wrongs are inflicted on you—and you've probably already faced something similar to one of these or you will eventually—you will discover to your despair that even if you're sitting pretty high on the ladder, it will be difficult for you to get justice, because you can probably never pay its price.

Every day, many just cases go begging a lawyer. In fact, more do than don't. Because most personal injury cases are accepted on a contingency-fee basis—that is, the lawyer's fee will be paid solely through a percentage of the winnings—just cases are often too costly in time and out-of-pocket expenses for the lawyer to take. Since, as Lincoln said, "A lawyer's time is his stock-in-trade," he cannot afford to gamble his asset unless there is a reasonable chance he can realize a fair return. Thomas Geoghegan, a well-known people's lawyer in Chicago, says: "It is so trite to say, but it angers me: We live in an over-lawyered society, but only the rich have lawyers. The other ninety-five percent, all the rest, are locked out of the courts. . . . [M]y fellow lawyers dump on each other our hapless would-be clients, not welfare mothers or ne'er-do-wells, but solid working people with serious problems. Every day I get calls from people I cannot help, referred from lawyers I have not met. Most of the time I tell them they do not have a case, because of some technical legal quirk, and they could not afford to bring such a case anyway, even if I took it on a mainly contingency basis. So they hang up the phone, and who knows what they do?" Daily, this is my experience as well.

In 1981, a young athlete from a western state went into the hospital for a simple knee operation. He died in the hospital as the result of malpractice when the anesthesia machine failed but the anesthesiologist administering the gases neglected to notice that the machine was malfunctioning. The problem went unabated until the pressure gauge on the machine actually broke and the young man's lungs literally exploded. By the time his condition was finally discovered, he was the color of a Concord grape and his face and chest were blown up like a balloon and the boy was dying from lack of oxygen, his lungs having been expanded to such an extent they could no longer take in air. Still the doctors failed to administer a simple life-saving procedure—the insertion of a needle into the lungs to relieve the pressure. Instead, they waited another thirty-seven minutes, while the boy died as they looked on.

Over eighty depositions of various witnesses and experts were taken in the case. Tens of thousands of pages of testimony were transcribed at a cost of $2.50 a page. Hundreds of thousands of dollars in out-of-pocket monies were expended in witness fees and travel expenses preparing the case for trial. After years of work, the case was finally tried to a jury in the summer of 1987. The trial lasted for over a month. I was assisted by two other lawyers, and we incurred thousands of dollars more in trial costs, and hotel and food bills. During the trial, there was evidence that the records had been altered, and in their testimony for the defendant three of the doctors changed their prior statements given in depositions. The defense now contended that the young man had died of an air embolism for which, they argued, there was no cure. Consequently, nothing could be done to save him, and even though the defendant may have been negligent, the negligence was not the cause of the young man's death. That was their new defense. But the jury wasn't fooled: They awarded $1.5 million in actual damages and $2 million in punitive damages, all of which might cause one to rejoice—the system works, the system is just.

This was as clear a case of malpractice as I have ever seen. Yet by the time it went to trial, it had become obscured almost beyond recognition with misleading factual issues and esoteric legal arguments. Six months after the trial, motions were still pending for a new trial and to reduce the jury's award. These were finally denied by the judge, but we must still win complicated and costly appeals to both the state's intermediate appeals court and supreme court that will consume at least two more years before the parents can collect a dime. If the appeals courts reverse the case, the whole procedure begins all over again. By that time, witnesses may be unavailable—some may be dead or their memories dimmed. If we win again, there can be the same appeals as before. These cases are too costly and too risky for most lawyers and most litigants. Only the insurance companies who refuse to pay just claims and the large corporations who are the perpetrators of much of the injury suffered by our citizens can afford this kind of "justice." Yet almost every case brought by individuals against corporations requires the individual to battle these unconscionable costs and delays. They are the evil tools utilized by corporate America to defeat justice.

In a system in which justice is delivered in money, it is obvious that unless there is money to satisfy the jury's award, those with even the most just case may not be able to find a lawyer to press it. None of us wants to put our quarters in a Las Vegas slot machine if the jackpot spews out only air. If the neighbor's vicious dog breaks through his fence and chews up your little girl but the neighbor is uninsured and has neither the proverbial pot nor the window to throw it out of, you will end up footing the bills yourself, and your child will receive nothing to compensate her for her pain and suffering or for the humiliation she will endure for the rest of her life from her permanent disfigurement. If the doctor cuts your wife's bladder in a routine hysterectomy and she continually leaks urine and has to wear a diaper until she is repaired in another painful operation, and the doctor is one of those who has decided to beat the system by going "bare"—that is, by not carrying any malpractice insurance—you will probably have to pay for the additional surgery, and your wife will receive nothing for her pain and embarrassment, because everything the doctor owns he's put in his wife's name or has mortgaged to the hilt.

In one of our recent cases, the defendant, a tough old rancher, had agreed to feed our client's saddle horses for the winter. Instead, the rancher left the horses to starve. One early spring morning when the snow had finally melted, our client traveled to the ranch to check his horses. He would never forget what he saw—his once-beautiful animals starved, most lying dead in the field, the few living wretches wobbling on stilt legs. Most of the survivors were too far gone and had to be shot. He brought his case to us, but a verdict against the rancher could never be collected, because the ranch was mortgaged for more than it was worth. It would cost us thousands of dollars to get the case to court and thousands more to try it—all to win an uncollectible judgment. Finally, it became clear to our client that he must take the small settlement the rancher offered him—that or nothing. The plaintiff, who used his horses to pack dudes into the mountains in the summertime, had worked for years to put his string together, one horse at a time, and he didn't have sufficient financial backing to buy replacement horses, even assuming the kind he needed were for sale. Now, he's back where he started ten years ago, with practically nothing except a bad taste in his mouth for the law.

I think of the teenager who shot his companion in a hunting accident, leaving him a paraplegic, and the pimp who beat his woman until her brains literally extruded from her skull, causing her to be institutionalized for the rest of her life. I remember the sleazy landlord who let his uninsured apartment building burn to the ground, killing and maiming scores of innocent people, and the village drunk who chose, of course, to pay his booze bill rather than his insurance premium, and thereafter squashed a little girl at a school crossing like a jackrabbit. These cases never get to the courthouse, because a jury's verdict against the wrongdoer can never be collected.

It is a pathetic irony that in this system the victim and the wrongdoer are joined together like Siamese twins served by a single heart, the heart being, of course, insurance. Justice in America has become almost exclusively the by-product of the legal games played by and against insurance companies, and the zealous commitment of that industry to defeat rather than pay victims has resulted in such inefficient and expensive procedures that much of the exorbitant cost of justice must be laid at the feet of that industry itself.

Let me tell you a story.

"If you have been to hell and back, no one needs to write you a travelogue about it," Maggie told me, "but maybe something could be salvaged by telling Roy's story." For many years, Maggie and I had been close, like prisoners exiled in some bleak place. I had known her husband, Roy, from the first day I came dripping-fresh out of law school to take up the practice in Riverton, a small Wyoming town dropped off in nowhere and surrounded by Arapahoes and Shoshones who live on the adjoining reservation. Our nearest neighbor of any size was Casper, a rowdy boomtown 120 miles to the east and, except for an occasional itinerant troubadour accidentally blown through the community, the principal source of culture, of intellectual energy, of communal spirit, gurgled out of the local newspaper like clear water from a desert spring. The paper was owned and published by Roy and his younger brother Bob. The "Peck boys," as they were often referred to by the locals, were to Riverton what John Winthrop was to Plymouth—its voice and its conscience.

Every Sunday, the Peck boys went to the Methodist church, where Bob strained in the choir and Roy passed the collection plate, and on Monday morning at an ungodly early hour, there they were at the paper again, nudging and coaxing the community into right acts and proper beliefs. They taught that Riverton's citizens were not poor souls condemned to outer Siberia, but rather, the chosen few who were privileged to live in that utopian garden. I remember in the early days flying home from one of my infrequent trips to the outside world. Roy and I were seated together in an old DC-3 that Frontier Airlines shuttled in once a day, mostly at the urging of the Peck boys, since there was little other reason for the airline to serve that sparse place. Roy had the seat next to the window. As the plane lumbered low over the town, he took in that whole inglorious little heap and suddenly exclaimed, "Isn't it beautiful!" I looked at him to see if he was serious. There could be no doubt of it. He turned to look at me when I didn't answer, and he asked me again, "Isn't it beautiful?" What is a man to say when his friend proudly holds up his child for praise?

"Yeah," I said. "It sure is, Roy."

Roy was an energetic, intelligent, happy man, with ambitious visions for his beloved town, a place he put ahead of himself, maybe even ahead of Maggie and the kids. As the years passed, he and Bob bought up other small-town papers throughout the state, and Roy acquired various businesses, including interests in uranium mines near Riverton and a hotel in Jackson. He was, indeed, one of those rare men who was able to succeed in business without sacrificing his virtue. Once, he ran for governor on the Republican ticket and was defeated by a better-known Republican who cut a larger swath, but several years later the people of the county sent Roy to the state senate at Cheyenne, where he was serving when this all happened.

On the morning of February 25, 1983, Roy had awakened around five-thirty, left his motel room about six for committee meetings, and had toiled through the day on the senate floor until adjournment, when he hurled himself into still more meetings. It was after 7:00 P.M. when he began the several-mile walk back to his motel in Cheyenne's raw, cold wind. He was a man who gave little thought to himself, and on this bitter night he was wearing only a thin suit jacket. When he came bursting in from the cold, Maggie knew something was wrong. He threw his briefcase down and fell into a chair.

"Roy, you look sick," she said. "I'm going to call Bill" (Dr. William Norton*, one of Roy's legislative colleagues). Roy demurred, insisting that he was going to be all right, and then lay down on the bed, coughing and complaining of chest pain.

Dr. Norton, an obstetrician, arrived with only a stethoscope to aid his diagnosis. He listened and thought he heard some congestion, so he called in a prescription for an antibiotic to the Safeway Pharmacy. Roy's going to bed was unusual, Maggie told me later. "I mean

* All the doctors' names have been changed.

that was a real 'uncle' for him, you know. He never gave in to symptoms of any kind. I can truthfully say that in all the thirty-seven years of our marriage, I had never known him to spend a day in bed." She called the hospital for an ambulance, and when Roy didn't protest, she knew for sure something was wrong.

The Peck family had been decimated by heart disease. Roy's father and mother both died of heart problems. His younger sister, Florence, had died of a heart attack, falling at Maggie's feet during a family reunion just a few years before, and Roy's brother Bob had recently undergone a coronary bypass operation. When the ambulance arrived, Maggie told the attendants, "He's too sick for me to drive him, and I'm scared he's dying." They examined Roy, and among other things monitored his heartbeat. It left an abnormal tracing on their chart. She reported the family's history to the attendants, but once at the hospital, the people there seemed more interested in the identity of his insurance company and a variety of statistics, one of which was the year of his birth, 1922. He was sixty years old. While Maggie waited in the corridor, she met a senate page who was an admirer of Roy's. "Listen, Mrs. Peck," the young woman said. "At Roy's age, you better be thinking about a heart problem," and she gave Maggie the number of a Dr. Carmen, who, she told Maggie, was a specialist.

Roy had already been examined by the emergency-room physician, Dr. Richard Appleton, and by the time Maggie was finally able to see her husband, a Dr. Howard Bennett, who happened to be the next up on the hospital roster, was completing his workup. X rays had been taken, and the consensus was that Roy had pneumonia, although Maggie told the emergency-room doctor, "This is a peculiar thing. Could it be his heart?" Dr. Appleton stuck to his original diagnosis, and Roy was put to bed with pain in his chest and nausea. He did not have the typical fever of pneumonia. He was feeling "woozy," and tired, but true to his grit he told Dr. Bennett, "Look, I have to get back to the legislature. I can't be laid up here," and Dr. Bennett replied that possibly Roy could return to work after the weekend. Maggie was still apprehensive, but after Dr. Bennett had gone home, there was nothing more to do, so she returned to the motel reassured by the nurses, that her husband would be quite all right. At about midnight, still worrying about Roy's heart, Maggie phoned her own Riverton physician, a cardiologist, asking if he thought it wise for her to call a local cardiologist into the case.

"I do, indeed," the doctor said, and since he was unable to recommend one in Cheyenne, Maggie decided that in the morning she would contact Dr. Carmen, whose name she had been given by the senate page. In the meantime, Maggie phoned her son James. Early the next morning, she called Dr. Carmen at his home, told him Roy's condition had been diagnosed as pneumonia but that her cardiologist in Riverton had advised her to consult a heart specialist in Cheyenne. She told Dr. Carmen the family's history of heart disease, and asked him to examine Roy.

According to Maggie, he said, "Mrs. Peck, I can't really enter a case unless I am invited by the attending physician." He'd be happy to consult if Dr. Bennett asked him, and although Dr. Bennett was not a cardiologist, Dr. Carmen assured her he was a competent internist and had a good knowledge of cardiology, and Maggie "should go with his recommendations." By eight-thirty, Maggie was back in the hospital looking for Dr. Bennett. He wasn't to be found. Roy looked desperately ill. His face was contorted. He was gritting his teeth and was nauseated, and his eyes squinted in pain. He usually had a florid complexion, but he was pale as paper, even his lips were white; he was sweating and said he was dizzy.

Still Dr. Bennett hadn't shown up, and Maggie began hounding the nurses. She wanted Roy transferred to the intensive-care unit. "I kept going to that nurses' station all morning long. That was the only hope I had of reaching the doctor. They kept saying, 'Well, he's on his way,' or 'He doesn't answer his beeper,' or 'He is over at the other hospital and we are trying to locate him.'" Finally, Maggie asked the nurses to get any doctor who could admit Roy to intensive care, but they didn't call another doctor. In the meantime, Roy's pain grew more intense: "He was writhing and vomiting and miserable in every single way," Maggie said.

At about 11:00 A.M., Maggie left the hospital at the invitation of the nurses, who had decided she was becoming a pest. "They were implying I was hysterical. They said, 'You are doing more harm than good. If you don't stop this, you will wind up in the bed right next to him.' The charge nurse said, 'We know what to do for him. He is not as sick as he thinks he is. Will you please go away. Get yourself some lunch.'"

Maggie began to worry that they might actually physically restrain her. What should she do? Roy was worse, and still the nurses hadn't been able to find Dr. Bennett. As Maggie saw it, "There was only one hope, and that was to get the physician in charge *to take charge.*" But she had no backup. "I was all by myself and I thought, Boy, if they decide I belong in that bed—I better get out of here for a minute and think about this." She went back to the motel and had a cup of soup in the dining room, and was in her room when Dr. Bennett finally called. He announced what Maggie had suspected all along:

"Your husband has had a heart attack." By the time Maggie got back to the hospital, Roy was in intensive care with a Dr. Peter Dunlap, a heart surgeon. As they wheeled him into the operating room, Roy looked up at Maggie and said, "Don't worry, honey, I'm in good hands." It was about one-thirty in the afternoon.

Their sons drove the fifty miles over the pass from the University of Wyoming at Laramie and were with their mother by three o'clock. There had been talk of flying Roy to Denver, but by the time the boys arrived, hospital staff were rushing into the intensive-care unit, where a Code Blue for emergency-revival techniques was flashing. After what seemed an interminable time, Dr. Dunlap came out. "Well, Maggie," he said, "it looks as though we won't be taking Roy to Denver after all. It doesn't look like he is going to make it." In a little while, Dr. Dunlap came back with Roy's watch and gave it to one of the boys.

I went to the funeral. The whole town was there, and Maggie was very brave and so was Bob. Several months later, when Maggie came to my office in Jackson, I could still see the grief hidden deep in her eyes. Nobody wanted to sue. Roy was a peaceful man, but he had left a widow and four children—two natural sons, David and James, and two Greek refugee children he and Maggie had adopted, Betsy and "Risty," and this widow and these children had a lawful claim for Roy's wrongful death—a potential fund that Maggie had the obligation to preserve, at least for the children.

We all thought the matter should be resolved peaceably. Lawsuits are long, expensive, and painful. It would be better to gather the various doctors, the hospital representatives, and the emergency-room people in one place and lay the case on the table—no games, no jockeying for position, just offer an immediate settlement for a sum less than the case was worth, but a sum that would mean something. Roy's death was a terrible waste, and none of us could bear the thought that he should have suffered and died for nothing. Justice requires change.

I wrote to the insurance carriers, and on June 10, 1983, I went to Cheyenne to informally present my case and to seek a reasonable settlement. The room looked like a presidential press conference. The lawyers were there, stuffy and reserved, and the insurance men, too, in their stiff white shirts and shiny black shoes, all wearing those polite smiles that befit gentlemen of stature. The room seemed icy. Then I said what I thought Roy would have said: "Well gentlemen, let's get right to the point. This is purely business. Nothing more and nothing less. We are here to make a fair offer that will put this troublesome matter quietly to rest without making a big show for the state and the papers. I don't want to hurt anybody. I am not here for revenge. I am here to do business and to do it fairly." They stared back. There was amusement on a face or two.

"How much do you want?" one of the lawyers asked.

"I want a million dollars," I replied. The lawyers looked at each other and smiled, and so did the insurance men. One cleared his throat and began to say something, but his lawyer interrupted him with a polite cough. I felt like a country bumpkin in his bib overalls laughed right out of a formal ball. But I was there to save my clients—and those doctors, too—a lawsuit, and my demand was reasonable. Roy's death robbed his family of his future earnings, a sum that would have exceeded several times the amount I sought. What if Maggie had run over one of the doctors on her way home from the grocery store? Wouldn't their families have asked the same?

"He was a million-dollar father," I said to the faces, and then I got very practical. I pointed out what they already knew. It would cost the several insurance companies more than a million to defend the case. And why drag the doctors through this public pain if they could settle it now for what they'd end up paying to defend the lawsuit, even if they won? They should all chip in like smart businessmen and pay the fiddler. They stared back as if I were the Whore of Babylon asking for their hand in marriage. After a long silence, one of the attorneys said, "Well, we will give this matter due consideration," and then the meeting was adjourned.

I was patient for more than four months. Then, having heard nothing, on October 20, 1983, I filed suit against the hospital and against Drs. Appleton, Bennett, and Carmen, and against the emergency-room corporation that had furnished Dr. Appleton to the hospital. The claim was for $14 million. I alleged the doctors had negligently failed to take a proper history, and to immediately administer an electrocardiogram, and had negligently failed to read the X rays that would have clearly revealed that Roy was probably suffering from a heart attack rather than pneumonia. The suit claimed the hospital should have provided another doctor when it became clear that Dr. Bennett was unavailable, but instead the hospital negligently permitted Roy's condition to worsen without providing competent medical care until finally his condition was irreversible, and I demanded that the case be heard by a jury.

Now, the legal game would begin. Now, I heard from the insurance companies. The lawyers for each of the insured defendants filed their papers—interrogatories containing hundreds of questions, scores of motions—motions to dismiss the case and motions for the production of documents and motions to elect remedies and motions for summary judgment and on and on, and all of the motions had to be briefed and argued. Answers were filed. The doctors each denied any negligence. It took hundreds of pounds of paper to provide the court and the numerous lawyers with copies of the legal instruments that were being filed. Each document was carefully drafted, then typed and carefully edited, and then filed by the attorneys at their standard rate of maybe a hundred dollars an hour. I couldn't begin to guess what the paperwork alone cost—maybe half a million, maybe more, because behind every instrument the lawyers filed were hours of research and preparation. Before the case was over, my own files filled eight large boxes to overflowing, each box containing approximately two cubic feet of space. Fifteen lawyers made their appearances in the case representing the various parties, and, of course, the attorneys had their support staffs totaling hundreds.

The court required both sides to list their experts, and both did—world-renowned authorities in the several fields of medicine: cardiology, hospital administration, radiology, pathology, emergency room, and nursing care—and the depositions of these and other doctors and witnesses would be taken so that at trial there would be no surprises. But before we took Dr. Carmen's deposition, we discovered he had prepared a written memo of what he recalled of the events leading up to Roy's death. He remembered Maggie's call, all right. "She told me that her husband had been admitted to the hospital the night before with the diagnosis of pneumonia and that he was a patient of Dr. [Bennett]. She went on to say that she was calling to see if one of my cardiologist partners would be able to see him. The reason she gave me was that he had a bad family history of heart disease and myocardial infarction and that she was concerned. I explained to her it was absolutely impossible for us to intercede or to see the patient of any other doctor once he was in the hospital until we had permission from that doctor to do so. She told me in our conversation at 7:30 that she understood this perfectly well and that she would talk with Dr. [Bennett] and get this arranged." But before he went to the hospital and began making his rounds, Dr. Carmen alerted his other partners, Drs. Raymond Elsworth and Edward Filmore, to his conversation with Maggie.

Dr. Carmen related in his memo, "[Dr. Elsworth] . . . was looking at some of the X-rays on our patients when he came across the chest X-ray on Mr. Peck and decided, since he had just heard this story, that he would look at it. He read the X-ray and called me *immediately*, at approximately 8:30 A.M., to alert me that if we were asked to see Mr. Peck that [*sic*] I needed to know there was a problem since the X-ray showed acute pulmonary edema and *not pneumonia*.

[My emphasis.] I said, 'Fine,' I would respond quickly when we got the request."

Pulmonary edema, the filling of the lungs with fluid, is a condition occurring in congestive heart failure. In a man of Roy's age and family history, it was appropriate that Dr. Elsworth, upon reading Roy's X rays, should feel it necessary to "immediately alert" Dr. Carmen to the "problem." At the very moment Dr. Elsworth was reading the X rays of the night before, Roy was only a few steps away, writhing in the last throes of a massive heart attack.

We took the deposition of Dr. Elsworth. Under oath, he said, "I knew at that time from the previous conversation of a half an hour ago [with Dr. Carmen] that Roy Peck was in the hospital with pneumonia. So, I thought, I will pick the X-rays up and look at them."

"In an attempt to be helpful to whom?" my young associate asked.

"Not necessarily in an attempt to be helpful to anybody."

"For what reason?"

"Because I knew that that name had crossed my pathway in the recent past and that one of my partners was likely to be asked to see the patient."

"So with the thought in mind of helping Dr. Filmore [he was one of the partners and the surgeon who would operate if called upon to do so by Dr. Bennett], but with the larger thought in mind of helping Roy Peck, you picked up the X-rays, correct?"

"I don't know that there was any conscious reference to helping Roy Peck."

Later, my associate asked Dr. Elsworth, "What, if any, attempt did you make to give that information to anybody besides your partners?"

"I made no attempt."

"Why?"

"Well, I guess I would have to have some idea as to why I should."

"Well, that information was important information, wasn't it?"

"Yes." To me, the words that followed sounded unconnected to Roy Peck's dying—words about X rays—the black-and-white evidence of a mere process, lifeless technical words that sounded like a clerk reading a set of statistics out of the Congressional Record.

Then my associate asked the doctor, "Was the pulmonary edema that you saw consistent with congestive heart failure?"

"Yes," Dr. Elsworth said.

"We talked to an ambulance fellow here in these depositions, and he told us that it was part of his protocol to treat as cardiac, if questionable; that that was good medicine for him and his ambulance service. Is that good medicine for a doctor?"

Elsworth's attorney objected and instructed the doctor not to answer. "He's not here as an expert to talk about his opinion as to the standard of care," the lawyer said.

Elsworth admitted he had looked for Roy's electrocardiogram at the hospital, but not finding it where they were usually kept, he took no further steps to locate the same. He admitted he knew Roy was not in intensive care, because he'd just been to the unit and saw that Roy wasn't there. As to the radiologist's report, Elsworth didn't agree with it, either. "Well, my conclusion that this represented pulmonary edema is in contrast to the statement [by the radiologist] that this probably represents a process such as pneumonia."

Next we tried to find out what was going on in Elsworth's mind when he called his partner, Carmen, to warn him Roy probably didn't have pneumonia.

"*Nothing* occurred to you?" my associate asked.

"Nothing."

"Any thoughts?"

"No."

"Just blank?"

"Yeah," Dr. Elsworth said, "about that."

"It's true, is it not, that you made no attempt to pass that particular information [about Roy probably not having pneumonia] on to Dr. Bennett," who he knew was the treating physician in the case.

Again the doctor's attorney objected, serving to warn him there was trouble ahead.

"Yes," Dr. Elsworth admitted. Yes, he had made no attempt to tell anyone of his discovery except his own partners, who were not in the case and who would not get in the case unless Elsworth's life-and-death secret were somehow unlocked by the magical word from Dr. Bennett, who couldn't be found.

"Did you make any attempt to convey that information into Roy Peck's medical record?"

"No."

"Did you intend to later convey that information to Dr. Bennett?"

"No."

"Why not?"

"I don't see any reason to do that. I don't have any idea why I would have been inclined to do that."

I whispered over to my young associate, "Stop." I didn't want to hear any more. But, dumbfounded, he asked one more question anyway. "Were things all right in your life?"

"As far as I know, they were fine; nothing is ever perfect."

The hours had passed, and Roy lay in agony, dying. No one, except Maggie, said a word. Dr. Bennett still could not be found, and the nurses called no one. By this time, it was noon. Dr. Carmen's memo continues the narrative: "I saw Dr. Bennett walking into 41 [Roy's room] and told him that he needed to know that Mr. Peck had had an acute inferior infarct [heart attack]. . . . I did not tell Dr. Bennett that I had talked with Mrs. Peck earlier that morning and that she had wanted us to see the patient. I decided it was simply best not to say that at the particular moment, realizing that he would hear about that soon enough. I went back to finish reading the electrocardiograms [they included those taken of Roy the night before]. Dr. Filmore [the heart surgeon in Carmen's group] came into the Heart Station and I told him that Mr. Peck had had an inferior infarct. He said, 'Okay, I'll be around awhile in case Dr. Bennett asks me to see him.'

"After finishing the electrocardiograms, I returned to the Intensive Care Unit just as Mr. Peck was being brought in. I said to him, 'Hi, Roy. I'm sure sorry this has happened to you. How are you doing?' 'Thanks,' Roy said, calling me by my first name. 'I'm having a terrible lot of pain.' I then left the building and, as I was going out the door at about 12:45, I got a page from the Exchange that Dr. Bennett was now in the ICU if I still needed him. I did not need him since I had just talked to him.

"I returned to the hospital at about 3:00 P.M. and, as I went into the Intensive Care Unit, undertakers were removing a body. This frankly alarmed me because we had several patients in the ICU. I immediately asked the nurses who had died, and was told Mr. Peck. I was honestly just plain upset at this because of my having known Roy for so long and because I knew we had never been asked to see him." He said he later learned that Dr. Bennett did try to page Dr. Filmore, Carmen's partner, but Filmore was not wearing his pager, although Filmore was in the hospital at the time. Finally Bennett found Dr. Dunlap, who operated on Roy. But, of course, it was too late.

Shortly after Roy's death, Dr. Carmen called Maggie on the telephone. "I told her I was very sorry and very upset at what had happened because I was a friend of Roy's. . . . I then said, 'I just have to know what had happened and I have to ask you some very hard questions.' She then told me that . . . she had tried all morning to reach Dr. Bennett and could not. She had tried to get the nurses to do something and they had told her they couldn't do a thing until they got an order from Dr. Bennett. Mrs. Peck said that the nurses also tried all morning to get Dr. Bennett and could not. Mrs. Peck said she kept asking the nurses if someone, anyone, could just go ahead and put him in ICU. Again, the nurses said they just didn't have that authority. I then asked her, 'Did you ever ask Dr. Bennett to let us see Roy?' She said, 'No, I didn't, because by the time I talked to Dr. Bennett he already had another cardiologist called and I decided I didn't want to cause a brouhaha over which cardiologist consulted him.' I said I understood and said again I was terribly sorry and please to let me know if I could help. That was the end of the conversation." His memo ended with the following observation: "These notes are dictated March 7, 1983, because there has been such widespread community concern about the death of Roy Peck and because so many accusations are being made as to who should have done what that these recollections seem to need recording while they are fresh in my mind."

Neither Drs. Carmen nor Elsworth had made any attempt to get emergency treatment for Roy despite their belief that he probably had been misdiagnosed. As they said, why should they? He was not their patient, and wouldn't be unless Dr. Bennett invited them into the case. It was as if Roy, upon becoming the patient of Dr. Bennett, was magically transformed into his *private property*. Carmen claimed he and his group owed no legal duty to Roy Peck—that was their defense, in part. But that wasn't the way I saw the case. I had already sued Carmen. Now, I added Elsworth and their partnership to the lawsuit. And I sued the radiologist and his partners as well.

We took the depositions of each expert. The object of the deposition game is to discover what the expert will say at trial, and it is also to destroy his usefulness as a soldier for the opponent—to pry admissions out of him, to undermine his testimony so that at the trial his deposition can be used to attack his credibility before the jury. Sometimes the questioning went on for several days, and always the words were transcribed to fill hundreds of pages of transcript. It is a vicious game played by attorneys who know all the tricks to kill the witness before he gets to court. I know how to play the game myself.

The costs, of course, were monumental. First, the expert witness must be paid for his time. He reviews the case, including the hospital records and the testimony of other experts. Sometimes he first consults other medical authorities, and usually he reviews the case with the attorney who has hired him. This consumes a lot of time, time that doesn't come cheap. A fee of $1,000 a day or more is not unusual, and the overall fees of each specialist in a case often reach as high as $20,000 or $30,000, depending upon the extent of the doctor's involvement. Court reporters charge $2.50 for every page of transcript they produce, and $1.00 a page for a copy. Already there were thousands of pages of testimony, not to mention the costs of round-trip airline tickets to wherever the doctor's deposition would be taken and the price of hotels and restaurants. There is no damned end to the money it costs to take depositions in a malpractice case.

And at the depositions, the lawyers never run out of questions. Those in the Peck case consumed months. Experts go on endlessly. They have an opinion on every subject. No one agrees with anyone. Wouldn't they agree that this X ray, even to a medical student, clearly shows Roy was more likely suffering from a heart attack than from pneumonia? Yes. But another doctor would insist that the X rays were consistent with pneumonia. They used words like that—*consistent*. A fast heartbeat is consistent with a heart attack, but it is also consistent with running, rowing, and sex. It was all part of the game. The experts admitted only what they had to admit, and took opposite positions from each other on questions crucial to the sides who hired them. They were persons of good repute, to be sure, but after all, there are two sides to the plainest of truths, and one such truth is that justice is a business game. Big business.

We crossed the nation several times taking the depositions of the experts in Roy Peck's case. In Eureka, California, we questioned an emergency-room physician, and in Denver and in Michigan we took the testimony of experts on hospital care. In Cheyenne, we took the depositions of both the medical director and the so-called director of risk management of the corporation that had provided the emergency-room physician, and we took Dr. Filmore's deposition in Texas, where he had moved his practice, and we flew to Hollywood to take the testimony of a certain professor.

Back in Cheyenne again, we took the deposition of one Dr. Howard Paul. Maggie, at the encouragement of her family physician, had consented to an autopsy, and Paul, a pathologist who with his partners did business with both the hospital and the doctors I had sued, had been assigned the job. Later, at his deposition, he told me his group's gross receipts from the hospital in 1983 were on the order of $1.2 million.

"Is that an important contract to you?"

"Certainly," he cheerfully admitted.

He also admitted that Dr. Bennett, as well as the doctors in Carmen's group, sent work to him. At the trial, the jury would have the right to determine what interest, if any, the witness had in the outcome of the litigation and to thereby assess his credibility. Paul had practiced as a pathologist for years, and then one day had decided to go to law school. He was just graduating at the time of Roy's death, and from my own alma mater, the University of Wyoming. Shortly after I filed the case, he swaggered up to me during a reception for one of our newly appointed justices of the Wyoming Supreme Court.

"I guess I'm going to be coming up against you before too long," he began. I thought of a young gunfighter who was itching to draw on the old man with the reputation. The newly appointed justice was standing there taking it all in, not knowing quite what to say.

"Why do you say you're coming up *against* me?" I asked, surprised.

He grinned and tossed his head back. "Because I'm going to be testifying in the Roy Peck case. And what I am going to say is that I personally think that Mr. Peck was a dead man when he walked in the door of the hospital." He looked over at the judge, but the judge had already started to move away.

That was the first I'd heard of this very easy defense that could let every doctor in the case off the hook. If Roy's fate was already sealed by the severity of a heart attack suffered before he got to the hospital, the alleged negligence of the doctors and the hospital *after* he got there would not have been the cause of his death. "And what would you say if I brought in the world's foremost pathologists who didn't agree with you?" I asked.

"They would be wrong," he said.

"How would you be competent to say that?"

"Well," Paul said with another wry grin, "I'm the only living human being who ever held Roy Peck's heart in his hands." I liked the man's confrontational style, but how would a jury take him? I could lose the case if I weren't successful in his cross-examination. Maybe the doctors and the hospital had known all along what Paul's testimony was going to be. Maybe that's why all I got from the insurance companies and their lawyers at the settlement conference was a room full of knowing smiles.

At Paul's deposition I'd find out if his testimony would stand up. Could I turn a jury against him? In a friendly fashion, I began with a simple question: Why had he gone into pathology? I never could understand why anybody would want to daily cut and hack on bodies or parts of bodies. Paul explained he'd been working in a morgue as an assistant when he was told by one of the pathologists that he wasn't bright enough to be accepted into medical school and get through it. "And I told him that I would not only go to medical school and get through, but when I came back and was chief resident I'd have him fired. And I did."

"I take it," I said, "that you got some satisfaction out of that?"

"Yes, substantial."

"Well, Doctor, you're now taking law, aren't you?"

"That's correct."

"What motivates you to do that? Somebody say you weren't smart enough to be a lawyer?"

"Along those lines," he said. Then he related how he had grown up on a pig farm in Illinois and how his father told him, "If you think someone is your enemy, he is probably just your enemy because you don't know him. So try to understand him."

" 'Know thine enemy'?" I asked.

"The old adage," he said. "When I got into the practice of medicine, every day I heard my medical colleagues talking about the asshole lawyers, and blaming a lot of their problems on them." He said he had some young attorneys as friends, and he had concluded it was a lack of understanding of the legal system on the part of physicians that caused the problem. He decided he was going to understand lawyers. He said he'd discovered that many attorneys didn't like medical malpractice cases, that they cost a lot of money to investigate, that expert witnesses came high, and that the cases were risky. "I don't think lawyers are the enemy of the doctors. Just a difference in systems." Ostensibly he sounded reasonable enough. And he was smart. And now he was a lawyer as well. But he was committed to the other side. What could I do with him?

He admitted he was not in the business of treating people with heart attacks, but had recently looked into a number of articles on the subject when his own father had undergone a coronary bypass. That Roy Peck "was a dead man" when he walked into the hospital seemed to me like an after-the-fact opinion by someone who didn't know Roy Peck very well. I turned to Paul.

"You wanted your father to have his chance to survive?"

"Yes, sir."

"That was important to you?"

"Yes."

"Do you think that is an important right that should be given to every human being?"

"If it's possible, yes."

"And your father was given that right?"

"He was given the chance."

"And he survived?"

"Yes, sir, so far."

"How long has it been since he's had his heart attack?"

"It's almost two years."

"And the cardiologist acted promptly?"

"Relatively promptly. There was about a four-hour delay from admission to his diagnosis." Then he said his father, too, had been misdiagnosed as having pneumonia, but that an EKG, as in Roy's case, revealed the heart attack, and he was put in an intensive-care unit.

"Was there any history of heart disease in your family?"

"Yes."

"Was that history taken?"

"I don't know that."

"Should it have been taken?"

"I would think so."

Dr. Bennet's attorney objected. I had touched a sensitive spot again.

"Why would you think so?"

"I think if somebody is having a heart attack that, as part of a routine history and physical, such an inquiry should be made."

"Did your father have pain in the chest?"

"My father had pain and shortness of breath."

"Did he have a temperature?"

"Not to my knowledge."

"Was he coughing?"

"Yes, sir. He told me that he was coughing."

"Did he say, 'I have a cold'?"

"Well, when I saw him, he thought that he probably had a cold or a cough, but because his brother and father had died of a heart attack, and because my mother was, in his words, 'overreacting,' he went to the emergency room."

"How old was your father?"

"Sixty." There it was—a perfect case of how a man who had been given a chance might survive a heart attack—and from the opposing pathologist's own father!

I decided to have Paul lead us through Roy's autopsy. In response to my questions, he stated that he opened the body in the usual fashion, cutting a Y-shaped incision that extended from the tip of each shoulder down to the tip of the sternum, and in a single line down to the pubic area.

"How did you make that Y-shaped incision, Doctor?"

"With a knife."

"What kind of knife?"

"A standard household knife."

"What does the knife look like?"

"It's about ten inches long, including the handle—about five inches of blade and five inches of handle. It is a standard steel kitchen knife."

"Like any housewife uses?"

"Yes."

"Like any woman might use to slice the bologna?"

"Yes, exactly. That's what it is." He didn't wince.

He explained that he could arrive at an approximation of how long Roy had been suffering from his heart attack by the color of the heart muscle between the right and left ventricle. It was gray-colored, dead muscle, instead of the dark brown color of healthy muscle supplied with blood. "Based on the coloration of the infarct, I felt that it had been there a minimum of eighteen hours and likely longer than that," he said. "You virtually never see the color changes in myocardial infarct before twelve hours."

"So the lighter the color, the longer the time since the attack?" I asked.

"Yes. If we're just talking about color, that's true."

"Is there any spectrum against which you could measure the color you saw?" He said not. "All right, would the pale gray color be about the same hue as the walls in the mortuary?"

"No, it was not that light."

"Would it have been about the same hue as the floor in the mortuary?"

"No, it was not that light."

Wasn't he just guessing? "I mean, we can't describe the color in any scientific manner, can we?"

"Well, we have not been able to do that, no."

"And so what I might consider to be dark might be considered by you to be darker, isn't that true?"

"Yes."

"And while I might consider it to be light, it might be considered by you to be lighter?"

"Yes."

"And these are just words. They are not scientific color gradations that have been correlated with times, isn't that true?"

"Yes." That was the best I could do with that, but I got him to admit that in his entire career he'd seen only two samples of heart tissue he could measure against an actual known date of the attack and a known time of death.

"You don't know when Roy Peck had his heart attack, do you?"

"I can't give you an exact hour, no, sir."

"And do you know anybody in the world who does?"

"No."

"And other than your opinion, can you tell me, as a matter of scientific fact, that Roy Peck had his heart attack *before* he came to the hospital?"

"No, sir." A lawyer needs to know when not to ask another question.

Before I let the man go, I decided to turn the defendants' own witness against them on an issue he obviously couldn't deny. "Would you say that the sooner a heart attack victim can be treated, the better off he'll likely be?"

"Yes, sir."

"Greater chance he has to live?"

"Yes, sir."

"A more severe attack requires faster action than a less severe attack?"

"Yes."

"That's well known in the medical community, is it not?"

"Yes."

I had hit another nerve. One of the lawyers objected.

"That's something you'd expect even an emergency-room nurse to know, isn't it?"

The lawyer objected again.

"Even a layman like myself?"

"Yes, sir."

A little while later, however, Dr. Paul hit me one more time. He said he had been talking to one of the doctors and that, speaking as a lawyer now, "I thought that if any damages [the awarding of money to the plaintiff] were actually found, they would be limited, because if Roy Peck had survived, the extent of his infarct was such that he would not have had a very long life expectancy."

"Did you tell him that you thought that there were some, just to use the vernacular, 'pretty obvious screw-ups' on the part of the doctors?"

"Yes. I said I thought the misdiagnosis of congestive heart failure versus bronchial-pneumonia was a screw-up."

Later, I asked him, "Relative to your conclusion that Roy Peck couldn't live, you don't state that as an expert cardiologist, do you?"

"No, sir."

"And you don't state that as an absolute fact, do you?"

"No."

I pushed it one step further. "Whether he could live or could be successfully treated is not in your field, is it?"

There was, of course, another objection.

"I don't think it's within my formal area of expertise."

"Thank you," I said, and I meant it.

Later, in accordance with the rules of the game of modern malpractice litigation, we presented our experts for the other side to now depose. One of ours was a Mayo Clinic–trained cardiologist living in California who was a member of the Royal College of Physicians of London, a man who had been a full professor of medicine and director of the Division of Cardiology at the University of Minnesota. Dr. Bennett's lawyer asked him a hypothetical question—to assume that Roy had an infarct the size of the one described in Dr. Paul's autopsy report. Could he have continued to live?

"In general," the doctor said, "inferior infarctions have a good prognosis. Something of the order of ninety-five percent of patients with inferior infarction will survive, maybe better—under age sixty-five, perhaps ninety-seven, ninety-eight percent will survive." He said this was a large infarction, but that Roy had a good chance to live. Bennett's attorney pressed on.

"I would ask you, sir, whether it is more probable than not that the patient would die given that size infarct."

"The answer is no."

Now, the doctor's lawyer nailed it down for our case. "You say it is more probable, then, that he *would* live?"

"Yes."

Bennett's lawyer was left with the last obvious defense. If Roy had lived, wouldn't his life be very comparable to an invalid's? Wasn't a robust man like Roy mercifully saved by death?

"I would have to say that the professional likelihood is high that he would have enjoyed a very adequate life-style," the doctor said.

The depositions went on. We questioned a pathologist at Stanford, and another who was the chief of pathology at the National Institutes of Health in Bethesda, Maryland. Radiologists in Cheyenne and in Birmingham, Alabama, testified and even the radiology technician in Cheyenne was deposed. And then one day the defendants' attorneys took the deposition of Maggie and the kids.

We gathered in the family home in Riverton and sat around the dining-room table. You could feel the spirit of Roy Peck there in that big old white frame house with the ponderous cottonwoods in front. The attorneys, all except one, were courteous and respectful as they attempted to discover the weak spots in the family's case. Roy was a hard man to fault. But Maggie, well, didn't she have a drinking problem? Not that her drinking had a damned thing to do with anything. Even if she were a staggering drunk, which she was not, it would provide no excuse to let Roy die in the hospital without treatment. Yet there is that nearly irresistible need for lawyers to smear their adversary, even a grieving widow. It was the radiologist's lawyer, who, when it came her turn, attacked with a vengeance.

"Are you learning to deal with your alcohol problem?"

Maggie was taken aback. She hesitated for a moment and looked at me. I said nothing.

"I trust I am."

"Okay. Where are you, at this point, in terms of dealing with your alcohol?"

"I am not drinking."

"Okay. How long has that been?"

Finally I interceded. "Let me ask you, what is the materiality of that question?"

The lawyer shot back. "Well, in terms of—I am entitled to know if this has increased the drinking problem, if it existed prior to, and that type of thing."

"Are you willing to admit that Roy's death has had an effect on her alcoholism?" I asked.

"I have no idea," she said.

"She has missed her husband, and she lost his care, comfort, advice, and society, and there is no claim in the case for alcoholism. I would think you would be aware of that."

But the woman insisted she had a right to inquire. I objected. "This is a miserable, embarrassing matter for her. I don't want her to go through it unless it has some honest material relevance in the case. If you are doing it for your own sadistic needs to cause the woman pain, I will stop it. If you can show me that there is some legitimate reason for her to go through that pain, I will have her answer. But I don't want it done carelessly. Put yourself in her shoes."

"It is a painful thing for me to have to ask, but I think it is possibly relevant," she replied, and turned to Maggie. "After your husband's death, was there a period of time when you went through more drinking?"

"Yes."

"To what do you attribute that?"

"I don't know the pathology of alcoholism any better than I did many years ago. I had been seeing a psychiatrist for the problem. Following my husband's death, I didn't have access to this person." The lawyer smiled.

I jumped up. "Do you find this amusing?"

"No, I don't find it amusing," she said.

I was hollering. "I don't know what the smile is about! Explain to me why you are grinning!"

"I am not grinning."

"Then do I misinterpret what I see?"

She turned away from me. "If I can have the witness answer my question."

"I am not going to allow you to leer at the witness and smile at her as she describes her alcoholism. I just won't have it! If you have something specific, ask her, go ahead, but I think we ought to be gentle and reasonable with her."

Now, the lawyer turned back to Maggie. The smile was gone. "If you can answer the question."

Maggie began in a very composed manner. Her voice was soft and patient. "I had been seeing the psychiatrist during that session on a fairly regular basis, like once every week or two in Denver. When I suddenly was in Riverton following Roy's death, I found it not practical—there are no psychiatrists in this area, and he had me on a fairly heavy medication of anti-depressants, and for some idiot reason I don't understand, I decided to stop that whole routine. One does that at one's peril, I have since learned." Maggie said that on the night she took Roy to the hospital and for the entire weekend she had had nothing to drink.

Under the prodding of the lawyer, Maggie talked about her terror of being alone. Roy had made a lot of the decisions, she said. "I don't think that means I was any less of a person, but he was just an enormous support for the whole family, and I was just plain scared for months. I still am to some degree."

"What is it that you are scared of?" the woman asked.

And Maggie tried to tell her as best she could, but I don't think she could ever say how it really was.

Maggie had tried to explain her feelings to her friends after Roy's death by writing about it in her column, "I Must Say," in the *Riverton Ranger*:

I am going to try to continue to write this column, not because I want to, but because, like the cod liver oil my mother used to give me, it's good for me.

My grief over Roy's death is fresh. I can think about it and talk about it, but at some deeper level I cannot deal with the terrible experience. Whenever I feel self-pity I just remind myself that I don't deserve pity; Roy does. He lost his life.

The reason I am writing this column is I have to tell you something:

During that first terrible week I was able to be calm. I was able to talk with visitors offering condolences, to endure two memorial ceremonies without falling apart. After everyone was gone for the night I cried myself to sleep. It is patent that one of the stages of grief is a "high," a time during which the attention to the fact, to the survivors, is a kind of upper period.

I think the reason I held up is that people were praying for me. I'm not a religious person, but I think the spiritual energy of prayer and vibes and love sustained me. Don't stop now! I need your prayers more than ever! And when you need me, I'll pray for you. On my unmitigatedly static filled line to God I'll pray for you.

I cried when I read that. My tears were for me and for all who have loved and I saw in Maggie's words the terrible shadow that walks beside all lovers.

After that, there were more depositions—depositions of anyone who had ever gotten near the case—of the six RNs and the two LPNs and the switchboard operator who took the doctor's call. The insurance companies had obviously given their usual carte blanche to the lawyers to beat Maggie Peck at any cost. Only when we ran out of people to depose did the depositions finally end. It was a *trial by deposition* conducted across the four corners of the nation. There had been no judge. There was no jury. But evaluations were made. The lawyers watched each other, and they watched the witnesses and tried to imagine how it would be to come up against them in the courtroom.

In the insurance companies' offices, the questions posed by the claimsmen are money questions. No one asks, "What is justice in this case?" No one asks, "What is our responsibility?" Money is justice, and the limits of justice are identified by the amount the company must finally pay. How hard will a jury hit us here? Can the plaintiff hold out, or can we starve her out? How much are we going to have to pay our own attorneys? What are the costs going to be? Dollars were pouring through this case as if it were a fractured sieve.

The claimsmen ask other questions. Is there a chance the company will be held liable for a verdict larger than its policy? What trouble is brewing with the excess carrier? Sometimes a doctor has, let's say, $5 million in insurance. The first million is provided by Company A, while claims over a million are provided by an excess carrier, Company B. Suppose that the plaintiff offers to settle the case for a million. Now, Company A may be pressured by Company B to settle the case so that B will have no further risk, and B may threaten that if such a settlement is not accepted, and if a big verdict comes down that requires B to pay, say, its other $4 million, the company may sue A to get its money back, claiming that A should have settled the case for the first million when it had the chance. That would make the claimsman who didn't settle look bad. He's not in the case for the sport of it. A man who can't settle the cases right will never ascend the company ladder. He thinks about that, too. That's where the lawyers come in, of course, with their ability to force out the facts in the depositions, and so the questioning goes on and the claimsmen are drowned in depositions, and they ferret through the facts and weigh the possibilities of a calamity at trial against the cost of going forward.

They are like hyenas, these claimsmen. They work best in packs. If there are other insurance companies involved, the claimsmen will get together. And if they do not get together, they'll take comfort that others are not settling their cases and, therefore, they cannot be criticized by their superiors if they take a chance on trial. If, however, some of the others settle, it affects the judgment of those remaining. If the plaintiff gets a large award, how will they justify their decision when the other claimsmen have settled out? No hyena wants to fight outside the pack.

The plaintiff, too, will have terrible decisions to make. The insurance companies make it hard for a widow. What if Maggie had a bunch of hungry kids to feed and a blizzard of bills piling up? Under these circumstances the companies would come in early on with a very small offer—maybe $100,000 in a case worth millions— I've seen them do it time after time, and God Almighty, if the widow doesn't accept it and goes to trial instead, it's like taking $100,000 the family needs to a crap shoot in Las Vegas while the banks threaten foreclosure on the house, and the car payments are due and the doctors want their money. Even the best case can be lost. Every lawyer knows that. And if the widow wins big, the insurance company will only appeal it, and starve her out, while a bunch of judges who don't know her and don't give a damn for the kids take a couple of years to deliver their opinion. And if the jury gave her a big enough award, well, you can bet the appellate judges will decide against her for one reason or another.

When the company finally makes a small offer to the widow, her lawyer will have his say, too. She'll usually look to him to decide. Lord knows she's never been through something like this before. That's why she hired a lawyer—to tell her what to do. But the lawyer has his own interests at stake. He took the case on a contingency basis, and he's spent thousands of his own hard dollars, too. When it finally gets down to it, he's in the case to make a living. Justice is just money. Justice is still business, and the system favors those who can take the risk.

So, in the Peck case, the day of reckoning was not at hand until, seemingly, the insurance-company lawyers had extracted from the case the last possible penny of hourly fees. It's not that lawyers are dishonest, it's simply a matter of economics—they get paid for the number of hours they bill. Once, as a very young lawyer, I tried to settle a clear case of liability early on for a severely injured client who was in desperate need of money. I went to the office of the opposing lawyer. I decided to leave my pride at home and simply beg him for an immediate settlement. The old attorney led me over to his filing cabinet and put his arm around me like a father as he slowly opened the drawers, one after another.

"See these files, Spence?" I nodded. "Every one of these files is worth a new Cadillac to me. Do you really expect me to give you one of my new Cadillacs?" And, of course, he didn't. A few days before the trial, the company made its offer and we settled—too cheap—because the company knew its lawyer could probably beat a kid fresh out of law school and I knew it, too.

As the Peck case neared trial, the pressure for settlement intensified. Into the great decision pot would be thrown the fears of the attorneys on both sides and the fears of the claimsmen and the fears of the litigants, and the pot would be stirred, and finally a sum of money representing the difference in the composite fears of both sides would rise to the surface. Between the attorneys there would be the ceremonial posturings like those of wild Africans who never go to war but only brandish their spears at each other and fake their jabs and dance their dances and holler. Perhaps a plaintiff's attorney would begin by demanding, say, $5 million, while the insurance lawyer would scoff and threaten to end the negotiations but would finally come back with $50,000—and no more! The plaintiff's lawyer would then protest, threaten the company with a bad-faith suit, shout that he was through with the damned talking, and absolutely vow to go to trial. He might then hang up and file more papers in court or write intimidating letters. He might even start preparing for trial. But eventually the lawyers would talk again. The plaintiff's attorney, only in order to show his good faith, might lower his demand to $3 million, and the insurance-company attorney would respond with an offer of $150,000—and no more. Not a penny! The threats of the previous scene would be repeated again, and finally the parties might agree at a figure reflecting the extent of their fear factor. A case in the hands of a young, inexperienced plaintiff's lawyer strapped for funds and representing a needy client might be settled for the last offer of $150,000. The same case in the hands of a veteran plaintiff's attorney with a long history of big wins in court and plenty of financial depth, representing a financially secure client, might end up with a couple of million for the same case. Justice is the sale of grief and pain in a money market under the inscrutable principles of laissez-faire.

One evening early in Roy's case, after the day's depositions had been completed, I asked the attorney who represented both Dr. Appleton and the emergency-room corporation to meet with me to discuss settlement. I knew it was too soon for any likely resolution— there was still milk left in the udder of this critter—but I never give up hope that someday a case will, in fact, be settled fairly before the lawyers trudge up the courthouse steps. I had chosen to start early negotiations with this particular attorney, because, as I assessed him, he would be my most formidable opponent in the courtroom. He presented himself as a handsome, decent sort the jury would probably like and trust, and if the jury went with him, they might find for the other defendants as well. He practiced law in a large midwestern city and specialized in the defense of medical malpractice suits. It would be a good investment overall to get him out of the case even if I had to severely discount our claim against his company. I intended to do just that.

"I will be frank with you," I said, after the pleasantries were over. "I've watched you in these depositions, and I think you will be very appealing to the jury. I'd like to get you out of the case now, and I'm willing to settle with your client for seven-hundred-fifty-thousand dollars." (As Mark Twain said, "Always tell the truth. It will astonish your friends and confound your enemies.")

He looked surprised. "Are you serious?" he asked. I couldn't tell whether he was amazed at the cheapness of the offer or dismayed at my overvaluation of the worth of my case.

"Yes," I said. He knew I would probably take less. One seldom makes his bottom-dollar offer first.

"I'll let you know," he said.

At the same time, I was trying to eliminate some of the doctors from the case, and I was also obligated to add some—I had no choice. If, for instance, the radiologist wasn't sued, the other doctors would be free to blame him. I could hear their lawyers arguing: "It was the radiologist who was at fault here, ladies and gentlemen. We relied on his written report telling us this was likely *pneumonia*. We had a right to rely on him. Why isn't he here? Why hasn't the plaintiff sued him? Where is justice?" But by the time I had added the radiologist and his partnership and Dr. Elsworth, there were ten defendants in all. I didn't want to go to trial with ten defendants against me. What one of the lawyers might overlook, nine others and their associates would not. They'd gang up. They always do. They'd take turns making objections. They'd meet and plan a joint strategy, and they'd stretch me out like a bull hide nailed to a board fence.

This case could last for many months, with ten lawyers each cross-examining every poor witness who took the stand, and finally ten opposing lawyers arguing their cases against me to the jury. By the time the case was over, the judge and jury would be exhausted. Tired juries are not usually generous. Moreover, many of the expert witnesses would have to be flown to Cheyenne, and some on special charters to accommodate their frantic schedules, and some of the prima donnas would expect to be housed in expensive rooms, to be wined and dined and to have their thousand-dollar-a-day fees paid in advance. I needed to settle at least part of the case. But the insurance companies hung together. It looked as though I was working against a solid front.

On September 28, 1984, now over a year and a half after Roy's death, I wrote a letter to all of the opposing attorneys setting forth an offer that would expire at 5:00 P.M. on October 15. I began: "I have spent a lifetime involved in cases with multiple defendants. Usually even at the courthouse steps I can't get them to agree, and I find myself in trial. Each defendant has his own idea of what his liability is, his exposure, and what everybody else's should be. As a consequence, there are a good many surprises for the parties when the jury returns its verdict." I wrote that I could make a good case against any defendant, depending on *focus*. For example, Dr. Appleton was given the first opportunity to save Roy Peck. His misdiagnosis was clear, and the other doctors could argue they had a right to rely on Appleton's conclusion that Roy was suffering from pneumonia. But Dr. Bennett was a specialist, and Appleton was not. And Dr. Bennett was the attending physician, and apparently wasn't to be found on the morning of Roy's death. (Dr. Bennett was later to say in his deposition that he was in another hospital in Cheyenne.) Depending on the *focus*, Dr. Bennett could easily end up being the one the jury hit the hardest.

"And look at the radiologist," I wrote. "He tries to be just a nice guy doing his job, but early on he, too, had the opportunity to save Roy. When the nurse called up later to find out what the X-rays revealed, she was reassured that the X-rays merely showed pneumonia and so the nurse advised Mrs. Peck that she was overreacting and should get out of the hospital's hair." I continued, "And the hospital's own negligence appears at every turn of the road. The plaintiff could zoom in on them and by that *focus* let some of the other defendants fade into the background." In short, which of the defendants wanted out with a reasonable settlement and which wanted to take the risk of my turning the total focus of the case on them?

"Moreover, the amount of insurance coverage affects everyone's ideas as to what his own exposure is. *Exposure*—always exposure! The emergency room corporation—most likely to be kicked around for hiring doctors at little more than starvation wages and taking 85% of the billings in the emergency room, has $11,000,000 in coverage and, therefore, has the greatest exposure. If they come into focus as the principal culprit, which I predict they will, there are a lot of ready dollars at risk." On the other hand, I argued that if we picked up a $6 million verdict against Dr. Bennett, his insurance companies might be liable for more than their policy limits. That was also probably true for the radiologist and Dr. Carmen.

I dug in. "So while there is room for all kinds of maneuvering among yourselves and between us, and every conceivable kind of argument can be made, and whereas this case provides a fertile ground for lawyers to strut their stuff and for insurance men to lift their eyebrows and gaze knowingly into their crystal balls, nevertheless, the case leaves me unable to propose an offer that will suit everybody.

"Roy Peck, already a millionaire at the time of his early demise, was one of the few decedents I've seen whose life can be easily valued at $6,000,000. Eddie [they all knew whom I meant—Eddie Moriarity, my wild Irish partner who strikes great fear into the hearts of the defense bar] just got $6,000,000 from a jury in Phoenix [considered a conservative area], for the life of a young unemployed wife without children, and the case was settled for $3,000,000. I need to do as well for Roy Peck, my personal friend. I need to do as well as my young partner. Fair is fair."

I proposed three separate plans for settlement. Plan A contemplated "all defendants chipping in like good folks." If they did so, they could get out for a total of $3,200,000. I arbitrarily suggested percentages of liability, putting the greatest percentage on the emergency-room corporation because it had the greatest exposure. Plan B was one in which all but one of the defendants would settle, leaving me to go to trial against whichever defendant would not settle out. "I will gladly shift the focus to that remaining defendant as my target," I wrote. Under such circumstances, it would cost those defendants who settled a total sum of $3,500,000, and I would still be able to proceed against the holdout. Under Plan C, any of the defendants could settle with me for the price I set opposite each defendant's name. The amount was $1.2 million for the emergency-room corporation and lesser sums for each of the other defendants, the total amount being $4 million. "Since time is so short, I ask that you use the telephone as much as possible and that you act *without delay.*"

Again, utter silence. Finally, months later, the defendants jointly offered to settle the case for a total of $980,000, just short of the $1 million I had offered to settle the case for in the first place. By this time, twenty-seven depositions had been taken and hundreds of thousands of dollars expended. I recommended to Maggie that the offer be rejected, and it was. I made no counteroffer as the companies probably expected. I stood my ground and waited.

To complicate things, Drs. Bennett and Carmen were both insured by the same company. Since Bennett could claim that Carmen was at fault, and vice versa, the company, to resolve its position of obvious conflict provided two separate claims managers to handle their files. These claims managers, although working for the same company and housed in the same office, presumably did not speak to each other about the cases—nor, presumably, did their attorneys. Dr. Bennett's lawyer was a veteran warrior of many successful battles on behalf of various insurance companies and other large commercial institutions. He represented his client with appropriate zeal and prepared his defenses with thoroughness and intelligence. Yet he was also the most pragmatic of the lot. He could foresee the problems of defending a client who simply was not in the hospital during those critical hours when the patient was dying. And the fact that both doctors were insured by the same company must have posed a serious problem for the company.

At the conclusion of the depositions of Maggie and her children, I pulled Dr. Bennett's attorney aside. The spirit of this wonderful family and the sense of their terrible loss still lay fresh in our minds, and I thought this as good a time as any to explore any chinks in the enemy's armor. I put my hands in my pocket and looked over at this veteran opponent, whom I did, in fact, respect, and I said gently, "Couldn't we find a way to resolve this tragedy?"

"You bet," he said. "How much do you want?"

"Let me come to the company's office and meet with you and the claimsmen." He agreed, and we set a tentative time. Then there was silence again. I sent a telegram that said, among other things, that a refusal to negotiate with me separately could be evidence that the insurance companies had joined in conspiratorial activity, and, in the event of verdicts over the policy limits, they might all be liable for the *excess*. Liability in excess of policy limits! The idea of it drives insurance men into a frenzy. How can they do business, how can their tables and calculations and reserves work, if the limits of their exposure are not set in concrete?

My telegram concluded, "I am sorry we were unable to get together. I do believe that if *good faith* efforts were made by the claimsmen, we could settle this case to Dr. Bennett's satisfaction." Good faith! Those are poisonous words that cause insurance men to retch. Could they be accused of failing to exercise good faith? I offered to meet with the insurance people on another date, this time in Jackson, and I concluded the wire as follows: "Would you please immediately advise the claims representative supervising this file, Dr. Bennett, and his personal attorney, as to the exact contents of this wire, and please rest assured that I have not lost faith in your good intentions to bring this matter to a timely and satisfactory conclusion."

Bennett's attorney wrote an angry letter in response. I had failed to make any counteroffer to the defendants' last joint offer of $980,000. And he had not refused to negotiate with me. The company was evaluating the case, and these evaluations were not made overnight. He concluded his letter with the following: "Please do not forward another such guileful and inaccurate document as I received on 3-11-85. . . . [I] need no reminder of my obligation as counsel to Dr. Bennett, whose interests are paramount in my mind." However, his last paragraph left the door open. "Please, however, forgive the terseness of this reply, yet recognize that which prompted it." Finally, on behalf of his insured alone, he offered $350,000, which I also summarily rejected. Previously, in my joint offer to the defendants, I had agreed to settle Dr. Bennett's case for $700,000. Now, I countered with an offer of $850,000. I explained that the prior offers had been made in the face of Dr. Paul's testimony that Roy was already a dead man when he walked into the hospital for treatment. We had a different case now. We had a renowned pathologist and an equally renowned cardiologist, both of whom would contradict Dr. Paul. The price of Dr. Bennett's case was, therefore, going up, not down.

But Bennett's lawyer wrote, "Not for a moment did I believe you would fail to find a pathologist to disagree with Dr. Paul and a cardiologist who would express the view that Mr. Peck was not a 'goner' when he entered the hospital. Consequently, I do not feel the value of your case has substantially changed. I am, therefore, prepared to roughly split the difference between $700,000 and $350,000, and offer the sum of $500,000." I rejected the offer.

On May 20, 1985, I finally decided to accept $690,000 cash that Dr. Bennett's insurance company offered in exchange for my client's "Covenant Not to Execute." That simply meant that both sides agreed that the trial could go forward with Dr. Bennett still in the case. So far as the jury would know, there had been no settlement. But if our verdict against Bennett was greater than $690,000, we would agree not to collect it. It was the first important step in breaking up the pack.

The settlement agreement recited that Dr. Bennett "has denied and still denies liability to the plaintiffs and has maintained that his diagnosis of bilateral bronchial pneumonia was well-founded, that the welfare of his patient, Roy Eugene Peck, was of utmost concern to him, and in the course of his treatment reasonable reliance was placed on information imparted to him from usually reliable sources, yet some pertinent information was withheld from him. Investigation and discovery in this case have disclosed that incomplete information as to his patient's condition was provided by the nursing staff of the hospital, that the reported interpretation of the X-rays by the radiologist was misleading, and the diagnosis made in the emergency room, based in part on information not shared with Dr. Bennett, was influential despite the independent evaluation required of and made by Dr. Bennett. A reading of the X-rays in the morning of February 26, 1983 by Dr. Elsworth as reflecting pulmonary edema inexplicably was not conveyed to Dr. Bennett and such an interpretation could have prompted a reevaluation of his patient." The other defendants were provided copies of our settlement agreement. If they tried to show the jury the agreement, they'd cut their own throats with it.

Next, the hospital settled with us for $750,000. We were now facing an impending trial, and on May 23, 1985, I sent a telegram to the attorney for the emergency-room corporation and Dr. Appleton—the young lawyer to whom I had early on made the first settlement offer of $750,000. It said, in part, "We offer to settle with your clients for $2 million, which offer remains open until, but will expire without further notice at 5:00 P.M., Mountain Daylight Time, Monday, June 3, 1985. Our demand at the time of the pre-trial conference will be $5 million, and we will be seeking in excess of your policy limits should you still be in this case at the time of trial. We strongly suggest an immediate meeting between us and those within your company who have authority over the $2 million." Within the time prescribed, the insurance companies for the emergency-room corporation and Dr. Appleton settled.

Finally there remained only the radiology group and the cardiologists, Carmen and Elsworth. I wrote each of the insurance carriers' lawyers, "If you want to be the only one to go to trial against me, so be it. But if [your company] is the last to settle, I guarantee you will pay a penalty for it." Perhaps the remaining claims managers had visions of how it would be for the jury to return a $14 million verdict against their doctor when the others had gotten out cheap. Perhaps they panicked at the last.

The radiologists were the first to settle—for $375,000. That left only Drs. Carmen and Elsworth and their partners. The insurance company, which remember, had also insured Dr. Bennett, was represented by an old friend of mine, one of the most honest and forthright, yet one of the most immutably stubborn, lawyers I have ever known in my life, and the insurance carrier was now following the advice of this inflexible litigator, who wouldn't recommend more than $200,000. Actually I knew he didn't want to settle for any sum, that he was able to stomach a $200,000 offer only because it would cost his company that much to defend the case. He was ready to go to court, he said, and I believed him.

But by this time I had reason to think that Drs. Carmen and Elsworth, who sincerely never felt they were in any way answerable for Roy's death, nevertheless wanted this painful case over, too. I am told they asked their private attorney to place demands on the insurance company to settle, failing which Drs. Carmen and Elsworth threatened to hold the company responsible for any losses they might sustain if, by chance, the verdict came in over their policy coverage. Bad faith! The excess! At the last moment, the company caved in. I turned them down on their new offer. I doubt that my stubborn friend, their lawyer, ever gave an inch, either. Now, as I look back on it, perhaps I was the more stubborn. I geared up for trial. I had given my word that whoever was the last to settle would pay a penalty, and Carmen and Elsworth's company would pay more than the radiologist's insurance company or we were on our way to the courthouse.

Finally their attorney came to me as a friend. Please. Be reasonable. Don't make me eat this. I was sorry, I said. And I was. But my credibility was also at stake. I had no other choice but to stick to my demand. Then the company relented once more, and, indeed, paid a substantial penalty for being the last to settle—the total for all of the cases being in excess of $4 million.

Throughout the litigation, each of the defendants had denied any negligence. In settling, all of the defendants continued to deny liability for Roy Peck's death. By this time, I estimated that the costs and attorney fees paid by the insurance companies to the various law firms and the medical experts they had hired totaled well in excess of the million dollars I first offered to settle for. But the issue is rarely what is the right thing, or even what is the intelligent thing, to do. The insurance companies showed no concern for the misery their customers, the doctors, were put through in this battle. The doctors had also become victims. In order to be protected by the insurance they had purchased, they, too, had to be dragged through this grinding machine. It was a money game, and the companies were committed to winning at any cost. They had set out with the clear intent of never paying a penny to the Peck family, not if it cost them the bank, and like almost every case involving insurance, the cost to bring the companies to their knees makes justice a luxury item that ordinary people cannot afford.

A few days after the Peck settlement, I received a call from a doctor in a small Wyoming town asking me to represent his wife against some of his fellow doctors. She was dying. He was weeping and could barely get the words out. He could not afford to hire a lawyer, he said. He had tried to hire several firms on a straight fee basis, but the estimated cost of the case was several hundred thousand dollars, not including the cash he would be required to advance for witness fees and depositions and other expenses. He couldn't come up with the money without mortgaging his home, and he couldn't risk that kind of money on a case he couldn't be sure he would win. He said, "I know we doctors have fought you tooth and nail. But they just don't understand. They all think this will never happen to them."

I told him we would look at his case. We had him send his wife's entire medical file, and we had our own physicians review it and give us an opinion. The case was a tragic one, all right. The doctors had missed the diagnosis, but any competent doctor under the circumstances could have. Doctors are not required to practice flawless medicine. They are only required to act *reasonably* under the circumstances according to the standards of their profession. These doctors had. The contingency fee usually sorts out the questionable cases to begin with. Even the unscrupulous lawyer who will sue anybody for anything won't usually risk his own time and his own cash on a meritless case.

The settlement I forced down the throats of Dr. Carmen's insurance company stuck in the craw of my old but stubborn friend, and a junior member of his firm, who hadn't had his day in court, took me on in an open letter to the *Casper Star Tribune,* Wyoming's largest newspaper. He started like a good lawyer always does—by saying nice things about the dead before he attacked. "Wyoming will miss Roy Peck," he began. "He will be remembered as an effective legislator, a concerned citizen, and a good man." As I read the letter, I had my own thoughts—yes, he was a good man, but you defense attorneys at your standard hourly rate would have done whatever you could, legally and ethically, to deprive that good man's family of a just settlement. If you could, you would have turned that family away without a penny. And you would have been proud of it. You would have insisted that justice was on your side. It would have been good business. The members of your firm would have congratulated you. And the company you represented would make due note of your success and would have sent you more cases against more widows and orphans. And whatever was kept from those widows and those children would, of course, stand as blessed profit for the company. Don't speak of good men to me.

The young lawyer continued: "It is my belief that Roy himself would have been appalled at the result in the Peck settlement." I think Roy would have slapped the table and said, "By damn," which was about the worst word I ever heard him say, "maybe the rest of the people will be safer now if they have a heart attack! Maybe those at the hospital will listen to our wives next time. Maybe we've made it too expensive for this to happen again." Roy would have been appalled, all right. But not by the settlement. He would have been appalled that he was never given a fair chance to live. "Don't worry, honey," he had said. "I'm in good hands." The betrayal of his own innocent faith would have appalled him.

Now, the lawyer leveled his attack at me. "But you, Mr. Spence, hold a gun to the doctor's head, a gun forged from your remarkable courtroom skills, your ability to persuade juries to award millions of dollars in damages, your ability to make juries detach themselves from the logical and the factual and succumb to your irresistible powers of rhetoric. You say to insurance companies, 'Pay me or I will use this gun.' And because insurance companies have seen the magic you have performed in courtrooms throughout the country they usually pay your demands."

But what of the great masses of Americans who can never get justice because the costs are too high and the risks too great? What of them, of the hundred thousand poor widows and their children who, every year, settle good cases for piteous sums because the insurance companies put guns to *their* helpless heads? Who weeps for them?

"I didn't file the suit for money," Maggie told me later. "I just had to do something."

She wrote her own letter to the paper in defense of me. "We decided to sue the parties we felt were responsible for Roy's premature death because we wanted to alert the public to the negligence we discovered in the treatment of my husband in the hospital. . . . We asked only for ordinary care. He did not receive it. . . . If any man believed in justice, Roy did," she wrote.

"Did you get justice, Maggie?" I asked when it was over.

"It's not that I'm not grateful," Maggie said. "It's just that the people think I did something wrong." Then she looked at me with those deep, gentle eyes. And the tears came. "Did I do something wrong?" she asked.

"No, Maggie," I said. "You didn't do anything wrong."

8 | LABOR

People as Property, Workers as Slaves

In the workplace, we sell our lives the way a street peddler in Katmandu sells his turnips. By that sorcery, both turnips and lives are converted to money. In the workplace, we wage our most important battles, with poor weapons and few rights, and then, like the slaves of old, many are irretrievably trapped and there many grind away their lives in drudgery and despair. Although no one could rightly contend that the American worker is truly in bondage, daily he lives with degradation and helplessness. He has the sense of being bound to a job he may despise. He is free to go, but he cannot leave. He and his family depend on the work, and what will happen to him if he does not measure up? Surely he will find himself once more on the dreaded auction block. And ask any worker about the treadmill, the maddening tedium. In flat voices, some will say they have grown used to it, and some have become so numb they cannot hear the question, and some have been transformed into machines. In even the best of arrangements, servility changes the worker from man to slave, for the will of the employer becomes the will of the worker. It is not that our condition is unimproved, but that we have such a long way to go. To the same extent that slavery is the supreme degradation of the species, so also is perfect justice its promise.

Our roots are deeply embedded in polluted soil. In 1619, a year before the Pilgrims landed at Plymouth, the first shipload of slaves was delivered to Virginia, and in 1637 the first American slave ship, the *Desire*, sailed from Marblehead for the coast of Africa, its holds partitioned into two-by-six-foot cells, and furnished with leg irons and bars. Once captured, the new slaves were stuffed into these cramped cavities without proper ventilation or sanitation. By the time the survivors were dragged out of the hold and into the blinding light of day in Virginia, they were encrusted with excrement and the slave deck was, according to one observer, "so covered with blood and mucus that it resembled a slaughterhouse." Some say one in five, others as many as one in three, died during the voyage, but profits were immense. Howard Zinn, in his painfully forthright *A People's History of the United States*, cites an account of slave-ship conditions:

> On one occasion, hearing a great noise from below decks where the blacks were chained together, the sailors opened the hatches and found the slaves in different stages of suffocation, many dead, some having killed others in desperate attempts to breathe.

Nearly 50 million humans were lost from Africa to the slave trade. By 1800, between 10 million and 15 million blacks had been transported to the Americas, representing perhaps but a third of the total human souls originally seized. By the time of the Civil War, the United States census recorded 4,441,830 slaves in America who had provided the foundation labor for this new "land of the free and home of the brave."

Yet already there was protest. In 1700, in Massachusetts, Judge Samuel Sewall sadly concluded in his tract *The Selling of Joseph* that no ground could be gained in spreading the word of the Lord until slavery was abolished. He objected to the dehumanizing slave laws, which he saw as an "oppression provoking to God," and he considered it obscene that the Massachusetts legislature should rate Indians and blacks with horses and hogs. James Madison, author of our Bill of Rights, boasted shortly after the American Revolution that he could make $257 annually on every slave he owned and was required to spend only $12 or $13 yearly on each slave's upkeep. Jefferson offered to include a paragraph in the Declaration of Independence denouncing the king for having engaged with the colonies in the slave trade and "suppressing every legislative attempt to prohibit or to restrain this execrable commerce." Although the paragraph was quickly purged by the Continental Congress, Jefferson's dissent must be juxtaposed against the hundreds of slaves he himself owned. A troubled master, however, he reflected, "I tremble for my country when I reflect that God is just." Few citizens trembled with him.

I am painfully aware of how we get caught up in our times and become contaminated by our own hypocrisy. My law firm employs perhaps forty people, and although we pay them in excess of the "going wage," we do not pay them as much as they are worth, or how could we profit from their labor? Most of our employees are wholly dependent on their employment with us for their survival. Of course, they can leave, and would if the cause were sufficient— even slaves run away. But there is always some *margin* of *bondage* in every employment relationship that is both painful and degrading, the width and depth of its slavelike properties varying with the worker's ability to tolerate the yoke and the employer's sensitivity to the worker's neck. Most workers have learned to tolerate its pain—so, eventually, did the slave. Within the margin of bondage applicable to my employees, they are as much my slaves as Jefferson's were his, bonded both to me as well as to the market that sets the price for all commodities—in their case, their skills; and, as Jefferson's slaves did for him, my employees provide me with a greater security and a better life-style than they themselves enjoy.

We are the offspring of our history. Indeed, the black man was not the only slave in America. Voracious in their quest for cheap labor, the colonists conceived of the indentured-servant scheme, whereby the poor, imprisoned in England for petty crimes or debt, entered into indenture agreements for their passage to the New World and freedom. Among them were also children gathered up by the hundreds on the streets of London by profiteers who sent them like slaves to the colonies, for the poor had not fared well in England. In 1572, Elizabeth decreed: "Unlicensed beggars above 14 years of age are to be severely flogged and branded on the left ear unless some one will take them into service for two years; in case of a repetition of the offence, if they are over 18, they are to be executed, unless some one will take them into service for two years; but for the third offence they are to be executed without mercy as felons." In America, indentured servants were bought and sold the same as slaves. An announcement in the *Virginia Gazette*, March 28, 1771, read: "Just arrived at Leedstown, The Ship Justitia, with about one Hundred Healthy Servants, Men Women & Boys. . . . The Sale will commence on Tuesday the end of April." Beatings, rapes, and suicides of indentured servants were, of course, common.

The Church traditionally condoned slavery in its numerous forms, too. In 1610, Father Sandoval, inquiring from the Americas concerning the Church's position on the issue, received the following reply from Brother Luis Brandon:

> I think your Reverence should have no scruples on this point, because this is a matter which has been questioned by the Board of Conscience in Lisbon, and all its members are learned and conscientious men. Nor did the bishops who were in Sao Thome, Cape Verde, and here in Loando—all learned and virtuous men—find fault with it. We have been here ourselves for forty years and there have been among us very learned Fathers . . . never did they consider the trade as illicit. Therefore we and the Fathers of Brazil buy these slaves for our service without any scruple.

The Church's logic made it easy, as is the office of logic. "All men are brothers in union with God," but in the temporal world, "slavery was a necessary part of the world of sin." Thus, "the bondsman was inwardly free and spiritually equal to his master, but in things external he was a mere chattel." The Church itself was a major owner of slaves. Even before the Jesuits began to promote the importation of Africans into the New World, the Church actively encouraged slavery. Pope Gregory XI himself viewed bondage as justice for those who had resisted the papacy, and ordered the enslavement of excommunicated Florentines wherever they were captured. In 1488, Pope Innocent VIII (who commissioned the writing of the infamous procedures for the identification and prosecution of witches, the *Malleus Maleficarum*) accepted a gift of a hundred Moorish slaves from Ferdinand of Spain and distributed them to various cardinals and nobles.

The industrious Puritan, to whom many American businessmen trace their ethical roots, understood such power as well. God heaps His riches upon the righteous, leaving poverty and sin somehow connected. Therefore, it was not sinful to exploit the poor. Even today, our poor remain the object of national scorn. The homeless and those on welfare are despised as lazy or dishonest. In the spirit of Christian Darwinism, our government, by its example, grants us permission to be cruel to the poor and the unfortunate.

Our welfare programs reveal that we are more dedicated to imprisoning those in the ghettos than in providing them an adequate education or an honest job. We are more committed to building another bomber than bringing our homeless children in off the streets. We honor power more than compassion, dollars more than people.

Power wielded without conscience is as dangerous as a gun in the hands of a lunatic, and to glorify profit making as a sacred right that drifts down upon the affluent, to sanctify the wresting of the last of the workers' creativity and zest for life in the holy name of gain, is the ultimate dementia of the privileged. In 1902, George Baer, the president of the Philadelphia and Reading Railroad and spokesman for the coal operators, answered piously to the appeal of the striking coal miners for Christian treatment. "The rights and interests of the laboring man," he proclaimed sanctimoniously, "will be protected and cared for—not by the labor agitators, but by the Christian men to whom God, in His infinite wisdom, has given the control of the property interests of this country." Shortly afterward, in Ludlow, Colorado, at John D. Rockefeller's Colorado Fuel and Iron, the tent settlements were burned to the ground, the tenants, including women and children, burned and shot—not by savage Indians but by Rockefeller's private army and the U. S. Cavalry. One of the Ludlow strikers, William Snyder, testified at the coroner's inquest over the death of his eleven-year-old son, who had been shot through the head.

"They set fire to the tent?" Snyder was asked by the coroner.

"Yes, sir. My wife then said, 'For God sakes save my children.' "

"What did they say to you?" the coroner asked.

"They said, 'What the hell are you doing here?' I told them I was trying to save my children and they said, 'You son of a bitch, get out of there and get out quick at that.'

"My wife was out by that time . . . I told them to hold on. I had a boy killed in there and they told me to get out damn quick. I picked the boy up and laid him down outside so I could get better hold of him.

"I asked some of these fellows to help me carry him to the depot and one said, 'God damn you, aren't you big enough?' I said, 'I can't do it.' I took him on my shoulder and [lifted his] sister on the other arm and then one of these militia men stopped me and said, 'God damn you, you redneck son of a bitch, I have a notion to kill you right now.' "

Another woman and five men, all strikers, were killed that night, and thirteen children were murdered in addition to William Snyder's boy. Rockefeller is said to have monitored the struggle at Ludlow with great pleasure. His son, however, took full responsibility for the massacre, saying it was the unfortunate outcome of a principled fight he was bound to make "for the protection of the working men against trade unions." But the miners did not see the Ludlow Massacre through Rockefeller's eyes. The miners erected a monument that still stands. Carved in stone are the figures of a man and his wife at whose feet lies their slain child. The inscription reads, "Erected by the United Mine Workers of America to the memory of the men, women and little children who died in freedom's cause."

By the time of the Industrial Revolution, Northern blacks and poor white farmers had drifted to the cities in search of work, and there, nearly helpless, they were bilked of their lives and cheated of their dreams as they labored, at piteous wages, in sweatshops owned by a new ruthless breed of robber barons, the revered heroes of American industry—John D. Rockefeller, founder of Standard Oil of Ohio, who had also moved into copper, coal, iron, and shipping and into the control of the Chase Manhattan Bank, and J. P. Morgan, who would soon form U.S. Steel after acquiring the sprawling interests of Andrew Carnegie. Empires were built, competition choked out, and wages smashed. Congress was induced to pass protective tariffs and to provide subsidies that established these industries as the first beneficiaries of the "welfare state." Men were used up. The Union Pacific employed twenty thousand workers—mostly war veterans and Irish and Chinese immigrants—to lay five miles of track a day, and the workers died by the hundreds in the heat and the cold and in battles with the Indians. Records of the Interstate Commerce Commission disclosed that in 1889 alone, twenty-two thousand railroad workers were killed or injured.

But, wrestling in frantic competition, the immigrants kept pouring in—5.5 million of them in the 1880's, and nearly that many in the following decade. In 1885, in my own state of Wyoming, desperate whites attacked helpless Chinese miners who had been imported by the Union Pacific to labor for miserable pay as a tactic to break the backs of the white strikers. Twenty-eight Chinese were killed. Elsewhere, factory workers toiled twelve hours a day, six days a week, and their hollow-eyed children worked with them. In this furious struggle against starvation and despair, a new American slavery emerged—and thus the seeds of the American labor movement were also planted.

In the beginning, the labor movement struggled helplessly like a beast caught in quicksand, and whenever its wobbly head rose above the surface, the heavy foot of the new industrial power forced it down again. Although there was feeble resistance—a wildcat strike at a factory, sporadic worker sabotage in a textile plant, a battle with police, as in East St. Louis, where seven workers died—the infant movement was taken for little more than transient lawlessness. But in 1881, the American Federation of Labor was formed, and hundreds of thousands of workers across the land began to strike for the eighthour day.

The South fared worse. Earlier, slave owners had at least minimal responsibility for slaves as property. Now, even that loathsome protection was gone, and in the South the old ruling class was reinstalled with its deadly spirit of despotism. From 1889 to 1901, there were 1,955 recorded lynchings of blacks. Thirty-eight died in 1917; fifty-eight in 1918; and seventy in 1919. Between 1885 and 1930, there were 3,256 recorded lynchings of blacks in the southern states.

During the same time, the robber barons called on state and local police and the National Guard to do their fighting for them. On May 3, 1885, police fired into a crowd of strikers in Chicago, wounding many and killing four. The labor leaders called for a meeting at Haymarket Square on the evening of May 4, 1885. It was said to be a quiet meeting, but a detachment of 180 policemen advanced on the speaker's platform and ordered the crowd to disperse. Then a bomb exploded, wounding sixty-six officers; seven died. In blind retaliation, the police fired into the crowd, killing several workers and wounding two hundred. Without evidence as to who threw the bomb, eight of the leaders were convicted of murder and promptly sentenced to death. When the Illinois Supreme Court turned down their appeals, four were hanged. Of the remaining four, one blew himself up in his cell by exploding a dynamite tube in his mouth. The executions aroused the nation. Twenty-five thousand marched at the funerals of the freshly hanged, and violence continued, with strikes, lockouts, blacklists, battles, and blood in the streets.

In June 1894, the workers at the Pullman Palace Car Company struck and petitioned the convention of the newly formed American Railway Union for support. On the platform, a speaker for the striking workers concluded his oration, shouting:

Pullman, both the man and the town, is an ulcer on the body politic. He owns the houses, the schoolhouses, and the churches of God in the town to which he gave his once humble name. . . . And thus the merry—the dance of skeletons bathed in human tears—goes on, and it will go on, brothers, forever, unless you, the American Railway Union, stop it; end it; crush it out.

Eugene Debs, one of the ARU's founders, along with other union leaders asked its members not to handle Pullman cars. Since nearly all passenger trains included Pullmans, a nationwide strike resulted. Lines leading from Chicago came to a dead halt. That the trains carried U.S. mail became the excuse for a government injunction against the workers, which was ignored, and President Cleveland promptly ordered federal troops to Chicago. Hundreds of railroad cars were burned by strikers. Thirteen people were killed in one day, fifty-three seriously wounded, and seven hundred arrested. Debs himself was arrested for contempt of court. At his sentencing, he told the judge, "It seems to me that if it were not for resistance to degrading conditions, the tendency of our whole civilization would be downward; after a while we would reach the point where there would be no resistance, and slavery would come."

Our American prophets, our poets, foresaw the birth of the corporate oligarchy, but they were largely dismissed as eccentric dreamers. Thoreau at Concord envisioned the enemy of man as the growing hierarchy of government dominated by the enslaving "weeds of commerce." A hundred years after his death, his stern warning was only the distant mumbling of transcendentalism—that man must follow his conscience regardless of cost, that life is too dear to be wasted trading oneself for the objects of one's own production, that the world of ideas and streams and forests is good, while the world of streets and crowds and things is bad, even insane. Emerson recognized the enemy and recoiled against it, pleading that the nation be rebuilt solely on the rights of man. The identification of the enemy was nothing new, nothing radical. The enemy was Power, a power that cheated man of the foundation promises of America, the right to self-government and the opportunity to forge his own destiny in the new land.

By the late nineteenth century, the far-off voices of Jefferson, Emerson and Thoreau were silenced by the clang and crunch of corporate commerce. Rugged individualism became only a celebrated ideal. The songs of Whitman were drowned out in the drone of the new producing-consuming machinery. Americans were told they were free, but felt weak and oppressed. They did not understand the forces descending upon them, nor could they separate the myth of their liberty from the truth of their new bondage to the corporate state. These forces struck at the heart of the American dream. In *The Greening of America*, Charles Reich posed the question: How could Americans, the most independent and self-reliant, the most jealous of their liberties, "have permitted themselves to be reduced to the impotent 'little man' of today, dominated by public and private power?"

How? Because power is the great domesticator. I see the savage dragged from the slave ship, frantic, eyes wild, searching for escape. I hear the whip at his back compelling him to shed his will, to stay in line. Most of us have long ago made our own solemn agreement to this. Most of us were born in captivity where domestication and maturation work hand in hand. When we corral a mustang on the

Red Desert in Wyoming, he must be "broken," that is, his will to resist, but not his will to work, must be destroyed. He will probably be "cut" as the cowboys refer to castration. An essential part of the domestication of any species is the continual sorting out of troublesome strains and replacing them with the more docile ones.

Consider the pressures placed on our children from the first day at school—not for learning, not for creativity, but that they contain themselves for their teacher's benefit. Children need to learn to "fit in," but a child who brings home straight A's in Conduct is evincing ominous signs. My eleven-year-old nephew, Aaron, recently came home with all A's except for a C in Deportment. His father inquired about Aaron's mediocre behavior. "Well, Dad," he argued, "that's a perfect grade! Only the wimps get A's. And the jerks get D's and F's." A child without fire is like a world without fire.

The "breaking" of our children begins the day they are born. For conformity we sacrifice spontaneity, originality, spirit. What is produced is a herd of predominantly submissive and passive humans who are easily managed for the benefit of their overseers. Notice how accepting we are of the idea that we must stand in line for long periods of time in order to gain the privilege of buying *their* groceries. Watch how people are seated in inferior places in a restaurant—say, in front of the kitchen door—when better tables are available. Observe people being herded like cattle through airports and theaters. We have been trained to accept what "they" give us, and how "they" treat us. We have been taught that to "make waves" is reprehensible; to resist slightly, antisocial. Rousseau observed, "Man is born free and everywhere he is in chains." What Rousseau saw is the relentless process of domestication.

My own mutinous spirit has caused me unceasing grief. My earliest memories include a pervasive sense of exile. I resisted the efforts of my teachers to make a gentleman of me. I was unpredictable and affronting. I could never win an office in the class elections—couldn't even get nominated. I was always the first to be dumped off after a party and the last to receive the nod when sides were chosen. At the university, no fraternity ever rushed me. I wasn't their type. I had no social graces. I had no money. I wasn't an athlete, or even a scholar. I was nothing except lonely. Rejection! It is an indomitable force.

I grew up as a smart aleck. I remember one time I spoke to my father about it.

"It's your fault, Dad," I said. "Why didn't you kick it out of me when I was a kid instead of letting me grow up this way?" My father waited for the energy of my attack to dissipate. Then he said very quietly, "Well, son. It's pretty easy to kick it out of a pup. But it's hard to get it back in him again."

Like any creature born free, we resist domestication. The colonists encountered the problem with runaway slaves. The preamble to the Virginia Slave Code of the 1700's recited that slaves "run away and lie hid alurking in swamps, woods, and other obscure places, killing hogs, and committing other injuries to the inhabitants. . . ." and their solution was to hang them. Today, many of our own misfits become our idealists, our fighters, and some can never be neatly constrained or bought. Many still take to desperate places—to our ghettos and streets, to our asylums and prisons. Our solution is similar to the colonists'. We flush the runaways from the swamps of poverty and oppression and dispose of them as the enemies of our society. Over half of the four hundred thousand people in our prisons are black. Our eagerness for capital punishment echoes the mentality of the old slave code. As recently as 1982, our Supreme Court heard an argument on the constitutionality of the death penalty imposed against a severely abused child who, at age sixteen, had fatally shot a patrolman. Attorney Jay C. Baker appeared for the boy and argued that he should be confined for life under psychiatric care rather than killed.

JUSTICE REHNQUIST: Why should the taxpayers have to foot the bill?

BAKER: It would be *cheaper* than executing him.

JUSTICE REHNQUIST: From the taxpayer's standpoint?

BAKER: More will have been spent on the defendant's case than would have been spent had he received some other sentence. [Baker was referring to recent statistics showing that the *dollar cost* to society for multiple trials and hearings in death-penalty cases usually exceeds the costs of housing the prisoner for the rest of his life.]

JUSTICE REHNQUIST: Only because of the protracted litigation.

JUSTICE MARSHALL: [unwittingly quoting the theme of the Virginia Slave Code] It would have been *cheaper still to have shot the defendant at the time of his arrest*. [My emphasis.]

BAKER: That's correct.

Judge Lois Forer commented in her book *Money and Justice*, "It is startling and dismaying to hear Justices discuss [such] matters of life and death in terms of money. . . . Despite lip service to the doctrine of equal protection of the laws, the courts have in effect put a price tag on justice."

Notions of a massive work force existing as units of labor, as machines, as consumables without rights, have deep and pernicious roots in American law, roots compatible with the very soil of the market society. We remember Dred Scott. On April 6, 1846, he sued for his freedom. Owned by Dr. John Emerson, an army physician, Scott had been taken to the several posts to which the doctor had been assigned, one being in the free state of Illinois and another in the free territory of Missouri. As a part of the Missouri Compromise, Congress had prohibited slavery within that territory. It was the settled law of the land that if a master took his slave into a free state or territory, the slave somehow magically absorbed the freedom of that place forever; and even though his master later returned him to a slave state, the slave could sue for his freedom and obtain it. Therefore, on his return to Missouri, both Dred Scott and his wife, Liza, sued.

During the eleven years of haggling in the state and federal courts, including the highest courts of both jurisdictions, Dred Scott remained in the custody of the sheriff in St. Louis and was hired out, like a rental car, by the sheriff to any who would use him, the proceeds of his labor being held by the sheriff for delivery in accordance with the final ruling of the court. On March 6, 1857, the United States Supreme Court handed down its decision, the opinion of the learned Chief Justice Taney becoming accepted as the majority. The Chief Justice held that at the time of the Declaration of Independence and the adoption of the Constitution, "history shows they [blacks] had, for more than a century, been regarded as beings of an inferior order and unfit associates for the white race, either socially or politically, and *had no rights which white men were bound to respect* [my emphasis], and the black man might be reduced to slavery, bought and sold, and treated as an ordinary article of merchandise. This opinion, at that time, was fixed and universal with the civilized portion of the white race. It was regarded as an axiom in morals, which no one thought of disputing, and everyone habitually acted upon it, without doubting for a moment the correctness of the opinion."

The Founding Fathers having regarded slaves as *property*, the court was without jurisdiction, since mere property cannot be elevated to the dignity of citizenship. Because Dred Scott was property, he could never become a citizen of any state. As property, he could not maintain an action in a court any more than a horse or a shovel could sue. But his citizenship was denied on yet another ground, namely, that he was *also a member of the black race*, and as such could never hold citizenship, slave or free.

Quoting from the "life, liberty, and pursuit of happiness" clause of the Constitution, Chief Justice Taney said, "It is too clear for dispute that the enslaved African race were not intended to be included," for this would be *flagrantly against the principles* that the framers of the Declaration of Independence held inviolate. "They knew that in no part of the civilized world were the Negro race, by common consent, admitted to the rights of freemen. They spoke and acted according to the practices, doctrines and usages of the day." Taney had his history right, but his personal principles and his law were wrong. By the same accident of birth that decided Dred Scott a slave, Taney had been born a southerner deeply committed to slavery, as were six of the eight other members of his court. The supreme law of the land did not measure justice. It measured the history, the prejudices, and the desires of the judges of the Supreme Court. It took into account the sayings of quiet mothers, and it measured the harsh laws laid down by tyrannical fathers. The justices were no more able to emancipate Dred Scott than they were able to emancipate themselves. Only the dignity and solemnity of the high court, their very black robes and their very starched language, hid their mortal souls from plain view.

"We have come to the conclusion that the African race who came to this country, *whether free or slave* [my emphasis], were not intended to be included in the Constitution for the enjoyment of any personal rights or benefits . . ." and consequently it must be clear to all "that Dred Scott is not a citizen of Missouri, and is not, therefore, entitled to sue in the United State's courts." But the court did not end its opinion there. It went on to declare that Congress had no authority to prohibit slavery in the Missouri territory, because to do so was an unconstitutional deprivation of the citizen of his *property.* Dred Scott represented two competing bodies of legal rights—one, the natural rights that are attributable to the human race, and the other, the right of man to his private property. In balance, the right to property has always seemed more enduring.

The domestication of American slaves, black and white, has proceeded relentlessly over the past 350 years. We have nearly forgotten the bequest of our grandfathers—the blood, the broken bodies sacrificed to narrow our margin of bondage. The heavy foot is on our heads again. The workers of the world and their hungry children vie with Americans for jobs. Recently, in Bangkok, I walked a mere block from my luxury hotel into a section of the city containing miles of pathetic hovels facing dark, narrow alleys. The day was hot and the doors were open, and as I strolled by, I peered into the dim spaces where children were sweating and squinting and sewing with skillful hands, producing the clothing that will pack the racks in American stores. The children would rather work than lie in the streets with bloated bellies. That is not a just choice for children.

Such competition is also not just for American workers. Yet upon the spoils of such exploitation, we have cheerfully elevated our own grand standard of living.

Elsewhere, American workers have been driven from the workplace by another horde of new immigrants, unconditionally committed to work without rest, without pay, without a mumble of complaint. Silently, faithfully, perfectly, they work. These new immigrants devour the jobs of millions. The draftsman no longer draws his plans. The repairman at the telephone company no longer makes his repairs. The lathe operator merely pushes a button. Already General Motors is being manned by these robots, mechanical men with tireless backs and stainless-steel souls. Experts project that by 1990, 17.5 million computer-driven electronic workstations will become the nerve system of the nation. Banking, telephones, machine tools, drafting, engineering—all are being computerized. The imperfect heads and the troublesome hands of living workers are being usurped. Machines do not march in the street and get sick and raise hell and fall in love and have babies and file lawsuits against the corporation. Computers are the perfect slaves. To compete, the American worker struggles to be more machinelike, more serflike himself, for perfect management demands perfect control.

Occasionally there is a puny rebellion. Occasionally the machines are sabotaged. But the workers have finally had to surrender, because there are fewer and fewer jobs. The unions grow impotent. What do they have to sell? To some modern corporate managers, the unions, like steam-driven locomotives, are historical relics. Some theorists claim the union movement is dead. "Today," say corporate sociologists John Naisbitt and Patricia Aburdene in their fine book, *Reinventing the Corporation*, "only 17 percent of the U.S. work force is organized. In the private sector, only 15 percent is unionized. And in the economically dynamic South and West, only 5 percent of the work force belongs to a union. Because unions don't understand the need to reinvent themselves to fit the information society, their decline and eventual demise seem certain."

Today, it is a common experience to see workers rejecting unions in favor of the new "enlightened" unionless workplace. According to two Harvard economists, Richard Freeman and James Medoff, most of the new "excellent corporations" are nonunion and, with the support of the workers, there has been a "slow strangulation of private sector unionism." In their book *What Do Unions Do?*, Freeman and Medoff cite statistics showing that in the mid-fifties unions represented 34 percent of the nonagriculture private-sector labor force. By 1980, the proportion had been reduced to 24 percent, a decline they contend is unprecedented in American history. By 1982, the figure was below 20 percent, the lowest since the Great Depression.

In *Brave New Workplace*, Robert Howard's brave new book, we are told of sensors that are attached to computers to record the workers' output, their mistakes, their efficiency, and when the worker rests, a little gong—the new, computerized whip—goes off. The worker has become a machine, monitored by a machine. The jobs in the brave new workplace are tedious and drive people insane. The use of drugs has become rampant. Workers are trapped. They cannot leave. They endure. They work for the computer, not the other way around. A woman (let us call her Mary McCafferty) is lucky to have a job. The machine operator she replaced is unemployed and too old to be re-skilled. Howard says, "It does not take long to realize that when the managers of the brave new workplace talk about expanding managerial control, they mean control over workers." And if the workers object, they are, of course, quite free to leave.

For the good of the industrial society, human beings have become as mobile and expendable as any other commodity required in production. Yet in the hierarchy of human freedom, there is now a level below that of the slave. It is that of the inanimate disposable object. Today, the American worker moves on the average of once every four years. Today, when the worker can no longer produce his quota, he is discarded. When the overseer for the new corporate master reads Mary McCafferty's printout and sees that her output is down, she, too, will be terminated, perhaps without notice and almost certainly without any right of redress. She is not a slave, or a thing. Yet even the old or unproductive slave was always the master's responsibility, while Mary McCafferty can be used up until she is useless to the corporation that hired her, and then one afternoon at quitting time she will get her pink slip, after which she will take her place alongside the other millions like herself in the great garbage heap of the unemployed.

And so Mary McCafferty labors away. She must stop thinking about it. The bell is sounding its alarm. She must concentrate. It is boring, maddening. She must concentrate. Some call it the terrible battle against detachment. She suffers chronic stress. She wants to cry out, she shakes, she is on tranquilizers, she thinks of suicide. She cannot escape. Her overseer says he can measure her every movement, and he laughs and pats her on the back and promises her a small raise if she meets her quotas. She is working for the minimum wage. It does not provide a living, but there are endless lines of new and hungry immigrants patiently, quietly waiting for this very job.

The federal government's National Institute of Occupational Health found that clerical workers like Mary McCafferty exhibited the highest levels of stress ever reported in their surveys—higher than those of air-traffic controllers. Another survey of four thousand working women conducted in 1984 by Nine to Five, the National Association of Working Women, found that the highest incidence of frequent health problems, including headaches, nausea, digestive problems, insomnia, irritability, depression, and other indicators of stress, was reported by women in automated clerical jobs.

The flood of toxic chemicals creates even more serious health problems in this brave new workplace. Workers become human litmus paper. After repeated exposures, many become supersensitive organisms no longer able to tolerate the usual levels of toxins we live with daily. They become walking invalids. They can barely lift their heads. They cannot think. They break out in rashes. They sob. Their symptoms are elusive. Sometimes the workers are even unable to prove they are ill and are adjudged lazy or dismissed as malingerers. And how can they prove that whatever is wrong with them— perhaps they are only crazy—is connected with the workplace? We are exposed to chemicals everywhere, in oven cleaners, detergents, patent medicines, hair sprays—everywhere. Some of the chemicals cause cancer, some sterility. That American workers may be destined to die for the sake of their jobs or sacrifice their right to parenthood for corporate profits are among the great tragedies of our times.

Now the corporate sociologists, understanding our human yearning for home and family and community and the need to devote our lives to worthy goals, invite the American worker to look to the brave new workplace for fulfillment. It is more than an invitation. As Thomas Peters and Robert Waterman assert in their best-seller *In Search of Excellence*, the model corporation has become "like good parents who care a lot and expect a lot." According to them, the "excellent company" has become a "mother institution." But mother expects you to be there whenever she wants you, and it is hard to satisfy demanding mothers, and harder still to leave them. "There is no halfway house for most people in the excellent companies. We either buy into their norms or get out." We either accept their "shared culture" and "guiding beliefs" and "transforming purpose," all of which contain haunting reverberations of Huxley's *Brave New World*, or we "opt out." But where can we go?

Like the slave, the modern worker has been separated from his family and from his traditional community, and so will his children be. His need for family and tribe, as genetic as the instinct of herding elk and flocking geese, are replaced by a new corporate community. Corporate social scientists now candidly admit that with the disintegration of traditional social structures, companies have filled the gap. Fellow workers have become his new family and his new tribe; his supervisor, his chief; the job, his contribution to the clan's survival. He is utterly dependent on the corporation for both his economic and emotional security. As in the days of the Civil War, when freed slaves would not leave the shelter of their masters, many American workers perceive their very right to life, liberty, and the pursuit of happiness as corporate perks.

I am wary. I do not wish to be captured, to be "loved" as a manipulation of the corporate mother. The corporation cannot love me, because the unalive cannot love. It can only love *what I produce*—money—not *who I am*. I recoil at the idea of opting in as strongly as I hurt at the implications of opting out. And I do not want to be mothered for money, because when the corporate mother is finished with me, it will haul me off to the junk pile as it does any obsolete machine. It is bad enough to be exploited. It is intolerable to be loved in order to make the exploitation "excellent."

In *Brave New Workplace*, Howard reports the frighteningly candid admission of a Harvard Business School student who reveals her newly acquired management philosophy: One "need only figure out what your employee's *hot-button* is." She talks of gaining the workers' trust as if she were establishing contact with the greater apes of Africa. "I wanted to make them feel that they had a little input into the decisions," but there was only one hitch—"of course, they didn't. People like to feel in control," she said. "So let them feel in control." It is what Peters and Waterman call the "illusion of control," an admitted manipulative tool by which more production can be milked out of the captured cow. "If people think they have even modest personal control over their destinies, they will persist at tasks," Peters and Waterman say. "They will do better at them. They will become more committed to them." I think of the pre–Civil War plantation, the indenture agreements, the company store, the sharecropper—all more direct devices designed to squeeze out the last drop of the worker's productive juices. Today, our overseers jockey our psyches instead of whipping our backs. Even Peters and Waterman understand the cruel game. "For us," they admit, "the most worrisome part of a strong culture is the ever present possibility of abuse."

I remember how a survivor of the Holocaust described his experience in a Nazi slave camp. The comparisons are not equivalent, but there are certain troublesome parallels. Ask any worker what management respects the most—the lathe or the lathe operator. The slave-camp survivor writes:

> We were not slaves. Our status was much lower. True, we were deprived of freedom and became a piece of property which our masters put to work. But here the similarity with any known form of slavery ends, for we were a completely expendable piece of property. . . . The equipment in the shop was well maintained. It was operated with care, oiled, greased and allowed to rest; its longevity was protected. We, on the other hand, were like a piece of sandpaper which, rubbed once or twice, becomes useless and is thrown away to be burned with the waste.

Mary McCafferty is free. Yet to her corporate master she is as disposable as the used-up sandpaper in the Nazi slave camp. Outside the door of the workplace, Mary McCafferty, the citizen, has constitutional rights. For one, she has the right to free speech. But if she belongs to the wrong church and does a little preaching to the other workers on their break and is discharged because she is an embarrassment or merely a nuisance to superiors, she has no rights so long as the overseers attribute no religious reason for her discharge. They need no reason. When the corporate master demands that Mary take a lie-detector test or subject her urine to sampling for whatever reason, she cannot resist if she wishes to keep her job, for in the workplace she has no constitutional right to privacy. She may be discharged in most states at will. And when a prospective new employer asks about Mary and her former employer writes the vicious lie that she is a lazy good-for-nothing, Mary has no rights, for the law protects her former employer so long as the lie is merely transmitted to other potential employers, and so long as Mary cannot prove that the members of this exclusive club have been malicious. The exceptions make the law a fascinating game. Perhaps Mary will find a way to bring a lawsuit, but should a jury return a just verdict, her case will receive wide coverage in the corporate press and Mary will be held up as one of those greedy troublemakers who contribute to the "lawsuit crisis." "We all pay the price," the ad in *Time* magazine reads.

The new corporate serfs have been de-skilled and dehumanized—familiar feelings to a slave—except, of course, there are the important differences. The slave knew his master, a human master to whom the slave was chained, and the same chain also enslaved the master. But in the new electronic workplace, the corporate serf cannot see his master, because his corporate master is a *fiction*. Fictions bear no responsibility. Fictions have no consciences. Fictions do not grasp the chains of slaves. That is the fortunate thing about fictions.

To claim workers today are, in fact, slaves would insult our ability to make obvious distinctions and ignore the long and bitter struggle of American workers by which they have elevated themselves to a position occupied by few others in the world. But there are certain similarities. The margin of bondage, like any venal organism, wishes to expand itself. It lies in wait. It wishes to cling and choke and consume until we are all slaves. The fact that our margin of bondage is expanded so easily and contracted with such agony, demands that we maintain a constant and intense vigil against it. Ironically, it seems almost natural, even harmless, to bargain away that which is so hard to feel and painful to exercise—our freedom.

Yet management itself is not free. Management, too, has become a commodity that is bought and sold like any other commodity in the marketplace. Even before the Civil War, many slaves were supervisors of sorts. In fourth-century Athens, bank managers were often slaves, and in Rome the emperor's principal secretaries and accountants were slaves who often became politically influential and did the work of secretaries of state and ministers of finance. The distinction between the slave and the free man, then as now, was not a matter of how high a position the slave occupied, or whether he asserted his authority over slaves beneath him, but whether the individual was totally subject to the will of another and existed essentially without rights. By this definition, the margin of bondage for both labor and management are often similar.

Today, in the marketplace, we behold these curious goings-on— the inanimate corporate master being managed by slave types, and the slave types from time to time selling their corporate masters to other corporate masters, thereby reducing their former masters to slave types. It has become the supreme achievement for humans to convert themselves into a property that can be marketed with ease. But it has created an insane specter—properties buying and selling each other, machines managing management machines—all humming, all slaving away for the love and affection of surrogate corporate mothers, all delivering their lives to property in order that they might have their "hot-buttons" punched.

And so I peer and I preach. I look for dangers and point into the dark. Sometimes what I see are only vague forms and vaporous apparitions—I admit it. But I take nothing on faith. Nothing for granted. I test what I see, or think I see, against what I know, or think I know. I test my visions against history, or what I believe to be history, and whether my sight is faded or fragmented finally makes no difference. It is all I have. In this war, there is the constant greater danger of turning one's head aside—even for a moment.

Out there, the "powers that be," as my mother used to call them, exert their relentless forces against us. In our childhood, it was "They" and "Them" with a capital "T" that controlled us. Theirs was not a human power; it was not a godly power, for one could pray to God, and we were told that we and the dogs and the frogs and the polliwogs were all heard, were all counted, were all important to the scheme, whatever the scheme was. God knew. But "They" and "Them" did not hear, or even care to hear. Theirs was, instead, a power even more mysterious than God's. It was an altogether evil power that constantly controlled us and against which we were helpless.

If overt slavery were essential to today's market economy, Dred Scott would fare little better in modern courts than he did in 1857, for he was mere property; to acknowledge his rights was contrary to the interests of Power. How then can today's worker—the mere cost of labor, the mere appendage to a computing machine—have rights, either? When the worker in the brave new workplace sues because he has been used up and discarded, when he beseeches the court to consider him as a human being and to distinguish him from a piece of disposable cotton engine wipe, his rights will be defined by judges who serve the interests of Power. Then the tears of that old slave will be shed over and over again, for although we have traveled many a bloody mile since the days of Dred Scott and occupy a higher perch on the perilous mountainside, the same pernicious spirit that embraced the sanctity of property over the rights of man still fills the ears of our judges with its enchanting songs, and clutches their souls with its acquisitive hands.

9 | INSURANCE
Unjust Profits
of Justice

If on Sunday morning the paperboy slips and falls on Harvey Householder's front steps, Harvey will be protected by his homeowner's policy.

And if, on the same Sunday morning, Harvey's automatic coffeepot explodes in his face, the manufacturer will be covered by its liability policy for Harvey's damages.

If Harvey survives the risks of coffee making and goes skiing, he will be covered with his own medical insurance; and the ski-lift operation will be protected from liability should Harvey be run over by a company snowcat as it grooms the slopes.

If the ambulance driver who takes Harvey to the hospital is drunk and runs into an oncoming car, the owners of the ambulance will be protected against the suits of both Harvey and the victims in the other car, and the hospital will be protected by its own insurance—even if in the emergency room he is treated for hives rather than for the internal injuries he suffered in his accidents.

Thereafter, should the attending physician conclude that it is not hives but heartache from which Harvey suffers, the doctor will be shielded from financial loss by his malpractice insurance.

When the undertaker buries Harvey in the wrong grave and his remains are lost to his loved ones, there will, of course, be insurance to protect the funeral parlor, and later, when the county commissioners construct a highway through Harvey's corner of the cemetery, the commissioners themselves will be protected by an insurance policy that saves public officials from personal responsibility.

Insurance has become as much a necessity in America as food and shelter. We dare not rest our heads in slumber, or, upon awakening, venture forth in the ordinary course of our lives without being snugly encased within the womb of modern insurance. Although most hospitals will not permit physicians to practice unless they are insured, a few brave doctors have elected to go "bare," as they like to call it. This disparate lot do not observe their patients for the ominous signs and symptoms of disease but, instead, for the first hint that these patients will name them in a malpractice suit. In America, peace of mind has also become a commodity, and it carries a very high price tag.

No one escapes the insurance company. It prods at our most tender spots, at our deepest terror. It reminds us that death and destruction are lurking just around the corner. It pokes at the very heart of our neurosis—that we will be victimized and dragged into court and held up publicly in infamy and cast into bankruptcy—or worse. Sensitive to our vulnerability, the industry fashions its product against both our fear of life and our fear of death, and godlike, it demands our tithing—that we pay our premiums promptly no matter how outrageous the price—failing which we will surely be condemned to dark and dreadful places.

The insurance company is the God of Money.

But the God of Money is not a benevolent god. It does not love us. It loves only its dollars, and it will hire the best lawyers in the land to keep them. When, as a result of the negligence of the airlines, a husband is killed in a plane crash, the insurance-company lawyers will fight to prevent the widow and children from receiving a just award, not because they despise widows and children, but because these lawyers are devoted to the cause of money. They are pledged to it with the fervor of Christian soldiers, and will fight for the insurance company's money as if their own lives depended on it. Indeed, they do, for if the lawyers lose too much of the company's money, the company will soon hire others to defend them. There are no moral constraints binding these lawyers, for to most, the very marrow of morality has become money. The insurance-company lawyers come to court not to ascertain the truth or to search for justice, but to fight for money, and they will do whatever is necessary to keep it. They will not bribe a juror or buy off a judge, but they will dig up any skeleton and make any argument, fair or not, so long as it is likely to influence the jurors. They will not offer perjured testimony, but most will mislead the jury if they can and most will cast the widow as some money-hungry hag offering up her dead husband for filthy lucre.

Such lawyers are not immoral. To the contrary, they faithfully reflect the souls of their clients. Insurance companies themselves are committed to the notion that it is better to pay unreasonable sums to attorneys to fight just claims than to pay reasonable sums for their settlement. Last year, the principal insurer of the doctors in Wyoming admitted it was not the sums paid to patients injured by doctors that hurt the company's profits, but the fees it was paying to its own attorneys to fight these victims' claims. Overall, the insurance industry profits from litigation. Often it can force frightened people in desperate need to take a pittance. Often its lawyers can accomplish a "good result," as they like to call it, which means they have persuaded the jury to award a sum substantially less than the injured plaintiff deserved. Often the company lawyers, skilled in every art of persuasion and supported with the best experts money can buy, can defeat just claims altogether, an "exceptional result."

We are told that in America the jury will deliver us justice. But how can the jury do justice when it is never permitted to know all the facts? No court will permit your attorney to inform the jury that the driver who ran you down, that nice old man sitting over there in his shabby suit looking poor and scared, is insured to the eyeballs, and that his attorney, one of the best defense lawyers around, was hired by the insurance company. No court will permit your attorney or anyone else to inform the jury that if they find for you, that nice old man over there, who, incidentally, was drunk, won't have to pay the jury's verdict, but that every penny of it will come from the bounteous coffers of the insurance company. It is an unconscionable farce that the largest, most powerful corporations known to civilization are permitted to masquerade as people and lead juries to assume that the person in court, the sad and the pitiful, will have to pay the jury's award. As every experienced attorney can attest, many a just case has been lost when juries have mistakenly believed that the person sued would have to personally pay the jury's verdict. Too often, the jury's compassion for *human beings* only saves the nonhuman—the insurance company—its money.

Recently, I witnessed a case in which a shop foreman failed to see to the proper repair of the brakes on a truck that was scheduled for a steep mountain run, and later, on the treacherous road, the truck went out of control, killing the driver. His widow brought suit on behalf of herself and her children, but under Wyoming's Workers' Compensation Act she was prohibited from suing the trucking company that had employed her husband. However, the shop foreman himself could be sued for "culpable negligence," as that phrase is technically defined in the law. Despite a clear case, the jury refused to find for the widow, not because the shop foreman hadn't been negligent, but because the jurors mistakenly believed that if they found him guilty, their verdict would bankrupt the poor man, who had a wife and kids of his own. He was, of course, insured for millions under the company's policy. But the jury was never provided honest answers to honest questions like, "How can this working man with a family of his own, who, himself, is obviously just getting by, pay any sum to this widow and children, much less the hundreds of thousands to which they are entitled?" Maybe, the jurors reasoned, "we should leave well enough alone. Maybe, in the end, we might just make things worse." From the standpoint of the deserving widow and her children, the bitter irony of the case was the jurors were guided by their compassion for the human issues, while the insurance company, which cared only for its money, played upon the jury's sympathy and was thereby able to preserve its profits.

While justice cannot be measured by the size of the defendant's pocketbook, the ability of the defendant to pay is as relevant to justice as is the victim's requirement for compensation. Suppose that an employee of the First Interstate Bank, while on an errand for the bank, was inattentively reading the racing form while driving, and his car veered to the wrong side of the road, where he ran into the plaintiff. After enduring serious surgery and two years of resultant pain, the plaintiff made a reasonable recovery. The jury calculates the plaintiff's damages (including his loss of earnings and medical expenses that exceeded $100,000) at a total of $200,000. Under these circumstances, where the bank has adequate resources, all of the plaintiff's damages should, in justice, be paid. But what if the negligent driver was a farmer whose attention was diverted when he saw one of his cows caught in the fence? True, he was on the wrong side of the road when the accident happened and admittedly was responsible for the wreck, but he has only $100,000 in insurance and $100,000 equity in his farm. If the plaintiff receives full justice from the farmer, the latter will lose his farm, and his family, who was innocent of any wrong, will be turned out on the street. On the other hand, full justice from the bank means the entry of a barely discernible figure on its profit-and-loss statement along with its write-offs of hundreds of millions in loans to Brazil. As a consequence of providing full justice to the injured plaintiff, the farmer must seek other employment—say, as a mechanic. In that line of work, he will be lucky to put food on the table, much less save enough to ever get back on the farm again. The jury's verdict sentences the farmer to leave his home, the land, and for the rest of his life to work in a fume-filled garage, while the jury's verdict against the bank will hardly be noticed at the bottom line. If the jury is to follow the court's instruction to render justice to *both* parties in the case, it must consider the ability of the parties to pay, lest that which is just compensation in one case becomes an unjust life's sentence in another.

Ceaselessly, we hear the piteous cry of the insurance industry charging that the injured present their crippled bodies and grieving hearts to gullible juries, plunk at the jurors' heartstrings, and rob the companies blind. My experience is to the contrary. Juries try very hard to be just. They are as repelled by money-grabbing, opportunistic plaintiffs as by reckless, gluttonous corporations. If a truck ran into the insurance company's office building in Boston, causing serious damage to its structure, no one would claim that the insurance company was soliciting the jury's sympathy when it displayed its cracked walls and crumbling foundations, nor would anyone criticize the company for seeking restitution for every penny of its loss. But when an injured workman comes into court displaying his stumps to the jury, or a mother holds up her maimed child in order that the jurors may assess the damages, both will be accused of a calculated attempt to inflame the passions of the jury. Like the damaged office building, the life of an injured person must be rebuilt brick by brick, often at great expense. Still, when the mother comes to court to get justice for her innocent child who was sentenced to life imprisonment in a spastic body as a result of the doctor's negligence at childbirth, she will likely be accused of being a greedy wench should she demand that the doctor pay every penny of her child's damages, including a sum for the last, agonizing spastic cramp he will likely suffer seventy years later as an old man. Her claim will be for millions. Yet who can rightfully argue that the child, whose life expectancy is in excess of seventy years, and whose pain and disability will span his entire lifetime, is not worth as much consideration as the insurance company whose office building has a similar expected life? If the jurors were told there was insurance, so the argument goes, such knowledge might improperly influence them to award a huge sum for the injured child. The opposite is more often true. Despite today's sophisticated jurors, the full justice they might otherwise award a deserving party is almost always adversely affected when the insurance company is permitted to hide behind a human being.

The law that permits insurance companies to sneak anonymously into the courtroom, and there, disguised as living persons, to wage their battles against the injured is a form of fraud founded on the law's congenital distrust of juries and argues that this capricious body is likely to deliver justice only if it is under the complete dominance of the court. Judges, bound by precedent and often by statute, protect mature, responsible jurors from the whole truth like a Victorian father shielding his children from the facts of life. Today, should a lawyer for an injured person even intimate the truth to the jury that the defendant is covered by insurance, the judge will likely declare a mistrial at the expense of the offending lawyer, and he may even hold the lawyer in contempt of court. The abominable word *insurance* must never escape the lips of the injured. He must never mention the threatening letters he received from the adjuster or tell the jury about the time the adjuster knocked on his door and told him in his own living room that if he took his case to court, the company would see him in hell before he got a nickel. While the law demands that the witnesses tell "the truth, the whole truth and nothing but the truth," it punishes them if they do. I don't argue against ruling out irrelevant evidence or prejudicial testimony that is intended to defeat justice. I argue that today's juries are composed of responsible, adult citizens who can be trusted to make a just decision if they are provided all of the relevant facts, and that the defendant's ability to pay is always an essential consideration. To hide the truth concerning the defendant's ability to pay stacks the deck for the insurance company that hides its wealth and its identity behind the human face of the defendant it insures.

Whenever we seek justice, be it for an injury to our bodies, our minds, or our good names, be it for the wrongful death of a loved one or for the injury of our child, the suit will likely be defended by the best lawyers the insurance company can hire. As the cases are finally settled by agreement, a jury's verdict, or the appellate court's decision, the issue is never justice. *Money*, not the restoration of a healthy body, not relief from pain, is all the insurance industry has to offer. *Money*, not the return of a husband to a grieving widow, not retribution or revenge, is the only form of justice the insurance company can provide. The industry carries no reserve on its books for sorrow or suffering or humiliation or disgrace except in *money*. As almighty as they are, the companies can only fondle their figures and make their computations, invest their policyholders' premiums and preserve—at whatever cost—their profit. Is it a surprise then, that in a system dominated by insurance, justice, too, has become a commodity—something cold and bloodless expressed exclusively in dollars?

The civil courts of America are no longer places where citizens come to settle their disputes. As insurance has become the voodoo of our culture—the instrument by which we are protected from all nature of evil—so an insidious, mostly unnoticed transformation has occurred in our courts. Today, our temples of justice are a network of administrative machines, equipped and staffed with hundreds of thousands of secretaries, clerks, bailiffs, and judges, who, at the sole expense of the taxpayers, labor to process the millions of claims that constitute the annual business of the insurance industry. The people furnish this machinery for the use and benefit of the industry—for the money-changers in the temple—most of whom contribute little to the communities in return. Instead, billions in premium dollars flow out of our towns and cities each year to distant centers where the great companies maintain their offices. There the wealth accumulates and overflows. There the companies merge and take each other over and buy banks and buildings and land. There sits Prudential, for example, owning two hundred office buildings, five hundred industrial buildings, seventy-five hotels, fifty shopping centers, fifty-five residential buildings, and six hundred thousand acres of prime American farm land.

In its more mathematical aspects, insurance operates on the same principle as the gambling business in Las Vegas, where the house sets the slots to keep all but a paltry percentage that will be paid to the players. In the delivery of justice, the insurance industry makes similar computations and adjustments in rates and payouts. But as in Las Vegas, the players are provided a different vision. They never see the casinos' mechanics manipulating the machines to guarantee that most of the players will lose. Instead, everywhere we look, people are pulling away on handles to which they are affixed, and every once in a while we hear the jackpot bell go off and the lights flash, and we see some little guy hollering and jumping hysterically up and down in front of a machine that is regurgitating dollars. The fantasy Las Vegas provides us confirms the notion that people win big at the casinos. Similarly, when we read of those sensational verdicts in the evening newspaper, we tend to believe that not only does the system deliver justice, if anything, it has gone wild, and momentarily some irresponsible jury somewhere is likely to render a million-dollar verdict for a sprained thumb. As in Las Vegas, we never see the great mute herd trudging homeward with their pockets empty. All gaming systems, whether conducted in the casinos or the courts, are founded on the myth of winning and require a jackpot. It is an illusion that allows the house to continue to build its empire on one simple principle—that most of the people lose most of the time.

I have spent many years laboring in the justice system knowing full well how it operates. I have spoken of it many times to my brothers and sisters of the bar. Yet we hide these simple truths from the people, not out of malicious intent, but because we love the law and are taught to respect it, and we repeat the gospel over and over— to our clients, to ourselves, until it has become the liturgy of our lives—that the system may not be perfect, but it is the best damned system known to man. We are patriotic. We sanctify the Constitution. We are Americans and are proud of our country, often with just cause. Yet after having fought and bled a lifetime in the courts for thousands of clients, I hold in serious doubt my own contribution to mankind. Perhaps I have obtained as many multimillion-dollar verdicts for those I have represented as any lawyer. I should be proud of that. But in the larger view, I have done little for the human condition by bringing home the jackpots. Instead, I have played straight into the hands of the house. The jackpot bell goes off. I provide the example of the country lawyer who has won big for the ordinary person. I supply a model for young lawyers to do the same, and I prove once more that the system is, indeed, working for the people. Those of us who represent the people often validate the fears of the public—that smooth-talking lawyers are bamboozling gullible juries into awarding ludicrous verdicts for undeserving litigants, and to protect themselves from being victimized, people must buy more and more insurance at higher and higher premiums. In the end, my life in court may have been spent as much in the service of the insurance companies as in the service of the people. That is a damnable legacy for any lawyer.

When the insurance industry goes into one of its normal cyclical loss periods, as it does about every tenth year, the industry, like Chicken Little when the acorn fell on his head, declares a crisis. It raises hell across the land. It cancels the policies of our day-care centers, and jacks up the rates on obstetricians so they can no longer afford insurance. Mothers can't find doctors willing to deliver their babies. Parks are closed because the companies have canceled the city's liability policy, and when the people panic, the insurance companies point to those big awards. It's the greedy lawyers representing their greedy clients! Soon waves of lobbyists descend on our legislatures, persuading them to take away more and more of our rights, to put caps on the amounts juries can award, and to limit contingency fees so that people cannot hire skilled lawyers to fight for them. I see well-meaning legislators across the land passing laws against themselves as if the victim will always be someone else. It will never be them or their loved ones who will be killed or injured or charged with a crime. The lawyers they cripple with restrictive legislation will never be their lawyers, for as they see it, the only persons who hire attorneys and sue are the greedy, the abstract "them," who wrangle for dollars in those infamous courts. But one day one of their sons or daughters will lie paralyzed from the neck down in a hospital somewhere, and an insurance adjuster will be knocking at the door, and then they, too, will have paid their stakes to play in the justice game.

These so-called insurance crises in America are costing us like hell. We pay our insurance premiums before we buy our groceries and send the kids to college, and when, in the panic of the latest crisis, the cost of insurance is jacked up again, we retch and we cry, but we pay. Yet the price is more dear than money. We pay by sacrificing our sacred rights. We are so easily led to pernicious solutions. We are, of course, a trusting people. We believe what we hear on the evening news and read in the morning paper. But the selected facts and partial truths and sometimes the whole falsehoods we take as the whole truth are supplied by the insurance industry. No coalition of consumers sponsor Dan Rather, who tells us about juries gone haywire and premiums that skyrocket to meet the costs. No workers' groups buy full-page ads in *Time* magazine from which we learn that insurance companies are refusing to insure us, that we are being left vulnerable because of an alleged crisis—one they say *we* have caused.

We, of course, are not told certain relevant, underlying facts—for instance, that the insurance business is exorbitantly lucrative. International Telephone and Telegraph owns twenty-five insurance companies. Gulf and Western owns eighteen, and Teledyne, fifteen. America's major corporations seem to lust for them. Beatrice Foods owns four; Control Data, fourteen. American Express owns Fireman's Fund. General Motors and General Electric both own insurance companies. Sears has earned more from Allstate than from its retail stores. Almost five thousand insurance companies are domiciled in this country alone, with reported assets approaching a trillion dollars, assets greater than the combined worth of the nation's fifty largest industrial corporations. The reported assets underlying State Farm Mutual Automobile Insurance Company alone are larger than those of either Citicorp or Bank of America, and double those of Chase Manhattan. In America, the business of insurance occupies the very heart of the corporate state.

Like the irresistible force of a glacier, the industry has carved out huge immunities for itself in Congress, and is this country's *only* major industry not subject to the nation's antitrust laws. Moreover, in 1980, the full Senate—77 to 13—passed a bill prohibiting the Federal Trade Commission from even investigating or reporting on the insurance business. How can this happen in America, where the people supposedly control their government? One might better ask, What is the power of a trillion-dollar industry? Or what is the power of sixty-six political action committees (PACs) that have been organized in the fire, marine, and casualty segment of the insurance industry, "committees" with a single purpose—to legally deliver money to so-called "deserving candidates" who understand the problems of the insurance industry better than the problems of the people who elect them. These insurance PACs pay millions every year into the campaign coffers of our representatives so that today the industry remains as free to squeeze and extort the helpless public as any of the robber barons of old. McDonald's and General Motors and USX and IBM are required by law to conduct their businesses in accordance with the rules of the game. But not this country's insurance companies. They are free to roll across America, state at a time, profession at a time, without the slightest fear of the antitrust laws that were designed to protect us. Unrestrained, the insurance companies conspire, combine, cancel policies, close businesses, raise rates, threaten, manipulate, set doctors against lawyers and citizens against themselves, and drive terror into the hearts of the people, so that finally, in panic, the people run hell-bent to their legislatures demanding that our laws, even our constitutions, be amended in whatever way the industry demands—and their demands are always the same—that the people give up more and more of their rights.

In 1984, another of these "insurance crises" erupted across the land during a typical bottom-of-the-cycle year for insurance profit. Before then, in the mid-1970's, we had been subjected to a similar "crisis" when the insurance industry had backed the nation up against the wall demanding that "adjustments" be made in the justice machine. The *Washington Post* editorialized in retrospect: "But look at what happened: [the industry's] profits skyrocketed to all-time record levels. Insurers learned that the state regulators would, during the panic, give away the store in rate increases. Insurers also learned that state legislators would act to reduce victims' rights. . . . Where will this raid on victims' rights end?"

One insurance expert, recently testifying before the Commissioner's Special Task Force on Property-Casualty Insurance, said of the current "crisis," "If premiums had been 5 percent higher, they would have earned a rate of return on net worth of about 13 percent." A 5 percent premium shortfall is hardly a national emergency. Yet at the same time, there were utterly unjustified 70 percent increases for ob-gyn physicians in Maryland, and 300 percent to 900 percent increases in lawyer and architect malpractice insurance premiums around the country. Day-care centers suffered increases of 200 percent to 500 percent, if they could even get insurance. Many couldn't. And there were 300 percent to 1,000 percent increases for public transit authorities. The list of the industry's victims includes almost every American. Yet the National Insurance Consumer Organization says that the industry's profits in 1985 were $5 billion. By 1987, the General Accounting Office found the insurance companies had profits of $8 billion, with a cumulative rate of return of 13.4 percent.

Wall Street knows what's going on. Property-casualty stocks have soared to record highs, more than doubling the explosion enjoyed by the Dow-Jones Industrial Averages in 1985. Best's Property-Casualty Stock Index was up by 44 percent compared with a 20 percent increase in the Dow-Jones Industrials. By the first quarter of 1986, property-casualty insurance profits had risen by $2.11 billion, or 1,227 percent. Admitted net profit for the first half of 1986, during the height of the "crisis," was $5.7 billion, up from $930 million the year before. According to the General Accounting Office, between 1976 and 1985 the property-casualty companies had net gains of $75.2 billion, on which not a single penny of federal income tax was paid.

Despite such poignant numbers, the insurance companies launched a multimillion-dollar propaganda blitz to convince the American public that those damnable ambulance chasers, the people's lawyers, were causing premiums to balloon from the outrageous awards they talked juries into and, of course, from their exorbitant contingency fees. The companies demanded "tort reform" to stem the crisis, and the people dutifully responded by slashing the traditional rights of the citizen and adding new restrictions and limitations that would presumably cure the crisis. In the process, the people often gelded themselves. They set limits on the amount they could recover, no matter how severe their injuries. They passed legislation that often made it impossible for ordinary citizens to sue for their injuries. As we already know, if the insurance company's building was damaged through the negligence of another, the company could recover for *all* of its losses against the guilty party, but under "tort reform" the amount a jury might award was capped so that many of the injured could recover only part of their losses. In some states, claims for pain and suffering were outlawed entirely or severely limited. In others, patients could sue their doctors for no more than a stated sum, often making it impractical to proceed in such costly litigation at all, despite the severity of the person's injury. In our office, we have been required to turn down many a deserving case for no better reason than the impossible economics of the lawsuit. Elsewhere, contingency fees were so restricted that attorneys could not afford to take a victim's case. Statutes of limitations were severely shortened so that people's claims were barred, sometimes before the injured persons had recovered sufficiently to discover the facts surrounding their own cases.

The press, often unwittingly, joined in the conspiracy. Major national publications hysterically reported stories of sensational jury awards, but usually ignored the masses of worthy cases that never reached the courts. Professor Marc Galanter of the University of Wisconsin, whose work was recently described in *The Wall Street Journal* as a "masterpiece in the field of social research on law," confirms that only a very small fraction of injured Americans ever get to the courtroom, and according to Jury Verdict Research, whose figures are often quoted by proponents of "tort reform" to prove the "legal crisis," only about half of those who obtain jury verdicts ever receive compensation. Neither does the media report the hundreds of thousands of cases settled out of court in which victims are forced, by unequal economic circumstance, to accept whatever token of justice they are offered. Timely and objective studies of medical malpractice cases are rare. However, several years ago, researchers following six thousand cases found that 43 percent of the malpractice suits filed were dropped without any payment. Fifty percent were settled out of court, with an average payment of $26,000. Only 7 percent went to trial, and once in court the victim was successful in winning only one in four, the average award being $102,000.16, a sum less than is often spent in such litigation on the costs alone. In short, we never hear the rest of the story.

Even if we were to conclude that it is in some way desirable to bargain away our rights for cheaper insurance, there is convincing evidence that "tort reform" does not lower insurance premiums. Two leading property-casualty companies—Aetna Casualty and Surety Company, and St. Paul Marine Insurance Company—recently notified the Florida Insurance Commissioner that even extensive "tort reforms" will not reduce insurance rates. In Wyoming, the president of a company that insures most of our doctors testified that if every "tort reform" the industry requested were enacted immediately, the company still would not guarantee our doctors continued insurance. In Pennsylvania, a law immunizing all municipalities from most kinds of suits and limiting liability to $500,000 was passed. Yet cities and towns in that state are still having their insurance canceled. A recent national study of the effectiveness of "tort reforms" showed that limits imposed on the amount of money a citizen might recover for pain and suffering in medical malpractice cases has had no statistically measurable impact on premiums. In Ontario, most of the "reforms" sought by the insurance industry have been enacted, including caps on awards for pain and suffering, restrictions on punitive damages, and a prohibition of contingency fees. Moreover, in Ontario, an unsuccessful plaintiff must pay the defendant's costs, and there is no constitutional right to a trial by jury, so that most cases are heard by judges. Still, in that Canadian province the insurance industry has raised premiums by 400 percent or more for many of its customers, has canceled coverage in midterm, and refused to provide coverage for some businesses at any price. The insurers have gone on treating their customers like some poor grocer on the Lower East Side who gets a gun put to his temple whenever a hoodlum selling "protection" wants more money. Yet a recent survey by the National Insurance Consumer Organization shows that the availability of insurance is increasing, even substantially, in some states where "tort reforms" have not been enacted. Simply put, the insurance industry has created the crisis and manipulated the people as it deemed necessary to increase its profits.

It has become faddish to join in the hue and cry against lawyers, especially those who accept cases on a contingency-fee basis for people who can't otherwise afford representation. Napoleon Bonaparte foresaw the value of the contingency fee. He said, "I wanted to make it a law that only those lawyers and attorneys should receive fees who had won their cases. How much litigation would have been prevented by such a measure." Sometimes I wonder if we would be better served if doctors charged us only when we are kept in good health and enjoy cures for our ailments. It is, of course, the American Medical Association that has led the pack against the lawyers' contingency fee—in fact, the only vehicle by which the average American can get to court. Doctors did so hoping to stem their patients' suits against them. That profession has the ability to make the most sophisticated kinds of diagnoses, but its collective intelligence has yet to discover an obvious truth—that attacking lawyers will not cure malpractice. Nor will limiting the rights of the people doctors injure cure the negligence of the medical profession. The only cure for malpractice is careful, competent, caring doctors. The alliance between America's insurance companies and her doctors makes an interesting spectacle—the doctors clinging to the insurance industry like frightened children, and the companies, in turn, with their arms around the doctors and their corporate hands wedged deep in the doctors' pockets. So joined, they march into battle against the people and the people's lawyers—a war waged not against malpractice, not against the needless injury of citizens, but against the right of citizens to get justice when they are wrongfully injured, maimed, or killed. In essence, the companies have convinced doctors that it is appropriate to further injure their already injured patients by limiting their rights to full justice.

Doctors and lawyers should join together to see that people receive adequate medical treatment, that the incompetent and the unethical are weeded out of both professions, and that the victims be given a fair chance at full justice. Doctors and lawyers should join together to bring the insurance industry under control so that these damnable civil wars between two honorable professions whose only reason for existence is to serve the people can no longer be fomented by the insurance industry for its private gain.

In the meantime, the people of America, not understanding the huge profits the insurance industry enjoys when jury awards are reduced even a percentage point or two, are being systematically brainwashed against the only justice system they have. We have been told that we will have to pay for these awards ourselves, through increased premiums. The industry plays on *our* emotions, spending millions for full-page ads in national magazines. A typical headline reads: THE LAWSUIT CRISIS IS BAD FOR BABIES. We see a doctor tenderly holding a newborn. The accompanying text provides the following information:

> A medical survey shows one out of every nine obstetricians in America has stopped delivering babies. Expectant mothers have had to find new doctors. In some rural areas, women have had to travel elsewhere to give birth. How did this happen?

The ads go on to say that, as good citizens (and we are all good citizens), we must stop these lawsuits with "tort reform."

Propaganda. Daily the public has been ruthlessly bombarded with propaganda against the American system of justice. In fact, it is a money system of justice almost entirely in the hands of the insurance industry. Millions have been spent on television and in the print media as part of the most pernicious campaign of modern times by an American industry against its own citizens. Victims of such propaganda, large numbers of well-meaning citizens were convinced they must go to war against themselves. Nurtured on the industry's contaminated word, Americans began to see the world through the eyes of the insurance adjuster instead of their own. It was an evil world out there, one populated by a hoglike species that will eat its own young for a dollar, a species that does not speak the truth or engage in reason because it speaks only through bloodsucking lawyers. And when citizens are called to jury service, most will not forget.

The industry's propaganda has influenced every potential juror in this country. If we attorneys who represented victims did what the insurance companies have done to influence jurors against deserving claimants, we would be thrown in prison for jury tampering. Suppose before my next trial began, I knocked on the door of every prospective juror in town to explain one simple truth: that the person my client was suing—say, the schoolteacher down the block who ran the stoplight and broke my client's back—was fully insured. Suppose I sat down in the juror's kitchen and argued to him that justice would best be served if he returned a full and fair amount for my client's injuries? The insurance company's attorney would have my license to practice law before the sun set. But through a national media blitz, the insurance industry has spoken repeatedly to every man and woman in America who will ever serve on a jury. Large jury awards are making a mockery of the justice system, we are told. You, the citizen, must pay for these awards in increased premiums, their advertisements say. As responsible citizens, you have the duty to, and can, avert these insurance crises.

The effects of insurance propaganda are already being felt by victims across the land whose just cases are, for the first time, being systematically rejected by their own neighbors. It is too early for meaningful statistics, but insurance adjusters are more arrogant than ever before. Today, I hear them laughing at reasonable demands they would have previously paid. One claimsman from New Mexico told me recently, "We used to be afraid of the juries. But not now. Jurors are on our side." In Oregon, a leading plaintiff's attorney told me he could no longer win a trial for a malpractice victim, no matter how just the case. "The people are being taught to distrust each other," he said. Other trial lawyers around the nation have told me that even in the strongest of cases lawyers are settling for pennies on the dollar, because they are afraid of today's juries. Some even say they get better justice from judges. Lawyers are unanimous that the reason for this sudden turnaround in the attitude of jurors against their neighbors is the jurors' reaction to the so-called "lawsuit crisis" in exactly the way Madison Avenue intended.

We have been told that Americans are the most litigious people in the world. Yet, per capita, there are no more suits today than there were in 1959, and the amount of the mean verdict, $8,000, has remained nearly constant since that year after adjustments for inflation have been calculated. People sue not because they are greedy or mean, but because they believe they have been wronged. That people sue establishes that our democratic institutions are still functional. But like rabbits in a cage that have been poked and prodded with sharp sticks until they are ready to bite at anything, we now attack our rights, our lawyers—even ourselves. The idea that we must respond to the insurance industry's demand for profit by abandoning our long-established legal guarantees not only begins to seem reasonable, it seems imperative.

Of course, the fifty states have regulatory agencies to police the insurance industry, but independent studies of these agencies are unanimous in showing that most states have failed to put meaningful controls on the industry. One government agency reports that 50 percent of the states' regulators were hired from the industry itself, and another 50 percent went back to the industry after having acted as the regulator—the classic "revolving door." When, in Wyoming, the insurance commissioner called for just rates, the industry threatened to withdraw from the state altogether, and pressured the state's legislators to restructure the insurance department. As a result, that agency, like those in most other states, is now essentially powerless to enforce any meaningful regulations to protect the people; it protects, instead, the industry it was originally organized to regulate.

But the final triumph in the industry's war of propaganda against the people has been to teach them to despise their own champions. How can people hope to prevent their final domination by corporate America if they reject their own warriors? The American trial lawyer remains the single remaining barrier standing between the average citizen and his total subjugation by the corporate oligarchy. Still, we believe what we are told—that our own lawyers are not to be trusted, that they are avaricious villains, feeding on the miseries of the innocent flock, that they are the cause, not the cure, of most injustices in America. Yet the civil suit brought by people's lawyers remains the only effective weapon to protect the people against the recklessness and the excesses of the corporate state. The prospect of paying large damage awards tends to deter manufacturers, drug companies, builders, doctors—and lawyers, too—from pursuing practices that harm innocent people. The right of the injured citizen to sue has protected untold thousands from further injuries and death by the Dalkon Shield, from death by burning in the Ford Pinto, and the horrors of lung cancer brought on by asbestos poisoning. Today, tens of millions of Americans are less likely to be injured because of the tort system that corporate America is now bent on "re-forming."

"Reform" must never lessen the rights of a free people, but should eliminate the wrongs committed against them. Better societies are built by reforming the wrongdoers, not by punishing the victims. Yet the ghastly trick has been to convince us that we can preserve our rights by giving them up. The sting has been to so divert our eyes and muddle our minds that we have finally come to pay tribute to the money-changers in the temple.

10 | CORPORATE CRIME

Profits of Injustice

Corporate crime is an institution in America, a phenomenon of the marketplace that piles up like manure in the horse corral. But we judge corporate conduct and human conduct by dual standards. When our neighbor kills another, the maximum punishment may be leveled against him. But what of the crimes of corporate America? Our outrage is reserved for the misdeeds of our own species, while we accept corporate crime like the weather, like some pollution that contaminates an environment we are powerless to control. Besides, there are no prisons for corporations. No electric chairs, no lethal injections.

One of the most staggering statistics to be revealed in modern times is that every year the dollar cost of corporate crime to America, as estimated by the Bureau of National Affairs, is over *ten times* greater than the combined larcenies, robberies, burglaries, and auto thefts committed by individuals. One in five of America's five hundred largest corporations has been convicted of at least one major crime or has paid civil penalties for serious misbehavior. Amitai Etzioni, professor of sociology at George Washington University, recently concluded that in the last ten years approximately two-thirds of America's largest corporations have been involved in some form of illegal behavior. A distinguished study completed ten years ago with the assistance of the Department of Justice reviewed the criminal administrative action brought by 25 federal agencies against the 477 largest publicly owned manufacturing companies in the United States: 60 percent of America's biggest and best had been filed against at least once; 42 percent had been charged with more than one violation, and 25 percent had been charged with "multiple cases of non-minor violations." Even *Fortune* admits from its own studies of 1,043 major corporations that 11 percent committed at least one major crime since 1970, leading the magazine to blandly conclude that "a surprising number of [major U.S. corporations] have been involved in blatant illegalities." If such an epidemic of crime persisted among the general population, we would call out the National Guard and declare martial law. But how can our uppermost tier go so berserk? Is some odd plague attacking only the blue bloods of America?

What if one in four of the leading citizens in every community in America were convicted felons? What if these citizens were quietly protected, even aided and abetted, by our elected officials? What if our courts were gentle on these offenders, their crimes handled by judicial taps on the wrist instead of by appropriate fines and imprisonment? What if evidence concerning these felons' crimes were routinely suppressed? What if the offenders were not Mafia bosses and dope peddlers but men and women we had been taught to respect because they represent America's aristocracy, those who have been mollycoddled in the elitist schools of the nation—the best of Harvard Business School, the best bred, the best dressed, the best maintained, the best connected, the best—the very best?

This raging epidemic of corporate crime is nothing new. Jefferson understood the problem: "Money," he said, "not morality, is the principle of commercial nations." Over forty years ago, information began to reach Johns Manville's top executives through its medical department implicating asbestos inhalation as the cause of lung cancer, a crippling lung disorder called asbestosis, and mesothelioma, an invariably fatal disease. Johns Manville suppressed research on the evidence and concealed essential information from its workers. In 1976, Manville's medical director, Kenneth W. Smith, was asked during testimony whether he had ever advised Manville to place warning labels on its asbestos products. His reply: "The company had to take into consideration the effects of everything they did, and if the applications of a caution label identifying a product as hazardous would cut out sales, there would be serious financial implications." Dr. Irving Selikoff, of the Mount Sinai School of Medicine in New York City, who has done "pathbreaking work" linking asbestos to cancer and asbestosis, estimates that within the next thirty years, 240,000 of the million who worked with asbestos will die from asbestos-related cancer—that's about one every hour.

More recently, the First National Bank of Boston pled guilty to laundering satchels of twenty-dollar bills totaling $1.3 billion in a transaction that included a group associated with organized crime. Thousands of bags of bills passed through the doors of the bank before the scheme was uncovered. E. F. Hutton & Company, that very large, supposedly very proper corporation that so fiercely and perpetually lauds its own ethics, recently pled guilty to two thousand counts of wire and mail fraud after having systematically bilked four hundred banks by drawing against nonexistent or uncollected funds in an effort to enjoy interest-free use of the money. "If this were a little guy, he'd be jailed," says Helen Scott, a securities-law professor at New York University Law School. "He'd be barred from the business for years, if not life." But no such sanctions were leveled against Hutton. Alpha Industries, a Massachusetts microwave manufacturer, paid $57,000 to a Raytheon manager, supposedly for a market report, but air force investigators charged that the transaction was a shenanigan to cover a bribe for subcontracts that the Raytheon manager supervised. The company was indicted for bribery, and its contracts were suspended. In 1984 alone, the Pentagon suspended 453 other companies for violating procurement regulations.

Ford Motor Company knew that, because of the location of the gas tank on its Pinto, even in low-speed, rear-end collisions, the tank could rupture, spewing gasoline and risking the death by fire of its occupants. They put it on the market anyway. A couple of years later, as part of a campaign against certain forthcoming federal regulations, the company applied a cost-benefit analysis to another safety problem found in U.S. cars and trucks that pit the cost of making a safer car *against the cost of paying for the lives lost!* (One measure cost only $11 per car.) This procedure would require Ford to view innocent American men and women and their families as commodities, something disposable in the course of commerce.

The National Highway Traffic Safety Administration had already made its own calculations: The damages for death averaged $173,300 per person. Add average medical costs of $1,125 and property damages of $1,500, insurance administration of $4,700, legal and court costs of $3,000, employer losses of $1,000, and the sum of $10,000 juries might award for the victim's pain and suffering. Finally, put in $900 for the funeral bill and $5,200 for "other costs." The "per fatality" damages averaged $200,725. Of course, some of the best lawyers in America would be called upon to represent Ford in these cases, and the entire resources of Ford would be available to the defense, billions against the meager resources an average American family and their hometown lawyer might scrape up for the battle.

A Ford Motor Company memo revealed that if the Pinto were sold without the $11 safety feature, an estimated 2,100 cars would burn every year, 180 people would be injured, and another 180 would burn to death. Taking the government's figure of approximately $200,000 and estimating the survivors' medical bills at $67,000 and a lost vehicle at $700 (presumably the depreciated value of an older Pinto less salvage value), and further given the market of 11 million cars and 1.5 million light trucks every year, the company could then draw up the following balance sheet:

BENEFITS *Money Spent for Safer Car*	COSTS *Money Spent on Safety*
180 deaths × $200,000 180 injuries × $67,000 2,100 vehicles × $700	11 million cars × $11 1.5 million trucks × $11
$49.5 million	$137.5 million

By putting its cars and trucks on the market without the $11 safety device, Ford, according to these figures, saved $88 million. Between 1971, when the Pinto was introduced, and 1977, an estimated five hundred men, women, and children burned to death in Pinto crashes.

Ford was later acquitted of the criminal charges brought against it, but troublesome questions won't stay buried. Why is Ford Motor Company, which dumped millions into its defense—or the Mafia killer, for that matter—entitled to better justice than the black in the ghetto who is charged with petty theft? Why is IBM, suffering from an insatiable thirst for profit, entitled to a better defense in the antitrust suit brought against it than the impecunious alcoholic who breaks into the local liquor store to quench his habit? And if, indeed, we assume that Ford reaped its $11 profit per car in exchange for the torching of 180 people a year, isn't this in the same league as the most heinous murders committed by the felons on death row? Why are the corporations in Cleveland that pollute the Cuyahoga River until it actually bursts into flame lesser criminals than the thug who steals a car or a bicycle? These corporate polluters and poisoners who destroy the earth and knowingly inflict incalculable misery and death on human beings in search of their private profit are our national leaders, our leading citizens, who sit on the president's councils and are held up to us as role models.

On February 29, 1984, Federal District Judge Miles W. Lord spoke from the bench of his Minneapolis courtroom to some of these industry leaders when he approved a $4.6 million products-liability verdict against A. H. Robins, manufacturers of the Dalkon Shield. Here is what he said, in part, to the firm's officers, Mr. E. Claiborne Robins, Jr., president, Dr. Carl D. Lunsford, senior vice-president for research, and William A. Forrest, vice-president and general counsel:

Gentlemen: . . . Today as you sit here attempting once more to extricate yourselves from the legal consequences of your acts, none of you has faced up to the fact that more than 9,000 women claim they gave up part of their womanhood so that your company might prosper. It has been alleged that others gave their lives so you might prosper. And there stand behind them legions more who have been injured but who have not sought relief in the courts of this land.

I dread to think what would have been the consequences if your victims had been men rather than women—women, who seem, through some quirk of our society's mores, to be expected to suffer pain, shame, and humiliation.

If one poor young man were, without authority or consent, to inflict such damage upon one woman, he would be jailed for a good portion of the rest of his life. Yet your company, without warning to women, invaded their bodies by the millions and caused them injuries by the thousands. . . . If this court had the authority, I would order your company to make an effort to locate each and every woman who still wears this device and recall your product. But this court does not. I must therefore resort to moral persuasion and a personal appeal to each of you. Mr. Robins, Mr. Forrest, and Dr. Lunsford: You are the people with the power to recall. You are the corporate conscience.

Please, in the name of humanity, lift your eyes above the bottom line. You, the men in charge, must surely have hearts and souls and consciences.

Please, gentlemen, give consideration to tracking down the victims, sparing them the agony that will surely be theirs.

Judge Lord's plea for corporate conscience was, instead, met with a head-on assault against the judge himself. Robins hired former Attorney General Griffin Bell to institute disciplinary proceedings against the judge. Bell had, as attorney general, passed on the appointments of several of the appeals-court judges in the circuit that would now hear the case against Judge Lord. The judge told me,

"The object was to cause me to resign, to be censored, or even impeached. It was an effort to silence men like me." Although the circuit court conceded that it did not have the power to discipline Judge Lord, it nevertheless struck his famous indictment from the record because it found that he had censured the Robins officers "without giving them notice" he was intending to do so. A. H. Robins reportedly expended more than $1 million in its attempt to undermine, discredit, and, I think, intimidate a judge with a conscience whose only misfeasance in office had been to make an eloquent, compassionate, and public plea on behalf of thousands of innocent American women. The spectacle of an honorable, compassionate federal judge who was helpless to do anything but plead with a multinational corporation to recall its product, which he saw as "a deadly depth charge in [the] wombs" of tens of thousands of women, "ready to explode at any time," typifies the arrogance of corporate power in America.

We may have read how SmithKline Beckman was charged with concealing information from the FDA about its product Selacryn (a drug used to treat high blood pressure), and how more than five hundred people suffered liver and kidney damage and at least thirty-six people died before the drug was finally taken off the market. We may have seen news articles concerning cases in which the manufacturers knew their products could injure or kill people and yet refused to discontinue sales or to recall their products until they were forced to do so by the government. Yet by the time the lawyers edit the evening news for libel and the producers require their changes to keep the program "even" and "balanced," the moral indignation that is finally communicated is as if they were reporting on some obscure accounting problem. And the anchorman doesn't even blink. He doesn't dare.

We have always felt a certain uneasiness about corporate crime, but America's view of it is one of cynicism, not outrage. We have come to accept presidents who commit felonies, politicians who lie, and corporations that steal and kill; and those who make waves about such things are noxiously labeled "environmentalists," "knee-jerk liberals," or worse, and too often the rest of us also adopt these labels and use them against the few who have bravely refused to accept these atrocities. That corporate America knowingly, cheerfully barters the lung tumors of its asbestos workers for profit, exchanges the brain damage of thousands of children from lead poisoning for earnings, trades the toxic-chemical contamination of whole populations for gain, and, without adequate testing, feeds carcinogens to an entire nation to secure a possible early market advantage, diminishes the likes of Charles Manson to a prankster at a Sunday School picnic. And Congress, with its hands in its pockets—wherein reside its true concerns—stands mutely on the sidelines.

Once in court, the cases go one of two ways: If the company can conceal its wrongdoing from the public, it will offer a secret settlement to the injured party. The attorney has no right to refuse a settlement that would be beneficial to his client even though the settlement is secret and the public has a vested interest in knowing. His duty is to his client—not to the public. I remember the case of Jody Bonney, a child born without arms, legs, a tongue, or a chin as a result of a hormonal pregnancy test taken by his mother. When it finally became clear that the FDA would require the drug to be withdrawn, the manufacturer's attorneys filed delaying appeals to give the drug company time to dump its supplies on the unsuspecting mothers of America. Jody Bonney was one of the by-products of that decision. Profit had been the issue—nothing else. But when we finally got the drug company into court, it offered a settlement. There was, of course, the usual hitch: The settlement had to be secret to protect the company from the hundreds, perhaps thousands, of other cases like Jody's that lay waiting.

On the other hand, if the injured party refuses a secret settlement, the companies will drag him through the courts in endless litigation and interminable appeals, and if the jury's award is large, an appellate court will likely reverse the jury's verdict. The court's conscience—that appellate judges' collective spirit dedicated to the commercial good of the nation—will usually be "shocked" at the multimillion-dollar verdict rendered by the jurors in their attempt to punish the criminal corporation with meaningful punitive damages.

In another of our cases, a large automobile manufacturer encountered a simple gas-tank problem different from that of the Ford Pinto. The corporation knew as a result of its own crash tests that in head-on collisions the gas tank ruptured, and often the vehicle caught on fire. A three-dollar conversion would have corrected the design defect, but the corporation chose to ignore the problem. In an ensuing crash, four persons were burned to death, while the fifth, a child, watched in horror as his parents perished in the flames. Again the corporation had something to conceal from the public courtroom and demanded a secret settlement, and again I was bound to my client. The settlement was one of the largest of its kind, but the public, including countless other victims, will never know, for the facts of the case must forever remain hidden in secret files.

In still another of our cases, a large electronics manufacturer had been told it should place warning plaques on its TV antennas reminding people to watch for electrical wires overhead during installation. The president refused, replying, "I've torn the notice up, and I will do the same in the future." Later, a Wyoming resident living in a small trailer house purchased that company's television antenna and during installation touched it to an overhead high-voltage wire, losing both of his arms and both of his legs as a result. Again the case was settled secretly. The client, almost totally helpless and in frightful debt, could not afford the risk of a public trial and the possible reversal of his case by the appeals court.

Although lawyers are charged with the duty to represent their clients, they have an affirmative duty not to assist them in the commission of crimes. Yet lawyers who advise their corporate clients on how to conceal the deadly effects of the corporation's products from the innocent public are lauded and rewarded for their skills by their corporate employers. Recently, a former research official of Liggett Group, Inc., testified that managers of that giant tobacco corporation suppressed a safer cigarette because allowing it to be marketed "would seriously indict them for having sold other types of cigarettes" that didn't contain the additives believed to protect smokers against lung cancer. James Mold, former asistant research director for Liggett Group, testified, "Whenever any problem came up in the [safer cigarette] project, the legal department would pounce on it in an attempt to kill the project, and this happened time and time again."

What if we were shown the real horror stories of corporate crime and told the whole shocking truth of those multibillion-dollar defense deals? What if we actually watched our clear rivers and pristine lakes being turned to muck and acid, and our virgin forests ripped and burned, all at the whim of some callous corporate overseer sniffing out an easy buck? What if we saw the trout floating to the surface and the elk running and running, aborting their calves, and we waited like children at the movies for the good guys to come until finally we knew there were no good guys, and that those in charge of our public lands were helpless bureaucrats who had been delivered over to the corporate mob along with the land entrusted to them? If we have learned anything from nearly a century of government regulation, it is that the administrative agencies of government are almost invariably captured by the industries they are created to regulate. As a consequence, the Interstate Commerce Commission becomes the protector of the railways, and the Federal Power Commission the partner of private power, the Federal Communications Commission lies paralyzed, unable to define any stan

dard of public interest that might cut seriously into the profits of
the broadcasting industry, and the Pentagon has evolved into the
guardian of the defense industry. All the while Congress stands by—
impotent as a herd of steers.

Our politicians rail about crime and fluff our dander up at election
time. But when bills are introduced in Congress to help curb the
epidemic of corporate crime, there is an eerie silence. We have no
representatives. They, too, were long ago transformed into commodities packaged and sold in the marketplace. The fashioning of
that sad product begins when the candidate is converted to an image
on the television screen, usually through the magic of corporate
money. Their faces carefully powdered, they speak to us with sincere
words composed by skillful writers. There are seductive visuals and
heart-rousing music. After months of such bombardment, and unable to distinguish between hype and substance, we finally deliver
up our power—not to a human being who will represent us but to
a full-color image on the screen already owned by its corporate fi-
nanciers. Elizabeth Drew writes in *Politics and Money*, "[Television]
is driving the politicians into a new form of political corruption. It
is making it very difficult for those who wish to avoid the corruption
to do so. . . . What is relevant is what the whole thing is doing to
the democratic process. What is at stake is the idea of representative
government, the soul of this country."

Before Watergate, we thought the merchandising of congressmen
was at least partially controlled by law. But Watergate taught us
about secret funds. The Committee for the Re-election of the President maintained a pot of nearly $17 million raised by the committee
from only 124 contributors, each of whom gave more than $50,000.
Over $1.7 million was received from contributors who were later
awarded ambassadorships.

Congress did make feeble attempts to regain its honor. A Federal
Election Commission was established to enforce the federal election
laws, but the limits on spending were soon struck down by our high
court in *Buckley* v. *Valeo* as a violation of the First Amendment.
The decision should have surprised no one; it probably didn't. The
court equated freedom of speech with the spending of money. At
the time of *Buckley* there were only eighty-nine corporate political
action comittees (PACs). Today, there are over seventeen hundred.
Kindred PACs have organized themselves into the National Association of Business Political Action Committees (NABPAC), an organization that can make or break a candidate. If the congressman
doesn't measure up, hasn't promised right, or voted right, the organization advises its members—and the candidate's money can dry

up. Worse, in the next election, his *opponent* may receive the blessed kiss of these dollars.

Sophisticated corporate lobbyists agree there is nothing to keep a contributor from putting a million dollars—or any sum, for that matter—into a campaign. Today, contributions of the size that shocked the nation in Watergate can legally be made. Drew says, "Now lobbyists sit right in the Committee room keeping score. Sometimes they even signal to a member how to vote on a certain amendment."

When congressmen take their handouts from corporations, we benignly call them "contributions," and then they report the same to the proper public authority, and that seems to cleanse the process. But when the time comes for the congressman to vote on a matter concerning those who have contributed to his campaign, our representatives seem neither to bear guilt nor to suffer embarrassment. Nor do they declare themselves disqualified. One and all will tell you they vote according to their conscience, not according to the special interests of those who have lined their political pockets. But do we really believe that Rosy Medina or Hank Herbinski, who gave nothing to the senator, have as much influence with him as the company that did?

What would happen to me if, while representing a client against a major corporation, I accepted a small "contribution" from that corporation? A police officer who takes money from a dope dealer may try to convince us that the payment had nothing to do with his attitude in enforcing the narcotics laws. He might even tell us, as one of my own congressmen once told me, "Why, Gerry, my boy, I call 'em as I see 'em. These contributions don't make a damn to me. I vote against 'em as often as I vote for 'em. I figure that if they're foolish enough to think they can buy me, they got it comin' when I give 'em the old double-cross." And he laughed as if it was a great joke he'd played on them—a sort of justifiable political sting. Whether a congressman has been bought outright or not, all lobbyists agree that money delivered to him at least assures them an audience for their case. Today, few congressmen represent any constituency. They represent their own longevity and those whose financial support perpetuates them in office. As long as our representatives remain purchasable commodities, we will continue to suffer unabated corporate crime. "Congress is," as Will Rogers said, "the best money can buy."

The well-known "dairy scandal" serves as a timeless example of how elected officials hear the rustle of raw money more clearly than the voices of Americans who were frightened by inflation. During

Nixon's administration, the dairy industry sought to increase the guaranteed price the government paid farmers for milk, which would raise retail food prices in an already inflation-threatened economy by hundreds of millions of dollars. Secretary of Agriculture Clifford Hardin found no cause for the increase and rejected the proposal. But less than two weeks later, the administration had changed its position, allowing a 6 percent raise—exactly what the milkmen had requested. The cost to America was an estimated $700 million per year. What the milk men had that the housewife didn't was a lot of "Grade-A cash." William A. Powell, president of Mid-America Dairymen, explained "that the sincere and soft voice of the dairy farmer is no match for the jingle of hard currencies put in the campaign funds of the politicians by the vegetable fat interest, labor, oil, steel, airlines and others." The dairymen accumulated a war chest of $1 million, and spread half of it in congressional elections. Next, the industry drafted a bill that would have taken the pricing decision out of the hands of the Department of Agriculture, making the increase mandatory. Fifty members of the House who had received dairy contributions jumped at the chance of becoming sponsors of the bill, and there were twenty-nine sponsors in the Senate. The dairymen paid thousands in installments to the Nixon election fund—the balance to be paid after "delivery," and, indeed, a $45,000 installment was paid just four days after their new price increase went into effect.

Mark Green, writing of the scandal in *Who Runs Congress?*, reported:

> What happened just before Hardin's turnabout announcement is revealing. The first big contribution was on March 22. It got quick results. The next day, President Nixon invited sixteen dairy and farm representatives to the White House. William Powell, president of the Mid-America Dairymen, gave a glowing report of what money can buy. "I sat in the Cabinet Room of the White House and heard [the President] compliment the dairymen on their marvelous work in consolidating and unifying our industry and our involvement in politics. He said, 'You people are my friends, and I appreciate it.' . . . Whether we like it or not, this is the way the system works."

But no one was there for the Rosy Medinas and the Hank Herbinskis who eventually paid the bill. Green, an expert on the nefarious congressional carryings-on, says, "The only thing unusual about the dairy campaign was the publicity it received." Senator Edward Kennedy complains, "Representative government on Capitol Hill is in the worst shape I have seen it. . . . We're elected to represent all the people of our states or districts, not just those rich or powerful enough to have lobbyists holding megaphones constantly at our ears."

James Madison, the father of our Bill of Rights, stated his dream of a democracy in the Federalist Papers: "Who are to be the electors of the Federal Representatives? Not the rich more than the poor; not the learned more than the ignorant; not the haughty heirs of distinguished names more than the humble sons of obscurity and unpropitious fortune. The electors are to be the great body of the people of the United States." What has happened in America that our representatives are conditioned to jump and sing to the jingle of money but cannot respond to the cries of our poor and our disenfranchised? The sodden sounds of our representatives beating their chest at the television cameras fill the halls of Congress. Only the weary bones of the original republic remain. At appropriate intervals, we are entertained and enthralled by hearings on Watergate and Irangate, but no one any longer believes there is justice. Congressmen fill the air with patriotic babble, but they do not represent us. They represent themselves.

Elsewhere, the "revolving door," through which many top-level government regulators pass to lucrative employment by the industries they have lately regulated, has become an accepted wickedness of our times. The practice fosters corporate crime, and the governing ethic—that public service ought not be parlayed into private profit—is often eclipsed. In the past seven years, more than one hundred Reagan officials have been caught up in ethical controversies. Resigned: Richard Allen, first national-security adviser, and Anne Burford, head of the Environmental Protection Agency, as well as former national-security adviser John Poindexter and Marine Lieutenant Colonel Oliver North, both submerged in the Iran-Contra scandal. Rita Lavelle of the EPA was convicted of lying. Paul M. Thayer, deputy secretary of defense, pleaded guilty to obstructing justice and lying. Under pressure, Attorney General Meese announced his resignation. Reagan's bland reaction: "Things like this have been going on for a long time."

In Washington, where there are over eight thousand paid lobbyists, the newest growth industry has become influence peddling. Besides Michael Deaver and Lyn Nofziger, both of whom were convicted, fourteen former aides in the Reagan White House are now selling their clout to American corporations, prompting one columnist to ask recently, ". . . [S]houldn't the electorate of this republic say that trust is not for sale? Isn't there a sacredness of shared power in a democracy that requires fidelity to the ideal, not adultery to profits?" Nofziger, at the time of his conviction, decried the Government in Ethics Act as a "lousy unfair law." But Herbert Robinson, a former postal worker and one of the jurors who tried Nofziger, when informed of the latter's comments said he was outraged that Nofziger had lobbied former White House colleague Edwin Meese on a $32-million army contract for Wedtech in 1982. "Would I go back to former officials I know and make connections that might involve the security of the United States? To make a buck?"

Bills have been introduced in both the House and Senate providing for severe penalties against corporate managers whose intentional misconduct injures us, but the corporate lobbies have repeatedly and easily killed them. Fines levied against corporate criminals are usually inconsequential. In the great electrical-equipment price-fixing conspiracy of the 1950's, the average fine imposed upon each corporate offender was a mere $16,500. General Electric paid the largest fine, $437,500, which amounted to 0.001 percent of its net profit. The Nuclear Regulatory Commission fined the operators of the Three Mile Island facility only $115,000, and Kerr-McGee, although cited over seventy times, was never fined a single cent for its violations. In the criminal case against Ford, the maximum fine Ford would have faced for the Pinto-induced deaths and injuries had it been convicted was a total of about $35,000, compared to the millions of dollars of profits generated by the decision not to install a safer gas tank in the Pinto.

The corporation is society's Frankenstein, containing most of man's darker traits and little of his light. Once loosed upon the world, the question has always been: How do we contain the thing? Over two hundred years ago, Lord Chancellor Edward Thurlow cried, "How can the beast have conscience with no soul to damn or hide to kick!" In 1250, Pope Innocent IV forbade the excommunication of a corporation that had been convicted of a crime upon the unassailable logic that since the corporation had no soul, it could not lose it. The corporate form has always been in ceaseless conflict with the edifying spirit of man. Thomas Hobbes, proclaiming the natural rights of man in seventeenth-century England, saw corporations as "worms in the body politic." He called them "chips off the block of sovereignty." The French in their famous declaration of August 18, 1792, proclaimed, "a state truly free ought not suffer within its bosom any corporation." Even Adam Smith, the venerated father of modern capitalism, opposed corporations as "stupid and medieval."

In America, our own memories fade too soon. By the time of the

Constitution, our countrymen had already endured a hundred years of harsh domination by the East India Company, a corporation chartered by the king in 1600 to carry on the business of the throne. It maintained its own army, conducted its private wars around the world, exploited the helpless masses of India, and eventually opened up China for the opium trade. For more than one hundred years before the Declaration of Independence, the Hudson's Bay Company, still another corporation, had exploited the Indians and the furred animals of this continent to near extinction. It was, of course, the East India Company's forcing of cheap, government-subsidized tea on the colonists that prompted the Boston Tea Party, a prelude to the American Revolution. Early in our history, our Founding Fathers rejected the corporate form as another of the king's tools for enslavement, casting it out with the remaining trappings of tyranny in favor of the simple rights of man.

But the regenerative powers of the corporate hydra were insidious. By 1791, the federal government had already organized the Bank of the United States—a corporation—and by 1816, corporations were again threatening the vision of the framers. In that year, Thomas Jefferson said, "I hope we shall crush in its birth the aristocracy of our monied corporations which dare already challenge our government to a trial of strength, and bid defiance to the laws of our country." In 1819, Chief Justice Marshall, in the celebrated case of *McCulloch* v. *Maryland*, confirmed the right of the federal government to form corporations under its "implied powers" for governmental or quasigovernmental purposes.

Then, in 1886, came the now infamous *Santa Ana* case. For the first time, the United States Supreme Court ruled that the corporation should have the same rights as a living person, and was entitled to the same protection of the Fourteenth Amendment of the Constitution. States were no longer permitted to deprive a corporation of its (non-)life, liberty, or property, without due process of law. Those laws that had been thrown up to protect the people from the corporate beast were ripped down as violations of constitutional due process. The *Santa Ana* case marked the demise of a nation of men and the coronation of the new king, the corporate state.

The rights of the new monarch now included protection against unreasonable searches and seizures under the Fourth Amendment, and corporate attorneys, taking advantage of the corporation's due-process protection, often delayed and deterred effective regulation designed to safeguard the public. Ironically, the same court that decreed that Dred Scott, a slave, was property, had granted to the corporation, a non-man, the sacred rights of citizenship. Yet the ageless question continued to plague us. As humans, we have inalienable rights. By what rationale does mere property have the same rights as we, the people? The Fourteenth Amendment provided that no state shall "deprive any person of life, liberty, or property, without due process of law, nor deny to any person within its jurisdiction the equal protection of the laws." It was to be a shield of freedom to protect the emancipated slave against abuses from the states. But the Fourteenth Amendment soon became a formidable weapon used to subject both black and white to the will of corporate America. We have not often heard that story.

In 1884, in *San Mateo County* v. *Southern Pacific Railroad*, the judges of the Supreme Court, on oral argument, were told by Senator Roscoe Conkling, a former member of the Joint Congressional Committee that drafted the Fourteenth Amendment, that the secret minutes of the committee would reveal Congress's intent that the word "person" include corporations. Although the court did not so rule in *San Mateo County*, it later did in *Santa Clara* v. *Southern Pacific Railroad*. In that case, Chief Justice Waite told the lawyers before the proceedings began, "The Court does not wish to hear argument on the question whether the provision in the Fourteenth Amendment to the Constitution, which forbids a State to deny to any person within its jurisdiction the equal protection of the laws, applies to these corporations. We are all of the opinion that it does." That utterance became the pernicious seed from which the beast was born—namely, that a fiction, a corporation, may hold rights equal to those of human beings. Later examination of the journal for the joint committee revealed no evidence to support Conkling's representation. But by that time, the constitutional doctrine of corporate personhood was firmly rooted in the cases. Justice Hugo Black observed in *Conn. General Co.* v. *Johnson* that of the cases in which the Fourteenth Amendment was applied during the first fifty years after its adoption, "less than one-half of one per cent invoked it in protection of the Negro race, and more than fifty per cent asked that its benefits be extended to corporations." In the century following the amendment's passage, only two members of our high court are said to have challenged the central fiction. Perhaps in the abstract, arming the corporation with rights identical to those of the citizen seemed fair enough, but in practice it was the equivalent of giving a bulldozer and an ant equal rights to run over each other.

Ours is an age of illusion and fiction. Sylvester Stallone and Clint Eastwood provide us our heros. Our president is the mythological "Gipper" reading his TelePrompTer. Our judges are in the fashion of *The People's Court*, our lawyers molded after *L.A. Law*. Justice is the happy ending of our movies. Even the United States Supreme Court has joined the ubiquitous game of fictionalization. By judicial magic, the court, in the 1986 case of *Pacific Gas and Electric Co. v. Public Utilities Commission of California*, supplied the fictional body of the corporation with a *fictional conscience*. Even Justice Rehnquist could not go that far. In dissent, he said, "Extension of the individual freedom of conscience decisions to business corporations strains the rationale of these cases to the breaking point. To ascribe to such artificial entities an 'intellect' or 'mind' for freedom of conscience purpose is to confuse metaphor with reality." Under federal law, where corporate influence is rife, it is still not a crime for corporate officers to knowingly market an unsafe product, or conceal a hazard in the workplace. As Edward Alsworth Ross, the father of American social psychology, bemoaned, "[A] corporation is an entity that transmits the greed of its investors, but not their conscience."

Television, potentially the greatest weapon for democracy ever invented by man, now totally in the grip of corporate America, is used to exert an inexorable control over our lives. And behind it, the new king hides its criminal face and its bloody hands. *Advertising Age* commented, "Network television, particularly, is largely the creature of the hundred largest corporations in the country." These "hundred largest" account for over 80 percent of all network advertising. Jerry Mander's conclusion, in his classic work *Four Arguments for the Elimination of Television*, is inescapable: "Broadcast television is available only to monstrous corporate powers. What we are permitted to see on television is what suits the mentality and purposes of corporations." Advertising has become an $88-billion industry—more than the whole country spends on higher education annually. Americans are exposed to an estimated one thousand advertising messages every day, a majority of which are broadcast over the three major networks. In a nation of four hundred thousand corporations, and over a quarter of a billion people, a technology dominated by the "hundred largest" belies the concept of democracy, and is, as Mander insists, incompatible with that form of government. Television is not the medium of the farmer or the factory worker or of the Chicano, or the teacher. It is not even the medium of the wealthy. Television does not belong to the people; it belongs lock, stock, and barrel to corporate America.

I am not against free enterprise. I am not against TV. I am against tyranny. I am against delivering the nearly perfect, nearly total access of our minds and our children's minds to the vicissitudes of the market and to its values. I am against fostering the myth of a free media when the media is, in fact, inaccessible to the people. I am against the media so taunting us with the crimes committed by our neighbors that we virtually hurl ourselves into the arms of the police demanding protection they only too willingly give—provided we adopt their view of our Bill of Rights as a pesky collection of loopholes through which criminals are permitted to escape. Already we are beginning to applaud the courts as they chisel away at the very pillars of liberty that have long distinguished us. Today, we are being trained to hate our hard-earned rights against self-incrimination and unreasonable searches and seizures as the weapons of crime, not freedom.

Control over people's minds has always been the goal of the tyrant. Aldous Huxley in *Brave New World* foresaw it half a century ago. To make them "love their servitude was the task assigned." Huxley believed that people would become standardized, and that technology would lead to a joyfully submissive population, a mass that required no wardens and no gates but only the opiate of perpetual entertainment. Mander demonstrates that the electronic media substitutes fantasy people and fantasy places for real persons and real places, and that we are taught to adore the false and reject the authentic. We are trained like baby ducks who learn to cuddle up to a warm light and a ticking clock and to snub their own, honest-to-God, quacking mother. Worse, television supplants our vision of ourselves and those around us with a new, treacherous tape of what is—an illusion that reshapes our minds. The corporate criminal spends millions creating an image as sparkling as Mary Poppins, and thereby transforms itself into a beloved member of the family of man. Have we become the Huxleyan mob irretrievably affixed to the tube and addicted to its terror and its trivia? The electronic medium elicits no serious conversation or thoughtful discourse. It diverts and beguiles. At feeding time, millions of us are attached by invisible beams to a feeding trough remotely controlled by corporate advertisers, from which we are provided simultaneously our daily ration of cerebral nourishment at periods in the evening called "primetime television." There we are twittered to death—that is, we become so soaked in it and stupefied by it that we are changed—to what, no one is sure. But this new being in his altered state has a frightening capacity to consume and be satisfied with the empty and the shallow. When our enemies commit this outrageous evil on their victims, we call it "brainwashing."

Some claim the constant barrage of television has changed us from inquisitive, self-reliant, resourceful, fiercely independent people to passive indolents who are distinguished chiefly by their obedience to the commercial purposes of corporate America. In contrast, compare the typical "Court Day" of the colonists at the time of the Revolution to a Sunday afternoon in America today.

"Court Day" provided the people an opportunity to get together, to exchange the news, and to exercise their newly won freedoms. Then candidates mounted the courthouse steps and delivered their speeches, and a barrel of rum was often opened. As the spirit of the day mounted, there would probably be horse races and wrestling matches to entertain the folks.

Surrounding the town square were numerous small buildings, including the courthouse. Some were brick, and some clapboard and log, and next to the courthouse stood the stocks and pillories, in which some poor miscreant was likely imprisoned for all to see and for all to scorn. Itinerant peddlers positioned themselves along the roadside to hawk their pewter, copper, and tin. If our scene were in Virginia on "Court Day," Patrick Henry—lately returned from the Constitutional Convention in Philadelphia, where he had protested the adoption of the proposed Constitution without a Bill of Rights—would have mounted the courthouse steps to address the crowd. You can hear his words:

"My friends, the Constitution should be like Caesar's wife—not only must it be beautiful but beyond suspicion. Can we embrace a document that all admit is defective in the hope that it will amend itself after we are married to it? I look upon the adoption of that paper, without it first including a Bill of Rights, as the most fatal plan conceivable to enslave free men." At this point, he likely would have removed his wig and twirled it to punctuate his oratory—a habit for which he was famous. "Our own Virginia Constitution did not dare speak for the people without first protecting them with a Declaration of Rights. Our burying grounds are filled with our loyal and our brave who have laid down their lives for freedom."

The man stood over six feet, and the sound of his voice was like thunder: "We shall not be captured by one general government with its terrible powers—with the purse in one hand and the sword in the other. Our struggle for liberty has but begun. Wise men who engage in this grave and arduous struggle, having eyes to see do not shut out their sight, and having ears to hear do not turn deaf. I have said it once to a prior assemblage and I say it again: 'I know not what course others may take, but as for me, give me liberty, or give me death.' "

Today, we would reject a proposed Bill of Rights out of hand.

Today, people do not gather and choose their great leaders from among themselves. Instead, the masses sit alone, watching the New England Patriots take on their Sunday afternoon opponents.

We live in an intellectual wasteland where creativity is replaced by the exigencies of the marketplace. We live in a dangerous corporate anarchy, where, like the victims of a school of piranhas, we are devoured in a feeding frenzy. Love is out. Neither fear nor law nor moral constant provide a deterrent. Unquenchable greed is the force that moves us. Crimes of pecuniary indecency have become standard corporate conduct. We have been captured. Our children, too. The enemy has not taken us by force, but by a technology we gratefully embrace, even demand. This new technology has made the military coup passé and irrelevant. We have a new king already—and the new king is mad.

We have abandoned the good earth to abide in concrete canyons of our own creation, and to roam the vast and desolate plains of billboards and buildings. We use up twelve square miles of farmland a day for new roads, shopping centers, corporate housing developments, and factories. That amounts to 3 million acres a year—in the last ten years an area equal to that of Vermont, New Hampshire, Massachusetts, Rhode Island, Connecticut, New Jersey, and Delaware combined. Of the nation's remaining tillable acres, 5 billion tons of topsoil are lost annually to erosion, a rate greater by 25 percent than we suffered during the infamous dustbowl days of Steinbeck's *The Grapes of Wrath*. In New York City, the level of carbon monoxide in the blood of most taxi drivers is too high for their blood to be used in transfusions for people with heart ailments. Our lobby-plagued government subsidizes the tobacco industry, which in turn, reaps its ignoble fortune from the disease and death of the masses—and we permit the farmers who supply our food to go bankrupt. We are told about our First Amendment freedoms, our right to express ourselves, but in the end our choices have become mere statistics in the race of the networks for ratings, and what we watch is all the same.

Behind the screen, like an evil magician, stands the corporation selling us what we do not need and committing its crimes of greed at will. More and more, we crave new excitement, new pleasure. Our minds, opened wide like the gaping mouths of baby birds, receive television's latest fare, and at the precise moment the corporation drops in the new American wisdom of No-Nonsense pantyhose and Preparation H. Television does not educate us. It tells us foolish bedtime stories in exchange for our promises to purchase the latest corporate goods and corporate services. At the going rate of half a million dollars per minute, there is no time for truth. We live in the dreaded land Lord Acton described, where "[P]ower tends to corrupt and absolute power corrupts absolutely." Our experience negates Marx: Religion is not the opiate of the people; television is.

When we decide to do so, we can emancipate the black child from the ghetto and render justice in the workplace. We have the power to make our representatives responsive to us. We can, when we decide to do so, curb corporate crime. We can, if we will it, break the stranglehold of the corporate king who uses our airways to control us. We can transform the media into an incomparable weapon of freedom. We are able, when we choose, to select and train new lawyers, who will fight for us and who will strive for an order where no longer the plaintive cry of the harbingers of gloom is "Justice for none," but where a free people can again be dedicated to the ideal of *justice for all*.

PART TWO

JUSTICE FOR ALL
What We Can Do

11 | NEW LAWYERS
The Champions Return

With the halls of the courthouses teeming with lawyers, the skyscrapers bulging with lawyers, the streets of our cities packed with lawyers, the people are still without fighters, for they have gone off to other wars for other causes. Like mercenaries, they wrangle and scheme for money wherever money can be found. Too often it flows in the corporate troughs. We would reject a surgeon who loved the dead more than the living, who attended only to those who paid him the most, who worked hardest to preserve our enemies, and ignored our cries of pain and the cries of our children. But people demand a fair chance at justice as surely as they demand medical care. They demand to be represented by professionals who care about them, who are devoted to justice and are properly trained to fight for it. They demand a system of justice that is responsive to them. The people do not hate lawyers. They hate only those whose fees are the single hint of their expertise, who love money more than their neighbors, who love money more than justice itself. These are not unreasonable expectations. We need no fancy studies to confirm them. It is what I wish of my own lawyer. The question, therefore, is very simple: How can the people obtain the kind of lawyers they expect? Surely among the 675,000 lawyers out there, there are those who can provide the service the people of America demand at a price they can afford to pay.

The system itself, usually deaf, usually locked in paralysis, has taken remarkable but faltering strides in the past two decades. That there has been any movement at all is, in itself, astonishing. In 1975, the Supreme Court for the first time ruled that minimum fees set by state bar associations were in violation of the antitrust laws. I remember when lawyers who cut fees were thought to have soiled their souls. In those days, it was pointless for people to shop for an attorney. I remember when it was considered unlawful for anyone but lawyers to close a real-estate sale, or give advice in estate planning. Now, lawyers must compete with accountants, real-estate agents, title-insurance companies, and bankers. In some states, no-fault insurance has made it easier for the citizen to collect for minor collison damage in automobile wrecks. People have become more aware of their right to invoke the jurisdiction of small claims courts because of television programs such as *The People's Court*. No-fault divorce makes it easier to dissolve hopeless marriages, where before our clients had to provide proof that their spouse's moral dereliction matched one of the grounds set forth in the statutes.

Next, the Supreme Court permitted lawyers to advertise. Over five thousand firms recently reported to the American Bar Association that they have done so. Some provide twenty-dollars-off coupons in the Yellow Pages. Others advertise on television, and still others have gone so far as to advertise on matchbook covers and bowling-alley scoresheets. The theory is that advertising opens up the profession to the people, breaks down the barriers of a closed shop, and encourages competition. The advent of the word processor has made mass production of mortgages and wills, and the formation of simple corporations and partnerships, matters that paralegals can easily handle, and paralegals themselves have taken the place of expensive associates to do routine interviewing of witnesses and legal research. Many years ago, my ethics were called into question when I first hired a paralegal. My hyper-ethical brothers of the insurance bar, who kept me under their constant and intense scrutiny and who claimed I would do anything to win a case, now had their proof—I had finally even stooped to aiding and abetting laymen in the unlawful practice of the law.

Prepaid plans for legal services are now available to over 2 million households as fringe benefits in union contracts. For as little as fifty dollars annually, participants are provided legal services at a guaranteed hourly rate, usually at about fifty dollars an hour, and there are fixed prices for wills and divorces. Less than a decade ago, the bar was contesting these efforts as the "grossest kind of champerty," and threatening those lawyers who cooperated in such programs with criminal prosecution. Today, well-managed production-line law services have begun to spring up. Similar to H&R Block, they advertise heavily, situate themselves conspicuously in storefront offices, and are not only taking business away from established law firms but changing the way the public views the law—as something purchasable, like a box of soap.

Legal clinics—high-volume, high-efficiency law firms—have become a permanent phenomenon in the profession. Linda Cawley and Rick Schmidt of Cawley and Schmidt Legal Clinic in Baltimore, Maryland, say, "We've organized routine services and payment plans for our customers. We've also set up flexible schedules with evening hours for working clients. . . . we have made up forms about mortgages, child custody and car payments. Our services are standard, and we don't charge for the myth." Hyatt Legal Services, founded in 1977, is the largest and fastest growing of these clinics, with more than 150 offices in more than 21 states. The goal of such clinics has been to make lawyers more available to the people. The method, however, has been the same weary approach of a market society. Too often what is being sold to the people is not a lawyer's thoughtful advice but what's on the lawyer's computer—an empty form.

I think of my own first client, who came wandering down the hall on the deserted second floor of the Masonic Temple Building on a Saturday afternoon over thirty-five years ago. Here was an honest-to-God client looking for a lawyer, and I was he! I was thrilled. What I tried to say sounded like a long string of spits and sputters from my mother's old pressure cooker at full throttle. I finally learned that he wanted a power of attorney, a form that could be readily supplied today with the touch of a key on the word processor. With the aid of a form book, it took me the rest of the afternoon to draft it, and after that I had to type it myself. Even framed with a "blue back," it wasn't very pretty, nor was the fee of ten dollars. Today, the same form, perfectly, beautifully regurgitated from a computer, might cost $100—but there would be something missing. As I typed away on the form, my client and I talked. He was a serviceman going overseas and was concerned for his family. He mistakenly believed that the power of attorney would give his wife the right to dispose of all of his property if he died, and thus avoid probate. Indeed, death would automatically revoke the power of attorney, and his wife would be stuck in the mire of an expensive and time-consuming estate. She needed the power of attorney, all right, to transact business in his absence, but she also needed her name on the family home and car, and more than the simple legal advice, my client required reassurance "that if something happened, everything would be taken care of." I was so delighted to have a real live client and to know that I had been successful in recognizing a real legal problem that I threw in the extra instruments it took for the price of the power of attorney. The point is not my poor business acumen, but that *lawyering is a relationship*, not a commodity. The computer does not sell the concern of the lawyer for his clients, or deliver to them much peace of mind.

While it is clear enough to me that certain tasks that were once jealously locked within the profession needed unlocking and that the requirements of a market society are responsible for throwing the door of the profession open to these services, in the end, the very thing people most deplore about both lawyers and doctors is that increasingly we withdraw ourselves from the people and serve up only a sterile, impersonal product. One doctor, recently musing on the cause of the so-called malpractice crisis, wrote, "We will still have malpractice suits until we physicians learn that these suits begin as a breakdown in the doctor-patient relationship. That is where we begin to control our destiny—in our own offices."

At the other end of the spectrum, young lawyers joining prestigious firms often have little opportunity to develop close client relationships. Most work at uninspiring tasks, pore over old court decisions and statute books, and draft memos for their higher-ups. They dig again and again in some tiny specialized area of the law, and rarely see the law as a whole, meet clients, or stand up to argue in court. They work punishing hours to bill clients 2,000 to 2,500 hours a year, and even though beginning stars from the Ivy League may earn $70,000 a year, or more, the big firms will charge their corporate clients accordingly. Thereby the business game of the law is made hugely lucrative at the top of the hierarchical structure—seven or eight "associates" to one partner, all of whom labor at a cost to the firm of, say, $50 an hour, while the firm bills the client $150 an hour for the same labor. Some lawyers have come down from the great towers of our cities to where the people are—and they must. Recruits in the big firms frequently jump ship. Michael Kearney, an attorney at M&M Legal Clinic in Washington, D.C., says, "I have been to the mountain—handled corporate matters in a prestigious law firm—and I like this a lot more." There is compensation in representing human beings—albeit, most often not in big money. Yet there remains a stigma against the storefront lawyer who has opened up a practice of his own. Says Michael Magness, who heads the recruiting arm of the law directory Martindale-Hubble, a firm that presumes to rate lawyers, "There was a time when the American dream was that you went out of law school, hung up your shingle, starved a few years and then started making money."

Now, Magness says, "Hanging a shingle is virtually a sign of defeat. It means a guy couldn't get a job."

But more than making themselves available to people, lawyers must be competent to fight people's causes in court. That is quite a different matter from filling in forms stored in computers and obtaining quickie divorces. The "people's lawyer" must be more "people friendly" than "computer friendly," more committed, more connected to principle, more the ruffian with a conscience than the gentlemen without. Unless we provide America with this new breed of well-chosen, well-trained fighters, the promise of justice for all will remain a tired refrain. We require, therefore, a new way to select our lawyers and a new way to train them.

The law student is the brick from which the entire justice system is built. That there are too few black lawyers in the ghettos, too few Hispanics in the storefront offices, too few lawyers in the small villages near the farms, too few lawyers who will fight for a Mary Wilson when she is sexually harassed by her landlord, too few lawyers to take on the landlord for a Henry McMillen when he is burned out of his tenement, too few lawyers to fight for our air, our skies, our rivers, our earth, too few lawyers to fight for simple things, for a man's good name, for a woman's right to keep her body private— that there is a scarcity of such lawyers is only the first glimmer of the tragedy, for when there are not enough people's lawyers there will also not be enough people's judges.

We have seen how those who would fight for just causes are turned away by tests that can identify neither fighter nor saint. One would never leave the defense of our country to Green Berets chosen by a computer. It would be comical to see who might appear in the ring to fight for the world championships or who might fill the slots in the National Football League if those fighters were selected by such tests. Yet the courtroom, for all of its niceties, its verbiage, its grand form and gesture, its gentlemanly tradition, is as much a place of fighting, of war, and of death, as any battlefield, and much of the same emotion and many of the same fighting skills are required to win there.

Recently a young man from Jackson Hole asked for advice. I had known him since he was a small boy. All his life, he had wanted to be a lawyer. He cared deeply for the human condition. In the summer, he was a white-water river guide, and I remember him telling me how hard he worked to see that the people on his raft had an exciting ride as well as a safe trip. He shared with his customers his love of the river and thrilled them with sightings of moose and otter and bald eagles. "Some of these people have been saving for years for this experience," he told me. "They come from big cities and poor places, and I try not to forget that." He, too, had worked hard. At the University of Wyoming, he had earned a high-B average, but his score of 25 (on a scale of 10 to 48) on the LSAT would not permit him entry into most of the nation's leading law schools—perhaps as yet an unidentified blessing.

I sent the lad to David White, director of Testing for the Public, a nonprofit educational corporation in San Francisco that offers a test-preparation course for the LSAT intended to aid minorities and the disadvantaged. In preparation for his second go at the test, this young man learned how to fashion his thinking to give him an advantage. White asked his students to envision the answers a slogan-type, conservative, white, elitist male would make. "In your mind, select a prototypical WASP and think like him. Act like him. Become him. When you are asked on the test to pick an answer, do so out of the mind of this prototype. What is true for him will also more likely be true for this examination." This mental set helps students, White says, because people tend to pick answers they like, and those who construct the test also select the answers—usually those more compatible with the corporate intellect, usually different answers than a kid from the Bronx or, for that matter, from the backwoods of Wyoming might choose.

White told me he began to examine the answers this young man made on the LSAT for cultural and political bias. White taught him that questions suggesting that "the police are right," that "doctors are right," that "the defense industry should be supported," that "poor people are likely to migrate to those areas where welfare benefits are highest," should be picked. Those who were the clones of the more conservative segment of our society seemed to have an advantage. But I discovered something even more frightening: On each exam given, a certain portion of the questions given will *not* be used in scoring the test. These are questions that have been included for testing to be used in later versions of the LSAT. White says those answered *correctly* by *low-scoring* students but *missed* by the *high scorers* are eliminated. White has shown that blacks, minorities, and ethnic whites who have not had much experience in taking sophisticated tests do less well than their affluent white counterparts. As a consequence, the elimination of test questions that blacks and the poor frequently get right and that more affluent white youths most often miss establishes a further bias against those who begin with a strike already against them.

By learning a few tricks from White on how to take the test, my young friend raised his score nine points, which will greatly increase his competitive edge for admission into law school. But what of the thousands who never learned how to take the LSAT? What if, indeed, we are witnessing a concerted and systematic scheme that tends to select students who are philosophically compatible with those who devise the test? Is it not possible that large numbers of those best suited to be the people's lawyers are never permitted to enter the law-school door?

White cites a study of 16,233 students made by Joseph Gannon of Boston College that showed that when blacks, Chicanos, and whites graduated from the same college in the same year with virtually the same grade-point average, the blacks and Chicanos averaged 100 points lower on the LSAT (referring to the 200–800 scale). More recent averages on LSAT's newer 10 to 48 scale is 22 for blacks, 27 for Chicanos, and 33 for whites. In another study, 13 percent of the blacks seeking admission to law schools had a 3.25 GPA or above, while 40 percent of the whites met this standard. But when the law school required a 3.25 GPA *plus* a 600 or above on the LSAT, using the old scale, 20 percent of the whites qualified, while only 1 percent of blacks did. The higher score on the LSAT only cut the whites that qualified in half. It literally eliminated the blacks.

Temple Law School was one of the first to realize the danger of allowing the LSAT to dominate the school's admissions program. Dean Peter J. Liacouras, now the president of Temple University, wrote:

It is a statistical fact that not only blacks, Hispanics and native Americans but other groups whose first or family language is not standard English . . . are outscored on such tests. This has little if anything to do with brains or ability or merit or predicting who will do best in the profession. These ostensibly objective tests are not the easy-to-recognize "Minorities Keep Out" obstacles of the 1900s and 1930s. But they are just as effective barriers, and they should be exposed as such.

As we have seen, the ABA sets standards the law school must meet in order to win coveted ABA accreditation. Standard 503 requires that every candidate take the LSAT or a proven equivalent. In forty-three states, unless the law student graduates from an ABA-accredited law school, he or she cannot take the bar examination. Most but not all states have surrendered. California, Vermont, Virginia, and Washington permit their students to take the bar even though they have not graduated from law schools that have earned ABA accreditation. Only these four states fail to see the relevance of ABA accreditation to the competence of a candidate to serve the public. Many schools rely almost entirely upon the LSAT and the student's grade-point average to select their candidates because it is a cheap and defensible way to reach their admissions decision. Even distinguished schools, such as Harvard and Stanford, set minimum LSAT scores. Professor Morton Horwitz of Harvard says that the admissions policy of every law school is an issue at the core of law-school responsibility: "We must break down the idea that the way to get into Harvard is to be a clever test-taker." Yet today the clever test-takers are the nearly exclusive population of our most prestigious law schools.

Recognizing that such discrimination was detrimental to the school, to the profession, and to society, Temple has for many years followed a "two routes admission policy"—the first, denominated "nondiscretionary" and accounting for roughly half of the entering class, is based almost exclusively on the LSAT and GPA scores. But the second route of entry, the "discretionary" route, sets different criteria for entry. Whereas the "nondiscretionary" route results in the admission of predominantly white men and women, the "discretionary" route seeks out and "carefully, individually and affirmatively selects those applicants . . . who have an outstanding performance record and an exceptional aptitude for the study and practice of law not necessarily reflected by their LSAT."

Temple reports that by the "discretionary" route it chooses students who have unique work experience, those who have picked themselves up by their own bootstraps—men and women of practically every race, ethnic group, economic class, religion, age category, and walk of life. Here is a typical class profile:

A youngster of Italian ancestry who worked in a gas station for forty hours a week from the age of twelve all the way through college; the children of working-class Kensington, Manayunk, and South Philadelphia ethnics; a white woman teacher who helped establish an alternative school; students with Puerto Rican ancestry who grew up in crowded sections of Manhattan and Vineland, New Jersey; policemen from across the Delaware Valley; brilliant Jewish students from Logan and Main Line who score below average in standardized tests; . . . black wounded Vietnam veterans who have earned the right to realize their share of the American Dream; a white farm boy from Chester County who was the first in his family, extending back to colonial days, to attend college; a native American raised on a reservation; a Japanese-American whose first memories of life were of a World War II detention camp . . . and on and on.

"At Temple Law School," Dean Liacouras reassures us, "all students admitted under [the 'discretionary' program] are highly qualified persons who we believe will become good lawyers and community leaders." Such reassurance is not necessary when one considers the alternative—entrusting the future of justice in America to the all-white sons and daughters of America's elite.

Several other schools have, to some extent, followed Temple's lead. St. Louis University School of Law has a "Special Admissions Program" "designed to identify students who have suffered the effects of racial discrimination, cultural deprivation, or economic disadvantage to such an extent that their undergraduate work or performance on standardized tests is affected." After taking a required summer course, the applicant is again examined by the committee on admissions for evidence that the applicant "will be able to overcome the effects of the disadvantage and study law effectively." McGeorge Law School in California and others have similar programs, but overall, and even in such schools as Temple, the LSAT and GPA remain the primary tool for administering the admissions policy.

Even San Francisco's New College of California School of Law, a heroic little school emphazing public-interest law and dedicated to preparing students for people-oriented practices, is under pressure from the California Bar to apply the same old measurements of the LSAT and the GPA to its applicants. Currently this school is one of the few that uses no specific numbers formula in its admissions policy. Dean Chris Gus Kanios says, "Students are from diverse backgrounds, of all ages, races, ethnicities, and sexual orientations. Over 50 percent of our students come from minority communities, and most come from working-class backgrounds. Many are parents, and most need to work to support themselves. (This is quite a different student body from the more dilettante profile generally encountered in the Ivy League schools.) In the admissions process, we rely heavily on a student's demonstrated commitment to public-interest work. And although we require the LSAT from all applicants, a low score, in and of itself, does not preclude admission to otherwise qualified applicants. We have shown that students with less sterling LSAT scores can obtain the skills necessary to pass the bar exam, but a law school has to offer more than just a 'Professor Kingsfield' pompously spouting doctrine if it is committed to such students." To fulfill its commitment to its students, the new college even utilizes one-on-one tutoring sessions.

Temple Law School claims it maintains its "populist tradition in making a superior legal education available to working men and women, and their children, irrespective of ethnic or racial or social origin or religious heritage or favoritism." Still, over half of Temple's students are admitted, not because they can demonstrate that they will more faithfully serve the people or their community, but because they are, even there, clever test-takers chosen by the computer. At St. Louis University, the disadvantaged students must still pay their dues for being disadvantaged by submitting to an extra summer's schooling, which they can least afford. At Stanford and Harvard, the selections are made almost totally by the numbers and on the students' written files.

But one day soon, the coupling of man and machine, by which each new year's crop of law students is conceived, will cease. Even the most mulish must finally see that numbers alone can never describe a whole person. Over fifteen years ago, Dean Liacouras called on the American Association of Law Schools to devise alternative tests to the LSAT. He called the matter "urgent" and of the "highest priority." He called it a "crisis in admissions." He said "[T]he perception that informed middle-class Americans have of legal education is that we have abdicated our responsibility to insure equal access by fair and rational standards." Both the dean and middle-class Americans were right. Today, the clamor for reason is growing louder.

But if not by impersonal numbers, how should the admissions committees make their decisions? First, they must define the kind of lawyers their communities require. Obviously, the traits and characteristics of those suited to work in the large New York City firms are not the same as those who will represent the citizens of Wyoming. Perhaps lawyers who will work in the sterile corporate environment, running through the impersonal mazes of government and business bureaucracies for corporate clients, can still be selected by the computer. All lawyers should not be trained in the same fashion. One may work for Skadden, Arps, Slate, Meagher & Flom in New York, a seven-hundred-lawyer firm highly respected for its expertise in takeover law, and the other may set up a small-town general practice and represent folks like Betsy Bowser, a widow whose husband lost his life in the mines. To win before a jury against a multinational coal corporation on behalf of the widow, that small-town lawyer must have different traits and different skills—yes, even a different heart—than his city cousin who shuffles paper for a brokerage firm on Wall Street. Yet today lawyers are selected and educated in substantially the same way whether they attend Harvard or the University of Wyoming.

If I were on a committee selecting Wyoming lawyers, I would prefer a student who worked as a waiter during undergraduate school and had average grades to a Phi Beta Kappa whose performance flourished under the shelter of a blank check from his father. I would want to know if the candidate had written poems or painted pictures, and I'd like to see them. Does the student like to perform? Let me hear his songs and see her dance. I would choose those who create over those who spend their spare time browning their bellies at the beach. I would pick one whose hobby was photography over one who plays golf and hangs out at the country club.

What about the student's grade-point average? Indeed, lawyers must be both diligent and intelligent. But the very narrow kind of intelligence reflected by grade-point averages does not assure us of the lawyer's survival in the wilderness of practice. One does not have great reverence for the intelligence of a mule until one is lost in the mountains in a raging blizzard. Then the mule's ability to return himself to the barnyard and his owner to a welcome fire becomes his genius. His owner's IQ of 140 has once again proved worthless, even counterproductive. Ours is an adversary system. Every encounter is a battle, every case a war. It is not that our fighters ought not to be intelligent. But they must possess a different intelligence—one surely not measurable by the LSAT.

I would *talk* to the candidates, and invite them to bring a cherished friend or a past employer, or their parents or grandparents. Perhaps I could learn how the candidates relate to others. Why does a young woman want to be a lawyer? What could this young man accomplish with the great gift of a good legal education? I would like them to share their dreams with me. I'd like them each to tell me the hardest thing they ever did in their lives, and I'd ask them, too, to tell me the worst. It's not that I would answer that question myself, but I would take great pleasure in hearing some young fighter tell me it was none of my damned business. I would pick the kid who confesses he is a recovering alcoholic over one who says the worst thing he ever did was steal a newspaper off the neighbor's porch. I would pick the one who had been arrested for civil disobedience or had spread herself in front of the bulldozers to stop a road through virgin forests over one who spent a year traveling in Europe on her parents' purse between high school and college.

There would, of course, be no uniformity in the choices from one school to another, since the people's requirements for lawyers are as divergent as the people themselves. Grades would still be important, for they often reflect the willingness of the student to study, and surely the practice of law is study. No standard would test the committee's choices except its judgment that the candidate would be dedicated to and successful at winning justice for the people. The committee's selections would not be as easily defended, for students would not have been reduced to digits. But I have never wanted a digit to represent me. First-year classes would tend to be larger, because the selection process would continue through that year, giving those students a chance who seem especially suited to hard battles but who would otherwise have been rejected. I am looking for the fighters, the missionaries, the preachers, and the reformers. Give me those who *test the system*, not those whom the system so easily tests. Give me the bleary-eyed idealist and the hard-bitten realist—those with fire, with passion, with dreams. But please— save me from the test-takers whose visions focus on the first paycheck at the large corporate law firm.

The defects in this proposed selection process are obvious. The kind of candidates selected would be those that appeal to the committee. That leaves room for favoritism and back-scratching, and puts a premium on hot air over hard numbers. Even so, we are better off trusting human beings to select people's lawyers than leaving it to statistics and machines. It is better to embrace a person than a number. That the student enters law school as a digit rather than as a unique individual is his lot. Administrators complain that interviews take too much time and are too expensive, and they are right. But nothing is more expensive to society than populating the ranks of the profession with lawyers who have no conscience or moral values. Nothing can be more costly to America than a huge, wallowing contingent of lawyers who have no commitment to the interests of society and who have no affinity for human beings, who pass, naturally, predictably, from the law-school hierarchy to the large-firm hierarchy, all according to the rules of the money game. Today, the victims of corporate America are our burden. The victims include most of us—those injured and contaminated by dangerous products, those cheated by false advertising, those who have fallen prey to corporate crimes, those wrongfully rejected and discarded because of age, race, or sex, those robbed of clear air and pure water, of forest and prairie and wilderness. These ravages against us could not have occurred but for lawyers. It is not that it costs too much for us to carefully, tediously, personally select our lawyers. It is that we can no longer afford not to.

One year at Temple University it took over 10,000 person-hours to sort through 2,000 applications, from which 158 students were finally selected. But no one complained it wasn't worth the trouble or that the cost was too high. Rather, the university seemed proud of its effort. "We have sought to fulfill our historic twin commitments to excellence and populism by doing the extra work. . . . Such allocation of resources is an indispensable reason for our success, and we reject the argument of others who claim that 'the benefits are so doubtful.' "

If at first there are not enough candidates of certain racial, ethnic, and social groups, it will be up to the school to find and recruit them, for their involvement in the revolution is critical to its success. We are a nation of uprooted families, our children scattered to the winds, the small farm towns abandoned, the whole country on wheels, brothers roaring by each other from coast to coast in wild pursuit of the dollar. We are losing the experience of family, of home, of place. It's not that black lawyers will always return to their neighborhoods or Poles to their ethnic communities. But most of our children do not "go home again" because they cannot, often because home has become a wasteland of opportunity. A responsible society would encourage its minorities to better themselves by utilizing their own abundant resources—their young men and women who will return from law school to take their place as community leaders. Dean Liacouras gives us a specific example of how Temple's admissions policy has assisted such goals:

Before 1972, there were some 13,500 lawyers in Pennsylvania and not a single Puerto Rican lawyer. The Puerto Rican community was leaderless and politically disorganized. In May, 1972, Nelson Diaz graduated from Temple Law School and in September was admitted to the Bar. He was the first Puerto Rican to graduate from a Pennsylvania law school and the first Puerto Rican to become a member of the Pennsylvania Bar. Within months of his admission—and even while a law student—Nelson Diaz began to serve the needs of his community. Within five years and with the help of other Puerto Rican lawyers since admitted to the Bar, Mr. Diaz has molded a politically effective community which today receives a greatly increased share of services and respect.

We seem to have no trouble supplying ourselves with excellent candidates for our football and basketball teams from a talent pool of black athletes. It is a bitter irony that at the same time our law schools are nearly pure white. The rewards to our country from lawyers committed to a just society would far outweigh those delivered to us by the athletic programs of our colleges. There is no better way for people to raise their status than to have their rights protected and their dignity preserved. Welfare in the ghettos will not benefit the nation nearly as much as assuring the black worker an equal chance at a job, fair conditions at work, and just treatment by his landlord.

Our 175 ABA-approved law schools supply us with enough lawyers, but not the right kind. In 1982, the enrollment of all minorities in ABA-approved law schools was only 9.7 percent of the total. A few schools do better. At Stanford Law School, about 20 percent of the student body are minorities, but overall, enrollment of minority students is on the decrease. Today, there are only 5,894 blacks and only 471 Puerto Ricans out of the total of 117,813 students attending our nation's law schools.

The justice revolution must begin in our law schools. The revolution demands a new and fair admissions policy. It demands that the cruel joke of the ABA's LSAT be exposed and rejected. It demands that we, the people, take direct responsibility for the selection of our nation's lawyers and community leaders. It requires us to look in the face those who aspire to the high ideals of the profession, to hear them as we wish them to hear their clients. It requires *us* to render justice. I hear the shrill scream of Power declaring that these ideas are impractical, even radical. Yet what could be more radical than if, knowing its opprobrious history, we continue to permit the ABA, long the corporate minion, to select and train the very lawyers the people engage to preserve their freedom?

12 | NEW LAW SCHOOLS

From Parts to People

The duty of the American law school is to train lawyers for the good of society. Amid vehement protest from most of the ivory towers, I charge that America's law schools are producing the same stale product that has been rejected by the people for decades. At public expense, we produce lawyers best suited to *fight* the people, best trained to represent corporate interests, and most inclined to enter the money game of the law. We take eager, fresh minds and dump them into hierarchical structures where there is a poverty of vision of a better world, a paucity of hope for its realization, and little commitment to try. Dean Roscoe Pound of Harvard viewed the law as an instrument of social change. Law professors must, he said, create a "true sociological jurisprudence." At the turn of the century in Pound's day, there was great life in the law schools, a contagious spirit that infected the student and teacher alike. One Chicago professor, speaking with an excitement and awe unheard of in most schools today, exclaimed, "Contemplate . . . what it means to be able to train the [students] who directly and indirectly are to exercise the most potent influence over the growth and development of our law!" Such, tragically, is no longer the idealism encountered in most of our law schools.

The occupants of our lawyer factories, professors and students alike, evidence the kind of dull vital energy typical of every captive. I have visited a variety of penitentiaries, and numerous law schools. In many of our law schools, I encounter the same gloom, the same latent hostility, a similar sense of despair and resignation to injustice, and a certain sadistic behavior among those in power that one observes in our nation's prisons, an existential resignation to futility acknowledged by both students and their professors. I remember being approached at one of our nation's great universities by a drawn, nervous-looking young man, who asked to speak to me privately. We moved back from the group that had gathered after my presentation on final argument. "Can you get me out of here?" he asked.

"You want me to file a writ of habeus corpus?" I countered, not fully realizing the seriousness of his plea.

"I can't take it here any longer," he said. He spoke of the appalling boredom, and how his deep disappointment in the law-school experience had smashed his vision of justice. "The professors actually mock you here if you talk about justice," he said. "You're some kind of a jerk—some kind of naïve dipshit—if you argue that something is unjust."

"What are they interested in?" I asked.

"Not much. Some get their kicks out of humiliating us. Some entertain themselves by playing their mental games. I don't know," he said.

"Why don't you leave?" I asked.

"I can't. It would break my parents' hearts. They've saved and scrimped all of their lives to get me into law school, and I've worked for as long as I can remember to get here, too. I can't leave."

"What do you want me to do?" I asked. We looked at each other for what seemed a long while, and then he shook his head and walked away.

Many law students suffer from this prison syndrome. I have spoken of it often to their teachers, some of whom claim to suffer from the same malady. A professor at a leading university recently told me of the impassioned arguments he had made at faculty meetings for a more meaningful curriculum. The schools are run by the faculty. "Most of my brethren are monks," he said. "They are trained to think in traditional ways. Ideas of change in the curriculum or the style of teaching threaten them. It's like suggesting that Jesuits abandon celibacy."

"Why don't you go somewhere else?" I asked. He was a man of considerable stature in academia.

"None of the major universities are really different," he said. There was resignation in his voice, and I have no doubt he passed along his sense of entrapment to his students.

Yet within our universities are found some of our great humanists, our legal prophets. Most are mavericks. Their thoughts are for the living, and their quiet labors have contributed much. At Harvard, one encounters Critical Legal Studies (CLS), a philosophy of legal education said to be laden with emotion and mystery, and there Roberto Mangabeira Unger writes deeply of its tenets. At Stanford, Robert Gordon, a prominent member of the group, tells how the CLS movement got its impetus in the late 1960's, when many students in those troubled times began to chafe against the insensitivity of the law. Students could not accept a justice that emerged out of the business-as-usual grindings of the same antiquated legal machinery. In a curriculum empty of ideals, the question they most often asked was: "Is law dead?" They began to demand that they be taught as human beings, persons with consciences who might espouse goals other than the mere caretaking of the wealthy, and the baby-sitting of corporate America.

Critical Legal Studies is but one of the several schools of thought that currently coexist in American law schools. The law-and-economics movement, one most closely associated with the University of Chicago, from which Judge Robert H. Bork graduated, sees the law as a tool dedicated to the economic requirements of a free-enterprise system. At the University of Wisconsin, a law-and-society approach examines the operation of the legal system through empirical research made from a sociological perspective. But the proponents of CLS do not utilize conventional concepts of economics or sociology to explain laws or institutions. As well as a scholarly approach to legal reasoning, it is a movement, and as such its members believe in a nonhierarchical, actively participating society at large. CLS emphasizes the futility of searching for any objective determinant for legal rules and legal institutions: Law becomes merely a description of our politics—a device for protecting the power relationships that exist within our society. Proponents of CLS hold the law responsible for the perpetuation of injustice and believe society can be transformed through the rediscovery of human rights.

The CLS professors see the legal profession trained for the most part as guardian of the corporate mass, as apologist for market tyranny, and as abandoning the people who depend so heavily upon the law to fulfill the American ideal of equal justice. Our lawyers, they say, should be trained not as mere systematizers of old cases but as active participants in making the difficult and delicate decisions that affect us all. We must, as Unger writes, tell the truth. Is it possible that we have descended to such abysmal depths that it is now considered revolutionary to tell the truth?

New ideas are always resisted. We fight them like hell. Yet it is curious that the idea that law and justice are somehow mysteriously related should be seen as new. It is odd that in a democracy we should see as revolutionary the idea that the law should support the rights of people as opposed to preserving a status quo antagonistic to their rights and their freedom. It is odder that such ideas should offend. Paul D. Carrington, dean of the Duke University Law School, decries the CLS professors who teach a law they do not endorse. They should resign, he argues, because it is immoral for professors to teach the young what they themselves do not believe. Should an atheist be permitted to teach theology? he asks. But who better to teach the truth than those who know it?

The law has always shrouded itself with a certain religiosity. Perhaps we have preferred to see it with our eyes closed, to blindly embrace it as sacred, to approach it as we approach God, who permits no criticism. Perhaps we have attributed to the common law a soul, a spirit, that does not exist, or that, indeed, is often incompatible with justice. Perhaps the law demands a faith that forecloses inquiry into basic questions of human need. Perhaps, like religion, the law obsequiously kneels at the feet of Power and repeats its timeworn creed rather than creating the new psalm justice requires.

Unger and the CLS movement are right. The revolt must begin in the law schools. At Harvard, it is said the faculty is too divided even to make appointments. In March 1988, President Derek Bok refused to grant tenure to Clare Dalton, a CLS professor. Derrick Bell, a law professor unallied to the CLS movement, boycotted commencement in favor of a four-day sit-in at his office to protest the faculty vote against Ms. Dalton, which he called a "threat to ideological diversity." But the movement has proponents and sympathizers in all the major law schools; and although some may not have identified their own aspirations with any movement, the fact is that in every school in the land there reside the concerned, the responsible, the liberated individuals who endow the law with ideals of social betterment, who argue that the law must be reinvented to provide a revolutionary new purpose, who demand that old power structures that inhibit democracy be torn down, and that hierarchies of Power that pervert the higher goals of our society be dismantled. The CLS movement has generated a massive literature. A few years ago, *Stanford Law Review* dedicated a six-hundred-page issue to a collection of comment on the subject. The revolt is inevitable. Were it otherwise, we should have to believe that the song of justice is perpetually caught in the throats of the good and the caring.

At a recent convention of the American Association of Law Schools, the nearly two thousand professors in attendance were again bombarded with criticism. Judge Harry P. Edwards of the United States Court of Appeals for the District of Columbia said, "Too many law professors are indifferent to or hopelessly naive about the reality of legal practice." The judge, a former professor at both Michigan and Harvard, told his academic colleagues they must change. They could no longer "afford the luxury of pure reflection," or demonstrate "active disdain" of the profession. Even Justin A. Stanley, a past president of the ABA, urged the professors to rededicate themselves to "principle" over "profit" and "professionalism" over "commercialism."

Today, students in most law schools are subjected to a curriculum reminiscent of the assembly-line manufacture of automobiles. Beginning with a piece of raw sheet metal, we force them into certain shapes, station at a time, course at a time, until what comes out is a body that looks like all the others. Deviations from predetermined specifications are discarded in the name of uniformity and quality control. Art, creativity, and individual courage stand in the way of the factory's goals. The end product is, consequently, standard and dull, and—because it has been stamped into shape instead of grown to maturity—its use is predetermined. One does not make the same demands of the car body that one does of a living tree. One rattles and rusts; the other blooms and bears fruit. Thus, void of most speaking and listening skills, bereft of an understanding of dramatic method, empty of experience either in the art of living or lawyering, the newly graduated lawyers can produce for their clients only as they themselves have been produced—according to convention, according to formula, according to rote.

It is a pleasant irony that the same law schools that so mechanized our students, that led us into these swamps and so cheerfully delivered our young to Power should now free them. Although such thinkers as Unger and Horwitz and others in the CLS movement may provide the intellectual rationale for the revolution, palpable progress comes from less esoteric sources. Clinical programs, in which students actually draft legal documents, interview living clients, or represent indigents in misdemeanor cases or the poor in landlord and tenant disputes, are now part of core curriculum in many schools. Although the Denver University Law School offered the first clinical program in 1910, most of the nation's law schools, including DU, scurried to line up in puppetlike imitations of Harvard, where the law was considered a very difficult science to be taught by professors whose experience was study, not practice. But by 1960, law students were demanding that their experience in law school be more relevant, and the seeds of the clinical approach to education, one greatly preferred by students, were planted. The clinical method of teaching saves the students from the bottomless boredom of studying long-dead appellate cases that often have little connection to the student's world. It momentarily silences the interminable drone of the professors, and proves to the students that what they study has actual application to living persons.

I remember how I, too, hated law school. I remember watching the professors pace the floor clutching their lapels as they gazed at the ceiling, filling the room with pedantic blather. It was as if we were asked to install permanently into our innards that which was lifeless and meaningless, like old phone books or wallpaper catalogs. But the new clinical programs, if they do little to train competent trial lawyers, still give the student's law-school experience a new dimension. While most of the clinical programs are focused almost entirely on poverty issues, they do tie the dry, abstract rule of law to the living client, and provide a vision of relevance to the otherwise nearly empty theoretical event called a legal education.

A few schools have done more. At City University of New York Law School at Queens College, an experiment in legal education is proceeding. The school's curriculum is aimed at the student who sees law as an instrument of social change rather than as a part of the world of business and finance. It emphasizes training for a public-interest practice involving civil liberties, public service, the environment, and defense of the indigent. It is meant to be affordable to those who could not otherwise acquire a private legal education. There, the curriculum departs from the usual. The law is not conceptualized as divided into separate compartments such as torts and criminal law. Instead, the student takes a single course on Responsibility for Injurious Conduct, which combines and synthesizes these traditional subjects. The study of contracts, corporations, and partnerships is likewise combined into a single course. Although the school utilizes the large lecture hall, it also divides the students into six "houses" of twenty-five students each, where the students work as teams handling simulated practice situations.

Northeastern University School of Law in Boston has done what most of our law schools must eventually do by joining hands with local attorneys to integrate the teaching of law with its practice. The experiment is an ambitious and exciting one. The students spend most of their first year receiving traditional classroom instruction, learning how to do legal research, writing, counseling, and negotiation. At the beginning of the second year, the class is divided into two sections—one academic, the other "cooperative." During the remaining two years, the students alternate between the two sections, so that by the time they graduate they have had a full year of work on actual cases in cooperation with local lawyers. The students at Northeastern are said to display a decided interest in public service. Michael Meltsner, who previously directed Columbia's clinical program for nine years and worked for the NAACP Legal Defense and Education Funds and until recently was the dean at Northwestern, says the school's program is "unique and is the only U.S. law school that demands systematic practice of law as a requirement for graduation." The demands of the market prevail. In 1987, Northeastern had 2,000 applications for 150 openings. Dean Meltsner said, "Frankly, we're benefiting enormously from our monopolistic position."

San Francisco's New College of California School of Law, which enjoys only California State Bar accreditation, requires its students to log six hundred hours of attorney-supervised apprentice work in public-interest law firms or public agencies, such as the Public Defender's Office, as a condition of graduation. In addition to traditional classwork taught in traditional ways, students, through the use of simulation, acquire skills in both civil and criminal cases in conjunction with their civil and criminal procedure courses. The students draft pleadings and argue motions, and each is responsible for conducting an entire mock trial, enlisting other college students as jurors. The school is not accredited by the American Bar Association, and Dean Kanios says, "We haven't even approached [the ABA] for accreditation, since their financial standards are so severe. Although we have a good working library of over twenty thousand volumes, it's still not close to ABA requirements. They also frown on part-time faculty (we rely heavily on experienced practitioners). . . . My guess is that they would also be hesitant about our flexible admissions criteria. I hope we can afford to get ABA approval someday, but not if it means the sacrifice of our ideals." The dilemma presented when a forward-looking school like the New College of California fails to earn the approbatory kiss of the ABA is that students who go to that college can take the bar only in California. In most other states, a candidate for the bar is permitted to take the same only after having attended an ABA-accredited law school.

At Stanford, one of the nation's prestigious law schools, less than half of the students get clinical training of any kind except that offered in a single freshman course called Lawyering Process, a very popular elective course that boasts the enrollment of nearly two-thirds of the first-year class. Dean Paul A. Brest says, "I think it would be desirable if more of our faculty understood the potential for that method of teaching, but it is only one method. I think those in the faculty who have not taught clinical courses tend to think that it is more complicated and more frightening than it really is, and many of the faculty members themselves do not feel qualified to teach clinically." Professor Nielsen of Hastings Law School said recently, "This reminds me of a cartoon I saw in the late '30s when commercial aviation was still in its novelty period. As I remember it, a pilot strolled nonchalantly up the airplane aisle past the nervous passengers holding a book entitled *How to Fly.* We laughed because no sane person would entrust his life or his airplane to someone who had never flown—even if he had been taught for three years 'how to think like a pilot.' "

Dean Brest admits, of course, that the direction a law school takes in its curriculum is controlled largely by the tenured professors. Most are still committed to the ghost of Christopher Columbus Langdell. While stubbornly clinging to their moldering thresholds, they curse at the light behind the door. I asked Dean Brest, "If tomorrow morning you decreed that hereafter Stanford would be run as a clinical institution, that couldn't, in fact, happen, could it?"

"That is very true," Brest replied. "That is one of the wonderful features of a major law school. It is largely run by the faculty. The dean doesn't tell people what to do." But faculty control has also become the mud in which our law schools are stuck.

Like a window in the dungeon, the clinical programs at most law schools provide the student with little more than a vision of the possibilities of the profession. They do not and cannot train competent trial lawyers. They do not purport to. The clinical programs at most law schools have become only stopgap programs at best, and an excuse for maintaining the status quo. Law schools can point to these programs and argue that they, too, have entered the twentieth century, after which they can go right on teaching the same old curriculum in the same old way. From Harvard to Stanford and from Michigan to Yale, the students are still bored and what these and most other schools in the country still produce are graduates essentially unqualified to represent human beings in the simplest of human affairs.

Dean Brest of Stanford admits, "If the student is likely to go into a solo practice, then our graduates would be badly prepared. The assumption underlying our law school is that they are going to work for firms in which they will be apprenticed. In medical school, the student is given clinical training with live patients. In law school, we turn them over to the firms for that training." Brest states that over 90 percent of Stanford's students eventually end up in large firms.

"How do you feel about that?" I asked.

"I think for their own good too many of our students go to work for huge megafirms. After a few years, they don't enjoy the practice. I wish they wouldn't follow the herd instinct."

If we are to train young lawyers who avoid the delirious sirens of lucre at the large corporate firms, the dominant force in the law schools must shift from the pedagogical to the practical, from the pedagogue to the practitioner. Already, UCLA and Stanford are offering tenure to their clinical professors. The idea that "those who know how" are inferior to "those who merely know" is an awesome idiocy. The notion that clinicians cannot be legally sound, that scholarship is limited to the academician, that trial lawyers are merely empty-headed actors without substance, is imbecilic. More and more, the new professors will be those who have been tried and bloodied in the pits, and who will have fought the good wars for people until they are bone-weary and street-smart.

The loss of academic freedom threatens our law schools more than most academicians care to admit. Our professors bow to the dictates of the Multistate Bar Examination (MBE) in much the same way as priests and bishops accept the omnipotence of the pope. The curriculum does vary slightly from school to school, but this is more illusory than real, for no matter how the school may assert its freedom, unless most of its graduates can pass the MBE, another of those uniform multiple-choice tests powered by a computer, it will soon close its doors. Since the test is the same for a law student who will be practicing in a small village in northern Oregon representing lumberjacks and their families as for one who will go into a large firm in Atlanta, Georgia, representing corporate interests, the basic curricula of law schools across the land are nearly uniform.

To the extent that all lawyers must possess a basic knowledge of the law, it is acceptable that they be tested for such knowledge. But the principal objective of our law schools should not be to satisfy the MBE's computer. Yet all states but Indiana, Iowa, Louisiana, and Washington require applicants for admission to the bar to take and pass that examination. While the scores required for passage vary from state to state, all applicants need demonstrate only their skills as test-takers to earn the nod of the bar. I know a lawyer who takes bar examinations as a hobby and has been admitted to practice in numerous states. Yet he does not possess the skills to make a coherent three-minute presentation on how to make pancakes, and he knows it. He edits technical trade papers for a living.

The idea of the MBE is to test the applicant's knowledge in six essential areas of the law. Yet, as with the LSAT, a single point can be the difference between acceptance or rejection by the bar. Hence, the student in Wyoming who scores 125 on his bar exam may pursue his life's work, while one scoring 124 may not. The difference may be the extent of the test-taker's fright or whether he slept well the night before or took a course on how to pass the MBE—or more recently, enlisted the aid of the blood-pressure reducing drug propranolol, which supposedly gives one an edge by helping to control anxiety. There is a nearly universal reaction of loathing to the experience: Those who take it feel that something other than knowledge of the law was being tested, something they can not exactly define. One student told me after he had taken the test he felt as if he had been "messed with."

"What do you mean by that?" I asked.

"I feel like they didn't care about what I really knew. It seemed like what they wanted to know about was something very private."

"What?" I asked.

"They wanted to know how my mind was constructed, how it worked. There was something insidious about it I can't put my finger on."

I have heard this pervasive complaint expressed in numerous ways. Some say they felt humiliated; others, that the experience was degrading, insulting.

One of my Chicago associates, who was brilliant as both a student and a lawyer, told me recently, "I have never felt so close to being inhuman in my life as when I took the Multistate. Weeks before the test, I was so nervous no one could even speak to me. I was disintegrating. I was afraid I couldn't make it through the exam because by now I was also suffering from uncontrolled diarrhea. I bought the largest bottle of Kaopectate they had in the drugstore, took it with me, and set it on the desk. I glanced around the room. The place looked like a convention of drug dealers. There were assortments of bottles and pills on the tables everywhere. While I was absorbed in the test, every so often I unconsciously took a swig from the bottle in front of me. By the time I had finished off all of the Kaopectate, my gut was bound up for three solid weeks."

There seems to be no uniform agreement on the correct answers to MBE questions. Law professors rarely agree on them. Professors at Georgetown Law Center could not agree on correct answers to 25% of the questions, which, of course, means that the student who was more empathic with one professor at Georgetown might fail the test, while one more in tune with the other would pass it. Each state gives an additional section in the bar examination, often using essay questions, that further tests the applicant's knowledge of the law peculiar to the state. Yet most states now accept the authors of the MBE as the nation's ultimate authority on basic law, an attribute that is difficult to justify. Who tests the testers? Who tests the tests? And what is the real purpose of the test? Leslie Whitmer, executive director of the Kentucky Bar, insisted, as do nearly all students who take the test, that the MBE does not accurately examine a student's knowledge of the law. "The multiple-choice answers are so close that many questions can have more than one answer." Most lawyers agree that the bar exams are not intended to test lawyer competence but to restrict membership in the bar. This issue was raised in New Jersey, where the pass rate dropped from 85 percent to 47 percent. The bar exam is always in the hands of the long-established and usually prosperous members of the bar. When one gets to the top of the mountain, it may be tempting to pull up the rope. Professor Jerold S. Auerbach, commenting on the efficacy of the bar examination, says, "Perhaps the burden of proof has by now shifted to the bar: to offer evidence, if there is any, that the exam does indeed test legal competence. If the evidence is lacking, so is any justification for existing bar admission procedure."

It is the duty of the law school in Wyoming, as it is in New Hampshire and Texas, to train lawyers with skills consistent with the needs of the communities they will serve within the state. The fulfillment of that mandate is greatly deterred by the massive energy expended by our law schools in training students to please the MBE computer. But the MBE, like the LSAT, is cheap to administer and can be graded in seconds. The MBE, as yet another obstacle our students must hurdle, contributes much to the deadly atmosphere of oppression in our law schools. There, professors become more consumed with the demands of the MBE than with new and more creative approaches to teaching, and students become more concentrated on techniques of test-taking than on lawyering. It takes time to select the best students, and time to train them, and it takes time to finally test the product of our efforts. However, it is time we must invest, for we invest it in ourselves.

As New Students enrich our New Law Schools, and as the pedants are gradually replaced with practitioners, and as ideals that link law to justice begin to predominate, these centers of learning will begin to host the most important and innovative movements in the law. I envision a New Law School in which the best practitioners in every state deem it a great honor to be asked to share their great gifts with students. The New Law School will be easily accessible to judges, who will also congregate there and mix freely with lawyers and students as colleagues. They would rejoin the profession in search of better ways to advance their own elusive skills in judging other human beings and in delivering justice to the people.

At the New Law School, production-line education will be abolished. The abstract lecture will become passé. There, students, teachers, lawyers, and judges will meet as colleagues, to share their learning. Professor Kingsfield of *Paper Chase* fame will be a pitied anachronism, the epitome of the frightened savant who wishes his students to be as frightened as he. As in all true teaching, the professors (now Senior Associates) will benefit from the experience as much as the students. The Senior Associates will be generalists— veteran practitioners who will have labored in the courtrooms, drawn wills, struggled for the custody of their clients' kids, and defended the indigent. Some will be full-time faculty, and some will be practicing attorneys on sabbatical.

Over the years, I have taught with many a trial lawyer at the National College for Criminal Defense Lawyers (now at Macon, Georgia), a three-week summer seminar devoted to advancing the trial skills of practitioners, mostly young public defenders. These lawyer-teachers contribute their time, and covet the opportunity to serve. They do so not only out of a giving spirit, but because the experience brings them great happiness, knowledge, and energy. They know we never teach more than we learn, never give more than we receive.

The New Law Students will learn from *doing*, the only method by which true learning is acquired. The carpenter does not learn his trade by reading how to hold a hammer. In their first days of law school, the students will be assigned to cases that local attorneys and their clients have offered, cases that would usually get short shrift in most private law practices. Let us say an old woman slipped on some grapes in the aisle of Safeway, broke her hip, and as a result was confined to a nursing home where she lay unattended until she developed festering bedsores. The sores became infected, and finally the old woman died. The nursing home, owned by a national corporation, failed to provide her with proper care. She was an old woman, whose only living relative was a niece. Even without the injury, her life expectancy would have been very short, so the anticipated damages in the case, beyond her medical costs, are somewhat limited. The claim would be hard-fought by the lawyers for the hospital's insurance company, so that the risk-recovery ratio would discourage many general practitioners from taking the case in the first place.

Our students will be divided into teams of no more than ten— two teams to a group. One of the veteran lawyers-turned-teacher will supervise both teams in his group. Concurrently, the other team will be assigned to another case, say, one of an employee who has been wrongfully libeled in his personnel file by a vindictive foreman at the place where he had previously worked, and who now cannot get a job. He has been turned down on over fifteen occasions. He is past fifty. Finally he will look no further. He cannot stand the humiliation. He will not venture out of his house. He is withering perceptibly each day. He cannot pay his bills. The bank has repossessed his car and sold it for a sum not sufficient to pay off his loan, and now the credit bureau has begun calling him at all hours, harassing him for the balance. He cannot sleep. His wife believes he is suicidal.

One night, some friends take the couple to a movie to try to raise the man's spirits. No sooner have they taken their seats in the theater than the man is called out of the movie by an usher. Immediately he thinks of his ailing father. The old man must have died, and with the adrenaline pumping through his body, the son rushes to the telephone, where he is greeted by the same hounding voice from the credit bureau demanding payment and threatening to turn him over to the police if he doesn't pay within twenty-four hours. That night, the man has a stroke.

Within the first days of law school, and under the guidance of the Senior Associate, the students will actually be driven out of the classroom and into the streets to gather the facts, to obtain the records, to seek and interview the witnesses, even to take photographs. Both teams will meet daily and review their cases, and hear each other's suggestions for the next day's work. Their Senior Associate will not only ask questions that open new doors of inquiry for them, but direct them away from dangerous places by showing how, for example, the students must observe certain rules of ethics in their interrogations so that both the witnesses and their opponents are treated fairly. Their minds unleashed and able to run free, the students themselves will discover new solutions to old problems. They will learn that the key to success is not genius, not good looks, not belonging to the right clubs or seeking the patronage of those in power, but the wondrous creative energy that is born of simply caring and hard work.

In the first week, the students will receive a concentrated course on how to use the school's library. They must learn the law, but the responsibility for doing so is principally theirs. They may discover something marvelous—that the law is a tool, and that they must have tools with which to shape justice. Their Senior Associate will suggest sources of reading and assign different students to various legal inquiries as the class develops. In the meeting place, the students will report on what they have discovered, and be encouraged to express their own views. They are expected to argue their positions freely and to ask questions. What conduct does society condone, and what acts does it prohibit and why? What principles should we follow in making the law? What is negligence? What are the elements of negligence? What is justice? From time to time, the Senior Associate may present small vignettes on the law that fill in the spaces or put foundation, structure, and form to what has been developing, but in most cases the students will teach themselves the law, not to pass the MBE, but because they must know it in order to solve the problems presented in their cases.

Before the suit is actually filed, the students must consider the most important first question: Do they have a case? Then they must draft pleadings. Perhaps they will be permitted by the local trial judge to argue the motions that arise before trial, and when the case comes to trial, the students can help the local lawyer prepare the witnesses and provide him with the necessary briefs on the law. By this time, these would-be warriors for the people will have observed firsthand how the law actually operates, how abstract cases in the law books do in fact apply to living people, and how their own work—yes, and their failures as well—can affect the lives of human beings.

In most law schools, the curriculum of the first semester typically includes a lecture course in torts, perhaps one each in property, civil procedure, and contracts. By the end of three years in a traditional school, most students have had no more than a passing brush with any live client; some have had none at all. In our New Law School, the students will have discovered how the law in several fields can come together to protect the rights of their clients. From just these two cases, students in the group will have already been introduced to important aspects of torts, contracts, labor law, corporations, insurance law, estates, mortgages, creditors' rights, evidence, civil procedure, and ethics. They will have learned to research the law, to write, and to argue. They will learn that it is all right to be afraid of failing, because much depends upon their success. But they will also learn that they can be adequate. No longer will they be late for their eight o'clock classes; they will be waiting for the doors to open. They will have to be driven from the library at midnight. Passion, not fear, will drive the New Law School.

At the end of each semester, the students will be tested on the body of law they have learned from their experiences in both cases, and they will be graded. Part of their learning will be to review their examination paper with the Senior Associate to find where they went wrong and to discover what they did not learn. They will also be judged on their participation in the business of solving human problems. It will be here that the Senior Associate will encourage those who obviously love the profession and guide those elsewhere who possess no true passion for it. That a student is able to post high scores on his written examination is obviously no indication that he or she will be a good lawyer or be happy in the practice of law; in the New Law School, students do not have to wait the three years until they graduate to discover whether the law should be their life's work. The early weeding out of those who have no actual feel for the practice will help raise the overall quality of the profession. Most students never have a chance to sense what the practice of law is really about until after they have already invested their three years. Then, for many, it is too late. Exhausted both mentally and financially, they have little choice but to pursue a career for which they have no passion, and, year after year, a lifetime of clients suffer and add their complaints to the grumbling concord.

As weeks pass in the New Law School and the cases are resolved, the students will become members of new teams led by other Senior Associates. By the end of the second year, they may have had direct experience in as many as twenty cases, including a divorce, a bankruptcy, a property dispute, and a case in contracts. They may have taken on the defense of several indigent persons charged with crimes. By the end of the second year, they will have expanded their knowledge of criminal law and constitutional law and become budding experts in the fields of evidence and procedure. They will have learned about taxation and have drawn up actual partnership agreements, formed small corporations, drafted contracts, and probated a will. They will have developed skills in interviewing clients, in dealing with both lay and expert witnesses, and in working as a team with their own colleagues. By the end of the second year, their eclectic experience will begin to take on a vague form—a sense of the mysterious *corpus legis*—the body of the law.

The favorite myth of the academician—that the law is a mass of tangled, perplexing, divinely abstruse rules that only the intellectually chosen can hope to comprehend—will be laid to rest. The law is not hard to grasp. Yet we have convinced both ourselves and the public otherwise. Perhaps such fables are necessary in order to justify our fees. But I could teach most legal principles to most eighth graders in a relatively short time, and a jury, contrary to myth, is very intelligent, often very wise. Were it not so, how could we instruct juries on the law and successfully argue legal principles to them and leave justice in their hands? Many lawyers and some judges refuse to acknowledge that ordinary people can grasp the law, but the problem has never been the intelligence of jurors, but of lawyers and judges who have not yet learned to speak plainly and precisely to ordinary people. Big fees, big positions, big prestige, and big reputations seem to depend on big words—and an unjustified big mystery surrounding the law and our justice system.

Plain talk! That is the secret to the art of advocacy. It is a wonder that we use such monstrosities—long, difficult, mysterious words—instead of spare, direct ones that do the same job, only better. Perhaps those who use highbrow words do not wish to be understood. Perhaps they are afraid of their thoughts or ashamed of them, or more likely, they have no clear thought at all.

I do not trust people who use large words, nor do juries. When I hear a speaker use strange words, I suspect he intends to elevate himself by them as he tramples over me, knowing I must either feign understanding or admit ignorance—either way he wins, and either way he has caused me discomfort. To look at it another way, plain speaking is plain caring.

In their third year, the New Law Students will continue with their in-school practice of the law, but now they will also take concentrated courses in the various subjects that every student must know. In this way, students may fill in any remaining gaps in their learning and prepare for their upcoming bar examination. Now, what they learn makes sense. Now, what they learn is more than boring, abstract principle. What they learn confirms what they have already experienced concerning the lives of people they have known and cared for.

So educated, the New Lawyers will graduate with a zeal for justice and with solid ideals of what is right and what is wrong. They will have learned that the truly elite of the profession are those who are expert at serving the human species. They will graduate yearning to work for people, because they will have learned that therein lies fulfillment. The old-time lawyer with his snout in the corporate trough who sells his life away, measured chunk at a time, the way the corporation sells its beer or its television sets, will lose prestige. The demand for the New Lawyer will explode, making the old law schools that roll out their production-line drones for corporate America curious anachronisms.

The New Lawyers will have had their dreams reinforced, not shattered, during their education. Indeed, that is one of its most vital functions. After three years at the New Law School, most graduates would not fit comfortably into the typical large corporate firm. They would only become troublemakers there. They would not respect senior partners merely because of their lofty social positions or their money. They would require their elders to earn their respect by what they do. They would continually question the motives of the law firm and refuse to be consumed by it as a mere money-making tool for a purely money-making machine. Simply stated, our New Lawyers would be trained champions *for the people*.

No longer will the bar examination be a means to lock out those who are people-friendly and computer-wary. The candidates will be judged principally for who they are, not how well they can take tests. I know many an inmate in our penitentiaries who could pass the bar with a little tutoring. How can our law schools produce lawyers who have a conscience when they are only required to have a brain that can make correct selections on multiple-choice tests? The applicant's record at the New Law School will weigh as heavily as the bar examination itself. There, his or her true mettle will have already been tested in real cases. There, they will have already proven their willingness and their courage. We will no longer need only to hope the graduates are ethical; their training from the beginning has demanded it and proven it. Although the applicant must exhibit a sound knowledge of the law, the MBE must, at last, be abolished.

Today, there are pitifully few lawyers who, in an entire lifetime, have acquired the requisite skills to adequately represent people in a difficult jury trial. After having met thousands of good men and women of the bar, dedicated and learned as they are, I would find it difficult to name three I would confidently hire to represent me in court in an important case. This is not an indictment of the many lawyers of this country who would lay their lives across the tracks for their clients, but of the educational system that has spawned them. And even after our New Lawyers graduate, they are not sufficiently trained to try a major case before a jury. That takes more. Fortunately, we can give them more. And we must.

No one would question that a general practitioner should take a residency in surgery if he intends to do other than simple procedures. But our trial lawyers are deprived of this training and are left to learn this difficult skill the best way they can—mostly through bitter mistakes—often at the expense of deserving clients. It is as if each of us must rediscover the wheel, as if each is destined to learn for himself by trial and error those skills that have been known for centuries but that have never been gathered in one place and passed on as an organized and teachable craft. Many are educated at the public expense as prosecuting attorneys or public defenders. Most of the good trial lawyers are sooner or later picked off by corporations to join their stables of litigators. But if we are entitled to a skilled surgeon to remove a diseased gallbladder, are we not also entitled to a competent trial lawyer to win justice for us? My own experience in teaching trial lawyers for the past decade at various law schools and bar seminars around the country has established beyond doubt that the art of advocacy *is* teachable. Trial lawyers are not born. They must be taught.

It would, of course, be absurd to argue that if the referee at a football game applies the rules fairly and evenly between the junior varsity and the Chicago Bears, justice will be the natural result. The right to a skilled advocate exceeds all other constitutional due-process considerations, because a system of justice that depends upon courtroom combat to fully distill the truth becomes a mockery when the skills of the people's champions are not comparable to those fielded by powerful corporations. What is offered is not justice: It is the cruel, senseless, often embarrassingly transparent caricature of justice.

Haywood Burns, dean of the City University of New York Law School at Queens College, says, "Too many lawyers are serving too few interests." He believes there are two distinct legal professions, one for the rich, the other for the poor, and that the gap between the two is widening. Even the ABA is beginning to see it. Justin Stanley, former president of that organization, said that the standard three-year program of study at law schools might not best serve a society in which lawyers for corporate interests perform very different services from lawyers for the poor. Curiously, *those who represent people in trials require more training than those who merely represent corporations*. The skills required—skills in advocacy, in communication with humans, skills in empathizing with the living—are more varied, more difficult.

How shall we train trial lawyers for the people? Let us begin by gathering together the trial masters of the country to discover what expertise they possess and how those skills can most efficiently be grafted to practicing lawyers. I envision what might be understood as a "residency" in trial law by lawyers who have first graduated from law school and passed the bar. In the laboratory courtroom, these lawyers will acquire reasonable trial competency in as short a time as a year. They will gain skills that most trial lawyers never acquire. In the courtroom lab, budding trial lawyers can afford to take chances, try new methods, and explore their own boundaries.

They can make that great final argument, and then get honest and immediate feedback, and they can make their argument again and again until they have learned how to form it and deliver it convincingly.

The budding trial lawyer can learn to excel in the art of cross-examination as most veteran attorneys can never hope to. There are two ways a lawyer can become skilled in taking on, say, the insurance company's medical expert. He can lose ten cases trying to acquire that skill, or he can practice cross-examining that expert again and again under the guiding hand of a master in the safety of a laboratory. Suppose that in our practice case, taken from an actual trial, a child is so injured during delivery that he is born hopelessly, permanently injured, a spastic quadriplegic. For many hours, while the mother labored away unsuccessfully, the doctor failed even to show up. When he finally arrived, the mother was exhausted, and the doctor, still inattentive, failed to respond to the clear signs on the monitor that the child was being literally strangled to death. The defense, offered by the doctor's expert, utterly at odds with the plaintiff's expert, was that the tracings of the infant's heartbeat on the monitor were not exceptionally abnormal and that the doctor acted in accordance with the standard in the community—that this was an unfortunate accident, a risk attendant to all deliveries.

With the defendant's expert witness, a board-certified ob-gyn physician, on the stand, we would begin the laboratory cross-examination. The witness would be a veteran of many trials and one the insurance company usually hires because of his skills, not in medicine, but in testifying. To win, our student—the parents' lawyer—must not only effectively discredit the expert, he must do so while the defendant's attorney protects his witness.

A lawyer usually doesn't win his case. His opponent loses it. It is in the cross-examination of the expert in every civil case that the best and clearest cases are lost. The student is young and probably angry or afraid. The expert on the stand may be a charlatan, but his qualifications are impressive, he appears calm, certain, and knowledgeable, and his opinions are always weighted heavily in favor of the defendant who pays his fee. The student naturally wants to attack. And he does. He has not yet learned that although it is all right, even imperative, to accurately communicate his feelings, he must be able to do so appropriately. He shouts at the expert, who answers quietly and reasonably. The student, having been taught that it is all right to feel angry, attacks again, this time pointing his finger and demanding that the expert tell him how he comes to his

ridiculous conclusions—and the expert does. The answer takes fifteen minutes. It is clear and precise and convincing. The parents'
case is lost.

When the time for feedback comes, the student and his colleagues,
under the guidance of their Senior Associate, will dissect the failure.
First, they will consider the *dynamic* created in the confrontation
between the witness and the attorney. What was really going on in
this affray? It was a contest between a lawyer, who in his outrage
at his clients' pain attacked a seemingly reasonable person, an authority well schooled and qualified to testify, the chief of his department in a large hospital, a man with years of experience. The
expert seemed honest and likable. Why should anyone attack him
so? The lawyer had unwittingly transformed himself into the villain.
Suddenly the jury wanted the witness to win.

After a real trial, the attorney, having lost a case of clear negligence, would probably never understand what had happened to him.
He would rage that he had a lying expert on the stand whom he
attacked vigorously but the jury was too obtuse to see the truth—
at least, that's how he would tell it. No one would have advised the
young lawyer that you cannot attempt to kill any witness until the
jury wants him killed—until he has been carefully, quietly exposed
as a fake.

In the courtroom laboratory, the student will now try again with
the same expert. Again he will fail. This time, having done his
homework, he may begin to duel with the expert on technical questions concerning fetal-monitoring devices. But the expert, of course,
knows more, or sounds as though he does. After all, whom should
the jury believe, a lawyer barely dry behind the ears, or the experienced doctor who testifies confidently and reasonably in his own
specialty? And once again the beginning trial lawyer will learn why
he lost. Again the lawyer will take on the same expert until he learns
how to persuasively display to the jury that this man is merely a
lackey whose job it is to convince them of a false theory in the case.
The student will learn that good cross-examination is not only sound
technique but also the result of tedious labor during many long
nights. He must discover: In what other cases has the expert testified? Have all his prior depositions been scanned for contradictory
testimony? What authoritative articles has he written? Does his
testimony match the themes of his published material? Has the
expert interviewed all witnesses necessary to his opinions? Can the
student change the expert to the man wearing the black hat by
causing him to become defensive, to give evasive answers, or to
display hostility? The methods of successful attack are many, and

the new trial attorney will learn those that can work and how, and those that will fail and why. In a few weeks, he will acquire actual experience that will be equivalent to twenty years of failure in the courtroom. And there will be no corpses stacked in front of the door of his psyche.

The New Trial Lawyers will become aware of the rhythm of dance, the texture and structure of painting, the music of poetry, and incorporate what they learn into courtroom skills. In the courtroom laboratory, the fledgling trial lawyers will learn to observe and analyze how their children can speak simple truths. They will learn more from the country auctioneer and the old Baptist preacher about making final arguments than they can learn from most speech professors. They must learn to listen as well as to speak. I can tell whether my adversary is making points that I need to answer merely by the sound of his voice. The arguments that could devastate my case may be falling on deaf ears because the sounds that carry his arguments are meager. The New Trial Lawyers must learn that it is all right not only to be afraid, but to express that fear and, at appropriate times, to communicate both love and anger, and to bear pain. They will learn that it is permissible to be real in the courtroom because *they* are the final focus in every case, and they are either honest with their feelings, and therefore believable, or not. *They* are their clients' case, and if they have seen nothing, heard nothing, and felt nothing, and have given back nothing except tricks and clever techniques, they will also receive nothing from the jury. The role of the trial lawyer is to complete the dynamic of "gift"— the giving of one's self to the client's cause in return for which the jury will—trust the jury—deliver back its greatest gift of all— justice.

The New Trial Lawyer will severely challenge the traditional view society has held of the criminal-defense attorney. Many hope that lawyers representing criminals charged with heinous crimes will not cause much trouble and will aid the state in getting them off the street. Even the judges' expectations of the criminal-defense lawyer today are not much different than those of the fifteenth century. The ancient authors of the *Malleus* admonished magistrates about a lawyer who dares defend an accused witch:

> His behavior must be modest and free from prolixity and pretentious oratory. Secondly, he must . . . not bring forward any fallacious arguments or reasoning . . . or introduce legal quirks and quibbles if he be a skilled lawyer, or bring counter-accusations; especially in cases of this sort, which must be conducted as simply and summarily as possible.

The New Trial Lawyers will recognize that to deprive the guilty of their right to a full and fair trial is to deprive the innocent of theirs as well.

Who will finance this additional year for the training of trial lawyers? Society must. For years, we have been training corporate lawyers at our public universities at the taxpayers' expense. No one has thought that unjust. I take it no one could object if we began to train people's trial lawyers at the people's expense as well. It is our turn. Loans for the education of the New Trial Lawyer should be made easily available. If the lawyer practices for five years representing the public or a clientele that he or she can demonstrate is principally composed of the poor, the debt should be deemed automatically repaid, for his service will have lessened the burden presently borne by society. At Stanford, such a program is already in place. To encourage students to go into public-interest work, the school has a loan-forgiveness program so that those working in low-paying jobs after law school will have to pay less back and at a slower rate.

At the same time and place that we train our New Trial Lawyers, we should also be training New Judges in the obscure art of judging. Since judges and lawyers labor together, it seems obvious that they should be trained together. Moreover, it follows that trial lawyers and judges who learn their skills together inside the trial laboratory will work outside the laboratory with greater respect and understanding. Such training should occur as psychodrama in a courtroom setting. Lawyer and judge alike will crawl inside the hide of every other human participant in the drama: the client, the witness, the juror, the judge—even the opposing counsel. The true issues that arise from the trial experience will be explored. Students will learn to hear what is *communicated*, rather than to listen to the mere words that are being spoken. They will learn in what manner their acts and words affect the other participants in the trial because they have *become* the others. The lawyer who erupts into an irrational rage in response to a harsh ruling from the judge will begin to understand that he is really fighting the authority of his psychic father, and that such battles should be resolved elsewhere. The judge may learn that his need to exercise power over the other participants stems from a terrorizing insecurity. We can train lawyers and judges for the people. We are capable.

Professor Morton Horwitz of Harvard Law School says, "The law school curriculum is frozen at the ideology of 1870," but he, too, is optimistic. In the next ten years, Horwitz sees prodigious changes ahead for Harvard, changes already seeded by the Critical Legal Studies movement and advanced by the younger professors who will gradually breathe new life into the law school, a new moral content, one that reflects a law school with a purpose, with a commitment to the needs of the society it serves, one that has a vision—of justice for all.

13 | NEW JUDGES

People's Judges
Judging People

If we could only raise the caliber of judges slightly, we could elevate the quality of justice enormously. Even a majority of ABA members believe that "a significant proportion of judges are not qualified to preside over serious cases." Perhaps we expect too much of them. Judges are usually not individuals born of expansive minds and spacious souls. Often they have enjoyed mediocre success in practice or in politics and have sought the judiciary to obtain respect and power. They have not been specially trained as judges, and may have had little experience as trial lawyers. Many have grown in the shade of the corporate roof or have been on the public payroll as prosecutors for most of their careers. When they take the bench, they do not leave behind their fund of experiences. Their viewpoints, their attitudes, their quirks and kinks, ascend with them. Like the rest of us, they are ruled by who they are, which includes what they have been.

How do judges make their decisions? The great jurist Benjamin Cardozo said, "If you ask how he is to know when one interest outweighs another, I can only answer that he must get his knowledge just as the legislator gets it, from experience, and study and reflection; in brief, from life itself." One wonders about Cardozo, this judge's son who might just as well have issued a lifetime of safe, predictable pronouncements from the bench, all in harmony with precedent, and then vanished through the waiting door of oblivion. But there was something different about Cardozo. He had a vision of a law that looked at itself, that was aware of its power to touch and change the way people live. Take his now-celebrated case of *MacPherson* v. *Buick*. Before this landmark decision in 1916, if you bought a new car that killed your family when its front wheel broke, you could not sue the manufacturer. After all, didn't everyone realize that there was no "privity of contract" between you and the manufacturer? But those are only words, you say—words that have nothing to do with blameless people dying in the carnage. And what does this strange word, *privity*, have to do with the right of people to receive justice? Naturally, MacPherson bought his new car from a dealer, not from the Buick Motor Company. Under the law as Cardozo found it, since there was no contractual relationship—no "privity" between MacPherson and Buick—the manufacturer was perfectly protected from liability and the public utterly unprotected. The choice was Cardozo's. He could cling to established case law that had long shielded the manufacturer, or he could abandon the fiction of "privity of contract" and deliver justice to MacPherson. His now-famous case overturned ages of unjust precedent and required the manufacturer to bear responsibility for its defective products, today an idea as common as cabbage. But what would Cardozo's decision have been had his pre-judge life been spent defending insurance companies against the claims of such as Mr. MacPherson? If, as Cardozo insists, the judges' decisions reflect their experience, then are we not entitled to have judges whose experiences most nearly match our own?

We are proud that we are "the melting pot of the world," and that across this broad, rich continent live people of all races and creeds—"a duke's mixture" of men and women of eclectic origins, religions, and dreams. To be sure, most of us are not wealthy. Most of us do not wield great power. Most of us cannot influence a politician or purchase the services of a movie star to speak for us on television. Obviously, there are as many women as men in the country, and we also know that over 20 percent of our population is minority. Yet our judiciary as a whole does not reflect who we are. As a composite group, it reflects, in fact, who we are not—the white, male, powerful elite. I wonder what the state of justice would be in America if our predominantly white male judges were turned out in favor of a cross section of judges chosen from women and minorities and from attorneys who have spent their lifetimes representing people instead of corporations? Why, in an alleged government of the people, has no reasonable attempt been made to match the judiciary to a likeness of the people it judges?

I harbor other grave doubts about the composition of the judiciary.

Even among the white, elitist males who dominate the judiciary, do we select the right personality types to judge us? By the very act of seeking a judgeship, doesn't a candidate disqualify himself? Should one who yearns for such power over other human beings be trusted with it? Plato spoke of that phenomenon in the *Republic*: "Whereas the truth is that the State in which the rulers are most reluctant to govern is always the best and most quietly governed, and the State in which they are the most eager, the worst." The Chinese in those great early dynasties never permitted their rulers to seek power. *They* sought the ruler. In a murder case where the jurors have the power to inflict the death penalty, would we permit citizens to serve on a jury who line up at the courthouse door pushing and yammering for the chance to do so?

The very nature of judging requires us to select judges differently and in a more random fashion, for if we are a people of dissimilar roots who cherish our individuality, do we not require that the collective experience of those who judge us be as wide and rich as our own? Judges must be chosen from the broadest possible assortment of qualified attorneys, not from the few who have been nurtured by powerful, private interests and who, by rearing and experience, are pledged to the goals of the corporate sector; nor should we nominate large numbers of those who, as prosecutors, have waged their wars on behalf of Power. How can they understand our trespasses and hear our pleas for mercy?

Two things seem very clear to me: First, there is no way to identify the lawyer who possesses the true judicial heart. Judging, like painting, is an art. We cannot know the master by the mere fact that he takes up his brush. We must view his canvas. Similarly, we are unable to predict those few among the many who will be the great judges. But this we know: Those who seek the power are those who more likely need it. The way we choose our judges is the way we choose our spouses—we usually get them for life, for better or for worse.

Second, the way we choose our judges, despite the deluding trappings of democratic selection, has deprived us of a representative judiciary. Dazzling exceptions may blind us, but in the end, Power in this country is vested not in Congress but, as usual, in the black-robed, wily, silent minions of Power. All the lobbying in Congress, all the maneuvering and wrangling for bills, all the positive, creative, reformatory legislative labor, is for naught—for the ultimate power rests in the hands of the judiciary. Roosevelt understood that and wanted to pack the courts; Reagan understands it and has. The people, too, must finally understand, and when they do they will see we have no alternative but to *draft our judges* in much the same way that we draft jurors—on a case-by-case basis. We would not select jurors to sit for life and assign every case that comes along to them for decision. We argue for a more eclectic jury, one constantly renewed from the wellspring of the people. We would not select a jury of twelve wizened old devils whose exposure to the dark side of the human condition has hardened their hearts and callused their souls. Yet we vest such judges with nearly unlimited power, even in their dotage, over the lives of all our citizens.

We must draft our judges. We have no other choice. Were we to install such a procedure today, the judges assigned to hear our cases would not, of course, reflect a true cross section of the population. However, as the New Law Schools begin to recruit a more representative body of students, so gradually will those who are drafted as judges become more reflective of the people they judge. But were we to begin drafting our judges now, even from our present imperfect fund of lawyers, we would enjoy astounding benefits. Immediately we would be relieved of those who arrogantly, uncaringly judge us from the safety of life tenure. Many who rule against us out of blind allegiance to Power would be out. Those who seek judgeships to exert their own personal power would never get in, except by chance, and then their rule would be quickly over. Although the redistribution of judicial power would not be complete or yet fully representative, the drafting of judges would at once sever the judiciary from its indecent umbilical connection to Power.

But wouldn't this process permit the unethical, the lowbrow, the ambulance chaser, the near idiot, to take the bench? Yes, of course, depending upon the requirements we set for those we draft. But the mischief is for that one case only, which hopefully can be corrected on appeal. And who argues that this kind does not already fill certain slots on the judiciary—for life? It is only more difficult to identify the crooked judge or rid ourselves of the incompetent. Who really believes that the average intelligence of the bench as a whole is better than that of the bar? One might wager in the opposite direction, for our best and brightest do not usually serve as judges. Drafting our judges from the total trial bar, including the best and the worst among us, could only improve the overall quality of the judiciary.

A draft system for judges would be easily implemented. The clerks of the various courts would keep records on the lawyers who practice before them and forward their annual reports to the office of an assigning judge. This judge would identify all who meet the qualifications set by the legislature for the various levels of the judiciary.

The qualifications of a trial judge might be, for example, that he or she be a member in good standing of the bar of the state, have engaged in the practice of law for no less than, say, five years, and have tried at least five jury trials to verdict. (Large numbers of our judges have never tried a jury case on their own in their entire careers.) When the attorney meets these qualifications, his or her name is automatically placed in the trial judges' box. When a case requires a judge, the assigning judge will, at a public session of court, reach into the trial judges' box and select a name at random, designating the attorney whose name has been drawn as the judge in that case. Matters of disqualification because of a conflict of interest or questions concerning the attorney's inability to serve would be resolved by the assigning judge.

When I discuss this plan with practicing lawyers, their most frequent objection is that they can ill afford to take such assignments. We, of course, must pay them as we pay jurors for their services, but hopefully not at such a penurious rate. What if a lawyer were picked as a judge for a trial that dragged on three months or even a year? What do jurors do? How is it that lawyers possess a superior exemption to public service? We lawyers never hesitate to demand that a jury hear even the most insignificant of cases nowadays. In a thousand-dollar fender-bender, the lawyer has the right to wrest twelve people away from their lives to hear his case at a combined expense to the jurors of many times the amount at issue. The lawyer argues that in America it is the sacred right of his client to do so, as indeed it is. Yet I argue that lawyers have an even greater duty to serve the system from which they themselves glean their living.

How would we select our appellate judges? In the same manner as juries, I should think, except their qualifications will be somewhat higher. We might set these kinds of qualifications: Lawyers with fifteen years' experience who have served as trial judges previously would have their names placed in the appellate judges' box. Now, whenever necessary, the assigning judge would select a panel of three judges from the box who will hear the appeals of several cases in one sitting. The first name drawn would be the chief justice of the panel. The trial experience of this drafted appeals court will exceed that of today's judges on the high court, some of whom have never practiced a day in their lives. Some are former law-school professors, or were trial judges with little prior experience in representing people. Some have merely been good at politics. The new appellate judges would be lawyers of adequate years and experience from which to have gained sound judgment. They would judge our cases whether their philosophy matched the governor's or his cronies' or not. Upon completion of their work, they would not be called on for service for the remainder of the year.

More magic would occur from our drafting of judges. Suddenly our court dockets would become current, because the assigning judge can appoint as many judges as are needed to get the work done. Lawyers can only be better lawyers for having experienced the justice system from the side of those whose duty it is to make heavy decisions, and judges will never forget how it was to once be a lawyer, because tomorrow they will be back in their law offices again. No longer will the judges' decisions be tempered with political considerations, because they will never stand for reelection or have political debts to repay.

There can be abuses, of course. But they will be fewer and easier to deal with. We won't need to impeach a dishonest judge. When the lawyer is disbarred, his name is also removed from the judges' box. Under this system, one might hope that lawyers would gain a new pride and would earn an improved public image, for they would have a personal stake in justice and would know that they, too, will be called upon to make just decisions and to share in the responsibility of creating a better society.

The drafting of lawyers as judges also requires us to teach judging as a part of the postgraduate trial lawyer's residency discussed at some length in chapter 12. My vision of the law school is one where lawyers, judges, teachers, and students assemble to learn the art of advocacy, to create and explore new methods of communication, and to search for better ways to deliver justice to the people. Part of that experiment would be to receive the feedback of those who have judged—to feel how it is to wear the judicial skin. Part of the experiment requires the judge, as well, to become an advocate again so that he does not lose the sense and the fear of it. The New Law School will become the training ground not only for our trial lawyers but for our judges as well, and as we become more successful in this endeavor, so, too, will the people's faith in the justice system gradually be restored.

While a timely revision of the judiciary is not a realistic expectation since the life tenure and the method of appointing our federal judges are established by Constitution, we can, nevertheless, take firm steps toward making our current judges more responsive. We might begin by realizing that when judges ascend to the bench, they tend to become isolated, and their experience in the outside world narrows. It is not easy to be a judge—to be served as a daily diet human conflict and human suffering. In defense, judges tend to pull back, to harden, sometimes to become cynical. Once they are securely on the bench, we usually give them no further guidance as to what we expect of them. Whereas lawyers in most states are required to take a minimum number of hours of continuing legal education each year, judges are presumed to be all-knowing and are required to take none. Teachers must periodically enroll in short courses to keep their certification. So must doctors and pilots. And so should judges.

There is a certain divine wisdom that flows from humble roots. I wonder how the quality of judging might improve if occasionally our judges were turned back to labor with the people. It would be a noble experiment. Perhaps those physically able should periodically work in a factory or carry hod, or wash dishes or wait tables. I wonder how many would seek to be judges if a condition of their ascension would be our requirement that they experience the human condition as much as they study the law. Perhaps judges should step down from the bench periodically to do social work in a neighborhood in the Bronx, or teach at the prisons where they can renew their acquaintanceship with those they have sentenced to these dismal holes. Perhaps they could even take on a few cases as lawyers for the indigent. Judges do not learn much about judging people once they become judges. Little is learned concerning that art from typical out-of-court activities many judges engage in—playing golf with certain lawyers, or giving luncheon speeches to the Rotary Club, or attending the political dinner of a party crony. Plato expressed this same idea in the *Republic*:

> The business of the founders of the State will be to couple the best minds to attain the greatest knowledge of all. They must ascend until they arrive at the good; but when they have ascended and seen enough we must not allow them to do as they now do. I mean they must be made to descend again among the prisoners in the den, and partake of their labors and honors.

Although Mao and I are not in accord in most things, I agree with his idea that the people's leaders should periodically rejoin the people as laborers in the fields and the factories and thereby gain the necessary humility and insight for leadership.

What would it hurt if judges were friendlier, more approachable? Perhaps we are the ones who fence them out with our fear of them, but once elevated they seem so haughty, so distant, so inhuman and frightening. When people come to court, they are already afraid, and so are their lawyers. Entering a modern courtroom resembles being admitted to the hospital for a serious operation and everywhere you look you see symbols of death that warn you that you will probably not survive the surgery—the doctors all wearing black robes and gloomy faces. It is hard for justice to grow in such a place as a courtroom with these solemn, frightening figures peering down at us. Perhaps we could find a way for lawyers and judges to meet together. Perhaps we could tell them how they frighten us. Perhaps we could hear them tell us how we disgust them with our endless, mindless arguments, our poor preparation, our reluctance to be responsible, and our sad incompetence.

I remember an old friend of mine telling me about his appearance before the justice of the peace in Glendo, Wyoming, a town of only a few hundred hardy souls. Court was being held in the judge's living room, where he presided from behind a card table. In court, when a lawyer wishes to go up to the bench, it is customary for him to ask the judge's permission to "approach the bench." (Imagine! One may not even come close to the judge without his permission.) My friend, needing to show the judge a document, said, "May I approach the card table?" Forthwith, the judge granted him permission to do so, and thereafter he invited the opposing lawyers as well, and they gathered around the card table and justice was done.

Besides new judges, we need new and more efficient judicial procedures. Cost and Delay continuously cripple justice. Both are favorites of the judiciary, for Delay is always snuggled in with the judges and hugs to the judicial covers like a bed dog, and Cost grows fat on the leavings of Delay. Of course, judges curse and kick at them, but they both bound back into the judicial bed at will.

Judges, of course, are very strict about certain kinds of delay. If they can punish delay and thereby avoid work for themselves, they will do so with a light heart. If a lawyer is one day late in filing his brief, his client's case, no matter how critical to life or to the cause of mankind, may be thrown out, thereby saving the judge the trouble of deciding the matter on its merits. But once the case is in the judge's hands, he may take years to announce his decision. I have never understood how a judge can demand that I file a brief within thirty days and then leave the same moldering in his files, sometimes for years. If lawyers conducted their business like most judges, we'd soon be bankrupt. I know judges who have time to write only one or two decisions a year but have ample time to join in the howl of their brothers against the alleged "litigation explosion" and the court congestion they claim results therefrom. I know judges with scores of cases piled high on their desks that have waited months, even years, for a first glance, while the same judges harangue the bar and the trial judges beneath them on the evils of delay, enunciating all the while through leathery lips such clichés as "Justice delayed is justice denied."

By the time a case gets to the appeals court, many litigants have already unjustly suffered to the point of exhaustion. The torture of waiting, of not knowing, the agony of relentless worry, is often an additional cruel and inhumane punishment inflicted upon those who have already suffered too long. The interest on the money tied up in the appellate logjam alone would likely pay the salaries of the entire judiciary of America. But they wouldn't know what that hardship is like—they get paid right on time. If you seek eternal life, be a judge. They seem to live forever. Their enigmatic good health and infamous poor tempers suggest they flourish on the mean, the dilatory, and the government payroll.

I do not indict all judges. There are many great judges who are embarrassed for their brethren. I know judges who put out thirty well-written, well-considered decisions a year, while the average for the court is ten. But who watches the king? The problem is that no one really supervises judges. How long would a worker last who, producing one unit, demanded the same pay as the average worker who produced twenty? In the end, we have a right to expect no less of our judges than they demand of us.

To fight judicial cost and delay, we should begin with the judges themselves. They, like any honest person, should not accept their pay unless they have earned it, and would presumably not object to a law requiring them to first certify in writing that their work is current, meaning that they have written all decisions in all cases assigned to them in, say, the past sixty days. The state of Washington requires its superior-court judges to make their decisions within ninety days from the date the case is submitted to them, and "upon the judge's willful failure" to do so, "he shall be deemed to have forfeited his office." Moreover, no county is permitted to pay a judge unless he shall have filed an affidavit to the effect "that no cause in his court remains pending and undecided contrary [to law]." I observe lawyers in Washington grieving less about delays in their trial courts than lawyers elsewhere.

The way many appellate judges marshal their time, one suspects they do, indeed, enjoy eternal life. Take the typical case before an appellate court. After many months and after hundreds, perhaps thousands, of person-hours, after lengthy briefs have been filed by both sides, and after oral argument before the court, the judges return to their chambers to argue the case among themselves. The arguments are secret, but one of the judges is eventually assigned by the chief judge to write the decision of the court. The judges have clerks to help them read the record and find the law. Yet it often takes them many months to come up with a first-draft opinion, which in turn is circulated among the brethren, who will likely disagree with not only the result that was reached but the method by which it was achieved. Judges may fight over the choice of words or the order of words or the implication of words or that there are not enough words or too many words. Dissents or concurring opinions are written, and finally, after many months, oftentimes several years, the decision is filed and published. If the excessive time in coming to their published decisions were reflected in the quality of justice rendered, we could wait; unfortunately, the opposite is usually the case.

We must help our appellate judges find a better way to do their business. I propose a conference method of appellate review, and submit that despite its arguable shortcomings, we would gamble nothing in adopting it, for no system of appellate review could be more costly, more irrelevant to living litigants, more unjust, than the current procedures in which the judicial process seems trapped. Let us begin with something simple—a plain round table in the center of a room. Let us seat there the three appellate judges assigned to the case and the opposing lawyers and a secretary with a pad. Since a round table has no head and no foot, there is no hierarchy to get in the way. Everyone has his feet on the same floor. This is a conference of human beings trying to identify where justice lies in this case. They will be guided by the law and respectful of precedent, but they will not be as enchanted by detached doctrine as they are absorbed in the discovery of justice.

Around this table the lawyers are not as fearful. Lawyers will no longer be left, as in the old courtroom, standing clinging to a podium looking up at judges who, in return, glare down at them in silence or hurl biting questions that confuse and humiliate. Around the table, in an informal fashion, the lawyers explain their view of the case and how they believe justice should be accomplished. The open and frank exchange of ideas is encouraged by the chief judge. If the judges have a fact wrong, or hold a correct fact in wrong perspective, that error can be straightened out immediately. If the judges do not understand a lawyer's position, they can ask questions until they do. In the presence of the lawyers, the judges will also begin to discuss the case among themselves. If a lawyer thinks a judge has gone astray, the lawyer can tell the judge so and why. The chief judge can bring order if the discussion gets out of hand, but the attitude brought to the table is not "Who wins?" but "How can we justly resolve this dispute?" Finally a decision will be reached in the presence of all. Most often it will be an obvious result—the document was or was not wrongfully admitted into evidence, and it did or did not cause prejudice to the appealing party. The judges may dictate a simple memo if no new principles of law are to be enunciated, and since the memo is of no important precedent-setting force, it will go unpublished. The case is over. A mandate will be drafted by the clerk and sent out that very afternoon. If the case is one requiring a published decision, a time limit will be set of, say, two weeks. If it is a very complex case in which a decision cannot be made immediately, the judges can order further assistance from their clerks and the attorneys and set a second conference.

While many an appellate judge believes he has a higher duty to the law than to the human beings governed by it, I argue that the divine calling of a judge must be to deliver justice to the litigants. The conference method would help remove the aura of black magic that shrouds the appellate process. Most lawyers are so in awe of it that they rarely get near an appellate court except when they are dragged into one. I know appellate judges who claim they go months at a time without a visit from a practicing member of the bar. No one questions the judges. No one demands that they answer to them. But why should we permit the justices to cloak their function with such secrecy, such mystery? We should be able to see them at work, join them in their effort to find justice, and guide them if they go wrong. One of the most frequent complaints attorneys make of appellate courts is that the judges do not read the briefs, much less the record, and that consequently they have little understanding of the facts or issues of the case. Frequently their decisions reveal the truth of these accusations. Moreover, many lawyers are not able to argue effectively in the fearsome environment of the appellate courtroom. The conference method is our best assurance that the judges understand our cases and that justice is swiftly rendered. In the typical case, this method will save hundreds of wasted hours and months of waiting. Half the court's routine caseload will be quickly disposed of, and most of the judges will find themselves suddenly current, with new time to devote to the more difficult issues of justice.

Unless our love of the status quo outweighs our regard for justice, we will soon be required to test the potential of electronics. Why, for instance, shouldn't the trial be recorded by video rather than by the costly and single-dimensional black-and-white record of only the written word? On appeal, the material parts of the trial could be shown to the justices so that they could see what *actually hap-*

pened rather than reading the sterile record. To initiate the experiment would require only an appellate rule in some states. On procedural matters that plague every trial—the admissibility of evidence, the alleged misconduct of counsel, or the correctness of a judge's instruction—we could obtain almost immediate decisions by the appeals court. Rather than, as now, first completing a costly trial and thereafter creating the written record at enormous additional expense, writing briefs by the hour at a price only a few can bear, and arguing the case and then waiting for months while the court makes up its mind on something that could have been decided in a matter of minutes, we might instead replay that portion of the trial in question using an instant-replay technique similar to that used to review the referee's decisions in professional football. It is nearly incomprehensible that this profession, presumably composed of the intellectual elite of society, cannot get unstuck from silly centuries-old procedural bogs. Our failure to do so causes one to suspect that we love our muck and our mire more than we love justice.

Facts! They are as essential to the rendering of justice as studs to the framing of a house, as bricks to the mortaring of a wall. One of the great challenges of our justice system is to devise efficient methods for ascertaining the facts. Under current procedures, many civil cases are actually tried twice—once when the depositions of witnesses are taken, and a second time when the witness testifies again in court. Many just claims never see the light of day because the cost of such discovery depositions is enormous. Telephone depositions recorded by both sides with their own inexpensive recording equipment and transcribed by their own secretaries would reduce the cost of the average deposition fivefold by cutting through the often impossible task of finding a single day when all attorneys can appear at some distant place at great expense to take the deposition of a witness in person. The $2.50 a page paid the court reporter to type up the endless harangues of attorneys—which consume thousands of pages in major cases—could now be absorbed into the regular office expense of the lawyer or, if the attorney chooses, he might not have the deposition transcribed at all. The verity of the recorded deposition is easily checked via the opposing attorney's own recording. Although the sound of the electronically recorded word may occasionally become garbled and require the translation of a present human ear, my experience is that the exactness of the court reporter's transcription is equally faulty. Words are often misheard by the court reporter as well, and although reporter transcripts approach the 90th percentile of accuracy, they also fail to record emphasis—tonal italics—and the clear meaning that can be transmitted only by the sounds of the syntax.

Today, most personal-injury cases become contests between experts hired at great expense by all sides, the object of the contest being to determine who can most convincingly call the other a liar. A fool with a small flair for acting and mathematics might be a more successful witness than, say, Einstein. Most often witnesses are not chosen for their knowledge but for their ability to persuade. Testifying has become not only an art but big business for many so-called scientists—engineers to reconstruct accidents, doctors in every speciality to testify against their peers, rehabilitation experts, economists, and psychologists. The swearing-for-hire business is immense and indispensable to nearly every case—and it is costly. Some medical-school professors I know make several times their annual salary by selling testimony to anyone who will retain them. Usually corporate America pays best—and most promptly.

Some reformers suggest that a single "court expert" be appointed by the judge. But in most cases, science, like the law, is many-faceted. A variety of interpretations, exceptions, and unknowns are honestly available to each side in every case. No just result can be obtained without fully presenting these viewpoints and weighing them. A single expert is no more capable of performing this function fairly than an attorney who is asked to represent both sides of the same case.

Perhaps we should also draft our experts and pay them a statutory fee that is assessed as a cost at the conclusion of the case. In general, the law has come to recognize that the expert's knowledge is his property and cannot be taken from him without just compensation. But this has not always been the law. Doctors used to be subject to subpoena and required to testify the same as anyone else. Why shouldn't the doctor who has treated his patient (for which he has received compensation) be required to testify as to the patient's history, condition, and prognosis the same as any other witness who is called upon to deliver his special knowledge to the court? If a lawyer is called to testify as to work he has performed for his client, shouldn't he be willing to supply these facts without compensation? A witness to a murder—say, a farmer—will be summoned before the grand jury and then to trial and paid only a statutory fee. He may have crops to harvest. Certainly his time is as valuable to him as the doctor's is to the doctor, who is the only eyewitness to the examination he performed on his patient, or the lawyer's to the lawyer, who alone knows the work he did for his client. Why should the jurors who receive their puny compensation sit patiently for months listening to the testimony of experts who log in their time at $1,000 or even sometimes $5,000 a day? Justice is the responsibility of all of us. Why shouldn't a professor who is on the public payroll make available his specialized knowledge to the jury at a fixed statutory fee? Why shouldn't doctors or lawyers who have received their schooling at a public-supported institution see it as their duty to give something back to the system? Many experts are the recipients of public grants for research but feel no duty to share their specially obtained knowledge in the furtherance of justice. If a corporation has contributed to a research grant—and most of the large ones do—the corporation seems to have no difficulty in obtaining the professor's testimony. Are we to assume that neither the corporation's grant nor its timely payment of the professor's handsome fee has any influence on his testimony? Experts on such diverse subjects as travel in space, how bones are set, ballistics, the functioning of the brain, the dynamics of human motion in automobile wrecks, infinite fields of inquiry in every variety of court case, are critical to the rendering of justice. We must dig out the truth. And we must have experts on both sides to present their arguments so that juries can weigh them.

True, when we ask a doctor to come into court and testify against a member of his own profession, it is disagreeable business. If the doctor does not have a strong sense of justice or is not otherwise committed to the betterment of his own profession, or has no stomach for the indignities that attend the courtroom brawl, he may opt not to get into such dirty wars without being handsomely paid. So, too, a doctor asked to defend a colleague he knows has grievously erred may not wish to offer support even though there are mitigating circumstances that the jury should understand. Perhaps the law should provide that no expert be paid in excess of an adequte statutory fee but that all experts be required to testify, if subpoenaed, as a part of their obligation to the justice system. There would doubtless be inequities. Sometimes it would be impossible to find experts who would testify at all. But compare such an injustice with the present state of affairs, in which experts can be obtained to testify to anything if the price is right. Competent, honest experts need to be equally available to both sides, just as both sides require attorneys of comparable skill. Otherwise, justice remains merely a purchasable commodity that is most available to those who can pay the price.

Sometimes the expert will face undue hardship under such a rule, and the court should grant relief where required, balancing the expert's duty to the system against the inequity that the duty may impose. If a reconstruction expert needs to perform out-of-court work to come to his conclusions, perhaps the Justice Fund, a public source financed in part from punitive damages, could provide the costs for litigants unable to provide such funds for themselves. The rules of evidence should be further relaxed to permit freer use of textbooks and other published material in the public domain as primary evidence.

The Defense Institute, an organization of lawyers who defend personal-injury cases for the insurance industry, has a computer bank listing willing witnesses in every conceivable field of expertise. Some of these witnesses bounce from case to case blithely testifying for whatever insurance company pays their bill. Even under our present system, we can better identify the whore, euphemistically referred to as the "professional witness," who will testify to anything for anybody who provides the price—and there are plenty of them. A simple rule requiring that several months before trial all experts designated in the case by either side file a sworn certificate that identifies every other case in which the expert has given testimony, the subject matter of his testimony, and the court in which the same was given, whether by deposition or otherwise, as a condition to his testimony, would greatly assist attorneys in defending against the "professional witness." Although this information can theoretically be obtained by deposition under our present rules, the expert most often forgets, sometimes conveniently, many of the cases in which he has actually previously testified. He knows that it is unlikely we will discover, say, a remote Arizona case in which he gave contradictory testimony, and if we do discover it, he can merely say it was one he inadvertently overlooked. Many experts have testified in hundreds of cases, but when asked the number of cases in which they have testified give only vague approximations that minimize their past testimonies.

The spectacle of pitting purchased experts against each other in the courtroom, the best performer taking all, is a barbarous throwback to the days of trial by duel. While these suggestions will never perfectly solve the problem created by the "expert-witness game," we can and must discover better ways to glean the truth in a scientific world so that experts, and consequently the facts, do not become merely the property of those who purchase them.

There is little chance that the vast reforms we require for a prompt and efficient justice can ever be accomplished by the bar, whose business has finally become *business*, not justice. We have had centuries to do better. We know what is wrong with the system, and we have the power to alter it. Yet we refuse to do so. The likelihood of the judiciary taking the necessary steps to bring about substantial change is also practically nonexistent. As the servant of Power, the judiciary is fully dedicated to the preservation of a status quo that favors Power. Nor will our legislatures bring about change. Too many of their members have become store clerks who cheerfully deliver the goods purchased by Power. Justice is one of those commodities.

Change comes only from the implacable demands of an informed people. But the people will never see the light of day so long as the shutters are closed against them. Yet the light will seep through where the louvers are most rotten. Light always prevails. Already it is leaking into our schools and our universities. The New Law Schools will produce a new, proud profession composed not of goods for sale, not of commodities, but of men and women dedicated to the rights of the citizen. And from these New Lawyers our New Judges will one day be chosen. More and more, they will be men and women committed to the speedy and efficient rendering of justice. And as the light seeps through, a new people will begin earnestly to strive for justice. For them, the love of justice will become as real as the love of art, as the love of discovery, as the love of truth.

14 | NEW LAW

Caging the Corporate Criminal, Curing the Corporate Plague

A corporation is a fiction that relieves man of his responsibility to his neighbor. It permits him to do in the name of the corporation what he would not do in his own name. It shields him from his human conscience. Like any mechanism, the corporation mindlessly obeys the commands of those who manipulate it and thereby commits some of the greatest crimes ever visited upon the human race. Yet a corporation has an independent life that, like the machine, possesses certain features of immortality. It can survive those who have created it. It can, like a runaway train, smash any and all who stand in its way. It consumes the energies of its workers like coal shoveled into the boiler. If it wrecks, many will be injured and many will be destroyed. It can be junked. It can be bought and sold. Professor Charles A. Reich of Yale Law School says, "The corporation is an immensely powerful machine, ordered, legalistic, rational, yet utterly out of human control, wholly and perfectly indifferent to any human value."

Over the next 30 years, it is estimated that 240,000 people will die of asbestos-related cancer. That's about one every hour. As many as forty thousand American veterans are likely to die of the effects of Agent Orange and other toxic chemicals dumped on Vietnam. The Dalkon Shield intrauterine device has already seriously injured tens of thousands of women and left many barren. Some have died of pelvic inflammatory disease. A million children throughout the world perished in 1986 because corporate America encouraged supplanting the mother's breast with formula from the corporate bottle. In 1984, thousands of innocent humans died and two hundred thousand were injured—thirty thousand to forty thousand seriously— when Union Carbide's affiliate in Bhopal, India, released a deadly gas over the sleeping city.

The problem was their penchant for profit. So it has always been. When a delegation of nuns concerned about the tactics of an international pharmaceutical house, Abbott, in marketing infant formula in the Third World visited the company executives, one of the nuns asked an Abbott executive, "Tell me, if you stop selling to people who are too poor to use the product safely, will you still make a profit?" After a long pause, the corporate executive reportedly responded, "That is the crux of the problem."

Agent Orange contains dioxin, one of the most deadly of synthetic chemicals. Three ounces of dioxin placed in New York City's drinking water would wipe out the city's entire population. In 1965, when the United States was destroying the forests of Vietnam, it was purchasing millions of pounds of Agent Orange, a herbicide containing dioxin. Dow Chemical's toxicology director wrote in an internal report that dioxin could be "exceptionally toxic to humans," and that the company's medical director had warned that "fatalities have been reported in the literature." Documents of that company also show that on March 24, 1965, four chemical manufacturers met at Dow headquarters in Midland, Michigan, to discuss the health hazards of dioxin. A scientist attending the meeting said later that Dow did not want the findings about dioxin made public, because the situation might "explode" and generate a new wave of government regulation of the chemical industry.

How can we protect ourselves from these corporations that destroy us—that pollute our earth—without reason, without regard, without justice? The corporation is a mechanism, but it is one loosed on humans by humans. We must understand that and hold those who guide the machine, who mastermind its performance, personally responsible for its conduct. "The best way to get management's attention is to punish management directly," says Professor John B. Matthews of the Harvard Business School. Why shouldn't the corporate manager be as responsible for what he does on the job as he is for what he does driving home from the job? If he negligently runs us down, we do not permit him to blame his car; nor should he be permitted to lay responsibility for the malfeasance of his company on the corporate machine.

Take a day in the life of the CEO of a large drug company: One afternoon at a products committee meeting, he orders the marketing of a new drug that had been released after questionable compliance tactics with the FDA. The drug had great potential as a profit maker, but it also put at risk the health and lives of thousands of citizens who would innocently consume it. That evening, the company officers and department heads give a small party to celebrate the birth of their new product. After the party is over, the CEO, while backing out of his private parking place, runs into the back end of the janitor's pickup truck. The CEO is personally responsible, of course, and the janitor will get his pickup fixed by the CEO's insurance company. Yet the thousands of Americans who will suffer, perhaps die, as a consequence of his reckless profit decision made earlier that day will likely be abandoned by our justice system and left without any effective remedy at all against the corporation.

That profit-seeking managers commanding the enormous power of their corporations are not personally at peril is like putting a cannon in the hands of a three-year-old and rewarding him with a sackful of lollipops for every pigeon on the schoolhouse roof he can kill. Corporate crime and corporate irresponsibility can be brought under control only by imposing on corporate managers the same obligations we owe each other in our daily lives. Think of it from the standpoint of Rosy Medina. What difference does it make to her whether her husband died in a car with a defective transmission that the manufacturer knew was defective, or that he died in the flames of their small Bronx store after it was torched on the orders of a Mafia warlord? He is as dead, and she as lonely and helpless to obtain justice. It might have been better for her had her husband been the victim of the Mafia thug, for at least there could be an identifiable person to be charged, tried, and punished.

Corporate crime is the most serious social evil facing America. It is the predictable product of limitless corporate power. In nature, even our most successful predators are governed by restraints the corporation will not acknowledge, nor abide by. The wolf kills only when it is hungry. That seems to be a natural ethos. Consider a forest in which the wolf kills solely for the purpose of "keeping score," and in so doing wipes out whole herds of elk and deer. Chaos would, of course, result, finally affecting every animal in the woods, and Mother Nature would soon make easy adjustments. So must we. When new, stiff criminal laws permit prosecutors to indict the CEO of the corporation, its board of directors, its department heads— when all who know or should have known that the corporation is cheating or injuring or killing innocent people are called to answer personally—then corporate crime will magically come under control.

How can we instill ethics into this beast? *U.S. News and World Report* recently printed a study revealing that 75 percent of the managers polled said they felt pressured to compromise their personal ethics to satisfy the corporate goal—namely, profit. E. F. Hutton started an ethics program after its check-kiting scandal, and most major corporations have so-called codes of conduct to guide their employees. Martin-Marietta even has a "director of ethics," but all the same, this corporate defense contractor recently pled guilty to mail fraud and withheld over $1 million in travel-agency rebates from the Defense Department. Most see the in-house ethics efforts of corporations being adopted more for public relations than for the good of the public. The truth is, corporations are no more capable of acting ethically than they are of acting lovingly.

In an attempt to turn money into morality, John Shad recently donated $30 million to the Harvard Business School to fund a business-ethics college. A donation to the Church to teach underworld mercenaries to pray would be as effective. It is a problem inherent in power. When we cloak corporate managers, some of whom have more power than heads of state, with nearly total immunity for their acts, and charge them with but one responsibility—to make a profit—we guarantee corporate crime.

The idea of using the criminal law to deter corporate crimes is not new, but its use is growing and is receiving public support. William Maakestad, legal counsel and associate professor of management at Western Illinois University, says there are more cases of corporate homicide currently pending in state courts than the cumulative number of those previously tried during our nation's history. A Justice Department survey of sixty thousand citizens found that Americans "view purposeful dumping of hazardous waste a worse act than some homicides." The murder convictions in the summer of 1985 of three officers of a small Illinois company, Film Recovery Systems, and the twenty-five-year sentences they received, sent "shock waves" through the world of executives. Ann Singleton, a Maryland prosecutor, recently filed involuntary-manslaughter charges against the owner of a truck-leasing firm who allegedly refused to maintain his fleet's brakes. She said, "Both the public and prosecutors are beginning to realize that some accidents on the job can be equally outrageous as someone who hits a guy over the head and takes his wallet." Says Kenneth Oden, county attorney in Travis County, Texas, who successfully prosecuted a construction corporation and its president for negligent homicide for a work-related death, "By God, it does impress people when someone comes out and says we have a warrant for your arrest, here are the handcuffs that go on your little wrists, and you get to go down to the courthouse and you get to start up a process whereby you personally answer up for your misconduct." A recent survey showed that nearly 70 percent of the public support prison terms for corporate executives responsible for corporate offenses leading to violent consequences.

But against whom in the corporate hierarchy do we proceed? Middle management will plead, like the criminals at Nuremberg, that they only followed orders. Those lower down the ladder will argue the same, with even more force. Top management will say that they were never properly informed. The "Don't tell me, I don't want to know" tactic that has protected the presidents of nations will continue to shield our corporate criminals unless we make all those along the line accountable. Judge Miles Lord says, "They used to call it a conspiracy if two or more people got together to commit either a legal act by an illegal method or an illegal act by a legal method. Now they have a process of deniability: the underlings do the dirty work and the top man can deny he knew about it." The lower echelons in the corporate structure must be held responsible for informing those above them. If there are dangers they know of or should have reasonably perceived in the performance of their duties, they must discover them and be bound under penalty of law to advise their superiors. The obligation for the welfare and safety of innocent people can no longer be some hot potato that can be tossed upward or downward. It is everyone's responsibility. The corporate managers will ignore such knowledge only at their own peril. It will be criminal for any person in authority, from a foreman to the chairman of the board, to cover up or conspire with others to cover up danger-laden facts. Management's attempt to intimidate those below them from revealing the truth as they discover it will cause the manager to be dealt with the same as you and I, should we attempt to conceal a crime or obstruct justice.

When we witness corporations enjoying their ill-gotten profits from deliberately infesting the market with known dangerous products, we can begin to understand how severe the penalties must be. We must acknowledge such corporate crime for what it is: the willful exploitation, killing, injury, and robbery of innocent people for profit—crimes we will not tolerate from persons, crimes for which we sometimes demand the death penalty.

Let's take a look at how the prestigious William S. Merrell Company marketed, some years ago, its MER/29, and how adequate criminal laws might have prevented it. Merrell was a major subsidiary of Richardson-Merrell, a Fortune 500 company (since divided and sold to Procter & Gamble and to Dow Chemical). It provides such quick nostrums as Vicks VapoRub (a vile-smelling substance my mother always plastered on my chest at the first sign of a cold, as if to punish me for having caught it in the first place) as well as prescription drugs of great sophistication. Merrell represented that MER/29 seemed to reduce the amount of cholesterol in the blood of monkeys and other animals and could be added to a heart patient's therapy with little change in diet. The successful marketing of MER/29 was intended to shore up the company's position in the drug industry. The company was in a hurry. It wanted the FDA's approval of the drug in time to launch an aggressive sales campaign at an upcoming convention of the American Medical Association. The test results submitted to the FDA were exclusively favorable. But one of the FDA's pharmacologists, Dr. Edwin I. Goldenthal, found that there was "little margin of safety with the drug," that there was an "inherent toxic potential," and that clinical studies should be made of people taking the medication over several years rather than a few weeks. Merrell stood its ground and laid on the pressure, and in a decision that is hard to understand, Dr. Frank J. Talbot, a medical officer in the FDA's drug branch, decided to approve the marketing of the medicine. What followed was a devious crusade by Merrell to conceal the growing body of evidence that the drug actually caused cataracts, loss of hair, and a variety of other frightful side effects.

When complaints came in from doctors indicating serious problems, Merrell was ready. It instructed its salesmen by memorandum: "When a doctor says your drug causes a side effect, the immediate reply is: 'Doctor, what other drug is your patient taking?'" It changed the data on its own tests. Monkeys were reported as fat and healthy that were not—some had even died. The company withheld information from their salesmen, who continued blithely to sing the drug's praises to the medical profession. A public-relations physician for Merrell wrote a Wisconsin doctor in response to the doctor's observation of blurred vision after MER/29 therapy that such a symptom was "unusual," and "we know of a paper soon to be published showing some improvement in vision in patients with diabetes and hypercholesterolomia." The company even planted a concocted laudatory letter in *Medical World News* that it would later use to convince the medical profession and the FDA that the drug was beneficial.

But when finally the FDA's statisticians were able to infer from the company data itself that people on the drug were three times as likely as those not taking it to develop cataracts, a letter warning doctors of all the potential side effects was at last agreed to by

Merrell. With that MER/29 became a doomed product, but Merrell still had a $2 million inventory it needed to dump. Within two weeks of the warning letter, Merrell wrote an update to the nation's pharmacists saying, "Physicians throughout the country are prescribing MER/29, and we urge you to make sure that your stocks of this high-volume specialty are adequate."

The FDA later prosecuted. Those indicted were: the William S. Merrell Company; its parent, Richardson Merrell, Inc.; and three scientists—two lab supervisors and their immediate superior. The lab personnel quietly pled "No Contest" to the charges. Merrell was fined the maximum—$60,000—and its parent firm $20,000. The maximum penalty provided under the law for the individuals was five years and $10,000, but the Merrell strategists received no fines and were given six months on probation. Sanford J. Ungar, an author and journalist who reported these nefarious goings-on, commented on Judge Matthew F. McGuire's sentencing: "If the crime is not one of obvious violence and the defendants are white gentlemen of pleasant demeanor and apparent good will, their punishment shall be mild." But what would happen to us if we robbed Merrell's main office of, say, a thousand dollars from the petty-cash drawer and in the process threw battery acid into the eyes of the president of the company, who happened by and tried to stop us? We would still be in prison. What of the money Merrell lifted from innocent citizens whose only crime was their desire to lower their cholesterol? What of their eyes, their health? Considering the profit potential and the small risk to the company and its managers, what other result could we expect?

Merrell's conduct and that of its corporate henchmen seem more reprehensible than the thieves and the thugs who leave us quaking behind our double-bolted doors. We cannot lock out the insidious crimes of corporations. It is one thing for a common criminal to break into our houses and rob us of our money and, in the process, do us injury. It is a manifoldly worse crime when someone in whom we have placed our trust robs us of our savings or injures us with their products. It seems worse yet when the crimes are committed by the corporate executive who goes to church on Sunday and belongs to the country club and sends his children to fine schools and is cited for community service, and who overwhelms us with his company's television ads that try to convince us his company cares about us. These corporate sneaks remind me of a stray cur that used to hang around the ranch. He would wag his tail and grin, but if you turned your head a second, he'd snatch the hamburger out of your hand and usually your hand with it, and then run like hell.

Adequate laws with mandatory jail sentences would have prevented the withholding of critical facts in the case of MER/29. If everyone in the company who had knowledge knew he was at personal risk, from the guy who fed the rats and threw the dead ones out, to the supervisor who dummied up the report, to the president and CEO, the Harvard Business School wouldn't have to spend millions to teach ethics. Ethics isn't any more teachable at the university level than morality. We must change the *object* of the game from profit at any cost to responsibility at every level of the corporation, so that *the greater the trust imposed, the greater the duty to be trustworthy.* My years of dealing with salaried corporate personnel confirm that, while most are loyal to their employers and will make great personal sacrifices on their behalf, most will not, in face of severe penalties, risk committing serious crimes in order to fill the company coffers.

If the battle against corporate crime is to be won, we must eliminate profit from corporate crime. Today, the penalties imposed often amount to fewer dollars than the profit the corporation realized from its wrongdoing. New federal laws should impose fines based on a percentage of the corporation's net worth. Ten percent might be a reasonable *net-worth fine* where potential injury or death is the foreseeable result of intentional corporate wrongdoing. No one would argue that if I robbed the local bank of $10,000 and wounded a bank teller in the process, it would be unreasonable for me to pay 10 percent of my net worth as a fine for that crime. Why should corporations be given carte-blanche opportunities to profit from their crimes?

Perhaps we should punish the corporation for its crime based on the corporation's income derived from the crime. In the case of Merrell's MER/29, after the jury found the corporation guilty, the prosecutor would inspect the company's books and establish the amount of the company's sales of the offending drug. (When a common criminal is found guilty of a crime, we allow no deductions for his hotel bills while he scopes out the bank, or for his getaway car, or for the cost of ammunition he loads into his gun. Why should the common criminal in the corporate world be able to deduct, say, its development costs, the cost of sales, it losses from undisposed inventories, or pro-rata overhead?) After the total sales have been determined by the jury, the corporation would be fined a sum perhaps three times that amount. No discretion would be vested in either the prosecutor or the judge in levying or enforcing the fine. The government's expenses, including the actual cost for attorneys, investigators, and support staff as prorated to the case, would also be levied against the corporation. Otherwise, as in the infamous IBM case mentioned earlier, a huge corporation can simply bankrupt the prosecuting arm of the government. Only when we have made the risk of loss from crime greater than its potential rewards will we begin to get corporate crime under control.

I have made mention of the death penalty and do not favor it for human beings, since we cannot stop killing by killing. Yet those who clamor for the killing of human criminals as punishment for human crimes most often accept corporate crime as part of doing business as usual. If the death penalty is in vogue for human felons, should it not also be used against corporate murderers? Why shouldn't those corporations who kill not a few but thousands of innocent citizens for profit also suffer the ultimate penalty? Most would not hesitate to put the cold-blooded Mafia chief to death if it could be proved he had engaged in murder for hire—for profit. When a corporation determines how much profit it can make by concealing deadly defects in a product, or how much profit it can retain by not revealing known life-threatening conditions to inno-cent workers, and hundreds, or thousands, die, no logical distinction can be drawn between such crimes of the corporation and those of a killer who murders for money. If for our protection the death penalty is ordered against the human murderer of a few, ought we not similarly protect ourselves against the nonhuman murderer of many? Shouldn't we permanently terminate the corporate entity? Shouldn't their assets be sold item by item to the highest bidder—right down to the last typewriter ribbon—and the proceeds, after the costs of termination, be returned to the public treasury? Perhaps we could use the monies to compensate the victims who might oth-erwise be left without remedy. These are not new ideas in the law: Under present statutes, when the federal government apprehends a dope dealer in an expensive airplane, the government can, and often does, confiscate the airplane along with the narcotics, and in ob-scenity cases the merchant may lose his entire stock of lawful goods as well.

To be sure, America enjoys the contributions of many corpora-tions that produce goods or perform services necessary for the public health, safety, pleasure, and security, and most provide jobs and contribute to the gross national product of the nation. I do not seek to restrain the free functioning of the business machinery of the nation. I wish corporations to be free. But I wish *us* to be free of their crimes. Freedom in any civilized society always demands responsibility.

Every state has the power to regulate those corporations that choose to do business within its borders. In Minnesota and in other states, laws permit the revocation of the corporate charter if the corporation misconducts itself. We have the right to set the rules by which corporations will be allowed to profit from doing business with our people. "Good character" is a personal trait required of anyone with whom we conduct our business. Lawyers, doctors, accountants, even bar owners and morticians, are required to demonstrate "good character" before they are granted licenses to do business in the state. We require such a showing because the state has a duty to protect its citizens. Even persons who immigrate into our country must be of "good character." Yet foreign corporations who invade the nation to do business with millions of us need make no similar showing. Is there any less reason to require corporations, foreign or domestic, with their greater power to do injury, to demonstrate "good character" as a condition of their right to do business with our unsuspecting citizens? The Federal Communications Commission (FCC) requires good corporate character of those it licenses to broadcast. The Nuclear Regulatory Commission has also enacted the character standard, as has the Department of Defense in regulating its contractors.

What is "good character"? Several generations of regulation and subsequent case law have developed a clear line by which the FCC analyzes the character of the applicant. The clearest evidence of bad character is evidence that an applicant has lied or made factual misrepresentations to the commission. In *Federal Communications Commission* v. *WOKO*, the Supreme Court said, "The fact of concealment may be more significant than the facts concealed." But there is a problem in enforcing the "good character" provisions of the law. Take, for instance, the FCC's regulation of Westinghouse.

In an application by Westinghouse for the renewal of a station license, the commission conceded Westinghouse's long history of antitrust violations, but nevertheless ruled that its superior broadcast record outweighed this evidence of bad character. In another case, General Electric had pled guilty in seven cases of price-fixing, and *nolo contendere* in thirteen others. It had paid $437,000 in fines. Nevertheless, the FCC ruled that even though it probably would not grant a license in the first instance to such a wrongdoer, the company's "long and honorable record in broadcasting" would permit it to retain its licenses.

Agency discretion in applying the "good character" test of corporate conduct should be limited. Michael Waldman, legislative director of Public Citizens' Congress Watch, says, "Legislation to require the use of character should include two elements: a statutory command, in unmistakable terms, that the standard be used; and specific criteria for the analysis of character." The model Corporate Decency Act proposed by the Center for Study of Responsive Law requires a set of criteria that is sweeping:

> Any corporate entity organized or doing business in the state shall have good corporate character. A corporate entity that through its actions or inactions . . . engage[s] in activities which are detrimental to the public health, safety, or welfare including: . . . deceptive practices, criminal activity, or patterns of regulatory violations shall . . . [violate] this provision.

Why should a corporation charged with a crime be given benefits of citizenship identical to ours—the corporation being presumed innocent, and the state being put to its proof against the corporation beyond a reasonable doubt—when the corporation is not held to the same standards of citizenship as we? We grant constitutional safeguards to the individual for *humane* reasons. The state's burden of proof was intended to equalize the disproportionate power of the state over the individual. But many multinational corporations committing the gravest crimes against our society have resources exceeding those of the state itself. General Motors has a net worth equal to Switzerland's. Even at the turn of the century, the renowned American economist John Bates Clark was compelled to observe, "If the carboniferous age were to return and the earth were to repeople itself with dinosaurs, the change that would be made in animal life would scarcely seem greater than that which has been made in business life by these monster-like corporations." That the burden should be upon the people to prove their case beyond a reasonable doubt against such giants only exacerbates the cost the corporation has already inflicted on society with its crimes. A corporation should be seen for what it is: a state-authorized fiction by which citizens are permitted to conduct their business—which privilege exists only so long as that privilege is not abused.

A little-known fact: Large numbers of multinational corporations *continuously* commit crimes. Like the habitual human criminal, they do not become rehabilitated. One study of seventy of the nation's largest manufacturing, mining, and mercantile corporations revealed that 60 percent had been convicted of criminal charges on an average of *four times each*. The author of that study said, "[T]he criminality of the corporations, like that of professional thieves, is persistent; a large proportion of the offenders are recidivists. Among the 70 largest industrial and commercial corporations in the United States, 97.1% were found to be recidivists in the sense of having two or more adverse decisions." Eighty-six percent of the corporations studied violated the antitrust laws, and 73 percent were guilty of multiple violations. In another study of 477 manufacturing corporations, 210 had 2 or more legal actions completed against them during one 2-year period and 18.2 percent had 5 or more.

General Electric is the third-largest American corporation, with a recent market value of $48.9 billion. How did it get to be so large? From 1911 to 1975, the Antitrust Division of the Justice Department brought at least sixty-seven suits against the company. One hundred private antitrust actions were brought in the early 1960's alone, and the company was a major participant in the Philadelphia Electric price-fixing case of 1961, when several of its executives received prison sentences. But the company had its defenders. On October 31, 1961, the *Los Angeles Times* received a letter condemning the jail sentences handed down to its executives, protesting that the firm operated according to the highest principles—"higher I might add than some elements of government which are so bent on destroying business." The author of the letter was Ronald Reagan, host of *The General Electric Theater* TV show, who was himself investigated—but later cleared—as part of a criminal investigation of the activities of the Screen Actors Guild, of which he was president, and MCA. But GE did not reform. Two decades later, GE's misfeasance and fraud was said to be so pervasive that the Department of Defense debarred the corporation from doing further business with the department, the first time it had taken such action against a major supplier. The suspension, however, lasted only a month. And infractions continue. Kidder Peabody, a subsidiary of GE, has recently been implicated in the exploding "Yuppiegate" scandal.

Not all corporations, of course, are essentially criminal. Some have understood that public responsibility is good business. Johnson & Johnson's response to the first Tylenol poisoning is often cited as a paradigm of exemplary corporate conduct. At a time when no one knew how the poisoning had occurred, Johnson & Johnson began a policy of complete candor with the press. It quickly recalled its product, risking the loss of a very profitable product line. But the result of its openness was that Johnson & Johnson's public image became that of an innocent victim, and the public's confidence in its product was soon restored.

Overall, the egregious corporate-crime rate in this country confirms that we have been utterly ineffective in controlling the corporate criminal. Despite the fact that prosecutors are required to resort to existing criminal codes to prosecute corporations and their executives, the obstacles confronting state and federal lawyers who consider taking on the large corporations, the most frequent offenders, are formidable. Some prosecutors are not able to take the political risks involved in such prosecutions. Many are overwhelmed by the size of the corporate forces aligned against them. In the end, only federal resources can counter those that are available to multinational corporate defendants.

The nation faces a crisis in corporate crime that demands a comprehensive federal code for corporate criminals. New, stiff criminal laws would shift the risk of our injury from us, as innocent consumers, to these not-so-innocent crea ures of commerce who know—or ought to know—of the dangers they impose upon us. In the end, America's corporations are the only ones who can protect us from their own acts. Indeed, as the television ad portrays, they have us in their hands. If they knowingly trade our lives and health for money, their executives must do so at serious risk to themselves, to their own resources, and to their own freedom.

Change, a commitment to do better—rehabilitation—is a part of justice. We require that our misbehaving children change, and we demand the criminal change his evil habits as a condition of his release. But we make no requirement that corporations change. Judge Miles Lord spoke of the need of corporate contrition when he pled to the officers of A. H. Robins, the manufacturers of the Dalkon Shield, for corporate responsibility:

> Gentlemen, you state that your company has suffered enough, that the infliction of further punishment in the form of punitive damages would cause harm to your business, would punish innocent shareholders, and could conceivably depress your profits to the point where you could not survive as a competitor in this industry. When the poor and downtrodden commit crimes, they too plead that these are crimes of survival and that they should be excused for illegal acts that helped them escape desperate economic straits. On a few occasions when these excuses are made and remorseful defendants promise to mend their ways, courts will give heed to such pleas. But no court will heed the plea when the individual denies the wrongful nature of his deeds and gives no indication that he will mend his ways. Your company, in the face of overwhelming evidence, denies its guilt and continues its monstrous mischief.
>
> Mr. Forrest, you have told me that you are working with members of the Congress of the United States to find a way of forgiving you from punitive damages that might otherwise be imposed. Yet the profits of your company continue to mount. Your last financial report boasts of new records for sales and earnings, with a profit of more than $58 million in 1983. And, insofar as this court has been able to determine, you three

men and your company are still engaged in a course of wrongdoing. Until your company indicates that it is willing to cease and desist this deception and to seek out and advise the victims, your remonstrances to Congress and to the courts are indeed hollow and cynical. The company has not suffered, nor have you men personally. You are collectively being enriched by millions of dollars each year. There is no evidence that your company has suffered any penalty from these litigations. In fact, the evidence is to the contrary.

The case law suggests that the purpose of punitive damages is to make an award that will punish a defendant for his wrongdoing. Punishment has traditionally involved the principles of revenge, rehabilitation, and deterrence. There is no evidence I have been able to find in my review of this case to indicate that any one of these objectives has been accomplished.

Mr. Robins, Mr. Forrest, Dr. Lunsford: You have not been rehabilitated. Under your direction, your company has continued to allow women, tens of thousands of them, to wear this device—a deadly depth charge in their wombs, ready to explode at any time. Your attorney denies that tens of thousands of these devices are still in women's bodies. . . . We simply do not know how many women are still wearing these devices because your company is not willing to find out. The only conceivable reasons that you have not recalled this product are that it would hurt your balance sheet and alert women who have already been harmed that you may be liable for their injuries. . . . You have taken the bottom line as your guiding beacon and the low road as your route. That is corporate irresponsibility at its meanest. Confession is good for the soul, gentlemen. Face up to your misdeeds. Acknowledge the personal responsibility you have for the activities of those who work under you. Rectify this evil situation. Warn the potential victims and recompense those who have already been harmed.

The disposition of any case must be tied to *change*. If a defective machine caused the injury and the case is settled, then a plan to correct the defect must be submitted with the settlement agreement, and a public ombudsman should see that the required changes are carried out for the protection of the public. If a doctor has committed malpractice, an appropriate plan to prevent similar injury should be submitted and approved by the court before the doctor is permitted to practice medicine again. And no wrongdoer should be entitled to buy off claims, leaving the rest of the nation secretly exposed to the corporation's further transgressions. The public has an interest in the outcome of all litigation. That is why the doors of the courtroom are open. They must not be closed to America by the secret settlement—secret settlements should be outlawed.

It is also our duty to outlaw other unconscionable devices used by corporations to defeat the rights of citizens. Judge Lord also pointed to the practice of corporations that attempt to eliminate the few remaining experienced people's attorneys from seeking justice for the injured:

> The courts of this country are burdened with more than 3,000 Dalkon Shield cases. The sheer number of claims and the dilatory tactics used by your company's attorneys clog court calendars and consume vast amounts of judicial and jury time. Your company settles those cases out of court in which it finds itself in an uncomfortable position, a handy device for avoiding any proceedings that would give continuity or cohesiveness to this nationwide problem. . . . In order to guarantee that no plaintiff or group of plaintiffs mounts a sustained assault upon your system of evasion and avoidance, you have time after time demanded that, as the price of settling a case, able lawyers agree not to bring a Dalkon Shield case again and not to help less experienced lawyers with cases against your company.
>
> Another of your callous legal tactics is to force women of little means to withstand the onslaughts of your well-financed team of attorneys. You target your worst tactics at the meek and the poor.

The power of the court to reduce the size of an award—the remittitur—can be used by concerned judges for bringing about reform. Take the case of Betty O'Gilvie, a wife and mother who died of toxic-shock syndrome from the use of Playtex's superabsorbent tampons containing polyacrylate fibers. The trial judge thought the award of $10 million in punitive damages against Playtex was justified. There was abundant evidence that Playtex deliberately disregarded studies and medical reports linking high-absorbency tampon fibers with the increased risk of toxic shock at a time when other tampon manufacturers were modifying or withdrawing their high-absorbency products. There was evidence that Playtex intentionally sought to profit from this situation by advertising the effectiveness of its high-absorbency tampons when it knew other manufacturers were reducing the absorbency of their products for the safety of their customers. Worse, an internal company memo admitted, "In being obsessed with 'absorbency' we lost sight of the fact that 'leakage' complaints did not decrease as the tampon absorbency potentials were increased"—that is, the added danger to the user did not make the product more effective.

The trial judge, U. S. District Court Judge Patrick Kelly, tendered to Playtex a "provocative proposition." He would substantially reduce the punitive award if Playtex would remove its tampons from the market. A number of other cases were pending against Playtex, and the judge thought that Betty O'Gilvie's case was just the beginning. But the Tenth Circuit Court of Appeals reversed Judge Kelly, saying, "Far from punishing Playtex, the trial court here rewarded the company for continuing its tortious conduct long enough to use it as a bargaining chip . . . [which would] encourage [others] to pursue the very behavior that the punitive award here was intended to deter, and thus would discourage voluntary cessation of injury-causing conduct."

Yet in certain cases the reduction of large punitive awards in exchange for good behavior by the corporation can be a tool that courts can use to force change for the protection of the public. A Utah court recently considered the reduction of a $10 million punitive award in a case against Seven-Up in which a bottle cap blew off, blinding an elderly woman in one eye. Thousands of similar incidents in the industry had placed the industry on notice of this danger. Avoiding the holding in *O'Gilvie*, the court made no "deal" with the corporation at all. The judge merely took the corporation's plea to reduce the punitive award "under advisement" for a month, awaiting defendant's showing as to the changes it intended in order to make its bottles safer.

In the same spirit of accountability, the *real parties* to a lawsuit should no longer be kept secret from our juries. If there is insurance, the jury should know it. Why permit the insurance companies of America to lurk secretly behind the human beings they insure? These men and women who come to perform their civic duty as jurors and who are required to take an oath of fidelity to the law did not, as part of the bargain, agree to a proceeding in which important data would be withheld from them. The practice of keeping the fact of insurance from the jury constitutes nothing less than a judicial fraud on the jury itself. In all but a few states, the attorneys, by judicial rule, are gagged. Insurance companies argue that juries would tend to grant larger and more frequent awards if they knew that the party sued is insured. But in fairness, the question has two sides: Juries sometimes refuse any justice to deserving victims when they are led to believe there is no insurance to pay the amount of their award. In any event, the insurance industry has already solved that problem in their favor. It has persuaded the public that large awards are reflected in an increase in the public's insurance premiums so that jurors hurt themselves in granting just awards to injured people. That notion, brought on by a recent media blitz by the insurance industry, creates a conflict of interest for every juror, and many experienced trial lawyers insist the idea is beginning to adversely influence the results in their cases, insurance or not.

Americans have always been self-reliant. Accordingly we should encourage, not limit, the rights of our citizens to self-help in the civil courts. Damage suits against corporations have traditionally provided some inhibiting influence against corporate irresponsibility and recklessness. Judge Lord claims the courts are "the only place that [corporations] haven't been able to buy into government. And now they are trying to cut off the contingent fee, and put limits on liability to make it more difficult to recover damages. . . . The only thing that is deterring [corporations] is the personal injury lawyer, who literally takes the victims out of their bed or their grave, goes with them to court, and asks for retribution and punitive damages."

But corporate lobbyists want to change all of this. Now, they press for caps that limit the amount of dollar justice an injured person may recover. This special legislation for the protection of corporate profit has been in response to massive campaigns conducted on a state-by-state basis by the insurance industry and large corporate combines. Already, such laws have been passed in nearly half of the states. Some are eliminating punitive damages against corporations. More and more, we are drowned in corporate propaganda. We hear of the "lawsuit crisis." We are left with the impression that it is neither moral nor American to sue for our injuries, because those who bring the suits are *ipso facto* greedy and threaten our great institutions—our medical community, our sports, the clergy, even the ability of American industry to compete against the Japanese. On the other hand, the people, poorly organized and underfinanced, have had little success in preserving their rights.

The Ad Hoc Insurance Committee of the National Association of Attorneys General studied the so-called "litigation explosion" and concluded, "The facts do not bear out the allegations of an 'explosion' in litigation or in claim size, nor do they bear out the allegations of a financial disaster suffered by property/casualty insurers today. They finally do not support any correlation between the current crisis in availability and affordability of insurance and such a litigation 'explosion.' Instead, the available data indicate that the causes of, and therefore the solutions to, the current crisis lie with the insurance industry itself."

What can we do to prevent this industry-manufactured "crisis" from recurring about every ten years? First, Congress should repeal the insurance industry's exemption from the antitrust laws and thereby enhance federal regulation, and permit Federal Trade Commission scrutiny. Congress should require insurance companies to regularly reveal—subline by subline—for day-care centers, obstetricians, trucking concerns, municipalities, etc., how much they take in on premiums and investment income and how much they pay out in verdicts and settlements. Such disclosure in the past few years would have made it more difficult for these companies to manufacture these nonexistent crises for the media.

There are other ways we can begin to even things up between the mightiest corporation and the merest individual. We should make it too expensive for insurance companies to refuse to pay just claims on a timely basis. Judge Lord saw this tactic clearly when he admonished the officers of A. H. Robins in the Dalkon Shield cases:

> . . . The policy of delay and obfuscation practiced by your lawyers in courts throughout this country has made it possible for you and your insurance company to put off the payment of these claims for such a long period that the interest you earned in the interim covers the cost of these cases. You, in essence, pay nothing out of your own pockets to settle these cases. . . . The only lesson [corporate officials] might learn is that it pays to delay compensating victims and to intimidate, harass, and shame the injured parties.

Interest on the amount of the jury's verdict of at least four points over prime should run from the date of the claim until paid. That's about the rate of interest most injured citizens pay the bank to live on (most cannot even get a loan) while they try to wrest their just dues from the delaying insurance company. Several states already have such laws in place.

Since most of the time-consuming trial business in the civil court is devoted to the processing of insurance claims—a service provided the insurance industry at the people's expense—the insurance industry should pay for that service at a rate sufficient to insure a fair profit for the state or federal government providing it. Thus, if the insurance company does not settle its case with an injured party, who must thereafter file his case in court, the actual pro-rata cost of operating the court throughout the entire process should be paid for by the insurance company—not the usual assessment of costs, which amount to little in the average case, but an actual fee that is charged for the court's services and that adequately pays the costs of all court personnel, as well as the cost of running the plant, the courthouse, and an additional sum as a reasonable profit so that the courthouse will become self-sustaining. This cost would not be charged to a citizen—even if the citizen should lose—because the citizen supports the court system with his taxes, while most insurance companies do not. Moreover, most citizens are not engaged in the business of processing claims—a business activity carried on almost exclusively by insurance companies. Today, we provide clerks and bailiffs and reporters and judges and records and offices—all at our expense as taxpayers and free of charge to the insurance company. It enlists the services of the same court system against us whenever it deems it good strategy not to pay our just claims but instead to force us to litigaton. If that company were required to pay the expense attributable to its business of claim adjustment *in court* the same way that they must bear the cost of their claims business *out of court*, there would be very few cases ever to reach the courthouse doors.

We should consider legislation requiring that punitive-damage awards be divided in a different fashion. Today, the injured party receives the jury's entire punitive award less the percentage paid his attorney. I propose that one-third should be awarded to the party bringing the suit and one-third to his or her lawyer. The remaining third should endow a Justice Fund to finance public-interest litigation, to underwrite deserving cases where the costs are prohibitive, or to provide the finances necessary to give postgraduate training to the people's trial lawyers. The fund should be administered by a board composed of ordinary citizens.

The changes I envision, of course, require vast brave new legislation. In a government owned and operated as a business asset of corporate America, it is as likely that Congress will pass such comprehensive reforms as it is that it will gnaw off the hand that holds its spoon. Perhaps America cannot endure too great a jolt of freedom all at once. Freedom is a frightening condition. But we must begin. We must begin by outlawing *bribery*—let us call it what it is—in Congress. We must pass legislation prohibiting anything but the most meager kinds of political contributions to be made to a candidate. Why should corporations, with their enormous resources, own our representatives? There are no polling booths for Ford Motor Company and Union Carbide. Voting is for people. Government is for people. Yet what is happening in Congress is akin to this: I take my horse to the races, where corporate America races against me but owns *my jockey*.

Elections have become futile. Do we really believe that anything would substantially change if we cleared out the entire membership of both houses and the presidency and replaced them with a new set of politicians, all of whom had waged their expensive campaigns on television? Much of this evil arises from the need to finance electronic public images. The millions expended by our leaders for their offices—it takes from $6 million to $20 million to elect a senator, and from $60 million to $100 million to elect a president—

must be repaid, and unless our leaders are enormously wealthy, in which case all but the rich are ineligible, the corporate mass will continue to buy and own our representatives.

I would rather choose a leader based on who sang "The Star-Spangled Banner" with the most gusto than on television imagery that merely reflects the talents of those who produce his ads and the bankroll it takes to finance them. We should limit campaign contributions to a candidate from any individual or any corporation—from *any source*—to, let us say, $100. I do not intend to disenfranchise corporate America. Exxon and Ford can each contribute their hundred bucks like you and me. The total that can be expended on a given campaign should be set so that running for public office is within the practical reach of everyone. Political advertisements should be outlawed. Television will carry the debates of the candidates as a public service.

Now, the politician will be forced to stump his state in person. The candidates will have to knock on our doors and show us their *real* faces. They will hold rallies in the public square and mount the courthouse steps for their speeches. They will square off with their opponents for Lincoln-Douglas-type debates in the community hall. Madison Avenue and the fabricating of false television images is out. Once again, people talking to people is in. The candidates' huge campaign debts need not be paid, because they have never been incurred. The impoverished farmer, the unemployed laborer, and the college teacher can run for public office as easily as the wealthy and the famous. The quality of leadership offered and actually demonstrated by a candidate will be the basis of an election campaign, not money. And as the people recapture their power, so will we enjoy the reforms from which we can more nearly realize justice for all.

The funding inequity has not been lost on the voters. Legislation for the public financing of campaigns just narrowly failed in the Ninety-fifth Congress. And in 1988 the big money interests in Congress again beat back a bill that would have severely restricted the amounts special-interest PACs could contribute to a candidate's election. Says Mark Green, author of the best-seller *Who Runs Congress?*, "Until [we] institute the public financing of congressional campaigns as the best way to cleanse the epidemic of purchased politicians or at least until it establishes free and equal access to television, radio, and the mails for bona fide candidates—the jingle of corruption and veiled bribery will continue to be heard in its halls. Until then the Golden Rule of politics will prevail—he who has the gold, rules."

We must also jam the revolving door between government and the private sector. Would we hire an attorney to sue the local power company if we knew he had his application in for the position of general counsel with that same corporation? Many executives now working for corporations at bountiful salaries once served as their governmental regulators. The revolving door spins and spins, and influence peddling that permits the privileged to whisper in the ears of those who should be listening to all of us continues to dominate government. Michael Deaver, recently convicted of perjury, went directly from the president's side as his deputy chief of staff to becoming a highly paid lobbyist for corporations and foreign governments. Ann McBride of Common Cause says, "[F]ew things are more discouraging and demoralizing to honest government employees— and the public—than the spectacle of public officials cashing in on their positions of trust, using their government service to launch lucrative post-government lobbying careers." Such practice makes toadying lackeys of officials who have visions of rich corporate positions in the future but whose sworn duty is to protect us against the corporate abuses of their prospective employers.

Many of America's Cabinet members have been exceptional men "on loan to the government," as they like to say, from large corporations that do business with the government. Sometimes it's the other way around: Like many Cabinet officials, General Alexander Haig became wealthy after leaving public office. Over the last two years, his international consulting firm, Worldwide Associates, Inc., paid him $2.7 million. He advises Boeing and Amway Corporation and serves on the boards of half a dozen major companies. Even during his campaign for president, he saw no reason to curtail his business activities, including acting as a paid consultant to a South Korean conglomerate. "It's ludicrous to say that because you're running for president, you can't eat," Haig defends himself indignantly.

The Ethics in Government Act, a law laden with exceptions and conflicting administrative interpretations, does little to protect us, and at best provides security from only limited kinds of influence peddling for a mere year or two after the public servant leaves the government.

One way to jam this revolving door might be to pay our government officials wages equivalent or better than their counterparts receive in private business so that the people can compete with the large corporations for "the best and the brightest," and so these officials, trained by taxpayers' dollars, need never return to the corporate bosom. The National Commission on Public Service, headed by Paul A. Volcker as its unpaid chairman, has been authorized to discover why America cannot attract first-rate people into government service. Volcker notes that many are attracted to the opportunity to serve their nation, but "there is a point where salaries are so bad they become a disinducement. We didn't get the best young people in the Federal Reserve," he said, "because the difference between a $27,000 salary and a $70,000 salary is just too much when you're coming out of law school and probably in debt." Patricia Schroeder, the Colorado Democrat heading a subcommittee to investigate public service in government, blames the White House. "We had two presidents back to back, Carter and Reagan, who treated public service as if it was the lowest form of human life. Can you imagine the president of a private company saying, 'You wouldn't believe the bunch of creeps I've got working for me.'" She says, "We absolutely have to restore the dignity of public service." In Japan, the public servant is honored as few nations honor their officials. The businessman, no matter how successful he may be, can never achieve the level of respect and social acceptance afforded the Japanese public servant, for the businessman is guided by self-interest, while the Japanese public servant has pledged himself to his country.

These proposals, incomplete, illustrative, and utopian as they obviously are, establish a single proposition—that tools are available *within* the system by which we can regain our freedom. The law should reflect the conscience of the nation, and often it does. As social attitudes change, so will the law: The system *can* be moral if we choose to make it moral. We *can* take back our government if that is our wish. We *can* control corporate crime if we decide to. We *can* realize justice in the courtroom and accomplish change if we desire it. Such sweeping reforms as are suggested here are not radical; but that a free people should accept conditions and laws that finally assure them there will be justice for none *is*. The revolution calls for two very simple events: that we appreciate and accept an uncomfortable idea—that justice for all is a cherished American myth—and that we act on that knowledge and demand what is rightfully ours.

15 | NEW VOICES

Leashing the Corporate Cyclops

Freedom cannot exist in a muzzled world. Free people must speak to each other and hear each other—they must test and protest and raise hell and shake their leaders by the napes of their necks. Our Founding Fathers gave us the supreme weapon of liberty—free speech—and with the First Amendment, guaranteed us that most sacred of rights. But the people have been silenced. They have been administered a new sedative. There they sit placidly, like patients on the third floor of the state hospital, where the bad ones are locked up—their mouths open, their eyes lifeless and glazed, watching television.

The thesis of Marie Winn in her landmark work *The Plug-In Drug* is that television is addictive. She writes, "Not unlike drugs or alcohol, the television experience allows the participant to blot out the real world and enter into a pleasurable and passive mental state." Passivity! It is a style of our times—the leaden robe of serfdom. A 1983 Nielsen Report claims even children in the two- to five-year-old age group spend an average of 27.9 hours each week watching television. Other surveys argue for higher figures—up to fifty-four hours weekly for preschool viewers. Even the most conservative estimates show our children watching television more than a third of their waking hours and the average adult six hours a day. We are raising children whose original experiences are not in the fields or the forests, not at their chores, not in books or in the sweat of play. Winn warns, "It is disquieting to consider that hour after hour of television watching constitutes a primary activity for them." She says that many of their important life reference points will be the fantasy of television, not the reality of genuine experience. "To a certain extent children's early television will serve to dehumanize, to mechanize, to make less real the realities and relationships they encounter in life. For them, real events will always carry subtle echoes of the television world," and to that extent the child becomes another machine, responding as planned and nodding as programmed. As an adult, then, the viewer's perception of reality has become permanently altered by the steady, insidious exposure to illusion. One group of researchers reporting in *Psychology Today* found that a single thirty-minute program could significantly alter basic beliefs, related attitudes, and behavior of large numbers of people. The researchers demonstrated that audiences could be caused to rethink even their fundamental values. With curious optimism, they observe that the power of television could be used for good—to bring freedom and equality into better balance. But, they warned, there is a darker side: The same media techniques can be used—indeed, I argue that they are—to cause Americans to reject their precious rights.

As newly freed people, our forefathers not only endowed us with the right but charged us with the duty to openly and lustily debate matters of public concern, to warn each other of new dangers to our liberty, and to hear each other and avoid the ensnaring traps of new masters. It is a certainty that the nation's airways, the most potent force for freedom ever invented by man, should be controlled by the people. Our right to uninhibited access to the means of free speech is as important as the right itself, for although we may be free to cry out our griefs and expound our beliefs, if our voices echo against dead walls, the right itself is as dead. The airways are ours like the sunshine, like the atmosphere. Yet in the hands of our enemies, the airways afford the most abominable tool of oppression ever conceived. They are the first seized by every tyrant. The despots of history would have traded whole kingdoms for such unbounded power. Nothing can stop it—not the Great Wall of China, not great flotillas, not whole armies. As we embrace it, unwittingly we are caught in its spell. Its power exceeds even that of the bomb, for that monstrous evil contains us only by fear, while television captures us by seemingly harmless, mindless pleasure.

The idea that in a democracy a free people should quietly accept the theft of their voice is, indeed, very radical. Our "eternal vigilance" must have flickered. Did we not understand what was happening to us? What was ours was transformed into the corporate

Cyclops, and then turned against us. Perhaps the greatest betrayal of America was the giveaway of our airways to the commercial corporations of America. Channels belonging to us were licensed, *free of charge*, to the three leviathans who now own, as their private property, our most effective means to communicate with each other. Although they are theoretically subject to regulation by the Federal Communications Commission (FCC), these corporations, as history has proved, are too large, too powerful, to be effectively regulated even when, as we have seen, their criminal activity has been continuous and blatant. The overall ad revenue for the networks alone was recently projected at $8.2 billion. These networks, the public property, are bought and sold among corporations for a king's ransom. In 1985, the smallest of the three majors, ABC, was swallowed up by Capital Cities Communications, for $3.5 billion. General Electric soaked up first-place NBC by purchasing its parent, RCA, for $6.3 billion.

The FCC, presumably our servant, itself a mammoth body tangled in its own bureaucratic tentacles and permeated with the political worm, could have orginally distributed these channels to a wide spectrum of interests that represent a free citizenry, to stations controlled by blacks, by the poor, by farmers, workers, and women. One wonders how our awareness would change if *Dallas* were sponsored by a consumer's organization rather than by Buick, or the advertisements on *The Bill Cosby Show* were composed by Madison Avenue on behalf of the National Organization for Women rather than Ford. How might America bloom if the Super Bowl were sponsored by a trade union seeking public support for worker conditions, by the Gray Panthers or the American Association of Retired Persons (AARP) demanding equal rights for the elderly, or by the Sierra Club seeking to preserve important places on this earth.

I can see such a commercial during a time-out:

EXTERIOR: ACROSS THE CITY SPRAWL—DAY
The camera takes us over the small project houses bunched up like boxes piled in the garage, the junked cars in the yards, old refrigerators and garbage in the rear. We fly across the billboards and onto the concrete freeways gridlocked in traffic, the noise, the horns, drivers with their heads leering out the windows, yelling, diesels vibrating—the smoke. We follow the concrete to the towering offices. Vertical concrete.

Like a feather sucked up in a powerful draft, we seem to bounce off the walls as we ascend. Upward we speed, past the windows where we see people glued to desktops like mannequin heads, dull, slothful, frighteningly stiff. Now, over the building tops, again we see the endless urban sprawl between us and the smokestacks towering in the distance. The camera moves up close as we are taken into the greenish smoky ooze.

cut to:

INTERIOR: THE SMOKESTACK
We descend—down, down into dark, as if we are falling into hell. Abruptly we emerge into the fiery furnaces.

cut to:

INTERIOR: THE BOARDROOM—DAY
The room is grand, sparkling—crystal chandeliers. A pleasant-looking man with neat gray hair, wearing a dark pin-striped suit, looking proud, and speaking with authority addresses his clones, who sit at a long, shiny table. They nod and smile back as he speaks.

CHAIRMAN OF THE BOARD
Gentlemen: Profits for the third quarter are up twenty-eight percent.

We watch the CHAIRMAN OF THE BOARD *continue in his speech while a deep, appealing* VOICE-OVER *speaks to us, quietly, and very confidentially:*

VOICE-OVER
What price do *we* pay for these profits?

cut to:

EXTERIOR: THE SHORES OF A GARBAGE-STREWN LAKE—DAY
A bedraggled seagull rummages through the trash. In the background, we see the stacks and the smoke. An OLD-TIMER *with kind, watery eyes and a sad smile walks into the picture and speaks into the camera.*

OLD-TIMER
Used ta catch two-pound bass here when I was a kid and the place was loaded with ducks and frogs and pollywogs.

He looks back at the stacks and stares silently for a moment.

PULL BACK: To reveal the OLD-TIMER *standing forlornly on the shore of that godawful floating junk pile.*

VOICE-OVER
Where are you taking your kids fishing today?

I wonder what it would be like if people were speaking to people about matters important to the human condition on this earth rather than being sold dish soap and beer.

But what about public television? The people presumably have a network, albeit most of us don't watch it most of the time. Public television was a creature of Congress born in 1967. Legislation permitted the linkage of dozens of local educational stations into a national network later named the Public Broadcasting System (PBS). The original idea of public television was to produce what the networks, bound by the constraints of advertisers and profit considerations, could not—excellent, provocative programs. Major networks rely on pure mathematics—ratings, advertising profits—and, therefore, TV executives direct their appeal to the greatest possible number of viewers, with the consequence that they usually forego that which has intrinsic value unless it also has commercial value. It was the lamentation we heard from critic Cecil Smith that public television was intended to correct: "When network executives, mostly lawyers and computer experts and advertising salesmen who couldn't create a fire with a mountain of matches, drive out the creative people whose work occasionally flickers on the tube, we shouldn't wonder that we have so low a level of bland and lifeless television." Public television was to be a new, exciting frontier for quality work, a place where journalists, too, could attack the important issues of the day. "That," says S. L. Harrison, former director of communications for the Corporation for Public Broadcasting (CPB) and an adjunct professor at the American University, "is how the myth of public broadcasting was born. It was a myth."

Harrison reports that those with the power of the purse had different ideas about what "quality" meant, so that over the years outside political interference imposed as many constraints on public TV as commercial sponsors have on the networks. "Not that PBS carries the overt propaganda of a given administration as in fascist states," Harrison says, "but it has become soft, non-controversial— and, mostly boring." The Corporation for Public Broadcasting was established by Congress to assist in the financial support of the network, and its members are appointed by the president. But rather than assisting PBS to achieve its goals, Nixon vetoed additional congressional funding. "We have men on that [CPB] board," presidential adviser Daniel Patrick Moynihan wrote in a November 30, 1970, memo to Nixon's chief of staff, H. R. Haldeman. "Why aren't they looking out for the president's perfectly legitimate interests?" Of The Advocates series, Moynihan wrote to the CPB, "It seems to me yet another example of a persistent pattern of biased treatment of the administration by public television." Within two years, Harrison says, "the shows that the White House found irritating, including *The Advocates*, were off the air. . . ." Documents released in 1979 under the Freedom of Information Act establish that CPB actually presubmitted to the White House its schedule of the programs and guest lists for upcoming shows and made efforts to feature participants who would speak in a friendly way of the administration. "CPB staff members met regularly with White House representatives to assure them that unpalatable programs were banned."

The Reagan administration, with a majority on the ten-person board, has renewed the effort to emasculate the network. In a 6–4 vote, the Reagan-controlled CPB board deposed three-term chairperson Sharon Percy Rockefeller, replacing her with a skilled political in-fighter, Sonia Landau, who had headed Women for Reagan/Bush. Now that more reliance on corporate financing was required, controversial programs were eliminated or depreciated. Bill Moyers said that corporate sponsors called many of the shots in making his TV documentaries. He spoke to *Variety* of his series *A Walk Through the 20th Century*, funded by Chevron. "I should have been able to air controversial views," Moyers said. "I wasn't." He said that another of his shows, *Bill Moyers' Journal*, had its corporate support withdrawn after three "controversial programs." Harrison states that while he worked for CPB, public-TV producers regularly showed programs to underwriters to make sure that they would not offend sponsors. And why not? Corporate sponsors admit, says Harrison, that they "do not throw money away on programs that don't promote a 'feel-good' image for the company."

Harrison writes passionately on the issue in *The Washington Monthly*, and has proposals. He thinks that for PBS to acquire the independence it requires, a small excise tax on the sale of radios and TV sets should be levied and the monies put aside in tamper-proof trust funds. He says, "If PBS didn't have to worry about where its next meal would come from, it would be free to cook up a more interesting array of public affairs programs." He predicts, "Without a wall between the politicians, the corporations, and the broadcasters, public television will continue to fail in its mission to provide alternative programming in the critical areas of public affairs."

We are television's product—an audience sold to advertisers. David G. Clark and William B. Blankenburg, in their book *You and Media*, said, "The networks are really in the business of manufacturing audiences, which are then advertised and sold to advertisers who wish to reach large numbers of people at relatively little cost." Ron Powers, in *The Newscasters*, tells a more graphic truth: "Television's first mission is not to inform. It is not even to entertain. It is to move goods, to round up viewers for the main event, the commercial." In America, even we, the audiences, have become commodities. By one means or another, the networks capture us and sell the housewives to Procter & Gamble, the sports fans to Anheuser-Busch, and the mothers and fathers to Chevrolet. The idea that the users of our airways should serve us, not merchandise us, has been lost in Madison Avenue pizzazz. Yet it is not that we protest our bondage to that "plug-in drug": We insist upon it. Like true addicts, we do not long to be free of our addiction. We wish only to freely satisfy our habit. Norman Corwin, in his insightful book *Trivializing America*, says, "[T]he people have been conditioned to want what they want mainly by years of having gotten what they have gotten." Frank Mankiewicz and Joel Swerdlow, in their book *Remote Control*, add, "Nothing in our [investigations] or in our interviews suggests that commercial TV programming in the United States will change significantly in the foreseeable future. So long as the industry is based upon engaging an audience and delivering it to an advertiser, present tendencies, in one form or another, will prevail."

In 1938, E. B. White issued this startling prophecy: "I believe television is going to be the test of the modern world, and that in this new opportunity to see beyond the range of our vision we shall discover either a new and unbearable disturbance of the general peace or a saving radiance in the sky. We shall stand or fall by television—of that I am quite sure." Edward R. Murrow said, "The instrument can teach, it can illuminate; yes, and it can even inspire. But it can do so only to the extent that humans are determined to use it to those ends. Otherwise it is merely lights and wires in a box." But it is more than mere lights and wires as the mind is more than nerve endings and impulses. Television is an irresistible force that has finally come to enslave us. Most who have given thought to the matter have not been exuberant over our prospects to free ourselves, for, as Huxley asks in *Brave New World*, how is freedom possible for those who have grown to love their servitude?

Todd Gitlin, in his book *Inside Prime Time*, considered the problem. "The networks do just what they set out to do. They are not trying to stimulate us to thought, or inspire us to belief, or remind us what it is to be human and live on earth late in the twentieth century; what they are trying to do is to 'hook' us. Meanwhile, the government regulatory agencies have been persuaded that 'the marketplace' is its own regulator, which means that no interest that cannot be expressed in Nielsen numbers counts." It is a sign of our times, he says, when a president who does not know what his own government is doing is dubbed "the Great Communicator."

Some in America think the European system of noncommercial television might resolve the problem. But here Gitlin is not optimistic, either. "The mass-marketing mentality pervades much of non-communist European television to almost the same degree as in America, though without the compulsion of the profit motive." In France, commercial television networks were recently licensed, and there were the familiar cries of "giveaways" and "political patronage"; we can understand this outrage, for there is no reason to believe that France's experience in the commercialization of television is essentially different from ours. Even after France's years of noncommercial television, the perception was that their airways were "property," so that even the opponents of the "giveaways" wanted the networks sold to the highest bidder. Gitlin finally throws up his hands. ". . . [T]he predicament of American television is the predicament of American culture and politics as a whole. Walt Whitman," he concludes, "wrote, 'To have great poets there must be great audiences, too.'"

Let us suppose a frightening scenario, the technology for which is already in place. We can measure our need for air. We can also measure any individual's daily intake of air. Suppose that at a time when pure air becomes even scarcer, Congress creates the Federal Air Board (FAB) mandated to insure each American his or her fair share of air to breathe. Suppose now, in accordance with ideals similar to those under which the Federal Communications Commission gave away our rights to television, the Federal Air Board grants free licenses for the sale of air to three major air corporations, American Breathing Company (ABC), National Breathing Company (NBC), and Consolidated Breathing Company (CBS), and these three corporations end up controlling 80 percent of the free air of the country. Suppose fifty years later, after we have all paid trillions for the very right to breathe, some idiot suggests that the right to the air has belonged to the people all along, that it was stolen from them and that it should be returned. Some would doubtless see that as a very dangerous and radical idea.

For another perspective, let us examine where we are by transposing our current state of affairs into history. Suppose we travel back to the days immediately following the Revolution. The Constitution has just been adopted, along with the Bill of Rights. Suppose we suggest to our friends Jefferson and Madison, perhaps even Hamilton, that there would one day be a new technology called "television," and that this means of communication would be given away by the government to corporate enterprises many times richer and more powerful than all of the thirteen colonies put together, and that these corporations, with this incredibly powerful weapon, would brainwash Americans to buy the commodities these corporations manufacture, most of which, parenthetically, the people would not need. Suppose we told them that in two hundred years the people would be further taught to believe this powerful means of communication did not actually belong to them, but instead belonged to these corporations, and that when someone proposed that the airways be returned to the people who had owned them all along, the majority of the people would rise up in protest, claiming that the idea of returning the airways to themselves was so seriously revolutionary, so un-American, that such a thought could not be tolerated, even in a country where free thought is guaranteed by the First Amendment. What would our Founding Fathers have said? Might we not see Jefferson shrug his shoulders and say something like this: "That vision, repugnant as it is to freedom, is equally repugnant to the imagination of men. It is as unlikely to occur as a man's journey to the moon. It is as unlikely to occur as the parceling out of the air we breathe, by the cubic foot, to be paid for shilling at a time."

Gitlin believes that a "democracy requires an active, engaged citizenry committed to determine and seek the public good," while the bulk of television causes us to think of ourselves first as consumers. He contends the fundamental responsibility of the media should be to help people more successfully pursue their rights and obligations as citizens, "not to sell goods, or serve as an amplification system for politicians, or shore up the prestige of the privileged or sprinkle flakes of celebrity or blips of disconnected facts upon the daily life of a society otherwise dedicated to private gain." I would not turn TV into a constant course in civics, and I have no doubt the people themselves, those lovers of soaps and game shows and multifarious cop shows and trivia, would protest as loudly the idea that we should make better citizens of them. But here we have come full circle again and face the same endless emptiness, requiring, as it does, that by legislation we graft a responsive scruple to the corporate creatures who own our airways.

The Federal Communications Commission has the power to demand that our networks devote significant portions of their time to the public good. But they, too, are bound by their own precedents. They, too, are committed not only to a system of their own creation but to the political exigencies of those who have created them. In the end, the FCC has been given over, body, heart, and soul, to the industry. It merely referees the games between the participants, which, for the most part, exclude the public. A new comprehensive Conscience in Communications Act should impose upon those to whom we have *lent* our airways a duty to pay reasonably for their use.

How should the networks pay us? Why not extract the usual and ordinary markups in the market? If a couch for your living room costs the retailer $200, he will likely sell it for $400. The cost of the ingredients in a beer that sells for a couple of bucks at the bar is less than a nickel. The ingredients in a dollar Coke cost even less. In the same spirit of fair commerce that sets the price we pay for goods, let us require both the broadcaster and the advertiser to pay a reasonable fee *in kind* for the use of our airways. It would go a long way toward the rededication of radio and television to the public good if, say, *one-third* of all advertising carried over commercial radio and television properly educated us on concerns vital to our welfare. For example, if Ford Motor Company wished to sponsor the Super Bowl in order to sell us their automobiles, and if in doing so it expects to use six minutes of air time (which, I am told, sells at $1.2 million per minute), then the networks and the advertiser must, at their expense, produce two minutes of public-interest advertising during the Super Bowl. Such ads might explain to us how air bags can save us in a head-on collision where seat belts won't.

Ford and the other major auto manufacturers have been notoriously against the mandatory installation of air bags in their automobiles despite the fact that their lifesaving capabilities are no longer in serious dispute. Despite Ford's tarnished safety record and its preoccuption with glitter and chrome, it is not unheard of for the government, in guarding the general welfare, to require sellers, at their expense, to inform the public against the seller's self-interest. For example, cigarette ads fully paid for by the tobacco company now carry various specific health warnings from the Surgeon General concerning heart disease, cancer, and complications to pregnancy. Our Conscience in Communications Act can provide for an ombudsman, similar to the Surgeon General, to see that the provisions of the Conscience in Communications Act are enforced and its intent realized. The ombudsman would be a person nominated by a committee composed of leading consumer, environmental, and public-interest groups, and appointed by the president with the approval of the House of Representatives (for a wider feedback from the people), and the Office of the Ombudsman would be supervised by the same committee that nominated his or her appointment in the first place.

When Kellogg's wants to persuade our children to purchase Frosted Flakes, it could be required to also spend one-third of its television advertising budget providing interesting and vital facts on nutrition—to sell us on the idea, for instance, that we must lower the sugar content of our foods if we are to conquer obesity and heart disease in this country. It can sell us on health rather than on unhealthy products. Coors might spend a third of its advertising space explaining to Americans the responsibility that goes with drinking. I could even see a muscular young man, as he launches himself on his surfboard, telling us that he doesn't need to drink to enjoy the good life. When drug companies want to sell their Anacin or Bayer, we can require them to also spend a third of their budget educating us about the dangers of drug dependence. When IBM wants to peddle its personal computers, it can also explain why we have antitrust laws and the dangers large corporations present to a free-enterprise system when they squeeze out small competitors, and it could educate us on the methods we might employ to protect ourselves against such abuses by the corporate giants.

What we seek here is neither unreasonable nor un-American, for fairness and decency have always been among our highest ideals. We should try to encourage corporations not only to return something to the public for the use of our airways, but to stop using the airways to manipulate our minds, to ruin our health, to sell us unsafe products, and quite simply to brainwash us against our own interests for their profit—at least for one-third of the time. What we are trying to establish here is an attitude of corporate responsibility, one that will finally be demanded by the public and accepted by the corporate sector itself.

Altruism is not an indigenous corporate trait. We have centuries of proof that the corporate conscience must be mandated by law. Edward Herman, acknowledged authority on the sociology of the American corporation, in his book *Corporate Control, Corporate Power* says contributions made by corporations strictly for the public good are "not only a rarity, [they] would be regarded as evidence of irresponsibility and softheadedness." The anonymous corporate gift is unheard of. Corporate gratuities are always made to forward the corporate interest. Mobil's sponsorship of public television requires a credit in its name in order that we may know of the corporation's generosity. Fifty times a day, Budweiser calls the whole world's attention to the fact that it made a contribution to the Olympics.

While Madison Avenue creates a Santa Claus persona for its corporate clients, the actual penuriousness of the typical American corporation would make Scrooge look like an irresponsible old spendthrift. Even though the law has permitted a corporate tax deduction for charitable contributions up to 10 percent of a corporation's taxable earnings, corporate giving has hovered around the 1 percent mark, and, ironically, as profits increase, corporate giving declines.

Naturally our corporate citizens will resist our attempt to graft a conscience to their empty hearts, as all organisms attempt to reject something foreign. Hordes of corporate lobbyists, armies of corporate lackeys—some our friends, some our heroes—legions of "the best and the brightest" attorneys from the great law firms of the nation, will descend upon us like the biblical horde and alternately deluge us with their obsequious smiles and their rattling swords. Interminable cries of anguish will echo across the committee rooms and shake the very walls of Congress. We will hear many arguments, among which will be the assertion that the additional cost will only be passed on to the people. Undoubtedly that will be true. But so is *every cost* ultimately passed on to the consumer, including the billions spent each year to keep us glued to the tube and to stamp on our brains until they are turned to mush. *Forbes* magazine reports that a well-crafted commercial these days costs between $125,000 and $1 million per 30 seconds of sales pitch, all of which is passed on to the consumer and is tax deductible. Just as well, our corporate friends could pass on the cost of truthful information.

We should consider another ethic: Corporations ought not be permitted to use our airways to delude us with false images of themselves. We are entitled to be informed concerning the true character of the corporate advertiser, particularly if that corporation is a criminal. What of the corporation that knowingly injures its employees, dumps its waste on us, pollutes the air, and produces dangerous products it knows will injure us, but presents itself as a benign good neighbor? What of the corporation whose criminal offenses would reduce those of the FBI's worst public enemy to the magnitude of a pestering flea, but which portrays itself as a company of "just plain folks dedicated to serve you"? These corporations are like the carnivorous plant in nature that disguises itself to look like a flower—it even smells like one—and when the unsuspecting butterfly comes to visit, it entraps it and eats it.

We are entitled to know the true character of our corporate advertisers. Telling the truth is a principle to which American business gives constant lip service. Nowadays, truth is required in lending and, to some extent, in certain kinds of advertising. We demand even to know the most intimate details of the lives of our politicians. For centuries, the courts have permitted us to reveal the criminal record of a human felon who takes the stand to testify in his own defense. Why, when corporations take to the airways, are they not required to tell us the truth about their criminal records? At the beginning or end of every ad, like the screen credits that precede a movie, we should be provided a very readable and accurate account paid for by the corporate advertiser itself, of the record of convictions, if any, of the corporation and its subsidiaries.

After Merrill Lynch shows us its *bull* (an icon fully symbolic of its principal asset) it should also be required to reveal its crimes, if any. If the corporation has never been found guity of a crime, that fact may also be made known. It is a simple device that, perhaps more than any other, would act as an inducement to corporations to behave themselves. It is the one method by which we can put the criminal corporation in the public pillories, a method of shame and humiliation the colonists found exceedingly effective as a deterrent against wrongdoing. No longer would the game be, "Let's see how well and how often we can fool America." The new object would be, "Let's see how responsible we can really be," because responsibility would ring clear bells of financial advantage, those endearing sounds to which the corporate ear most readily responds.

Television, as we have seen, has become the favored means by which our attention has been diverted from the greatest crime wave in the history of our race—corporate crime. The trick is very simple. On the news—every morning, noon, and night—our eyes are diverted to victims of human crime. Television crews speed by helicopter to the scene of every revolting murder and every repulsive robbery and rape. We are taken up close to the fire and the blood and the horror, and the cameramen spread brutality full face across the screen until we are gripped with an ineffable loathing for the human race.

Mankiewicz and Swerdlow, in *Remote Control*, claim that television sells more than cars, hair sprays, and life insurance: It sells a view of the world, and that view helps change our image of ourselves. ". . . [I]f the TV world contains more victims than perpetrators of violence, that will create a society in which most people view themselves as potential victims and [they will] respond to life more fearfully." What effect does television have on the perception that adults hold of reality? Larry Gross and George Gerbner, two professors at the Annenberg School of Communications at the University of Pennsylvania, studied the effects of television "reality" on people's ideas and beliefs pertaining to the concrete world. Viewers were asked to guess their own chances of encountering violence in any given week as fifty-fifty, one chance in ten, or one chance in one hundred. Statistically, the chances that a person will encounter violence in any given week are less than one in one hundred, but heavy watchers of television consistently chose fifty-fifty or one chance in ten, reflecting the "reality" of television violence. We get benumbed by it. Thirty-seven people looked on while Kitty Genovese was murdered in their own courtyard. The people watched passively while it happened, as if it were just another television drama. Television not only destroys human sensitivity, it "conditions [viewers] to deal with real people as if they were on a television screen."

But the most cruel, calculating, and accomplished criminals of all time, the corporations of this country, are rarely held up to close public scrutiny. And when they are, they quickly buy prime time to create new images for themselves, having learned long ago that a corporate reputation in America today does not flow as easily from good deeds as from good advertising. That the media does not so readily and so graphically focus on corporate criminals as it does on individual felons is accounted for, not simply because the corporate culprits are their advertisers, as much as by the ease with which some poor devil is filmed as he is being dragged off to prison in handcuffs. It is quite a different task to present the crimes of Johns Manville and face its troupe of well-paid lawyers. Yet the spectacle of corporate crime with all of its heinous aftermath to victims—as horrid as any of the crimes committed by the living—is there ready and waiting to quench our daily need for butchery and misery. Instead of enthralling us with close-ups of the bloody body of a murder victim in the Bronx, why not tell us the truth about an industrywide rash of a different sort of mass murders?

By 1950, asbestos had been linked with asbestosis and lung cancer in the medical journals and was already a well-kept industry secret. Why not interview the son of an honest workman who, as a victim of corporate profit, died of an asbestos-induced cancer? Put Phil Lemere, Jr., on the screen. Let him tell a national television audience what he told the *Los Angeles Times*. His father was best man at his wedding. He was with his father the morning his father died. Let America listen to a tearful son, only one of the thousands of victims of that industry's crimes, tell his story:

"The fluid was building up. He was as big as a whale. His arms were like this big around, filled up with fluid, and I stayed with him all night," the son said. "I woke up hearing him gurgling and stuff and, you know, I just leaned over him, just talking to him, and I said, 'Dad, you know, it's OK. We all love you. It's just time to go . . .' I told him. 'I'll be with you again some day . . .'

"He just knew it was time to let go and he just stopped breathing. He just stopped breathing." He was fifty-one years old.

Why not take the viewers to the scene of a mass crime—to a plant where the deadly asbestos fiber was processed. Perhaps one of the workmen could be interviewed. In a deposition before his death, Milton Wheeler said one of the machines raised so much of the deadly dust "you couldn't see from one end of the machine to the other."

"You were covered with dust and the fibers. . . . It would be in your ears, it would be in your nose, even through the mask. It would be under your pant legs, it would be inside your socks. You'd just be literally covered with it. You'd be blue." A media dedicated to the exposure of corporate crime could not only provide us our daily fix of horror, it also could focus on issues critical to our very survival. Yet so long as corporate criminals remain in control of our airways, so long as our airways are the tool of profit, not social betterment, our head will continue to be turned from the masses of unpunished corporate crimes to the blood and gore and terror of our own crimes instead.

Ironically, the race for ratings is beginning to expose a variety of corporate criminals. That America yearns for a broader truth is demonstrated by the enduring popularity of such programs as *60 Minutes* and *20/20*. Take, for instance, this confoundedly visible man who runs Chrysler—Lee Iacocca. We see him daily on television. His company spends millions with the networks each year, and he has easy access to the camera. Two bestselling books recount a fascinating success story. We see him in charge of cleaning the Statue of Liberty. We see his rough, smiling, fatherly face on TV every day telling us to *trust* Chrysler because it has a wonderful automobile with the best warranty in the business. Then one day we see the same face and hear the same voice on the evening news explaining to us that Chrysler was "just stupid" (not criminal) for having sold thousands of used company-executive cars as new. Presumably we should still trust his company. But corporate carryings-on can be quite entertaining.

I have composed the following as if it were a scene in a screenplay. It is condensed from the actual transcripts of the now-infamous Nixon tapes. The dialogue has been edited to cut the numerous false starts and nonsensical filler of these national leaders who, in actual conversation, sound as if they suffer from some serious, undisclosed handicap. But for such merciful edits, the language is verbatim.

Iacocca, then president of Ford, convinced the president of the United States that the already-proven lifesaving device the air bag should *not* be installed in the nation's automobiles.

INTERIOR: THE OVAL OFFICE—DAY (between 11:08 and 11:43 A.M., April 27, 1971)
Seated in front of the PRESIDENT *are* HENRY FORD II, JOHN EHRLICHMAN, *and* LEE IACOCCA. PRESIDENT NIXON *leans back in his chair and dry-washes his hands.*

NIXON

My views in this field . . . my personal views—Henry, you will not be surprised at this but, uh, we, uh, uh, the, uh, uh, whether it's the environment or pollution or Naderism or consumerism, my views are extremely pro-business. Uh, we are fighting, frankly, a delaying action. There is pollution and maybe there are safety problems. I think they're greatly exaggerated, but we can't have a completely safe society or safe highways or safe cars and be pollution-free or we would have to go back and live like a bunch of damned animals. And these environmentalists aren't one really damn bit interested in safety or clean air. What they're interested in is *destroying the system*! They're the *enemies* of the system.

HENRY FORD II

Right.

NIXON

The safety thing's the kick, 'cause Nader's running around, squealing about this and that and the other thing. I try to fight these demagogues the best we can. Now tell me the problem you're having with the Department of Transportation and let me listen.

HENRY FORD II

We represent the total automobile industry—about one-sixth of the G.N.P. Now if the price of cars go up because of the emission and safety requirements—well, what's at stake is the economy of the United States. They'll buy more foreign cars too and you'll have a balance of payments problem.

A waiter brings the president some tea and he slowly stirs in his sugar.

NIXON

I see. It'll kick up the price of cars.

IACOCCA

This brings up the issue of safety. We didn't have to kill fifty
people on the highway. But inflation is eating us alive and it's
going to be bad as far as our labor contracts are concerned. . . .
. . . I think that they have said in the Department of Transportation that we are dedicated to passive restraints. The citizen
of the U.S. must be protected from his own idiocy, so we will
put him in a sophisticated device that will blow up on impact
and package him in an air bag and save their lives [*sic*]. . . . This
is the law of the land for '74.

NIXON

The air bag?

IACOCCA

We have on our cars today a hundred and fifty of, I don't say all
gadgetry, 'cause the steering columns, I think, are saving lives
. . . but the shoulder harnesses and the headrests are complete
wastes of money. The air bag is gonna be very expensive and if
on our Pinto by 1990 we haven't deterred the Japanese at $3,000,
the ball game's over.

NIXON

You can't mean $3,000 would be the *lowest* price!

IACOCCA

Yeah. That's what I mean! It'll go that high! We're up to fifteen
percent foreign cars when we've given them our best shot at the
$1,919 Pinto using German componentry to do that. In Cali-
fornia, about twenty-seven percent of all cars are foreign. In
Vancouver, Toyota outsold all Ford products! And this safety is
gonna make inflation look like child's play. We're gonna price
ourselves right out of the market. . . . The Japs are in the wings
ready to eat us up alive. We want these people to cool it a little—
to give us a break. Our time on air bags is up in sixty days, and
we're taking 'em to court Monday.

NIXON

To court? On air bags?

IACOCCA

They backed off once before—that was about three years ago.

NIXON

John, what's the presidential authority in, in, uh, uh—do I have
authority to review what the Department of Transportation
does?

EHRLICHMAN

Right. I take it that DOT could suspend its order right now.

IACOCCA

I checked this with our lawyers and the Department could say because of further evidence or because we want continuing discussions we will suspend this order and not force this court action on Monday. We talked to them on the phone. They used your name, Mr. President. And they told us *they* wanted us to take this one to court.

NIXON

Let me take a look at this whole thing and see what I can do here. I want to see what the hell the Department is doing in the future.

EHRLICHMAN

Right.

NIXON

They need to know exactly, uh, uh, uh, how decisions we make may make our industry noncompetitive with the Japs. I can see that, as we have these damn gadgets, and the [*unintelligible*] . . . seat belts is enough. [*Unintelligible*] . . . Not on my car. Never!

Everybody laughs.

I think this goes beyond the DOT. It involves America's competitive position. It involves the health of the *economy*.

HENRY FORD II

There are many things you could do in DOT just by calling them up, Mr. President.

NIXON

Yeah, yeah, yeah. You see we are becoming obsessed with the idea that industrialization is ipso facto bad. The great life is to have it like when the Indians were here. You know how the Indians lived? Dirty, filthy, horrible. *(Turning to Ford)* John is your contact.

HENRY FORD II

Thank you very much.

NIXON

I will not judge it until I hear the other side.

I do not know what the president heard, if anything, from those who had fought for the inclusion of this safety device in our nation's automobiles. Ford's own crash films would have doubtless been convincing had the president seen them. Safety officials estimate that air bags could save as many as eight thousand lives a year. During the more than fifteen years that have passed since responsible government agencies designated air bags as a necessary safety device on our cars, over 120,000 Americans have died—over twice the number killed in Vietnam. How can we defend this needless slaughter of Americans? Fifteen years ago, the estimated cost of an installed air bag was eighty dollars. Who spoke to the president for the hundreds of thousands of orphans and widows and the bereaved? The intervention on behalf of corporate interests by men who seem barely literate but who wield great power resulted in a deliberate presidential choice of profit over the lives of people. To me, that is criminal. It is also poor business. Dead drivers do not buy Fords— or Chryslers.

How we are fooled and how we are used! Iacocca's view of the American public is no better illustrated than by his current advertising campaign as president of Chrysler Motors *for* air bags. As if we have forgotten his arguments to Nixon that undoubtedly contributed to the decade-and-a-half delay in air bags becoming standard safety features in our cars, we are now subjected to the following national newspaper blitz praising air bags and giving Iacocca credit for Chrysler's inclusion of them on the driver's side of its late-model cars. The ad brazenly reads as follows in bold print an inch high:

No one can guarantee safety. But that doesn't mean the car industry shouldn't keep trying to do more. (signed Lee Iacocca)

Below the headline, we are treated with the nearly life-size smiling face of Iacocca. Across from this full page, we are shown another full page with headlines again an inch tall that read as follows:

Chrysler is the first and only American car company to make air bags standard equipment.

Now follows a laudatory, illustrated explanation of how air bags work, as if Chrysler, ahead in technology, and with deep concern for the public's welfare, has finally convinced the federal safety authorities that air bags should be included in American cars. The ad actually reads as follows:

Today's air bag technology has earned the confidence of the federal safety authorities. And Chrysler Motors takes the leadership role in bringing that technology to the car buyer.

There is no shame. There is no truth. There is only the blinding light of profit to guide the corporate conscience.

Yet honesty has always been good business, even for American corporations. Fully informed people are usually healthier and happier and, consequently, will probably live longer and more prosperously, and they will, therefore, likely buy more products during their lifetimes. People who are told the truth may eventually learn to trust corporate America because it has finally become trustworthy, and consumer reluctance will tend to diminish.

When we have taken business and profit out of politics, when we have taken the money and false images out and television out, when we have outlawed political campaigns that are produced for television like gala spectaculars and have chased the lobbyists from our chambers of government the way one would run the hogs out of the living room, when we have rid ourselves of the politicians who lick the boots of corporate America and once more uphold those public servants who fight for the people, when we outline clearly to our representatives that there is but one way for them to enchant us and that is by their dogged performance of duty, when we have taken back our airways and put this greatest of all tools for justice to the service of the people to whom it has belonged all along, then once more the people will rise and flourish again.

Yet we are still a free country—and that includes our freedom to be indolent, apathetic, and mindless. We are still a people who would rather be entertained than uplifted. I was recently discussing the age-old question of "the meaning of life" with a very charming and successful Santa Barbara businessman. He owns a great estate. He is married to a gracious and beautiful woman, whom he adorns with jewels and furs. His garages are filled with expensive cars, and he owns paintings by the immortal artists. He counts among his friends the rich and the famous. He personifies success, and his station in life would be coveted by most Americans. How does he view life?

"I see life," he said, "as a giant Disneyland, and I wander through it looking for the next fun ride." Hosts of television viewers would agree with him. Most continue to prefer watching sitcoms and second-run movies to public-interest programming. Our freedom includes the right to fritter our lives away. I have no right to demand that television be altered to conform to my vision of the world. In a free society, the people must be free to choose pleasure over responsibility, although this is also the identical argument made by those who would legalize the use of narcotics.

We are commoditized because we allow it. We'll tolerate brainwashing commercials in order to enjoy the proffered pleasure of commercial television. If controversial news programs and debates were the viewer's choice, corporate advertisers would serve them up instead of game shows. But I think it is clear that if corporate America with its enormous power over us is free to seduce us with our compulsion for pleasure, at least a pittance of social responsibility should be mixed in for decent balance. That the networks offer us sweet tripe in exchange for their right to brainwash us, and that we are willing to make the bargain, only emphasizes the need for an effective regulation of our nation's airways.

But the change must begin with us, for the frightful carryings-on we abhor are only our reflection. We elect our representatives and tolerate their betrayal. We *are* the pathetic programs we endure on television. We watch them, cherish them, even demand the right to be enslaved by them. We have, as Huxley predicted, grown to love our servitude. We must learn once more to love, instead, our freedom.

Once more!

16 | NEW PEOPLE

Workers as Partners, People as Peers

The first step toward freedom is admitting our margins of bondage. When they are exhibited to us, we respond in anger, not against those who bind us, strangely, but against those who rattle our chains. Then, all the more fervently, we embrace our myths of freedom. We accept our margins of bondage because we feel powerless. We turn on the TV to be reassured that we are free, that "we can have it all," that "it doesn't get any better than this." Then we uncap another Strohs. We are, indeed, advantaged over those who starve in the streets of Mexico City or silently labor in the rice paddies in China, or march mechanically to the state's music in the Soviet Union. We are, indeed, the privileged among the great hopeless hordes who thirst for liberty. But when the defects in our democracy seem inescapable, we surrender to old clichés: It is "the best system we know."

Like any domesticated creature, we tend to accept our status, accept the omnipotence of the "powers that be," accept that "they" are endowed with the final intelligence and trust "them" to deliver us justice. We see ourselves as free but obedient workers, as free but well-behaved students, as free but passive consumers, as free but unprotesting taxpayers, as free but helpless victims, as free but dutiful voters who secretly cast our ballots for candidates who will likely make no difference. Too often we have woven the bright myths of our freedom into the dull cloth of our bondage so that only the glitter is seen. But it is the same harsh garment that lies next to our hides. It was Lenin who said, "It is true that liberty is precious—so precious that it must be *rationed*."

But we must not ration freedom in America—not any or to any—and freedom must abound in, of all quarters, the place where we labor. Workers can still be workers and be free. Workers can still produce and have justice. Yet we tend to see ourselves as we are seen—as the mere cost of labor in the factories of Detroit, as beasts of burden in the lettuce fields of California, as but disposable units in the foundries of Ohio. And whether we serve the government or the corporate conglomerate, we are absorbed in a massive bureaucracy defined by Eric Fromm as "a method of managing in which people are dealt with as if they were things." Henry Ford admitted it. He said, "A great business is really too big to be human."

But today's multinational corporations make Henry Ford's little factory look like the corner grocery store. In 1776, Virginia had 493,000 inhabitants. By 1976, General Motors already had 681,000 employees. In 1776, Massachusetts had 252,000 citizens, while 200 years later, International Telephone and Telegraph had 367,000 employees. Delaware had 41,400 souls within its boundaries at the time of the Revolution, while by the time of the Bicentennial, J. C. Penney had 186,000 employees, the Postal Service 696,100, and the Department of the Treasury 129,000.

Robert E. Woods of Sears Roebuck acknowledged that the largeness of American corporations tends to create many dictatorial substates within the shelter of a democratic nation. He said, "We stress the advantages of the free enterprise system, we complain about the totalitarian state, but in our individual organizations we have created more or less of a totalitarian system in industry, particularly in large industry." The Soviet Union, having stifled worker dissidence by outlawing strikes, bargaining, and every other effective means of worker expression, pays dearly in worker apathy. Nowhere are workers more callous toward quality and indifferent toward achievement. In America, millions of workers are stricken with the same disease—one that empties them of motivation, that leaves them numb and causes their managers to judge them lazy and dull.

Out of the lethargy-bound doldrums of American labor, a remarkable and simple idea has of late dazzled the consciousness of corporate sociologists, their corporate customers, and workers themselves: It is the realization that workers are human, not digits; resources, not units of labor; assets, not a begrudging commodity on the production line. That cliché has not always been at the forefront of American management. What is occurring at last is industry's long-overdue abandonment of the nearly century-old teachings of one Frederick Taylor, the father of "time and motion" studies, who both analyzed and dealt with workers as if they were insensate machines. Taylor thought, for instance, that a good pig-iron handler should be strong and "so stupid and phlegmatic that he more nearly resembles in his mental make-up the ox than any other type." He admonished workers, "If you are a high-priced man, you will do exactly as this man tells you, from morning 'til night. When he tells you to pick up a pig and walk, you pick it up and you walk, and when he tells you to sit down and rest, you sit down. You do that right straight through the day. And what's more, no back talk." Henry Ford was enthralled with Taylorism. Men actually worked until they dropped in front of their machines. Ford, an absolute tyrant, once told a journalist, "I have a thousand men who, if I say, 'Be at the northeast corner of the building at four A.M.,' will be there at four A.M. That's what we want—*obedience*."

As if he were studying machines, Taylor divided jobs into their numerous narrow parts. Assembly-line production became the great melding of machine and man into a greater machine. His enormously popular book, published in 1911, *The Secret of Saving Lost Motion*, was said to have had as large an impact on economic production as Keynes or Marx. American factories were soon governed by rigid job classification and work rules. Unions, too, became Taylorist, by negotiating employment rules that kept workers classified and in straitjackets. A plumber could stop a construction job until a carpenter appeared to drill a hole for his pipe to go through. The drill might be lying there and it might take thirty seconds to drill the hole, but the unions' response to Taylorism required a plumber to be a specialized plumbing machine and a carpenter an equally specialized woodworking machine, and there dared not be any crossover. The workplace became stratified, unwieldy, mechanized, and finally dehumanized.

Mark Green and John Berry, in their book *The Challenge of Hidden Profits*, say that by 1972 Taylorism had gathered such force that its ethic was incorporated into GM's state-of-the-art assembly plant in Lordstown, Pennsylvania, where 101 Vegas per hour zipped past. The movement of each worker had been mapped and measured. Each worker was allowed thirty-six seconds to complete his task. The plant, although the most modern in the industry, was plagued with absenteeism, sabotage, and finally a bitter twenty-two-day strike. That "spasm" (the strike), Green and Berry say, "was of a system that assumed the worker to be a 'stupid ox,' but who was in fact a smart American." Taylor's totalitarian view of management gathered such impetus that before its breakup most subsidiaries of AT&T

required their workers to get permission to go to the bathroom. Those few worker rights guaranteed by the law were habitually and intentionally violated by the giant corporations. Under Taylorism, workers became stagnant, unproductive, and haters of management. America's workplaces became ubiquitous pockets of oppression, laden with strife, crippled by strikes, and diminished by stultified workers. Green and Berry report that labor grievances in the United States are seventeen times those in West Germany. The average number of days annually lost to strikes in the United States is double that in Great Britain and six times that in Japan. Taylorism became the method by which workers were transformed into machines and the philosophy under which workers were dominated like slaves. Freedom in the workplace became a lost concept, an ideal that has only recently begun to interest American corporations as a tool to increase productivity.

In the 1920's and 1930's, a group of psychologists began to question Taylorism. Dr. Elton Mayo of the Harvard Graduate School of Business Administration studied a remarkable new concept—"employee participation"—a notion that the worker had a brain that the employer not only had to contend with but could profit from. Mayo discovered the "Hawthorne effect," as he called it, which held that production could be boosted by paying more attention to workers, by actually consulting them. Mayo found that "[t]he group unquestionably develops a sense of participation in the critical determinations and becomes something of a social unit." Like most great discoveries, it was an awakening to the obvious: The production gains realized by "employee participation" were due to the workers' propensity to cooperate in groups, as tribes. Mayo's studies gave rise to the notion of "human relations" in the workplace, an idea at odds with Taylorism, and a threat to both labor unions and corporate management alike. Labor leaders resisted reforms based on cooperation between the worker and management. They saw any coalition between workers and management as a divisive means of weaning workers from the union, advancing the allegiance of workers to the company, and thereby undermining the union movement itself. There were, therefore, clear management-rights clauses in all labor contracts leaving management in charge of management and unions in charge of grieving. Douglas McGregor, in his book *The Human Side of Enterprise*, reported his widely known comparisons of Taylorism (which he designated as Theory "X") versus his own Theory "Y" approach—one that assumed that workers needed to be respected, involved, and satisfied. Again his discovery seemed obvious: Workers do not perform to their maximum in a state of servitude. Over twenty years ago, MIT Professor Jay Forrester, in a now-famous paper entitled "A New Corporate Design," called for an elimination of the superior-subordinate relationship that provides the traditional corporate control. Forrester said, "A substantial body of thought . . . exposes the stultifying effect of the authoritarian organization on initiative and innovation and suggests that . . . such control is becoming less and less appropriate. . . ." "Commitment," Forrester asserted, succeeds over "authority." These notions were to slowly take root and grow; and a new generation of corporate sociologists, facing powerful world competition that had left America behind, began to realize that if American industry was to survive, management must be "in search of excellence." The workplace must be "reinvented."

In the new workplace, employees were provided a surrogate family, replacing the real families from which they had long been separated. A new community was to emulate the tribe, from which they had long been alienated. The new workplace was to create a warm and fertile atmosphere within which workers might thrive and grow—and, incidentally, work at maximum levels of production. Yet within the fiber of this alluring structure were woven the cords of strangulation. That people should produce at optimum levels is, indeed, desirable both for workers and their employers. But to achieve its goals, management is being charged today with intentionally manipulating the psyches of its employees, not out of concern, not out of a spirit of joint enterprise, but to milk them of the last drop in the name of the same old god—profit. Workers claim they are receiving false signals of the corporation's concern for them, that they are enticed by the indicia of control where none exists. They say they are continuously reassured that they are important as individuals, but in the end—after they are bled of their talent and their loyalty in the name of the "company family"—they remain the same old dehumanized statistics in the company books. Wherever Taylorism has been replaced by such psychic exploitations, the worker, from the standpoint of freedom, may, indeed, have been better off with the whip at his back, for the whip is more easily recognized than feigned love in the fictitious eyes of his corporate employer.

Warmly enfolded in the new "excellent" corporation, the modern worker, like the cow in the air-conditioned barn listening to soothing Muzak and chewing molasses and oats, is thought to pay no mind to the milking machine. Too often the corporate goal has not been to uplift the worker but to raise his production, not to make employees happier, but to bring joy to management from elevated profits. Management consultant Thomas L. Quick says to employers, "Your being nice, patient, considerate . . . putting [the workers'] welfare above all other considerations, may add a pleasant frosting," but, Quick argues, the purpose of this paternalism is easily read by employees. "It is a means by which management gets what it wants, without genuine concern for the objectives of the employees. As one worker puts it, 'That's how they buy us.' "

The plan, of course, is to make unions obsolete. So thoroughly will workers be absorbed into the community of the "excellent" company that they will need no representation, which, of course, puts the proverbial fox to guard the chickens. Under these new schemes, the workers' every need and desire, indeed, their whole lives, are defined and realized within the corporate structure. One shivers at the prospect. Yet today only 17 percent of the U.S. work force is organized, and only 15 percent in the private sector, while in the South, only 5 percent have turned to unions. Some proponents of the new "excellent" corporation proclaim unions dead because they have become irrelevant. The prevailing wisdom of corporate America holds that labor unions should be altogether eliminated from the American scene as anachronisms that have become too big, too powerful, too corrupt, and too greedy, and that, alone, are responsible for the defeat of American industry in world competition. But we have heard little of the dire consequences that nearly a century of Taylorism has wrought on American labor and labor's ability to produce. Infrequently does management confess its own abandonment of American workers in favor of the Third World poor, who are more easily dominated and who will slave in their dingy sweatshops for a daily wage that wouldn't buy a loaf of bread in this country.

Today, many of the enlightened corporations are employing methods of management some claim are akin to brainwashing. New Age consultants are reteaching employees of some of American's largest corporations how they *should think*. At Pacific Bell, for instance, California's largest utility company, sixty-seven thousand workers are required to undergo "new-age thought training." Other corporate giants—Procter & Gamble, Ford, and Polaroid, to name a few—are signing on motivational gurus to change the way their workers think. Estimates are that as much as $4 billion is being spent by corporations each year to transform the minds of workers into a homogeneous gob—one that, of course, conforms with the goals of the company. The idea is to create employees with more uniform values and norms—workers who will labor peaceably, quietly, productively as a unit—more on the order of their counterparts in Japan.

Some of the programs use unorthodox methods, such as meditation or hypnosis, and others use the corporate version of "encounter groups." The methodology has a name. At Pacific Bell, it is called "Kroning"—elsewhere, "Breakthrough Learning" and "Transformational Technologies." The idea is to teach workers to be aware of their motivation. Workers being "Kroned" are taught to ask themselves whether their behavior is the result of (a) external stimuli, (b) themselves, or (c) and the preferred answer—a "purpose that is beyond self," i.e., the company purpose. They are even taught a new glossary of words because, as Charles O'Reilly, management professor at the University of California at Berkeley, says, "If people speak the same language and approach problems the same way, then, in fact, they'll be coordinated," a euphemism meaning subordinate to a single unit—as cells join together to make a thumb on the corporate hand.

Werner Erhard, the founder of a national personal-development craze known as *est*, has taken his methods to the corporate world to transform workers. His Transformational Technologies sells its services through fifty franchise operations, and Trans Tech's clients include such giants as RCA, Scott Paper Company, and Boeing. Innovation Associates of Boston helps firms become "metanoic," a Greek word meaning "gaining clear vision," and it claims General Mills, Red Lobster Restaurants, and Hanover Insurance as customers. Several of Pacific Bell's employees have filed suit, and complaints have been made to the utilities commission that these Kroning exercises, based on the mind-control techniques of Georges Gurdjieff (a controversial Armenian philosopher and mystic), are harmful. But Pacific Bell executives think the $147 million they intend to spend for Kroning is worth it. They attribute a 23 percent productivity increase in their operations department to Krone training.

More than ever, workers require a New Union, one that can identify not only with the needs of the worker but with those of their corporate employers as well, one that builds American competition on honest and mutually desirable goals. The New Union will join with an enlightened management to provide a workplace where American men and women can create and produce—one that insures justice for worker and industry alike. Already some of our major corporations have shared this vision and are joining with a more enlightened labor to put America back in business.

In 1980, when Phil Caldwell took over Ford and became the company's first chief executive who was not a member of that venerable family, some wondered if he or the company would last. In that year, Ford lost $1.5 billion, and in the next year another $1.1 billion. Even with a company in trouble, for the next five years Caldwell spent some $3 billion annually to update Ford's uncompetitive facilities. Green and Berry tell of Ford's commitment to change in their interviews with Peter J. Pestillo, the new vice-president of labor relations, and Donald Ephlin, a United Auto Workers vice-president who had been assigned to Ford. What these two did was to "bridge the chasm between labor and corporate management." For the first time, workers were asked by Ford to do what Dr. Mayo and others had been urging for decades: They were asked for their help in building a better product. Pestillo says, "At Ford, I guess we have gone from a more nearly authoritarian managerial operation to one that is more participative. We're not social reformers. We're trying to run a business, and asking people to help solve your problems is a pretty useful way to do it." Ephlin, on behalf of the UAW, was also more committed to worker participation than were others in the union hierarchy, who saw employee involvement as undermining union power.

Pestillo for Ford and Ephlin for the union arranged a trip to Japan for a union-management team that learned how the Japanese system demanded trust and goodwill between workers and management, attitudes that were said to have been noticeably absent at Ford. Eventually the union agreed to a ceiling on cost-of-living increases and eliminated certain paid holidays. Green and Berry tell how the company established a retraining program for laid-off workers and provided guaranteed income to those employees who, after fifteen years with the company, might find themselves out of work. In 1983, the plan's first year, each employee collected about $400. By 1985, employees collected 6 percent of their 1984 paychecks—an average of $2,000 per employee. Ford's staff salaries in North America alone cost the company something like $4 billion a year, twice the cost of its larger competitor, General Motors, and in an effort to further economize on the management side of the business, Ford let some twenty-one thousand salaried employees go, a 28 percent reduction.

In *The Challenge of Hidden Profits*, Green and Berry describe how communications between labor and management became a religion, and "E.I." (Employee Involvement) a way of life. At the once-troubled Louisville plant, where "E.I." was introduced in 1980, workers during the next three years made 749 proposals to improve the Ranger and Bronco II trucks. The company adopted 542 of them, and by 1983, industry experts claimed these products were equal in quality to their Japanese competitors.

My hope for the future is that the new union will join with new management to recreate at the workplace a more natural social structure, one modeled on the *just* tribe, for in the end we all seek our tribes. We join clubs. We belong to a softball team. We root for the New York Yankees. We have a need to flock, to hunt and gather together, to belong. Knowing that we work better in groups approximating the size of a tribe, the corporate sociologists are paring down the working unit to approximately 150 employees. Thomas Peters and Robert Waterman, in their best-seller *In Search of Excellence*, describe in detail the "hoopla, celebration and verve" they claim is emitted from many excellent corporations—where people feel like winners, where they slap each other on the back and gather clannishly at company picnics. But they also warn against the "lip service disaster" and the "gimmicks disaster." People do not want to be merely told that Mother Management loves them or to be jollied into a "temporary high" from the CEO's smile while the company stashes away its profits. The reinvented workplace will never succeed if it becomes simply another device to more easily strip the alienated worker of his life and his pride.

But the inventors of the new management keep dragging corporate America back on the path. John Naisbitt and Patricia Aburdene explain in their book *Reinventing the Corporation*, "The hierarchical structure where everyone has a superior and everyone has an inferior surely is corrupting of the human spirit no matter how well it served us during the industrial period." Even at General Motors, in its Fitzgerald, Georgia, plant, work teams are now making many of the decisions that management once made. At Honeywell, James Renier describes the shift from middle management to people management: "Let people do their jobs and tell you what expertise they need," and as John Welch, chairman of General Electric, now likes to say, "If you pick the right people and give them the opportunity to spread their wings . . . you don't always have to manage them." In my own state of Wyoming, the government's General Accounting Office (GAO) investigated twenty similar coal mines whose operations were essentially the same. Production ranged from 58 to 242 tons per workday. The GAO concluded that the most productive operations had uniformly provided their employees with more individual responsibility and involvement in decision making. Green and Berry studied ninety-eight employee-owned firms in the United States and Canada and found that "the more equity the workers own, the more profitable the company, other things being equal, and the more equity, the higher the employee morale." Why should these studies surprise us? The people who know the most about daily production are obviously the workers. The idea that they should be consulted seems too obvious for argument. Yet that small groups of supervisors and employees should meet regularly to spot and solve workplace problems was a plan that did not take hold until recently. Some years ago, a General Motors chairman complained of Chevrolet, "It is such a big monster that you twist its tail and nothing happens at the other end for months and months. It is so gigantic that there isn't any way to really run it. You just sort of try to keep track of it." A current study of the twenty-three GM assembly plants that have the most groups engaged in "quality of work life circles" (QWL), in which employees participate in the management decisions that affect them, showed that these plants had higher product quality, higher customer-satisfaction ratings, lower absenteeism, fewer grievances, and lower labor costs than other GM facilites. Already more than 14 percent of American firms with over one hundred employees are said to be using some form of QWL.

Frederick Herzberg, Distinguished Professor of Management at the University of Utah's School of Business, finds that workers around the world are similarly motivated. His studies show that 80 percent of the factors that workers identify as satisfying come from intrinsic elements of the job such as achievement, recognition, enjoyment of the work itself, responsibility, advancement, and growth. Only about 20 percent of the satisfying job events involve such things as working conditions, salary, and job security. The results of Herzberg's investigation should convince management that good labor relations and better productivity don't necessarily cost money. People want to be useful.

Although it is now established doctrine in enlightened management circles that if America is to survive in world competition it must do better by its workers, not since the days of the robber barons have American workers been so mercilessly exploited. Today, they have been forced to make drastic and unconscionable concessions in order to hold their jobs. Cutbacks in wages and other benefits have dominated the dreary scene. Management, eager to exploit labor's weakened position, has devised new schemes to undermine the advancements labor has won in hard-fought battles over the last half-century. One of the most insidious of these tactics has been the creation of pools of "contingent workers" to replace regular forty-hour-a-week employees. Contingent employees—those who are employed by outside contractors or who are permitted to work only part-time—have doubled since 1980 and compose nearly 17 percent of the work force. These are the "dispensable employees," the throwaway workers. Kathleen E. Christensen, a professor at the City University of New York, says, "We're creating a second-class tier in the labor force." According to the Bureau of Labor statistics, 3.8 million part-time workers would like to find full-time jobs. Little wonder. Recent government statistics show that part-timers earned an average of $4.17 an hour compared to $7.05 for full-time workers performing the same job, and most have no retirement plan, and 42 percent have no health insurance. Companies are now even leasing workers as one might lease a car or truck, the ultimate in worker commoditization. Motorola's ninety thousand workers are divided into three classes. About a third are regular employees with ten years' service and a guaranteed job. Forty percent are regular employees who don't have absolute assurance against layoffs. The rest have a six-month contract that can be canceled on twenty-four hours' notice.

Seventy percent of the value of each car Chrysler makes is subcontracted. One man with ten years' seniority at USX's Gary, Indiana, steel plant was laid off two years ago and immediately went back to work for a small company that subcontracted the same work to USX. Before, he was making thirteen dollars an hour. Now, he is paid five dollars an hour for the same work. If USX terminates the subcontractor, it won't have to pay the unemployment benefits it would have owed its own employees as union members, another advantage to corporations in turning core workers into disposable employees. This doesn't sound much like the loving care of corporate America.

Unions must work with management to make workers' jobs more meaningful but at the same time to protect them from the exploitations of the new robber barons and from new sirens that sing dangerous if enticing songs. At the sensitive and patient urging of the new union, the new corporation must be taught to think of its workers differently, not out of an impossible altruism but in deference to its own survival. Profit sharing is nothing new in America. Melville spoke of it on the early New England whaling vessel in *Moby Dick*:

I was already aware that in the whaling business they paid no wages; but all hands, including the captain, received certain shares of the profits called *lays*, and that these lays were proportioned to the degree of importance pertaining to the respective duties of the ship's company. I was also aware that being a green hand at whaling, my own lay would not be very large; but considering that I was used to the sea, could steer a ship, splice a rope, and all that, I made no doubt that from all I had heard I should be offered at least the 275th lay—that is, the 275th part of the clear net proceeds of the voyage, whatever that might eventually amount to.

Worker ownership is nothing revolutionary. Employee stock ownership was widespread in New England factories before the Civil War. John Stuart Mill's famous work *Principles of Political Economy*, published in 1848, advocated employee ownership. That idea is far from embracing socialistic ideals, for socialism calls for *state-owned* enterprises. When workers own a share of the company, that is *worker-capitalism*. And labor makes no demand that profit sharing be equal. It seeks only to be included in the great adventure. Winning players in the Super Bowl and the World Series share in the rewards of their victory. The more farsighted corporations are already beginning to see the light.

Workers at Cummins Engine Company receive a payment based on productivity. Their total profit sharing averaged more than $2,000 per person. The result of this incentive was to turn the company around from years of dismal performance, of low profits and actual losses. In a wide range of profit-sharing plans, Marion Laboratories is making a number of their workers millionaires upon retirement. All seventeen hundred employees are designated "associates" and given stock options, which have shot up more than 1,000 percent in the past ten years. Understandably, Marion associates take an active concern in how the company is doing on Wall Street and state, "An employee of a company thinks and performs differently [from] someone who has an equity interest. One of the reasons for Marion's continued strong performance and high productivity is that its associates participate as part-owners." Employees at Andersen Corporation recently gave their boss a standing ovation. This manufacturer of windows and patio doors distributed $105,894,743 to 3,700 employees as their share of 1987 profits that rose to $72 million from just $10 million ten years ago. Andersen started profit sharing seventy-four years ago by distributing $1,428 among its workers. Randy Cloutier, a fifteen-year Andersen veteran, says, "It's always a fair factory. That's why everybody gives 100%." Andersen's president says that the total profit-sharing dollars to be paid in 1987 increased tenfold in the last ten years. Cloutier's wife, Laurie, who worked at the factory for six years, says, "I'd say it's the American dream."

If the profit motive truly powers the capitalist system, if the opportunity to gain is truly mankind's moving force, then how can intelligent management bypass this greatest of motivators with its own workers? In the last decade, China has begun its "great leap forward" with profit providing the carrot, and the Soviet Union, too, has lately, begrudgingly, begun to acknowledge that if it is to keep pace it must fuel any new surge in its production by giving more, not taking more, from its workers. But profit alone will not cause the productive flower to bloom and flourish any more than a rose can grow only on a diet of water. *Passion* is an essential food upon which all human excellence thrives.

A couple of years ago, I gave the commencement address to the Jackson, Wyoming, High School. I told the graduating seniors I hoped they would never work—not another day of their lives—and from that day forward they would only play. I paused a long while. The kids giggled a little. The parents looked distressed and moved uneasily in their seats. That was hardly the way for an allegedly responsible adult to be talking to their kids. What about the work ethic—the honor in honest toil and all that? Then I told the kids that I owed my success to the fact that I had spent most of my life playing, which I defined as doing what I had a passion to do. Passion! It is so precious. And so few have it. Ask most of today's youth the simplest question: "What is it that you *must do* in your life?" Most shrug their shoulders and only stare curiously back. They have a vague suspicion that passion has something to do with being alive, but, in fact, all of the signals they are getting from the world around them—from their schools, their parents, their workplace—is that the natural and preferred state is apathy. It is *passion* that distinguishes the living from the living dead and drives us to our genius. Wilt Chamberlain had a passion for basketball, and Kimerli Jayne Pring for the baton. Mozart had a passion for music, and I know folks who have passions for art and gardening and photography and rock climbing. I have a passion for the law. It is not work. It is immensely more than work: It is my life. Naisbitt and Aburdene tell us the other side of passion: "Working for most companies is so demeaning to the human spirit that many talented people are forced out the door."

Work is the drudgery many endlessly endure to obtain the manufactured playthings civilization provides its captives—fast motorcars and motorboats and motorcycles and snowmobiles and mountain bikes and an evening around the campfire with a beer, exclaiming in the immortal language of the television commercial, "It doesn't get any better than this." I keep my parrot satisfied in the same way. Every week or so, I change his toys. Every morning, I open his cage door and he crawls up and down the bars both inside and out. But he never leaves his cage. He plays with his toys. He squawks, and he is learning to say, "It doesn't get any better than this."

In the new corporation, people must work less and play more—that is, they must follow their passions. At W. H. Gore & Associates, Inc., makers of the water-repellent fabric Gore-tex, there are no titles, no bosses, and only two objectives: to make money, of course, and to have fun. The people are said to manage themselves by organizing around voluntary commitments. When they are hired, some are merely told to find work that is interesting to do. As proof that one can turn passion into profit, Gore's sales have grown 35 percent a year for the last ten years. Yvon Chouinard, one of the nation's leading manufacturers of outdoor wear and equipment, told the Yale School of Management that he manages Patagonia by committee. His primary objective is not profit. Yet his company's sales have soared from $3 million six years ago to $83 million last year. He wants to make money, all right, but not mindlessly, endlessly. He has as great a compulsion to give it away, for somehow he equates its ownership with its ownership of him. He lives in a very modest home with his family, and has become one of the major contributors to environmental causes in the country. He tries to encourage creativity and pride among those who work for him. Says Chouinard, "When you are obsessed with profit you lose sight of the real costs of doing business. For instance, you put the screws down on your employees to work harder, so they lose respect for you and do the opposite, or quit. You don't need to manage self-motivated people, and nearly everyone is motivated when they are doing a job they enjoy and believe in."

Happy workers without rights in the workplace are only happy slaves. More than ever, workers need to rise up in a single powerful voice that reverberates through the paneled walls of the corporate boardrooms and demand that they no longer be deprived of justice in the workplace. It is *their* workplace. There, breath at a time, drop of sweat at a time, day at a time, they trade their lives for their sustenance. As David Ewing, author of *Freedom Inside the Organization*, sees it, "A business corporation . . . is now a lifetime experience for many of its members. Necessarily, therefore, it can no longer be an instrument satisfying a single end . . . only turning out its goods and services—but it has to be a satisfactory way of life for its members." He continues, "The Constitution and Bill of Rights light up the sky . . . but not so over employees. The employee sector of our civil liberties universe is more like a black hole . . . like the giant black stars in the physical universe, light can scarcely escape."

It is an astounding anomaly that in America, this great land of the free, there should be two worlds for workers: one outside of the workplace, in which their rights are protected under the Constitution, and one *inside* the workplace, where they are substantially without rights. Our workers enjoy the least rights where they spend most of their productive time. In that one place where the most consequential events of their lives occur, where they will succeed or be swallowed up into oblivion—in that one place where they labor for their very existence—workers' rights are least in evidence and the most poorly protected.

American courts have traditionally held that employers may dismiss their employees *at will*—for good cause, for no cause, or even for unjust cause, without thereby committing a legal wrong. That means if the employer doesn't like the part in the employee's hair, he may deprive him of his livelihood. Although current law is more subtle than that and refined by specific exceptions, the general rule of discretionary firing still defines the operative spirit of American labor law. Not long ago, a company's employee with twenty years of service came to my office seeking justice for his wrongful discharge. As the senior in his department, he had been elected to take a complaint concerning plant safety directly to his supervisor, to whom he protested that he and his seven fellow employees were suffering a variety of ill effects from dangerous toxic fumes that were escaping from outdated equipment. The next day, he and the other seven employees were discharged. They were told that the company had decided to close down that department, although the workers were confident that they would have kept their jobs had they chosen to suffer the rashes, the headaches, the swollen limbs, and the coughing. But wrongful termination could not be proven under these facts and under the law of their state. Often workers are discharged without recourse for justly criticizing their employer, as well as for protesting perilous working conditions, rights that would be clearly protected outside the workplace under the Constitution.

Workers can be fired for refusing to perform what they consider unethical or immoral acts demanded of them by their employer. I know a salesman who, despite his boss's urging, refused to offer a county commissioner a bribe in order to land a sale of several hundred thousand dollars' worth of heavy road equipment. The sale went to another dealer, who presumably did make the offer. The next day, the salesman was discharged over a minor complaint concerning his expense account. In any legal action, it would have been the salesman's word against the employer's as to the real cause of his firing. A worker who cannot tolerate corporate crime can lose his job for whistle-blowing. Ewing says, "Within the organization itself the worker is expected to sit at the feet of the boss's conscience." The employer needs only the flimsiest pretext to search workers' lockers, desks, and files. Employees have no right to resist the demand of the employer that they take a lie-detector test or give urine samples—rights afforded the common criminal outside the workplace.

Although citizens cannot be punished for the friends they choose or the organizations they belong to or the political positions they take, in the workplace employees can be fired for any of these reasons so long as the employer does not admit to them. Nearly any excuse will do. Except for civil-service employees and certain union employees who by regulation or contract must be given a hearing before dismissal, most employees can be discharged without a hearing. Workers can be and are presumed guilty by their employers. They may be discharged on mere hearsay. A common criminal charged with stealing ten gallons of gas from the company has a right to a jury trial, but the loyal, longtime employee of the same company who is wrongfully accused of violating a company policy may be summarily discharged. Workers have little protection against an invasion of their right of privacy. At a nationally known brewery, interviewers allegedly ask prospective employees such questions as "Have you ever been involved with a homosexual?" or "Have you ever done anything with your wife that could be considered immoral?" According to the American Polygraph Association, 25 percent of the Fortune 500 companies routinely subject their employees to the polygraph—a procedure that one AFL-CIO official says is used not to discover the truth but to intimidate workers, a procedure the police are prohibited from using against us without our agreement.

Justice in America demands a Bill of Rights for workers. Not only must workers demand it, employers must support it. Corporate America is slow to learn. But it is learning. IBM now recognizes the right of privacy at the job. It has learned that if you want productivity and profit, the company must treat its workers as it most important asset. In *A Business and Its Beliefs*, Thomas J. Watson, Jr., says: "IBM's philosophy is largely contained in three simple ideas. I want to begin with what I think is the most important: our respect for the individual. This is a simple concept, but in IBM it occupies a major portion of management time. We devote more effort to it than anything else. This belief was bone-deep in my father." Xerox and several other corporations that have embraced the principle that it is good business to be an ethical employer have hired ombudsmen to protect employees who resist unethical directives or unfair discrimination. But no American corporation has yet voluntarily put into effect a simple Bill of Rights that fully protects its employees in the workplace.

Ewing has defined the matter with great clarity. In the simplest form, the new Workers' Bill of Rights could provide, in part, as follows:

> No public or private organization shall discriminate against an employee for criticizing the ethical, moral, or legal policies and practices of the organization; nor shall any organization discriminate against an employee for engaging in outside activities of his or her choice, or for objecting to a directive that violates common norms of morality.
>
> No organization shall deprive an employee of the enjoyment of reasonable privacy in his or her place of work, and no personal information about employees shall be collected or kept other than that necessary to manage the organization efficiently and to meet legal requirements.
>
> No employee of a public or private organization who alleges in good faith that his or her rights have been violated shall be discharged or penalized without a fair hearing. . . .

Scholars have suggested various ways to implement such a Bill of Rights, the simplest being for Congress to pass a bill covering all government employees and those working for employers engaged in interstate commerce. Such a bill would immediately liberate the majority of American labor, and most states would doubtless follow with their own legislation.

In the tribe, every member had a revered station, a purpose, and every member was respected because each contributed to the survival of the whole. Each performed according to his or her genetic equipment and, like most of us, took great pleasure in that gift. The fastest runner was the esteemed tribal messenger; those with stealth and courage, the lauded hunters; and those with grace and artistry, the honored basket-makers. The way of the tribe afforded its members great freedom.

Today, our Constitution sheds its full beam of liberty only on certain privileged places. The American corporation, itself only non-living property, is protected under the Bill of Rights for the sake of profit, but its living employees have no such protection in the place where they labor for their daily bread. The law may provide the shackles that enslave us or lead us to the promised land. After the Civil War, American blacks were freed *by the law*, by the Thirteenth

Amendment that promised justice for all. Once again the law has the power to free American workers, not as the product of blood and war, but of conscience and reason—even as the product of profit, for we have learned that the American system of free enterprise thrives best where workers are also free.

ENDING UP

Justice For All

My goal here has been too lofty—to write a single true sentence. I doubt that has ever been done. I have thought a good deal about the kinds of injustices I have unjustly omitted from this book. I know, of course, that labor unions have been unjust to their members, and to their employers as well. I know that they are subject to the same unalterable rules that in the end foul all power. I know of their corruption. I know of their arrogant refusal to shift and to alter their methods in a changing world. I know of their failure to remain useful. I understand the war on both sides of the trenches. But what interests me most are the soldiers who are lost in the war—a war like all wars—where Power seeks more power.

I know we cannot realize justice by embracing an economic system committed to the division of goods, because when we do so we make a trade, and I take it that what is bargained away is freedom, that what is lost is the person. To dictate to people how things are to be divided up is as erroneous as to fervently demand the right to hoard it all. In either the socialist or capitalist way of things, it is our obsessive attachment to property that generates the wrong. The answer, of course, is simple: to love one another. But one knows that such an ideal is also at odds with the Darwinian scheme. What, of course, we have here are Christians who purport to love God but hate man. What we have here are those who claim to love mankind but who are only too willing to blow the world to hell while they bow at the feet of another religion—profit. I retch when I observe

"Christ's ministers," as they like to call themselves, engaged in their own unholy wars on television—not for the betterment of mankind but, like warring goat herders, for the ownership of each other's flocks. Like all Power, "the ministry" does not serve the people. It has become the sleaziest form of capitalism—one that trades on our nascent fear of death, that twiddles with our alienation and loneliness and asks us to give our possessions to God, to them, in exchange for eternal life.

My discussion of justice in this book assumes that man will continue to survive, at least for a while. Yet we must make room for the possibility that our unjust treatment of Mother Nature may soon change all that, and in retaliation she will let loose of the delicate balance she patiently holds, for I believe that justice goes to the core, and that Nature herself knows the heart of justice— revenge—and will one day set things straight again. Nothing in the grand plan permits man to dominate the earth. This is a matriarchy, with Mother Earth the old dame, and although she is uncommonly patient, at last she, too, will demand justice. In the end, all of us are defeated by the injustices we impose. That unalterable rule requires us to be more just to our worldly neighbors, failing which, much of what I have said herein may no longer be relevant.

Man's most resolute search has not been for eternal life but for justice. He has not often found it. I think that is, in part, because he has been born into injustice, either that which has been imposed on him by his parents, his fellow man, by the systems and structures that unjustly control him, or by God. Marx saw justice as the product of economics and sought justice through the distribution of goods. Jesus approached justice as a matter of the soul and sought justice through the elevation of the human spirit. The fruit of those ideas, however, has not been justice but further exploitation, enslavement, and injustice. The reasons seem simple enough to me.

Marxism does not take into account the anxiety of a mortal organism that is conscious of its finite being, one who, at the moment of its birth, is shoved off the cliff. The organism looks around and sees that it is falling. It is terror-stricken. Instead of letting go, instead of taking the trip, it grasps at anything and everything—money, property, power—and since none stop the fall, in panic it grabs again and again. The metamorphosis that corrects the grasping genes has not yet occurred, and to expect man to override them with the same brain that perceives his terrible predicament and that records his panic is more or less equivalent to asking a fish trapped in the goldfish pond to pick up its fins and walk.

Marxism is as much fascinated with goods and gold as capitalism is. One says it is immoral to hoard them, the other argues it is unjust to dictate how they should be distributed. But in the end, the Marxist view refuses to acknowledge that its precepts of justice cannot be successfully imposed upon the species once it has left the Garden and abandoned the tribe.

Christianity, on the other hand, commits a similar error. It, too, does not take into account man's genetic plan. He has survived not by love but by war. His propensity for hostility has spread the species over the face of the earth as it has fought, conquered, escaped, and sought refuge in the remote jungles and distant mountains. Although man can forgive, and does, his forgiveness is not preceded by turning the other cheek. Forgiveness does not arise out of a loving heart but from one who has experienced justice.

Marx thought religion was the opiate of the people, and I quite agree. But Marxism and capitalism as well have also become religions. We will never induce man to truly love his neighbor. We can cause him to put a Jesus look into his eyes. We can teach him to turn his other cheek and to speak of love. But we cannot teach him to indeed *be* loving. Nor is it possible to wean him of his violent nature. We can force man to share his goods with his neighbors, but we cannot separate him from his acquisitive nature. We cannot stem his greed without allaying his mortal anxiety.

In the end, Marx and Jesus preach the same thing—a demand that man do better by his fellow man. I should think we might stand a better chance at justice if we accepted man as he is, for any betterment can only begin after we recognize the way things are. I should think it would be preferable if we did not bear unreasonable expectations for the species but recognized the nature of the beast, which also includes giving man credit for his virtues—among which is his intractable desire to do the best he can. Man is driven by the same forces that cause the Alpine buttercup to fight storm and snowbank with its tender shoots and fragile petals and to burst forth as the first flower of spring in the mountains. It does as well as it can, as does the weaning fawn who did not make it through the winter and the raven that pecks at its bones. All would share and share alike and love one another if their genes would but permit it.

Man, too, does the best he can. The problem is that we trample his most divine efforts, and lock them in poverty and mock them with injustice. If we are to rid ourselves of crime in the ghettos, we must take our children out of the ghettos. They and their parents before them have turned their cheeks until their necks have become swivels, and still they suffer injustice. The children of the world do not demand an equal cut of the pie. But even the slowest among them can understand the injustice gnawing out of their bloated bellies. The children of the world do not need the likes of me to assert their right to an adequate diet and a decent shelter. Such is their right to begin with—one that accrues to them by virtue of their membership in the human race, and every human knows that—the leper begging in the streets of New Delhi as well as the wealthy idling by their marbled pools. Every child was born with the right to the best education he or she can absorb, and the children, better than I, better than anyone, understand the injustice of a system that, having the power to be just, perpetuates injustice in the name of a religion based on laissez-faire. Starve a herd of baby rabbits, cage them in a filthy box, poke them with sticks through the cage, and some will grow up to attack you. Despite our efforts to smash the children of this world for our profit, they do the best they can. A few rise out of poverty and filth to acquit the species. Most do not. Most began with blessed genetic gifts but were too fragile to return to us much more than what we gave them—rejection, pain, and hatred. Yet even our victims do the best they can with what have been our gifts to them—which too often include a psyche twisted from injustice through which the remaining effort of their lives is filtered. For us to expect justice of our children, we must be just to them. The gifts we give are not complete until they are returned to us, love and hate alike.

I think people who seek to change the world by changing man are destined to fail. The world is what it is. People are what they are. Until we have the power to alter the genetic plan of the species, its basic nature cannot be changed very much. What can change is the perception we hold of ourselves and the world. What can change is our awareness of what is happening around us. We can become aware of our unjust treatment of nature and save ourselves from near-term extinction. We can discover the immutable laws of justice—that the injustice we seed grows a poison fruit, one that we inevitably end up eating.

Ultimately we need follow neither Marx nor Jesus. We ought not render justice merely because it is the right thing to do. We should be just for altogether selfish reasons, which acknowledge the unalterable laws of justice. We should be just for our own well-being, for our safety—our own survival. For our own sake, let us be just.

This book ends up being no more than it set out to be. I wished to tell what I have seen. I wished to hold up our system—this device by which we supposedly deliver justice—for inspection, to see how it works and how it fails. I wanted you to know what I have seen. Whether they are truths for anyone else is not important. I have been the farmer who has spent his life on these forty acres of rocks trying to grub out a crop of oats. I know something about farming hard ground, and it doesn't do me any good to keep what I have learned to myself.

To know the truth—therein lies the key to our elusive salvation, when everything and nothing is the truth. We must cut away the myth, snatch off the masks with their false smiles from our faces, and look each other boldly in the eye. We must smash the trick mirrors, and do the best we can. We must begin by understanding what *is*, not what we are taught, not what the preachers or the politicians or those in power say it is. I have tried to do that here— that is, to tell you how I see it. It is not that I have no respect for lawyers or judges or the various institutions of our system. It is that I respect them *too much*. Too often, like the father of an ordinary child who expects him to read and appreciate Lucretius by Friday, I demand too much. But the change will come only when we have slammed the system up against the wall and stared it down, and made it responsive to us. It is not unpatriotic to criticize one's country: It is essential. I think of the wife of a drunk who covers, apologizes, and makes excuses for him because she loves him too much, and thereby enables him to continue in his oppression and destruction. In the same way, we must stop enabling our system to continue its injustices because we, too, love it so unconditionally that we fail to demand that it reform, that it be responsible. But, finally, we *can* make this system respond to us, for *we* are the system.

Mine is not a religion of economics or one of the spirit, although I am interested in both. Mine is a religion of ideas. We ought not worship the dead, whether they be men, ideas, or structures— whether they be Marx, Christ, or their hopes for mankind that have been stultified into dogma. We ought not bow down to the corporation, or enter the infinite emptiness of its mansions. We ought to cherish our visions. Justice itself is merely our *idea*, and its only limits are the boundaries of those creative minds that constantly strive to perfect it—of a people resolved to a simple notion: *Justice for all*.

Notes

CHAPTER 1:   JUSTICE
No notes.

CHAPTER 2:   LAWYERS

27   These statistics were taken from a consortium of sources, including those compiled by Lawrence S. Wrightsman in his revealing book *Psychology and the Legal System*, Brooks/Cole Publishing Company, Monterey, California, 1987; Richard Greene's article "Lawyers vs. the Marketplace," *Forbes*, January 16, 1984; and *Total Justice*, Lawrence M. Friedman, Beacon Press, Boston, 1987, together with current statistics provided by the ABA.

28   The colorful historical references to lawyers were gathered by Jerold S. Auerbach and appear in his thoughtful book *Justice Without Law?*, Oxford University Press, New York, 1983.

28   I found the California Bar Association statistics in the *Santa Barbara News-Press*, February 1, 1988.

29   Anthony Lewis and John Dean are quoted in Jerold S. Auerbach's prize-winning book *Unequal Justice*, Oxford University Press, New York, 1976, p. 301.

31   Mr. Sherman's quotes are from my personal interview with him.

32   The Lincoln quote was reported in *The New York Times*, February 11, 1988, "What Kind of Lawyer Was Lincoln?"

36   Judge Grady's speech is reported in *The Lawyer's Professional Independence: An Ideal Revisited*, American Bar Association, Chicago, 1985.

38   *Total Justice*, Lawrence M. Friedman, cited above.

40 The information about Ralph Nader in this chapter is based on an article by Allan Fotheringham, "Recognizing the Raider's Legacy," appearing in *Maclean's*, December 2, 1985.

CHAPTER 3: LAW STUDENTS

44 The statistics on dropout rates are from Lawrence S. Wrightsman's book *Psychology and the Legal System*, cited above.

44 The statistics concerning black lawyers in the legal profession in Chicago were quoted by Jerold S. Auerbach in his book *Unequal Justice*, cited above.

44–45 The numbers of black and Hispanic students were provided by the ABA.

45 Dean Liacouras's quote is from "Toward a Fair and Sensible Policy for Professional School Admission," *Cross Reference*, Vol. 1, No. 2.

45 Jerold Auerbach's quotes are from *Unequal Justice*, p. 125.

46 The statistics and quotes concerning the LSAT are from an article entitled "Startling Admissions," by Ralph Nader and Allan Nairn, which appeared in *Student Lawyer*, March 1980.

46–47 The quotes from Dean Liacouras are from his article cited above.

47 The Stanford statistic was taken from David Margolick's article on Stanford Law School appearing in *The New York Times Magazine*, May 22, 1983, as are the quotes of President Bok and John Hart Ely.

48 Nader and Nairn undertook an in-depth study on the efficacy of the LSAT as an admissions tool for law schools. "The Reign of ETS, the Corporation that Makes Up Minds," Learning Research Project, P.O. Box 19312, Washington, D.C. 20036.

48 Dean Liacouras's comment came from his article cited above.

48 The quotes from Professor Roger Crampton are found in his article "Change and Continuity in Legal Education," *Michigan Law Review*, Vol. 79, p. 460.

48 Nader and Nairn make their assertion that the LSAT filters people according to the income of their parents in their article, "Startling Admissions," cited above.

48–49 Dean Liacouras's discussion concerning Slavic and Polish-American students versus MIT students can be found in his excellent article cited above, p. 170.

49 Nader and Nairn quoted Barbara Lerner in their article cited above.

49 The statistics on the mushrooming of our law-school enrollments are supplied by the ABA Section of Legal Education and Admissions to the Bar. *A Review of Legal Education in the United States*, Fall 1979, p. 64.

50 I found the statistics as to where our law students go after graduation in Lawrence S. Wrightsman's book *Psychology and the Legal System*, cited above.

50 David Margolick's article in *The New York Times Magazine* cited

above is the source of the statistic relative to Stanford students and public-interest law firms.

50 The studies concerning the attitudes of lawyers themselves as to the relative prestige of specialities within the profession came from a paper by Laumann and Heinz, "Specialization and Prestige in the Legal Profession: The Structure of Deference," *Am. Bar Foundation Research J.* (1977), p. 155, and were cited by Roger Crampton in his article cited above.

50–51 The quote from Ralph Nader is from his article, "Law Schools and Law Firms," *Minnesota Law Review*, Vol. 54, p. 493.

51 Harvard's President Derek C. Bok made his statement concerning the "massive diversion of exceptional talent" into our law schools in his 1983 annual report to the Harvard University Board of Overseers.

51 The comments of Professor Duncan Kennedy of Harvard were made in his April 5, 1982, paper "Dissent from the Report of the Committee on Educational Planning and Development."

51 I am further indebted to David Margolick for the quotations of Professors Frank and Friedman and Cohen and Haverford College's President Robert B. Stevens, whose quotes appear in David Margolick's article cited above.

51–52 The costs of educating a medical student versus a law student are based on figures supplied by Professor Crampton in his article "Change and Continuity in Legal Education," cited above.

53 The quotation from the Indians of the Six Nations comes from a wonderful book I have quoted to juries and lawyers many times, *Touch the Earth*, by T. C. McLuhan, Simon and Schuster, New York, 1971.

CHAPTER 4: LAW SCHOOLS

56–57 The quote from Professor Nielsen is from his essay, entitled "The Flaw in Our Law Schools," in *Newsweek*, June 11, 1984, p. 15.

57 Professor Dershowitz's confession is from his book *The Best Defense*, Random House, New York, 1982, pp. 16–17.

58 Joe Branney, a leading plaintiffs' attorney in Denver, told me that young nurses were often more useful to trial lawyers than young lawyers. The quote is from my conversation with him.

59 The quotes of Christopher Columbus Langdell are from Arthur E. Sutherland's *The Law at Harvard: A History of Ideas and Men*, 1817–1967, Harvard University Press, Cambridge, Mass., 1967.

59–60 Judge Lois G. Forer's quote is from her insightful book *Money and Justice, Who Owns the Courts?*, W. W. Norton & Company, New York, 1984.

60 Herbert Croly's opinion of the American lawyer is from his book *The Promise of American Life*, Harvard University Press, Cambridge, Massachusetts, 1965 ed.

60 The cost of lawyers by the hour in major New York corporate law firms is from *The Wall Street Journal*, March 19, 1987.

61–62 The quotes of Roosevelt, Wilson, and Brandeis appear in Jerold S. Auerbach's book *Unequal Justice*, cited above.

63 I have quoted from *Final Report and Recommendation of the Task Force on Professional Competence*, American Bar Association, 1983.

64 The Cravath partner quotes are from Auerbach's book cited above.

CHAPTER 5: JURIES

70 The book about the Silkwood case is *Gunning for Justice*, Gerry Spence and Anthony Polk, Doubleday & Co., Garden City, N.Y., 1982.

83 The percentage of libel awards suffering reversal at the hands of appellate courts is from an article by Martin Garbus in *The New York Times Magazine*, January 29, 1984, entitled "New Challenge to Press Freedom."

87 The quotations by Adams, Hamilton, and Jay were gathered by Jon M. Van Dyke in his very insightful article "The Jury as a Political Institution," *The Center Magazine*, Vol. III, No. 2, March 1970.

87 The de Tocqueville quote is from *Democracy in America*, Vintage Books, New York, 1945 ed.

88 The quotations concerning the emasculation of a docile jury are from Van Dyke's article, cited above.

91 Van Dyke quotes the juror in the Spock case.

91 The quote from de Tocqueville is from *Time* magazine, September 28, 1981.

CHAPTER 6: JUDGES

93 The figures of Reagan's appointments are from *Newsweek*, June 3, 1985.

93 The profile of Reagan's appointees is from Sheldon Goldman's "Reagan's second term judicial appointments: the battle at midway," in *Judicature*, April–May, 1987.

93–94 The description of the approval procedure instituted by Reagan came from *Time* magazine, November 4, 1985, as did the quotes of Elaine Jones and Archibald Cox. The statistics on the judges' racial origins are from Goldman's article cited above.

94–95 The analysis by *The New York Times* of the high court's decisions was published July 8, 1984.

95 Burt Neuborne's quotation was supplied by the Associated Press, July 8, 1984.

95 The discussion of the Streetman case came from an editorial in *The New York Times*, "When a Tie Vote Means Death," January 18, 1988.

95–96 Judge Warren's comments concerning the ABA were part of his address to the Association of the Bar of the City of New York on April 9, 1970, as the twenty-seventh annual Benjamin Cardozo lecturer, *The Benjamin N. Cardozo Lectures, 1941–1970*, Matthew Bender, New York.

96   The discussion of the ABA's Standing Committee is from Harold W. Chase's *Federal Judges: The Appointing Process*, University of Minnesota Press, Minneapolis, 1972.

96   The Judicature Society's conclusion on the ABA's evaluation of judges came from Elliott E. Slotnick's "The American Bar Association's Standing Committee on Federal Judiciary, A Contemporary Assessment," 66 *Judicature*, 385 (1983). See also 65 *Judicature* 311 (1982). The ABA's rating of Reagan's first term appointment is from *Time* magazine, November 4, 1985.

97–98   Robert E. Woodside is quoted in Judge Lois Forer's book, cited above.

104   The quotations from Henvy VIII and the story of Dr. Fian came from *Liberty and Power 1600–1760*, Oscar and Lilian Handlin, Harper & Row, New York, 1986.

105   Summers's praise of the *Malleus* is contained in his introduction to the 1948 edition of that tome. See *The Malleus Maleficarum of Heinrich Karamer and James Sprenger*, translated by the Reverend Montague Summers, Dover Publications, New York, 1971 ed.

106   The quote from the *Malleus* is from pp. 222–223.

107–8   The quote from the *Malleus* is from p. 232.

108   The statistic on blacks in our prisons is from *Time* magazine, September 13, 1983.

109–10   Morton Horwitz is quoted from his authoritative book *The Transformation of American Law, 1780–1860*, Harvard University Press, Cambridge, Mass., 1977.

CHAPTER 7:   TRIALS

121   I write of how I "saw the light" concerning the representation of insurance companies and banks and other corporations in *Gunning for Justice* (with Anthony Polk), cited above, and *Of Murder and Madness*, Doubleday & Co., Garden City, N.Y., 1983.

125   The story of the battle between IBM and the Justice Department is detailed in James B. Stewart's fascinating book *The Partners*, Simon and Schuster, New York, 1983, and the quotes of the Cravath attorney are from that book.

CHAPTER 8:   LABOR

163–64   The story of the ship *Desire* and the facts surrounding the slave trade in America were taken from Howard Zinn's wonderful book *A People's*

History of the United States, Harper & Row, New York, 1980, including Madison's computations on the profit in slavery, the decree of Elizabeth in 1572, and the slave announcement in the Virginia Gazette.

165 The quote concerning the attitude of the Church toward slavery came from Time on the Cross, Robert W. Fogel and Stanley L. Engerman, Little Brown, Boston, 1947.

166 The statement of George Baer was reported in Corporate Control, Corporate Power, Edward S. Herman, Cambridge University Press, New York, 1981.

166 The story of the Ludlow massacre can be found in a remarkable book, Labor's Untold Story, Boyer and Morais, United Electrical Workers, 3rd ed., 1982.

168–69 A comprehensive story of the labor struggle in the United States may be found in Zinn's book and is the source for the statistics on lynchings and the history of labor found on these pages.

169 Reich's quote is from his book The Greening of America, Random House, New York, 1970.

171 The statistic on blacks in prison is from Time magazine, September 13, 1983.

171 The case involving the sixteen-year-old boy was Edding v. Oklahoma, 455 U.S. 104 (1982). The argument was reported in 50 U.S. Law Week 3363 and was reported by Judge Forer in her book Money and Justice, cited above.

174 The Naisbitt and Aburdene quote is from their book Reinventing the Corporation, Warner Books, New York, 1985.

174–75 The Freeman and Medoff statistics can be found in their book What Do Unions Do?, Basic Books, New York, 1984.

175 I am indebted to Robert Howard for his insight concerning the American worker and the American workplace. His excellent book is Brave New Workplace, Viking, New York, 1985.

177 The quotes regarding excellent companies are from In Search of Excellence: Lessons from America's Best-Run Companies, Thomas J. Peters and Robert H. Waterman, Jr., Harper & Row, New York, 1982.

178 The description of the slave camp is from William Manchester, The Arms of Krupp, Little Brown, Boston, 1968.

CHAPTER 9: INSURANCE

187 Prudential's ownership of assets was taken from Andrew Tobias's great exposé of the insurance industry, The Invisible Bankers, Pocket Books, New York, 1982.

189 The statistics regarding corporate ownership of insurance companies are from Andrew Tobias's book, cited above.

190 The editorial in the Washington Post appeared on November 3, 1976.

190   J. Robert Hunter, federal insurance administrator under Presidents Ford and Carter and now president of National Insurance Consumer Organization, testified on December 11, 1985, before the Commissioner's Special Task Force on Property-Casualty Insurance in Wisconsin, and later before Congress in 1986. His testimony included statistics on insurance rate increases, insurance profits, and stock increments that have been referred to herein.

191   The statistics from the General Accounting Office came from a statement of John C. Finch, senior associate director, General Government Division, before the Subcommittee on Oversight, Committee on Ways and Means of the House of Representatives, on the profitability of the property-casualty insurance industry on April 28, 1986.

192   I am indebted to the Public Citizen, 215 Pennsylvania Avenue, S.E., Washington, D.C., in whose December 1986 "Briefing Paper" prepared by attorney Joanne Doroshow appeared the quotation of Professor Marc Galanter. *The Seattle Times*, July 1, 1986, reports on the irrelevance of so-called "tort reform" and rate decreases.

192   The insurance company providing most Wyoming doctors with malpractice insurance is New Mexico Physicians Mutual Liability Company.

192–93   The facts showing that tort reform and resulting insurance availability are not connected were gathered by Public Citizen and are detailed in its December 1986 "Briefing Paper." The study of the effectiveness of "tort reforms" on premiums was reported by the National Insurance Consumer Organization in its paper "Six Insurance Fibs," August 27, 1986.

195   For statistics that show America is not suffering from a so-called "litigation explosion," see the study by Peterson and Priest, *The Civil Jury: Trends in Trials and Verdicts*, Rand Institute for Civil Justice, 1982.

196   The failure of the states to regulate the insurance industry is footnoted and detailed by J. Robert Hunter in his testimony, including the statistic by the General Accounting Office on the operation of the revolving door in the insurance industry.

CHAPTER 10:   CORPORATE CRIME

198   The Bureau of National Affairs statistics on the comparative cost of crime were reported by Jenkins, 44 U.S.L.W., April 13, 1976 at 2.

198   The numbers concerning misconduct of large corporations in the last ten years is from a study by Amitai Etzioni, professor of sociology at George Washington University, as reported by Saul W. Gellerman in his article "Why 'good' managers made bad ethical choices," *Harvard Business Review*, July–August 1986.

198–99   Marshall Clinard and Peter Yeager undertook a massive study for the Law Enforcement Assistance Administration (LEAA) of criminal administrative action brought by 25 federal agencies against the 477 largest publicly owned manufacturing companies in the United States. See their book *Corporate Crime*, Free Press, New York, 1980.

199 The *Fortune* statistics can be found in "How Lawless Are Big Companies?," Ross, December 1, 1980. These statistics, along with those cited by Jenkins above, and Clinard and Yeager above, were gathered in a very insightful article by William J. Maakestad, "State v. Ford Motor Company: Constitutional, Utilitarian and Moral Perspectives," 27 St.L.U.L.J. 857.

199–200 The passages concerning asbestos are from "Industry's Lethal Cover-up," *Multinational Monitor*, April 1987. See also "Outrageous Misconduct: The Asbestos Industry on Trial," Paul Bordeau, Pantheon Books, New York, 1985. (*Multinational Monitor* is published by Essential Information, Inc., P.O. Box 19405, Washington, D.C. 20036.)

200 The reports on First National Bank of Boston, E. F. Hutton, and Raytheon were gathered in Saul W. Gellerman's article "Why 'good' managers made bad ethical choices," *Harvard Business Review*, July–August 1986.

200 Helen Scott's cogent quote appeared in an article by Stan Crock entitled "How to Take a Bite Out of Corporate Crime," *Business Week*, July 15, 1985.

201–2 The facts surrounding Ford's Pinto trial and the documents supporting the same are gathered and reported in *Reckless Homicide?*, Lee Patrick Strobel, and books, 1980.

202 Quotes from Judge Lord's eloquent speech to the A. H. Robins officers are from "A Plea for Corporate Conscience," *Harper's*, June 1986.

202–3 The details of the attack on Judge Lord were told to me by the judge in a personal interview.

203 Deaths and injuries from Selacryn were reported in *The New York Times*, September 14, 1985, and, along with the references to GM and Firestone, dangerous products were included in an article, entitled "White-Collar Crime," by Joan Claybrook appearing in *Trial Magazine*, April 1986.

204 The case of Jody Bonney, a fictitious name used to accommodate the terms of the settlement agreement, is reported in *Gunning for Justice*, Gerry Spence and Anthony Polk, cited above.

205 James Mold's statement concerning the Liggett Group, Inc., comes from the *Washington Post*, February 13, 1988.

206–7 Elizabeth Drew's book *Politics and Money*, Macmillan, New York, 1984, is my source for the information pertaining to PACs, federal election laws, and the Committee for the Re-election of the President.

207–9 The dairy scandal is reported in full in Mark Green's valuable book *Who Runs Congress?*, Viking, New York, 1979, as is Senator Kennedy's remark.

209 The facts concerning the corruption of the Reagan administration were reported in *USA Today*, February 11, 1988. President Reagan's attitude toward the same appeared in *USA Today*, January 19, 1988, as did the facts pertaining to lobbying wherein Cal LeMon made his comment about trust being for sale.

209–10 Nofziger's statement after his conviction and the juror's reply appeared in the *Los Angeles Times*, February 12, 1988.

210 Concerning GE's fines, see 45 FCC 1592, 2 RR 2d 1038. The information on the citations issued against Kerr-McGee is from evidence adduced at trial in the case of *Silkwood* v. *Kerr-McGee*.

211 Jefferson's quote is from *Multinational Monitor*, May 1987.

212 The report on the *San Mateo* and *Santa Clara* cases and the secret minutes of the Joint Congressional Committee on the Fourteenth Amendment are from an extraordinary unpublished paper entitled "Controlling the Corporation: The Corporate Character Approach" by Michael Waldman and others, directed by Professor Harry First. Waldman is legislative director of Public Citizen's Congress Watch, Washington, D. C.

213 The principal statistics concerning television and corporate America were gleaned from Jerry Mander's classic *Four Arguments for the Elimination of Television*, Quill, New York, 1978.

215 The picture of Patrick Henry on Court Day was exquisitely painted for me by Henry Mayer in *A Son of Thunder, Patrick Henry and the American Republic*, Franklin Watts, New York/Toronto, 1986.

CHAPTER 11: NEW LAWYERS

222–23 The discussion of prepaid plans, production-line law services, and clinics is from "Lawyers versus the Marketplace," Richard Green, *Forbes*, January 16, 1984, and "Shopping for Legal Alternatives," Goody L. Solomon, *Working Woman*, November 1985.

224 The musing of the doctor on the so-called malpractice crisis is from "Is the Malpractice Insurance Crisis Over?" *Physicians Management*, July 1987.

224 The discussion of the life of the young lawyer in the big firm comes from "Rattling the Gilded Cage," Richard Lacayo, *Time* magazine, August 11, 1986.

224–25 The Michael Kearney quotation is from Goody Solomon's article, while the Magness quote is from Green's article, both cited above.

226–27 David White's quotations and materials are from a personal interview. White has pioneered the attack on the LSAT and has written extensively on this subject. He is director of Testing for the Public, 1308 Perlta, Berkeley, California 94702. White tells me that the current average scores for blacks, Chicanos, and whites on the LSAT are unpublished but widely known by admissions personnel at law schools. For the statistics on the comparisons of blacks to whites for a 3.25 GPA plus a 600 or above on the LSAT, White cites a 1977 study entitled *Applications and Admission to ABA Accredited Law Schools: An Analysis of National Data for the Class Entering in the Fall of 1976*, published by Law School Admission Council.

227 Dean Peter Liacouras's work is entitled "Toward a Fair and Sensible

Policy for Professional School Admission," *Cross Reference*, Vol. 1, No. 2.

228   I quote Professor Morton Horwitz from a personal interview.

228–29   The statements concerning the admissions policy at Temple and the typical class profile are from Liacouras's article, cited above.

229   The information on admissions at St. Louis University School of Law and McGeorge Law School is from their catalogs.

229   The quote from Dean Kanios is from a personal interview.

230   Dean Liacouras's statement to the American Association of Law Schools is from "A Call to Action on Our Disaster Area, Law School Admissions," 4 *Black Law Journal* 480, 1975.

233   The quotations from Temple Law School are those of its former dean, Peter J. Liacouras, as is the statement concerning Nelson Diaz. See Liacouras's article published in *Cross Reference* and cited above.

234   The statistics on minorities attending law school are from the ABA.

CHAPTER 12:   NEW LAW SCHOOLS

235   Pound's quote as well as the exclamation of the Chicago professor are from *Unequal Justice*, Jerold S. Auerbach, cited above.

238   The Clare Dalton story was published in *The New York Times*, March 11, 1988.

239   The quotes of Judge Edwards and Justin Stanley came from *The New York Times*, January 15, 1988.

241   The summary of the changing face of our law schools together with the quote of Dean Meltsner are found in an article by Bill Blum and Gina Lobaco entitled "The case against the case system," *California Lawyer*, March 1984.

241   The quotes from Dean Kanios are from my personal interview with him.

241–43   Dean Brest's quotes are from my personal interview with him.

242   Professor Nielsen's quotation may be found in his cogent essay "The Flaw in Our Law Schools," cited above.

245   The statistics on the New Jersey Bar pass rate and Jerold S. Auerbach's comments are found in "The Bar Exam . . . a Fraud and a Hoax," *National Law Journal*, January 28, 1980. Leslie Whitmer's quote is from an article entitled "Multistate bar exam challenged in Kentucky," by Vicki Quade appearing in the publication *Bar Leader*, Vol. 8, No. 4, January/February, 1983.

252   Dean Burns's comments are from *The New York Times*, January 15, 1988.

255   The quotation from the *Malleus* can be found on p. 218.

256   Professor Horwitz's quote is from my personal interview with him.

CHAPTER 13:   NEW JUDGES

258   The statistic on the attitudes of a majority of ABA members concerning the qualification of judges came from *American Bar Association Journal*, May 1982, p. 554.

258   Judge Cardozo's quotation is from his famous book *The Nature of the Judicial Process*, Yale University Press, New Haven, 1921.

CHAPTER 14:   NEW LAW

274–75   The statistics on the ravages of corporate crime were gathered in an editorial by Russell Mokhiber in *Multinational Monitor*, April 4, 1987. The quotation of the nuns came from the same issue of *Multinational Monitor* in another article by Russell Mokhiber, entitled "Infant Formula: Hawking Disaster in the Third World."

275   The history of Dow's knowledge of the hazard of Agent Orange is contained in Russell Mokhiber's article "Agent Orange: Bringing the Battle Home," cited above.

275   Professor Matthews's statement is quoted in "How to Take a Bite Out of Corporate Crime," Stan Crock, *Business Week*, July 15, 1985.

277   The *U.S. News and World Report* statistic appeared April 13, 1987.

277   The report on the murder convictions of three officers of Film Recovery Systems was reported in Stan Crock's article cited above.

277–78   The quotes by Ann Singleton and Kenneth Oden and the statistic for the public's support of prison terms for corporate executives are from "Redefining Corporate Crime," William Maakestad, *Multinational Monitor*, May 1987.

278   Judge Miles Lord's quotation is from "Judgment Day, an Interview with Miles Lord," *Multinational Monitor*, May 1987.

278–81   The MER/29 story, entitled "Get Away with What You Can," is by Sanford J. Ungar and appears in *In the Name of Profit: Profiles in Corporate Irresponsibility*, by Robert L. Heilbroner and others, Doubleday & Co., Garden City, N.Y., 1972.

283   *WOKO* is reported at 329 U.S. 227.

283   The price-fixing case I refer to is *General Electric Co.*, 45 FCC 1592, 2 RR 2d 1083.

284   The quotation from John Bates Clark is found in the book *The Bigness Complex: Industry, Labor and Government in the American Economy*, Walter Adams and James W. Brock, Pantheon Books, New York, 1986.

284–85   The study of seventy of the nation's largest manufacturing, mining, and mercantile recidivist corporations is from *White Collar Crime: The Uncut Version*, Edwin Sutherland, edited by Gilbert Geis and Colin Goss, Yale University Press, New Haven, 1983.

285   The study of 477 manufacturing corporations was conducted by

Marshall B. Clinard and Peter C. Yeager, and reported in their valuable book *Corporate Crime*, Free Press, New York, 1980.

285 I would like to again give much credit to Michael Waldman, now legislative director of Public Citizens' Congress Watch, Washington, D.C., who, under the direction of Professor Harry First, gathered the materials dealing with the control of corporate crime as set forth in an unpublished paper, "Controlling the Corporation: The Corporate Character Approach," which included, among other sources I have utilized and heretofore mentioned, the facts concerning Reagan and the history of General Electric's malfeasance.

286–88 Quotes from Judge Lord's eloquent speech to the A. H. Robins officers are from "A Plea for Corporate Conscience," cited above.

290 Judge Lord's quote here is from "Judgment Day, an Interview with Miles Lord," cited above.

290 The facts negating a "litigation explosion" are gathered in "Briefing Paper," December 1986, prepared by attorney Joanne Doroshow for Public Citizen, 215 Pennsylvania Avenue, S.E., Washington, D.C. See also *Consumer's Report*, August 1986, "The Manufactured Crisis."

291 This quote from Judge Lord was part of his sermon to the officers of A. H. Robins reported in *Harper*'s, and cited above.

293 The report on the defeat of a bill limiting the contribution of special-interest PACs was by the Associated Press, February 27, 1988.

294 The quotations on the revolving door are from *USA Today*, January 19, 1988, p. 12A.

294 Haig's quote is from *Time* magazine, January 18, 1988.

295 The Volcker and Schroeder quotes are from *The New York Times*, January 15, 1988.

CHAPTER 15: NEW VOICES

296–97 I have quoted from Marie Winn's very valuable book *The Plug-In Drug*, revised edition, Viking, New York, 1985.

297 The reference to the study on the altering of beliefs is from "The Great American Values Test," Sandra J. Ball-Rokeach, Milton Rokeach, and Joel W. Grubb, *Psychology Today*, November 1984.

298 The statistics on network income and the facts concerning the purchase of ABC and NBC are from *Time* magazine, September 22, 1986.

300–301 On these pages, I have drawn from S. L. Harrison's fine article, "Prime Time Pablum, How Politics and Corporate Influence Keep Public TV Harmless," *The Washington Monthly*, January 1986.

301–4 *You and Media*, David G. Clark and William B. Blankenburg, Canfield Press/Harper & Row, New York, 1973; *The Newscasters*, Ron Powers, St. Martin's Press, New York, 1977; *Trivializing America*, Norman Corwin, Lyle Stuart, Secaucus, N.J., 1983; *Remote Control*, Frank Mankiewicz and Joel Swerdlow, Times Books, New York, 1978; *Inside Prime Time*, Todd Gitlin, Pantheon Books, New York, 1983.

306   The Edward Herman quote is from *Corporate Control, Corporate Power*, cited above.

307   The statistic on the cost of a television commercial is from *Forbes*, September 21, 1987.

308   *Remote Control*, Frank Mankiewicz and Joel Swerdlow, cited above.

309   For an account of the Kitty Genovese murder, see *The New York Times*, April 12, 1964.

309–10   The account of the death of Phil Lemere Jr.'s father and the Wheeler quote are from the *Los Angeles Times*, January 19, 1988.

314   Chrysler's advertisement for air bags appeared in leading newspapers across the nation, including *The New York Times*, May 24, 1988.

CHAPTER 16:   NEW PEOPLE

318   The statistics and Wood's quotation are found in David W. Ewing's important book *Freedom Inside the Organization: Bringing Civil Liberties to the Workplace*, E. P. Dutton, New York, 1977.

319   Taylor's admonition to workers came from the praiseworthy work of Mark Green and John F. Berry, *The Challenge of Hidden Profits, Reducing Corporate Bureaucracy and Waste*, William Morrow, New York, 1985. From time to time in this chapter, I have drawn on their sound premises and thought.

319   I have borrowed many of the quotations and statistics gathered by Patricia Aburdene and John Naisbitt in their most insightful book, *Reinventing the Corporation: Transforming Your Job and Your Company for the New Information Society*, Warner Books, New York, 1985, including the statement of how men worked at Ford. The quotation concerning Ford's boast on workers being where and when he wanted them, even at 4:00 A.M., is from David Halberstam's book *The Reckoning*, William Morrow, New York, 1986.

319–20   The facts surrounding Taylorism came from Green and Berry, in their book cited above.

320   Douglas McGregor's book is *The Human Side of Enterprise*, McGraw-Hill, New York, 1960.

321   Professor Forrester's paper was quoted by Aburdene and Naisbitt, in their book cited above.

322   Thomas Quick's quotes are from his book *The Quick Motivation Method*, St. Martin's Press, New York, 1980.

322   Again I quote statistics gathered by Aburdene and Naisbitt on the percentage of the work force that is unionized.

322–23   The discussion about brainwashing American workers came from an article entitled "Corporate Mind Control," by Annetta Miller with Pamel Abramson in *Newsweek*, May 4, 1987.

323–24 The story of Ford and the United Auto Workers is from Green and Berry, in their book cited above.

325 *In Search of Excellence*, Thomas J. Peters and Robert H. Waterman, Jr., cited above.

325 The examples cited where workers are making many of their own decisions in industry I gratefully drew from Aburdene and Naisbitt in their book cited above.

326 The quote by the chairman of General Motors is from "Too Big for Business," *Multinational Monitor*, June 1987.

326 The QWL quotes, facts, and examples I borrowed with equal gratitude from Green and Berry's book cited above.

326–27 The facts and discussion of the "disposable employee" are from "The Disposable Employee is Becoming a Fact of Corporate Life," Michael A. Pollock and Aaron Bernstein, *Business Week*, December 15, 1986.

328 The examples gathered concerning worker interests in business and profit sharing were drawn from Aburdene and Naisbitt's book, cited above.

328 The story on profit sharing at Andersen was reported in the *Los Angeles Times*, January 19, 1988.

330 I found the report on W. H. Gore & Associates, Inc., in Aburdene and Naisbitt's book *Reinventing the Corporation*, cited above.

330 Chouinard's quotes are from an unpublished paper he delivered at Yale, and from my personal interviews with him.

330, 332 David Ewing's quotes are from his book *Freedom Inside the Organization*, cited above.

332 The attitude of IBM management was reported in *In Search of Excellence*, Thomas J. Peters and Robert H. Waterman, Jr., cited above.

333 I happily give great credit to David W. Ewing for the clear and just thought behind his call for a Workers' Bill of Rights and his suggestions for the same.

Acknowledgments

This book would not exist but for the contributions of life and love by Sandra Lambert, John Turner, Rosemary McIntosh, Imaging Spence, Lisa Drew, Sarah Trotta, and Jonathan Segal. There were others who know I'm grateful.

354

Index

FOR THE BEST IN PAPERBACKS, LOOK FOR THE 🐧

In every corner of the world, on every subject under the sun, Penguin represents quality and variety—the very best in publishing today.

For complete information about books available from Penguin—including Pelicans, Puffins, Peregrines, and Penguin Classics—and how to order them, write to us at the appropriate address below. Please note that for copyright reasons the selection of books varies from country to country.

In the United Kingdom: For a complete list of books available from Penguin in the U.K., please write to *Dept E.P., Penguin Books Ltd, Harmondsworth, Middlesex, UB7 0DA.*

In the United States: For a complete list of books available from Penguin in the U.S., please write to *Dept BA, Penguin*, Box 120, Bergenfield, New Jersey 07621-0120.

In Canada: For a complete list of books available from Penguin in Canada, please write to *Penguin Books Ltd, 2801 John Street, Markham, Ontario L3R 1B4.*

In Australia: For a complete list of books available from Penguin in Australia, please write to the *Marketing Department, Penguin Books Ltd, P.O. Box 257, Ringwood, Victoria 3134.*

In New Zealand: For a complete list of books available from Penguin in New Zealand, please write to the *Marketing Department, Penguin Books (NZ) Ltd, Private Bag, Takapuna, Auckland 9.*

In India: For a complete list of books available from Penguin, please write to *Penguin Overseas Ltd, 706 Eros Apartments, 56 Nehru Place, New Delhi, 110019.*

In Holland: For a complete list of books available from Penguin in Holland, please write to *Penguin Books Nederland B.V., Postbus 195, NL-1380AD Weesp, Netherlands.*

In Germany: For a complete list of books available from Penguin, please write to *Penguin Books Ltd, Friedrichstrasse 10-12, D-6000 Frankfurt Main 1, Federal Republic of Germany.*

In Spain: For a complete list of books available from Penguin in Spain, please write to *Longman, Penguin España, Calle San Nicolas 15, E-28013 Madrid, Spain.*

In Japan: For a complete list of books available from Penguin in Japan, please write to *Longman Penguin Japan Co Ltd, Yamaguchi Building, 2-12-9 Kanda Jimbocho, Chiyoda-Ku, Tokyo 101, Japan.*